Annotation in
Eighteenth-Century Poetry

STUDIES IN TEXT AND PRINT CULTURE

General Editor: Sandro Jung
Herzog August Library Wolfenbüttel

This series focuses on up-to-date, text-specific, and text-theoretical approaches to the literature and culture of Britain, Europe, and America from the fifteenth to the mid-nineteenth centuries. It publishes innovative scholarship that promotes an understanding of literature as closely related to, and informed by, other discursive forms, especially the multifarious visual cultures of a given time.

Sandro Jung, *James Thomson's* The Seasons, *Print Culture, and Visual Interpretation, 1730–1842*
Betsy Bowden, *The Wife of Bath in Afterlife: Ballads to Blake*
Michael Edson, *Annotation in Eighteenth-Century Poetry*

Annotation in Eighteenth-Century Poetry

Edited by Michael Edson

LEHIGH UNIVERSITY PRESS
Bethlehem

Published by Lehigh University Press
Copublished by The Rowman & Littlefield Publishing Group, Inc.
4501 Forbes Boulevard, Suite 200, Lanham, Maryland 20706
www.rowman.com

6 Tinworth Street, London SE11 5AL, United Kingdom

British Library Cataloguing in Publication Information Available

Library of Congress Cataloging-in-Publication Data Available

ISBN 978-1-61146-252-4 (cloth : alk. paper)
ISBN 978-1-61146-254-8 (pbk. : alk. paper)
ISBN 978-1-61146-253-1 (electronic)

∞™ The paper used in this publication meets the minimum requirements of American National Standard for Information Sciences—Permanence of Paper for Printed Library Materials, ANSI/NISO Z39.48-1992.

Contents

List of Illustrations   vii

List of Tables   ix

Acknowledgments   xi

Introduction   xiii
    Michael Edson

Part I: Georgic Annotation

1   Annotating Georgic Poetry   3
    Karina Williamson and Michael Edson

2   William Falconer's *The Shipwreck* and the Birth of the *Dictionary of the Marine*   23
    William Jones

Part II: Nationalism, Antiquarianism, and Annotation

3   The Afterlife of Annotation: How Robert of Gloucester Became the Founding Father of English Poetry   47
    Jeff Strabone

4   Topographical Annotation in Thomas Percy's *The Hermit of Warkworth* and John Pinkerton's *The Bruce*   67
    Thomas Van der Goten

5   Marginal Imprints: Robert Southey's Notes to *Madoc*   89
    Alex Watson

Part III: Varieties of Annotation

6   A Translator's Annotation: Alexander Pope's Observations on
    His *Iliad*   105
    David Hopkins

7   Allusion and Quotation in Chaucerian Annotation, 1687–1798   129
    Tom Mason

8   Looking Homeward: Thomas Warton's Annotation of Milton and
    the Poetic Tradition   151
    Adam Rounce

Part IV: Annotating the Canon

9   Zachary Grey's Annotations on Samuel Butler's *Hudibras*   169
    Mark A. Pedreira

10 William Hymers and the Editing of William Collins's Poems,
    1765–1797   189
    Sandro Jung

11 Paratexting Beauty into Duty: Aesthetics and Morality in Late
    Eighteenth-Century Literary Collections   207
    Barbara M. Benedict

Index   231

About the Contributors   239

List of Illustrations

Figure 3.1.   Thomas Hearne, ed., Robert of Gloucester's Chronicle,
               2 vols. (Oxford: Printed at the Theater, 1724), 1:xxxvi.
               Reproduced by permission from a copy in the Mathewson
               Library, University of Nevada, Reno.   57

Figure 3.2.   Glossary entry, Thomas Hearne, ed., Robert of
               Gloucester's Chronicle, 2 vols. (Oxford: Printed at the
               Theater, 1724), 2:665. Reproduced by permission from
               a copy in the Mathewson Library, University of Nevada,
               Reno.   58

Figure 11.1.   Title page, *Fables by Mr. Gay*, 7th ed. (London: Printed
               for J. Tonson and J. Watts, 1727). Reproduced by
               permission from a copy in the collection of Sandro Jung.   212

Figure 11.2.   Title page, Vicesimus Knox, *Elegant Extracts; or,
               Useful and Entertaining PIECES of POETRY* (London:
               Printed for C. Dilly and Poultry, 1789). Reproduced by
               permission from a copy in the collection of Sandro Jung.   217

Figure 11.3.   Frontispiece, designed by Isaac Cruikshank, engraved by
               Inigo Barlow, *Roach's Beauties of the Poet's* [*sic*] *of Great
               Britain; Carefully Selected & Arranged from the Works of the
               Most Admired Authors*, comp. John Roach (London: By
               and for J. Roach, 1794). Reproduced by permission from
               a copy in the British Library. ©The British Library Board.   226

List of Tables

Table 1.1.   Authorial Notes in English Georgics   6
Table 1.2.   Authorial and Non-authorial Notes in Selected Georgics   11
Table 2.1.   Types of Notes in *The Shipwreck*   29
Table 2.2.   Specialist and Non-specialist Notes in *The Shipwreck*   30

Acknowledgments

I began to consider the functions of printed annotation as a graduate student at the University of Delaware. The subject has remained in my mind ever since, first at the University of Alaska Fairbanks and now at the University of Wyoming. My thinking about poetry and notes benefited from panels on the topic at meetings of the American Society for Eighteenth-Century Studies (ASECS), one panel in Cleveland, Ohio, in 2013 and another in Williamsburg, Virginia, in 2014. Foremost, I am grateful to Sandro Jung, who encouraged this collection. My thanks are also due to the eleven contributors; I am grateful for their hard work and illuminating discussions of the interactions of poetry and prose notes. Others with whom I have had the great pleasure of discussing annotators and annotation include M. A. Box, John Dussinger, Anna Foy, Rhona Brown, Theresa Covich, Dallin Lewis, and Don Mell. As always, Cedric Reverand II challenged my ideas in productive and supportive ways. My appreciation goes to the Modern Humanities Research Association (MHRA) and the editors of the *Modern Language Review* for permission to reprint Sandro Jung's chapter. To those at Lehigh University Press: I am grateful to Kate Crassons, Trish Moore, and the two anonymous readers for their help in guiding this book through review and into print. My thanks also goes to Brooke Bures, Paula Williamson, and the rest of the design, production, and marketing teams at Rowman & Littlefield. I am also grateful to the staffs at the British Library and the University of Nevada Interlibrary Loan office for their assistance with images. Finally, special thanks goes to Evelyn and Cecily Edson, who endured another editorial adventure with patience.

Laramie, Wyoming
May 2017

Introduction

Michael Edson

Whenever the subject of printed annotation comes up during a conference on eighteenth-century topics, the ensuing discussion will likely feature one or more of the following. Someone will refer to the mock apparatus of the *Dunciad Variorum* (1729) and rehearse Alexander Pope's distaste for the pedantry and triviality of notes. Samuel Johnson's warning about the distraction of reading notes ("the mind is refrigerated by interruption[,] the thoughts are diverted, . . . and at last [the reader] throws away the book") will also be mentioned.[1] David Hume's complaint about Edward Gibbon's annotations to *The Decline and Fall of the Roman Empire* (1776–1788) might wrongly be offered as evidence of a general dislike for the practice, notwithstanding that Hume was, in fact, urging Gibbon, who had used endnotes, to adopt footnotes instead so as to spare future readers the dislocation of turning to the back of the book.[2] In the process, several commonplaces about eighteenth-century annotation will be reaffirmed: notes originated with arrogant, hectoring scholiasts set on obtruding their own erudition at an author's expense; notes signaled the dumbing down or commodification of literature; and, while faux or mock notes delighted poets, utilitarian annotations reflected the machinations of editors and money-minded booksellers catering to an increasingly assorted and ill-informed readership.

Drawing on methods of book history, print culture, and histories of reading, *Annotation in Eighteenth-Century Poetry* tells a different story about the comments attached by authors, editors, and booksellers to poems appearing in the British Isles between 1700 and 1830. In what follows, annotators and poets are not always rivals but often collaborators; annotations are not simply distractions but often devices to appeal to distracted readers. This story complicates the stereotyped narrative in which eighteenth-century authors, and poets especially, waged a heroic but futile struggle against printed notes and their many sponsors: pedantic scholars, hack writers, overreaching editors, ignorant readers, and profiteering publishers.[3] Of particular interest to this collection are the myriad purposes to which poets put notes at the same time they voiced concerns about their effects on reading and literature. Printed head-, foot-, side-, and endnotes—what will throughout this volume be collectively termed *annotation*, in contrast to the handwritten notes or *marginalia* of readers, and in contrast to the sustained and often freestanding remarks referred to as *commentary*—were a more widespread component of the eighteenth-century poetic page than has been hitherto recognized. Sometimes a single poem displayed several systems of annotation, including head-, foot-, and endnotes. The mock apparatuses attached to Pope's *The Dunciad*, John Gay's *The Shepherd's Week* (1713), and Thomas Parnell's *Battle of the Frogs and Mice* (1717) are famous, but most poetic annotation in this era was meant and taken seriously. Many of the canon-making editions issued after 1700—both of single poems and complete works by ancient writers as well as homegrown poets such as Geoffrey Chaucer, Edmund Spenser, John Milton, Samuel Butler, and Pope—boast non-authorial notes by such editors as Richard Bentley, John Upton, Zachary Grey, William Warburton, Thomas Tyrwhitt, and Thomas Warton. These non-authorial notes perform, in often roundabout or self-indulgent ways, the earnest tasks we today expect from annotation: citing sources, defining terms, and identifying allusions. Many poets were ardent (if reluctant) self-annotators as well. From Pope's *Windsor-Forest* (1714) to Thomas Gray's *The Bard* (1757), some of the period's most recognizable poems carry authorial notes.

The note's development is well known. Manuscript glosses had existed from ancient times, but as an advanced convention of print, annotation was infrequent before the seventeenth century. Having first appeared in writings by Pierre Bayle and Richard Simon on the Continent, notes soon entered into biblical criticism and classical editing.[4] From there, notes found their way into poetry and poetry editions. To establish a canon of vernacular classics, editors gave English poems the same editorial treatment associated with Greek and Roman texts. For poets and editors eager to locate poems in national literary traditions (Irish, Scottish, British), notes offered a convenient receptacle for commentaries identifying both the antique character and the national characteristics of such poems.[5] Only in the eighteenth century did printed annotations become so ubiquitous in poetry and poetry editions as to receive extensive comment from readers and poets.

The rise of the printed note also represents a development from pedagogical rituals of humanism such as note-taking and commonplacing, practices that even during the Renaissance sometimes resulted in printed compilations. Compiling notes by hand or in print extended the humanistic interest in collecting objects and medals to the artifacts of the textual realm: the dusty anecdotes and philological oddities especially common to eighteenth-century antiquarian apparatuses.[6] Not surprisingly, many of the earliest commentaries self-identifying as "notes"—Elkanah Settle's *Notes and Observations on the* Empress of Morocco *Revised* (1674), or Patrick Hume's *Annotations on Milton's* Paradise Lost (1695), among others—constitute independent volumes. Freestanding collections of notes continued to appear into the 1700s.[7] For this reason, eighteenth-century foot- and endnotes probably never seemed to contemporaries to be as subordinate to the "main text" as they seem today. Such notes, in many cases, had enjoyed a past existence as the centered text (Hume's notes become footnotes in later editions of Milton's poetry) or retained a lingering association with commonplace books, which held priority over their source-texts by virtue of their distilling important passages from them. The life cycle of many notes, like those to William Falconer's *The Shipwreck* (1762), notes recycled into his freestanding *Dictionary of the Marine* (1769), attest to annotation's humanist beginnings.

Before we go too far into this history, two preliminary matters demand attention. Why talk of *annotation* at all? If notes share some of the functions of the prefaces, glossaries, and titles treated in Gérard Genette's *Paratexts* (1987; trans. 1997)—the authoritative analysis of textual appendages of all kinds—should we not adopt Genette's terminology? The present volume discusses *annotation* and only secondarily *paratext* for two reasons. First, though scholars today frequently refer to notes as paratext, Genette is reluctant to categorize them so. Authorial notes for Genette embody "a local detour . . . in the text, and as such belong to the text almost as much as a simple parenthesis," whereas non-authorial notes "fall outside" the paratext category.[8] Non-authorial notes are excluded because the paratext always reflects authorial intention; paratext is commentary "legitimated by the author."[9] By contrast, this volume largely focuses on either *un*-authorized annotations by later editors or authorial notes that challenge (visually, politically) the priority of the main text. Second, the volume focuses on *annotation* not simply because the term was current around 1750 and therefore suits a historical study.[10] The choice of terminology also emphasizes the uniqueness of our undertaking. Paratexts such as indexes, illustrations, titles, and printer's ornaments have received attention.[11] By contrast, annotation has been neglected, either submerged in larger discussions of editing or mock-editing[12] or sidelined in sweeping theoretical studies of margins and marginalia.[13] Isolating notes for analysis helps distinguish their functions from the workings of the titles, illustrations, and other paratexts by which scholars have already mapped literature's relation to early print capitalism and the class-specific production of books.

Another preliminary matter relates to genre or form. Why limit the volume to poetry? The obvious answer is this: plenty of good scholarship already exists on the notes accompanying works of prose fiction and history.[14] Annotated poems by some late-century poets, including Robert Burns, Robert Southey, William Wordsworth, Charlotte Smith, and Richard Llwyd, have garnered analysis.[15] But among annotated poems from earlier in the century only Pope's *The Dunciad* has received wide study, and then often only singly or in relation to Gibbon's *Decline and Fall*, as if a comparison of the *The Dunciad* to a later prose work offers more insight than a consideration of the poem in relation to the practices of notation specific to poetry.[16] The reluctance of scholars to recognize a long tradition of annotated poetry reflects, I think, a lingering eighteenth-century view of notes as distractions from the proper business of verse. As Genette suggests, the intrusiveness of annotation is felt acutely with poetry, which aspires to timeless statements beyond the factual and topical concerns of history and other prose genres.[17] If the poetry of the eighteenth century is much more topical than Genette allows, it nonetheless remains clear that poets after 1700 protested more loudly about notes than prose writers. This should come as no real surprise: by explaining references, translating languages, and indicating textual and factual errors, foot- and endnotes threatened a literary kind premised on both its exclusiveness (owing to allusive range, imagistic density, and linguistic difficulty) and its alleged transcendence of drab factuality, the latter the purview of prose forms such as the novel. But by overlooking poetic annotation, we ignore how notes through their presence on the page confirm the exclusiveness of poetry while helping less-educated readers acquire the cultural capital associated with this elite form of literature. That is, to ignore these notes also ignores how poetry's claims to prestige, durability, and aesthetic superiority over prose depended on the same prose notes that appear to promise to disenchant poetry both by enumerating its errors and untruths and by recounting the grubby facts of its origins and production. By treating notes as worthy of attention, this volume discloses the cultural work of annotation that goes unseen when we regard notes as distractions.

One thing will become immediately evident from the essays in this collection: few poets altogether rejected notes, and the reasons for their ambivalence about annotation were more complex than is typically realized. When Thomas Gray heard the call for notes to alleviate wide public confusion about his odes, *The Bard* and *The Progress of Poesy* (1754), he initially dug in his heels: "I would not have put another note to save the souls of all the *Owls* in London."[18] Gray later caved to such calls, and, though he claimed to have added explanatory notes in 1768 only "out of spite," the change of stance nonetheless suggests that Gray realized the problem was less the obtuseness of his readers than his mistaken confidence in the transparency of his historical allusions.[19] This change of heart reflected not the urgings of a publisher but the pleas of friends such as William Shenstone, and therefore Gray's annotations might in some sense be considered collaborative. A more clear-cut example of collaboration comes with *The Dunciad*: when Jonathan Swift, among Pope's other friends, requested notes identifying the satiric allusions in the poem, Pope asked Swift to write them.[20] When Edmund Curll embarked on an edition of Shakespeare's poems in 1709, he advertised his desire to crowdsource the annotations: "To make the Notes as perfect as possible, any Gentleman that will please to communicate anything of that kind, shall receive a Gratification."[21] Complaints from the period that notes were either plagiarized or derivative—that every edition was a sort of unacknowledged variorum edition—suggest that collective labor, as much as rivalry, defined annotative practice.[22] The best example of such collaboration can be found in the negotiations between poets and booksellers. From a 1717 letter of Pope's instructing his printer to add a note to the *Essay on Criticism* (1711), we know poets were active in the production and layout of notes.[23] In a move suggestive of larger trends in the annotation of both poetry and prose, Hume directed his request for the conversion of Gibbon's endnotes to footnotes not to Gibbon, but to Gibbon's publisher, William Strahan, the author and publisher being in matters of annotation "the same thing."[24] And many times it was booksellers who resisted notes. When working on his *Aeneid* translation (1697), John Dryden wrote to Jacob Tonson the elder, who had either rejected the addition of notes or had refused to pay for them: "I am not sorry that you will not allow any thing towards the Notes; for to make them good, wou'd have cost me half a yeares time."[25] Publishers as often opposed annotation as they demanded it.

The notes to eighteenth-century poems did much more than elucidate meanings, interpret passages, and authenticate documents. They did all these things, but they served other agendas in the process, including financial ones. Bottom line: notes enhanced a volume's marketability. Similar to illustrations, notes were elements of the material packaging by which booksellers distinguished their wares from earlier and competing editions. That much is clear from the frequency with which title pages advertise the notes ("With Explanatory Notes . . . Never before Printed"). Fly-leaf advertisements and subscription proposals present notes as a kind of "illustration" beautifying a volume, as is apparent from the 1737 proposal for an edition of the works of the laboring-class poet John Bancks, a volume to be "Adorned with Sculptures, and Illustrated with Notes."[26] The ubiquity of the suspicion that notes were added to "swell . . . volumes into costlier sizes," a suspicion that Johnson voiced in relation to Pope's *Iliad* (1715–1720), further hints at the potential commercial benefits of annotation.[27] Even the placement of notes to some degree reflected economic calculations; endnotes were easier for typographers to set, and footnotes saved paper and therefore money.[28] To allegedly compete with an imported translation, Bernard Lintot in 1720 issued a duodecimo edition of Pope's *Iliad* that traded the usual endnotes for cheaper footnotes.[29] In later decades, the need to accommodate Pope's *Iliad* to affordable multivolume collections led often to the omission of some or all of the notes.[30]

Annotation frequently entered into debates about literary property in the years from the 1709 Statute of Queen Anne to the *Donaldson v. Becket* copyright decision of 1774. Much like abridgments and extract books, heavily annotated texts were often treated by the courts as new works and therefore outside the rights of the publisher of the unannotated original.[31] In 1774, William Enfield identifies annotation as one unconvincing strategy by which publishers sought to conceal piracies.[32] However, in an era where the 1709 statute was interpreted variously and the ancient privileges of the booksellers persisted, notes sometimes convinced copyright jurists. In the 1752 case of *Tonson v. Walker*, which focused on Tonson the younger's 1749 Milton edition, the court issued an injunction against Robert Walker's reprint, for although the copyright on *Paradise Lost* had expired Thomas Newton's notes remained Tonson's property. In the 1765 case of *Millar v. Donaldson*, the court cleared Alexander Donaldson of the accusation of piracy in his printing of an edition of James Thomson's *Seasons* but found against him in a reprint of Andrew Millar's 1755 *Works* of Swift because the notes by John Hawkesworth stood "within the Statute."[33] In these two instances, notes appear to have helped publishers to defy copyright law or at least to extend their copyrights in time. By recovering the note as a dynamic textual object whose existence reflects the diverse agendas of poets, publishers, and other agents of print, this volume contributes to book-historical inquiries into the materiality of texts, the growth of audiences, and the practices of the book trade.[34] One of the ambitions of this volume is to reveal the place of notes in attempts by poets and publishers to secure both property and profit.

To emphasize commercial incentives, however, risks overlooking annotation's broader functions. One consideration was durability. It is no accident that the eighteenth century, which saw an explosion in printed matter and a perceived increase in novice readers whose knowledge of literary tradition was lacking, boasted much annotated poetry. Poets and publishers of this era no longer assumed readers knew poems by heart or possessed libraries for looking up references. Readers required education on literary-historical contexts: they needed explanations of forgotten persons, archaic terms, and unfamiliar mores. This also held true for satires such as *The Dunciad*, whose topical allusions were said to be unintelligible "twenty miles from London" at the time of printing, though such explanation was especially needed for the ancient and vernacular classics.[35] As the century continued and older poems were repeatedly reissued, the gentlemanly faith in the ability of poetry to communicate across time yielded to a professional, historicist notion of poetry as specific "to a particular period of social development" and therefore as inaccessible without some explanatory supplement.[36] Concerns about the remoteness of the classics prompted the so-called battle of the ancients and the moderns.[37] The historicism embodied in the growing number of annotated poems was strongly committed to reconciling commercial with aesthetic value. Where notes appear to degrade poems in the service of profit by making them accessible to supposedly uneducated readers, annotations, in fact, heighten the aura of difficulty associated with poems in the high-cultural canon. At the same time notes assisted readers, they signaled how poetry required special expertise to be understood; at the same time annotations alleviated difficulty, they reinforced a view of poetry as a demanding and recondite form.[38]

To attribute the spread of annotation simply to a periodizing mind-set overlooks how notes ensured present relevance, too. As even so fierce a critic of the miscarriages of annotation as Pope could admit when imagining a posthumous edition of his own poetry, notes supply "a Crutch to the weak Poet to help him limp a little further than he could on his own Feet."[39] By notes even bad poetry could be perpetuated, as Pope observed of the "mediocre" Michael Drayton, who "is yet taken some notice of, because [John] Selden writ a very few Notes" on *Poly-Olbion* (1612).[40] If the mock annotations to *The Dunciad* satirize the conceited debunkery and pointless precision of editors, themselves mockingly embodied in characters such as the "Tom Folio" of *Tatler* no. 158 (1710), the poem's notes at the same time perform the serious work of explanation, ensuring the intelligibility of Pope's satiric allusions even today.[41] If annotation destroys a poem's air of universality by calling attention to its historical embeddedness in the process of explanation, then such explanation heightens its transparency and ensures the poem another kind of timelessness.

The drive to educate readers was matched by a desire to accumulate information. Similar to the Enlightenment rise of dictionaries, encyclopedias, and their paratextual cousins, the index and the glossary, the spread of annotation reflects broad cultural concerns, as Ann Blair, Seth Rudy, and Chad Wellmon have shown, with the storage and hierarchizing of comprehensive knowledge, a concern displayed prominently in the sprawling apparatuses associated with ballad editing.[42] The annotated page archived information and facilitated its retrieval; notes singled out anecdotes and excerpts from "a mass of texts that readers lacked access to or time to consult."[43] The reader of notes heavy with extracts could, technically, like the reader imagined in *Guardian* no. 60 (1713), "wander over a number of Books almost at the same Instant."[44] Some saw such accessibility as a shortcut by which pretenders to learning could obtain "knowledge without study."[45] However, notes just as often reinforced the gap between professional and lay audiences. The footnotes to John Theophilus Desaguliers's *The Newtonian System of the World* (1728) do not explain Isaac Newton's theories; instead, the notes supply technical details. Erasmus Darwin's notes to his poems of the 1790s likewise archive specialist information from the field of botany.[46] The drive to stockpile and organize information is clear from the frequency in many poems of single notes running across page breaks, thus often reducing the poetry to a thread at the top of the page. While annotators did recognize limits on content—most annotators, as Marcus Walsh has shown, aimed to recover what "authors meant" to the exclusion of private associations[47]—the desire to curate information often hurried them into what today looks like saying too much or "commenting even when [they] had little of relevance to say," especially when listing possible sources for images, metaphors, and allusions.[48] By marking a poet's supposed borrowings from other poets, such notes drew texts into a tradition or canon at the cost of undermining ideologies of originality by presenting every poem as a tissue of commonplaces. If the desire to store data prompted irrelevant notes, notes nonetheless enabled poets to square comprehensiveness with cohesion.[49] Notes supplied needed explanations without damaging the continuity of the poetry.

At times the archival impulse, the drive to accumulate information, yielded to aesthetic considerations. When Gray added notes to his odes in 1768, he left their placement, as he told James Beattie, up to his publisher Robert Foulis: "M^r F: will also determine, whether the few notes there are shall stand at the bottom of the page (wch is better for the Reader) or be thrown to the end with references (wch improves the beauty of the book)."[50] In turn, Beattie urged Foulis to use endnotes "as being most consistent with elegance."[51] The number and placement of notes in a volume reflected financial, educational, *and* aesthetic concerns. Readily available footnotes "better" educated readers about literary contexts, but distant endnotes preserved an uncluttered page. A decade earlier, having downsized the notes for the 1753 small octavo edition of Pope's *Works*, William Warburton directed the printer John Knapton to use endnotes for similar reasons:

> My reasons are these, first it will be a variety from the other Edns. but principally I think the small chara[c]ter of the notes in the specimen you have, deforms & hurts the beauty of the Edn. it appears to be much more elegant to have nothing but verses in the page or nothing but prose. besides if the notes be thrown together as I propose they will be in

the same letter with the text, which will make the Edn. more beautifull, & what is still
of more consequence will swell it out a little more.[52]

Warburton has a low reputation among editors today, and his annotations certainly
represent "the last trumpet call" of a now-obsolete aesthetic editing dedicated to the
identification of "poetical beauties."[53] But this statement perfectly captures the competing concerns surrounding the writing and placement of notes in the eighteenth
century. In mixing economic calculations (to "swell" the edition) with aesthetic
judgments (to make it "more beautifull")—together with his infamous use of notes
both to settle scores with scholarly enemies and to secure Pope's posthumous reputation—Warburton illustrates the many agendas guiding the annotation of poetry.
Notes mediate some of the important developments of the time: the rise of literary
scholarship, the shift from the amateur to the professional reader, and the division of
economic from aesthetic value.

As with all of the book's physical features, notes shaped and reflected consumer
tastes and, in turn, influenced how eighteenth-century readers read and related to
poetry. To view notes as tools for controlling interpretation would be incorrect, even
when acknowledging that control was perhaps what some annotators sought. Notes
could always be ignored or read selectively regardless of their visual prominence on
the page. Nevertheless, notes have much potentially to teach us about reading practices. As complaints about their powers of distraction suggest, notes worked against
linear reading: they invited a desultory practice of toggling between poem and notes.
Printed annotations may have discouraged dialogical reading by filling the margins
with other voices, or notes may have simply limited the extent to which such adversarial reading was manifested in scribbled responses by readers, marginalia more
readily recorded in the wide margins of expensive books than amid the cramped
footnotes of downmarket formats.[54] Since the visual subordination of footnotes on
the page cannot be easily replicated orally, annotations possibly discouraged reading aloud, too, but notes were just as likely ignored during recitation. The relation
between notes and distraction was equally complex. According to one printer, notes
served as time-savers, giving readers the option to read the footnotes "first" as a
preview before they consult the rest.[55] Notes surely distracted readers, but perhaps
some welcomed the diversion. Eighteenth-century detractors of annotation such as
Johnson privilege a unifocal form of attention in relation to which notes necessarily
become interruptions. But perhaps readers of the time exercised the multifocal attention familiar to scholars today who read both text and notes without any noticeable
loss of concentration. As these speculations suggest, notes offer an alternative approach to histories of reading. This collection aims to explore the ways in which this
new textual feature transformed, or did not transform, Enlightenment approaches
to poetry.

In denying Pope and Johnson the last word on annotation, this volume argues
neither that hostility toward notes was absent from the eighteenth century nor that
notes, contrary to their associations with a mean-spirited "criticism," did not some-

times take an adversarial relation to the main text.[56] The point is to show that such hostility was rarely unqualified and, anyway, it never stopped most poets from using annotation. Pope "liked notes" and added them to his poems both in manuscript and in print. His mockery of editorial practice coexists with a respect for annotation and a sense of its affordances.[57] Likewise, Johnson's remark about the "refrigerat[ing]" effects of notes acquires a gentler aspect when taken in its original context, where Johnson urges his readers to skip over notes on the initial encounter with a text and then return to them on a subsequent rereading: "When the pleasures of novelty have ceased . . . read the commentators."[58] Beyond Pope and Johnson, too, further complexities in viewpoint emerge. Poets may hold one view of notes in theory and endorse another in practice, and these practices will be the focus of the eleven chapters to follow. For now, let us consider the following list of quotations, which indicates the wide variation in eighteenth-century attitudes about notes:

1. Dryden, preface to *Sylvae* (1685), on Thomas Creech's 1682 edition of Lucretius: his "excellent Annotations . . . I have often read, and always with some new pleasure."[59]

2. Henry Felton, *A Dissertation on Reading the Classics* (1715): "Notes and Comments . . . crowd the Authors, and perplex the reader. I must own, I have not that Respect for the Company of *Annotators*, which they generally meet with in the World. . . . Comments are generally an art of making Authors difficult, under a Pretence of explaining them."[60]

3. Matthew Concanen, "Of Commentators" (1730), on Pope's 1725 edition of Shakespeare: "some tolerable Comments upon the Works of our celebrated Poets are not only expedient but necessary. . . . But it has been common among us, thro' a false Delicacy, to condemn and depreciate this kind of Criticism. Pedant and Commentator have been hitherto considered as Terms synonymous. Weak and idle Cavilling!"[61]

4. Joseph Spence, *Polymetis* (1747): "What is the usual aim of our commentators at present? Why really their usual aim seems to be, to shew their own erudition; at least, I am sure, they generally go but a very little way toward clearing up the meaning of their authors. . . .
   "This way of studying, by drawing your eye off (at every line almost) to the side lights, instead of keeping it steddy [*sic*] upon the proper object you ought to view, makes one often neglect the real intention of the author; and almost always loses the thread of his thoughts, and the connexion of the whole piece."[62]

5. Thomas Edwards, *The Canons of Criticism* (1750), on Warburton's 1747 Shakespeare edition: "The Profess'd Critic, in order to furnish his quote to the bookseller, may write NOTES OF NOTHING, that is notes which either explane things which do not want explanation, or such as do not explane matters at all, but merely fill up so much paper."[63]

6. Gray, letter of 1757 to Horace Walpole: "I do not love notes. . . . They are signs of weakness and obscurity. If anything cannot be understood without them, it had better not be understood at all."[64]

7. Tobias Smollett, review of James Grainger's translation of Tibullus (1758): the notes have been "borrowed from *Brockhusius* the Dutch editor of Tibullus. Indeed the sluices of annotation have been opened so successfully in the Batavian taste, that Tibullus is floated round with criticism, and stands *a l'abri*, like a fort in the Low-Countries. . . . This, we must own, is a huge farrago of learned lumber, jumbled together to very little purpose, seemingly calculated to display the translator's reading, rather than to illustrate the sense and beauty of the original."[65]

8. William Shenstone, "On Books and Writers" (1764): "It seems to me that what are called notes at the bottom of pages (as well as parentheses in writing) might be generally avoided, without injuring the thread of a discourse. It is true it might require some address to interweave them gracefully into the text; but how much more agreeable would be the effect, than to interrupt the reader by such frequent avocations?"[66]

9. Oliver Goldsmith, *An Enquiry into the Present State of Polite Learning in Europe* (1774): "Libraries were loaded, but not enriched with [editors'] labours, while the fatigues of reading their explanatory comments was tenfold that which might suffice for understanding the original, and their works effectually increased out application, by professing to remove it."[67]

10. Percival Stockdale, *An Inquiry into the Nature, and Genuine Laws of Poetry* (1778), on Gray's *The Bard*: "as a considerable number of explanatory Notes is . . . necessary, the flow, and warmth of the reader's mind, while He accompanies the poet, is checked and broken, whenever He is obliged to consult the Anecdotes at the bottom of the page: and after this interruption, He recovers not, even with the assistance of the Notes, that ardour which a well-written Poem should not only inspire, but maintain."[68]

11. George Colman the elder, preface to his edition of Horace (1783): "I have reserved the Notes to this place [i.e., at the end of the volume], that the reader might be left to his genuine feelings, and the natural impression [of] reading."[69]

12. Anna Seward, letter of 1785 to Court Dewes, on Thomas Warton's 1785 edition of Milton: "Mr Warton's two last notes on L'Allegro, Il Penseroso, are some of the most exquisite writing I ever beheld; and the last sentence but one in his preface, is of the sublimest species that oratory has been known to produce. I read them with the same thrill of delight, that the poetry on which they comment inspires."[70]

13. John Pinkerton, letter of 1787 to David Steuart Erskine, eleventh Earl of Buchan, on Pinkerton's 1790 edition of John Barbour's *The Bruce* (1790): "The notes are to be at the bottom of the page, as in [Thomas] Tyrwhit's [*sic*] Chaucer, to relieve the reader in so long and uniform a poem."[71]

14. Vicesimus Knox, "On the Use and Abuse of Marginal Notes and Quotations" (1788): "Though something may be said against notes, quotations, and mottoes; yet more, I believe, may be advanced in their favor. If a reader thinks them of little use . . . it is easy to neglect them. It is true that they occupy a space of the page, and increase the size of the volume; but these are inconveniences of little consequence, compared with the pleasure and information which they afford."[72]

15. Germaine de Staël, *Essay on Fictions* (1795): "People may call *Hudibras* a witty poem, but we have to hunt for the author's meaning . . . with innumerable notes to understand his jokes, and preliminary instruction on how to find it funny or interesting. The merit of this poem is therefore no longer generally appreciated. A philosophical work may require research, but fiction can only produce a convincing effect when it contains within itself whatever the readers need for a complete impression."[73]

16. Francis Hodgson, preface to *The Satires of Juvenal* (1807): "I like to read a poem quite through before I examine it in detail. We must compound for a little temporary ignorance of the full meaning of particular passages by this method: but pleasure is the great end of poetry; and it is impossible to judge of the general effect of a poem, if our attention is called off every moment to quotation and reference in the notes. This must be the case, if they are at the bottom of the page. There is a sort of compulsion in the plan; a reader is forced by his natural curiosity to look for an explanation."[74]

17. Charles Lamb, "Detached Thoughts on Books and Reading" (1822): "I do not care for a First Folio of Shakespeare. I rather prefer the common editions of [Nicholas] Rowe and [Jacob] Tonson, without notes."[75]

18. Leigh Hunt, "Among My Books" (1823), on Warton's edition of Milton: "his edition . . . is a wilderness of sweets. It is the only one in which a true lover of the original can pardon an exuberance of annotation; though I confess I am inclined enough to pardon any notes that resemble it, however numerous. The 'builded rhyme' stands at the top of the page, like a fair edifice with all sorts of flowers and fresh waters at its foot."[76]

19. Thomas de Quincey, "Style" (1840): "The question ["of how far the practice of footnotes . . . is reconcilable with the laws of just composition"] is . . . how far, viz, such an excrescence as a note argues that the sentence to which it is attached has not received the benefit of a full development for the conception involved; whether, if thrown into the furnace again and re-melted, it might not be so recast so as to absorb the redundancy which had previously flowed over into a note."[77]

Several inferences can be drawn from this collection of remarks, which, I should add, are hardly exhaustive and must be read in their original contexts, where they acquire a range of implication impossible to canvass in this overview. There is hostility toward notes, but no consensus about notes as evil or "necessary evils."[78] Endnotes appear to be preferred (Colman, Hodgson), yet the dynamic between notes and text, rather than the type of note, matters most. One thread of response (Felton, Goldsmith) assigns the dislike of notes to their making things more difficult rather than less so. There is a Johnsonian emphasis (Spence, Stockdale, Hodgson) on the aptitude of notes for defeating concentration. The most damning criticisms view annotation as a stylistic defect (Gray, Shenstone, de Staël, de Quincey). Yet these quotations also reveal admiration for notes. For Dryden, reading Creech's notes is a pastime, and for Hunt, the annotated page holds aesthetic appeal. In spite of their distance in time, Concanen and Knox articulate two parts of the same perspective: notes help readers understand poetry from other times, and, when explanations are not needed, notes can be ignored. (Though compare this view to Hodgson's understanding of footnotes as compulsory reading.) In a reversal of the expected relation, Pinkerton presents notes as a welcome distraction from the toils of poetry! It is difficult to draw a general conclusion from these statements except that notes were far from universally despised. To establish whether such statements align with actual practices of annotation, we must turn to the chapters in this collection.

OVERVIEW OF THE CHAPTERS

The collection begins with two chapters on one of the most extensively annotated of eighteenth-century poetic forms: the georgic. In their chapter 1 survey of georgic poetry from John Philips's *Cyder* (1708) to Charlotte Smith's *Beachy Head* (1807), Karina Williamson and Michael Edson reveal notes to be one of the few regular aspects of this protean genre, the quantity of annotation reaching its height around midcentury in poems such as James Grainger's *The Sugar-Cane* (1764). The purposes of this extensive annotation ranged from establishing a poet's expertise in a technical field to listing borrowings from Virgil's *Georgics*. The mix of goals differed from poem to poem depending on whether the georgic poem was more didactic or descriptive in nature and also whether the notes were by the author or an editor. In all cases, the annotation to georgic verse negotiated similar cultural forces. Following the rise of science-based disciplines after 1700, poets enlisted notes to give experimental proofs without violating ancient rules of decorum. As poets and editors became increasingly aware of these poems as parts of a Virgilian tradition, they recruited notes to define what kind of poem—didactic or descriptive or both—the category of "georgic" would encompass. Such pressures are illustrated in the chapter's closing example of Charles Dunster's 1791 edition of *Cyder*, in which the notes exhaustively document Virgilian imitations while impugning the scientific accuracy of Virgil's *Georgics*.

Turning, then, to an analysis of a single, heavily annotated georgic, William Jones, in chapter 2, traces the three waves of authorial annotation in William Falconer's *The Shipwreck* (1762, 1764, 1769) to changing readerships. Unique among English poems for its heavy use of nautical terminology, *The Shipwreck* of 1762 addressed primarily sailors, the footnotes defining nautical terms in the absence of a marine dictionary. Following the poem's success, Falconer revised and expanded the poem in 1764 to appeal to general readers, introducing, among other elements, a sentimental subplot of doomed love. The shift in audience registers in the content of Falconer's notes, which in 1764 and 1769 integrate more explanation of literary allusion while reducing the amount of technical instruction. Falconer's attempts to expand the poem's audience came at the cost of the delivery of technical information. Just as his notes in 1762 arose in response to the perceived deficiency of existing nautical dictionaries, so Falconer later drew on the notes to *The Shipwreck* as the basis of his own attempt in prose at rectifying this oversight: the *Universal Dictionary of the Marine* (1769). In charting the movement of Falconer's notes from the bottom of the poetic page into a freestanding work of reference, Jones presents annotation as an effort to link georgic poetry with the professional knowledges that by the 1760s were increasingly disseminated in prose.

The next three chapters, gathered under the heading "Nationalism, Antiquarianism, and Annotation," explore the links between antiquarian editing and national identity. In chapter 3, Jeff Strabone considers the function and afterlife of the notes in Thomas Hearne's 1724 edition of the Chronicle of Robert of Gloucester. As Strabone demonstrates, Hearne used his notes to present the thirteenth-century Chronicle as an object, not of literature, but of history, as a source of historical information and a resource on Anglo-Saxon language. Hearne's goal was not to make understanding the poem easy: in addition to printing the Chronicle in mix of blackletter and unfamiliar Saxon characters, he attached notes in Latin. Hearne instead stressed the poem's archaism and, through the Latin annotation, softened the perceived barbarism of the poetry. As Hearne's neoclassical distrust of the medieval gave way over the century to a scholarly desire to trace English nationhood to a native poetic tradition, the authority of Hearne's notes sustained the Chronicle's importance. In later years, the Chronicle served new purposes, from justifying Thomas Percy's theory of Anglo-Saxon prosody to inspiring Coleridge's meter in *Christabel*. Hearne's notes ensured that Robert's Chronicle was regarded into the nineteenth century as the founding text of an English literary tradition, a tradition unrecognized by Hearne himself.

Next, in chapter 4, Thomas Van der Goten considers the identity-fashioning work of an overlooked kind of antiquarian annotation: the topographical note. Unlike notes documenting sources or providing historical context, topographical notes employ the material fragments of the past—ruins, castles, statues, monuments—to create national landscapes. Such notes enact a tour of the monuments referred to in a poem; they present landscapes as catalogs of landmarks. In Thomas Percy's ballad *The Hermit of Warkworth* (1771), the topographical notes serve as a substitute form of national memory, recovering destroyed buildings and faded inscriptions. The destroyed castle at Wark is presented less in its hermeneutic role, as a symbol of medieval conflict, than as a token of Northumbrian identity. Specifying the etymology of place names and recuperating forgotten ruins, the topographical annotation in John Pinkerton's edition of John Barbour's *The Bruce* (1790) likewise constructs an authentic Scottish geography of iconic castles, churches, and statues. Through such examples, Van der Goten shows British and Scottish identities to be articulated not merely in literary traditions but also through canons of castles and monuments.

In the final chapter of this unit, Alex Watson explores the eclectic notes to Robert Southey's epic *Madoc* (1805). Featuring extracts from both Welsh histories and Spanish colonial writings, Southey's endnotes at first appear to espouse the imperialism of the main text, which depicts the defeat of the Aztecs by an invading Welsh army. However, the miscellaneousness of the perspectives collected in the notes undercut any straightforward message. While the poem celebrates the Anglo-Welsh union as a civilizing step, the notes document the English violence against the Welsh and the illegitimate origins of the union. While the poem stresses the brutality of the Aztecs to justify the Spanish conquest, the notes imply the cruelty of the Spaniards. Such self-defeating notes reflect more than Southey's antiquarian delight in amassing facts at the cost of coherence. On the one hand, this conflicting quality points up the fractured nature of the same national and imperial identities that Southey naturalized and celebrated. On the other, such contradictions document the poet's changing identity: from the radical he was in the 1790s, when Southey began work on the poem, to the pro-imperialist Tory he had become a decade later.

True to its title "Varieties of Annotation," the third set of chapters historicizes the apparent extravagances and impertinences alleged against eighteenth-century annotators. In chapter 6, David Hopkins starts by questioning the persistent view of Pope's *Iliad* translation as a distortion of Homer's original to suit the politeness of Pope's age. Such a view, Hopkins argues, depends on ignoring Pope's annotations, which, in eighteenth- and nineteenth-century editions, were either shortened or omitted and continue to go unread today since editions are hard to find. In fact, Pope had a sophisticated awareness of historical difference, and his notes captured both Homer's familiarity and otherness. An enemy of pedantry but not of scholarship, Pope combined his own insights with information from previous commentators in order to clarify the language and explicate the mores of the Greeks. Far from bowing to politeness, Pope's note on the death of Lycaon in book 21 praises Achilles at the moment when the hero seems to be farthest from gentlemanly ideals. When Pope altered the comparisons of heroes to low creatures, as in the case of the description of Menelaus in book 17, Pope acted not out of a regard for decorum but conveyed the intended meaning while acknowledging that the original comparisons would have carried more dignity for Homer's audience than for English readers. Through these and many other examples, Hopkins reveals Pope as a more historically sensitive translator than is often supposed, the poet helping Homer speak across time without bowdlerizing the epic to suit eighteenth-century sensibilities.

In chapter 7, the second chapter in this group, Tom Mason examines the transchronological quality of eighteenth-century annotation. In addition to anticipating modern editors in quoting from contemporaneous works as potential sources or analogues, Chaucer's early annotators cited passages from significantly earlier or later texts on the basis of mere similarity. The implication sometimes was that a modern author borrowed from Chaucer; more frequently, the point was that both writers thought in similar ways. For instance, in a 1737 note on the "Knight's Tale," the editor Thomas Morell quotes a similar passage from Pope's *Iliad* and speculates that Chaucer and Homer held similar views of honor. Despite his own strictures against such wide-ranging comparisons, Thomas Tyrwhitt in his 1775 Chaucer edition notes a resemblance between the "Reeve's Prologue" and Gray's *Elegy Written in a Country Churchyard* (1751). For readers today for whom such resemblances are largely irrelevant, such notes will seem gratuitous. But, as Mason argues, these chance associations (conveyed by phrases such as "this reminds me" or "I cannot help quoting") reflected an important aspect of eighteenth-century reading experiences.

To close this section on allegedly wayward annotators and annotation, Adam Rounce investigates in chapter 8 the apparent excesses of annotation in Thomas Warton's edition of Milton's non-epic verse (1785). At first glance, Warton's explanatory notes embody everything avoided by modern editors: digressiveness; tenuous claims of allusion; and accumulation of parallels without explanatory benefit to the passage annotated. However, as Rounce demonstrates, Warton's weaknesses are also his virtues. In extending his source-hunting to obscure and non-canonical poetry from the medieval and Renaissance periods, Warton better reconstructs Milton's intertextual element than other early editors, who limited their searches to scripture, the classics, and the vernacular canon of Shakespeare and Spenser. For example, when Warton explains the usage of *stops* in the opening lines of *Lycidas*, he gives clarifying quotations from William Browne, Shakespeare, and Michael Drayton; when he explicates the use of *free* in "L'Allegro," he gives excerpts from Chaucer, Shakespeare, Ben Jonson, and the romance *Sir Eglamour of Artois*. Even when such inventories of parallel passages or possible influences yield no new insights, Warton's notes promote historical thinking and an appreciation of the literary, religious, and historical culture around Milton in the eighteenth century. In defying the claims of hierarchy and canon when contextualizing his poet, Warton anticipated modern editorial values, and, for this reason, his Milton edition is one of the most important editions of the eighteenth century.

The collection's last set of chapters, "Annotating the Canon," addresses the role of notes in the creation of poetic traditions. In chapter 9, Mark A. Pedreira discusses Zachary Grey, one of the earliest editors of Samuel Butler's *Hudibras* (1664, 1678). In addition to explicating Butler's topical references, Grey seeks in his 1744 edition to establish the poem's canonicity. To this end, Grey uses footnotes to catalog Butler's borrowings from both the ancient and modern classics. But Grey also uses notes to negotiate different readerships. To satisfy expert readers, he quotes classical sources in original languages; to serve novice readers, he explains stories from unfamiliar or inaccessible works. Grey's educational aims frequently lead to the sort of over-annotation Mason and Rounce discuss in other contexts. For example, Grey's annotations go beyond making the implicit comparison of Hudibras to Virgil's hero Aeneas explicit. His notes include unnecessary details about Aeneas's genealogy and the loss of his wife Creusa during the flight from Troy. The necessity of such details might be questioned today, but in providing readers information available to Butler's original audience and staying consistent to Grey's own editorial principles, the 1744 notes prove to be more modern than they at first appear.

Moving from a published edition to manuscript notes, Sandro Jung in chapter 10 examines the editorial practice of the scholar William Hymers, who at his death in 1783 was preparing an edition of William Collins's poetry. After contextualizing Hymers's unfinished edition both in terms of the other Collins editions produced by John Langhorne and Anna Barbauld in 1765 and 1797, respectively, as well as the contemporary handling of other canonical poets, in particular Gilbert West's edition of the *Odes of Pindar* (1749), Jung argues for Hymers's unique approach to drawing Collins's verse into the vernacular canon. In identifying both classical and modern sources for the poems, Hymers positions Collins within two competing models of literary historiography, one a progressive model of increasing literary refinement favored by Pope and Addison, the other a narrative of literary decline from a purer, more authentic past advocated by the Warton brothers and Thomas Percy. Through analysis of Hymers's notes to Collins's "Ode on the Poetical Character" and "Ode to Fear," among other poems, Jung documents Hymers's attempts to situate Collins's poetry in a national, bardic tradition while simultaneously celebrating the stylistic elegance that links Collins to eighteenth-century "modernity." As Jung suggests, Hymer's unpublished notes give insight into annotation's role in defining poetry and offer an exemplary window into the relationship between annotation and canon formation.

To conclude the collection, Barbara M. Benedict in chapter 11 demonstrates how British literary anthologists employed notes and paratexts to sell volumes to new readers, including children, women, and the self-taught. Taking the annotating of fables early in the century as illustrative of the challenges facing later compilers, Benedict stresses how anthologists aimed to control interpretation without alienating readers through the forcefulness of the attempt. To present literature as both a luxury item and tool for self-improvement, Vicesimus Knox in *Elegant Extracts* (1789) employed notes sparingly, instead using frontispieces and topical headings to guide interpretation while allowing the uncluttered pages to imply literature's status as an art object. To promote literature as national sensibility, John Roach deployed notes in *Beauties of the Poets* (1794) to prompt sentimental response. For example, one of Roach's notes presents the historically specific attack on enclosure in Goldsmith's *The Deserted Village* as a generalized portrait of the corrupting effects of wealth. To represent literature as timeless morality, the Reverend George Glyn Scraggs in *Instructive Selections* (1801) combined short excerpts with overbearing annotation, detaching the excerpts from time and genre by arranging the extracts thematically. Far from simply giving identifications or defining terms, the notes and other paratexts in late-century anthologies, Benedict argues, market specific views of literature—as social capital, patriotic sentiment, and timeless morality—to novice readers.

* * *

Finally, a few words about the compilation of the collection. The possible frames for analyzing eighteenth-century annotation exceed the four themes that structure this volume. In focusing on georgic and antiquarian annotation, on the one hand, and on notes as devices to historicize and canonize, on the other, I made no attempt at exhaustive coverage. It would be impossible for a single volume to cover all the important annotated poems, all the annotators, and all the functions that notes served. A whole (long) book could be devoted to the Scribleriads, Hilliads, Diaboliads, Lousiads, and other poems imitating Pope's *The Dunciad*, not to mention other poems with mock apparatuses.[79] The annotatory methods specific to eighteenth-century classical editing likewise deserve several book-length studies.[80] Certainly annotations by women merit more attention than they receive in this collection.[81] To stir broader interest in the study of poetry and notes, this volume focuses on selected aspects of annotation that seem most relevant to ongoing discussions in the fields of eighteenth-century literature, book history, and print culture. Our volume therefore presents a series of snapshots, or case studies, gesturing at a larger mass of annotations and annotated poems awaiting future contextualization and analysis. Our limited generalizations may not satisfy readers looking for sweeping narratives or theories. But the caprices of annotation defy generalities; as Pope observes, notes have a disintegrating effect on theoretical systems and everything else: "How Prologues into Prefaces decay, / And these to Notes are fritter'd quite away."[82] If the chapters collected here reflect something of the quirky particularism of their subject, it is hoped that they at least appeal in their miscellaneousness.

Although the division of chapters in this collection seeks to foreground common themes, alternative groupings are possible. For those interested in annotation as a collaborative form of textual production, Pedreira and Williamson/Edson touch on the topic. For those intrigued by the ways in which annotators use notes to address diverse groups of readers, Jones, Hopkins, and Van der Goten offer something of interest. Mason, Jung, Rounce, and Benedict deal with notes as actual or potential sources of evidence about eighteenth-century reading practices, while Jung, Mason, Strabone, and Watson consider annotators whose goals exceed mere explication. Other configurations of the chapters in this volume are possible, too. If nothing else, the links between the chapters indicate paths for future inquiry.

Ultimately, to understand the pressures shaping the annotation of poetry in eighteenth-century England is to acquire a more critical perspective on the annotatory practices unique to our own print-to-digital moment and, specifically, on the ongoing production of new annotated editions of such poets as Swift and Pope. In the so-called age of ECCO, when—on account of the availability of early editions via electronic databases, and on account of the decline in the non-specialist readers most needful of notes—the continued compilation of expensive annotated editions of eighteenth-century poets is in question, a better understanding of past practices may advantage the editors and annotators of these poets today.[83]

NOTES

1. *Johnson on Shakespeare*, ed. Arthur Sherbo, vol. 7 of *The Yale Edition of the Works of Samuel Johnson* (New Haven, CT: Yale University Press, 1968), 111.

2. David Hume to William Strahan, April 8, 1776, in *The Letters of David Hume*, ed. J. Y. T. Greig, 2 vols. (Oxford: Clarendon Press, 1969), 2:313.

3. For studies endorsing this narrative, see Alvin B. Kernan, *Samuel Johnson & the Impact of Print* (Princeton, NJ: Princeton University Press, 1987); Joseph M. Levine, *The Battle of the Books: History and Literature in the Augustan Age* (Ithaca, NY: Cornell University Press, 1991); and Anthony Grafton, *The Footnote: A Curious History* (Cambridge, MA: Harvard University Press, 1997).

4. For Bayle's notes, see Grafton, *Footnote*, 190–222; for Simon's notes, see Marcus Walsh, "Swift's *Tale of the Tub* and the Mock Book," in *Jonathan Swift and the Eighteenth-Century Book*, ed. Paddy Bullard and James McLaverty (Cambridge: Cambridge University Press, 2013), 103–4. For the technological impetus behind the abandonment of marginal glosses for notes, see Lawrence Lipking, "The Marginal Gloss," *Critical Inquiry* 3, no. 4 (1977): 609–55.

5. For antiquarian editing, see Nick Groom, *The Making of Percy's Reliques* (Oxford: Clarendon Press, 1999); Maureen N. McLane, *Balladeering, Minstrelsy, and the Making of British Romantic Poetry* (Cambridge: Cambridge University Press, 2008); and Maureen N. McLane, "Mediating Antiquarians in Britain, 1760–1830: The Invention of Oral Tradition; or, Close Reading before Coleridge," in *This Is Enlightenment*, ed. Clifford Siskin and William Warner (Chicago: University of Chicago Press, 2010), 247–63.

6. Ann Blair and Peter Stallybrass, "Mediating Information, 1450–1800," in Siskin and Warner, *This Is Enlightenment*, 143. For humanist excerpting and commonplacing, see also Rebecca W. Bushnell, *A Culture of Teaching: Early Modern Humanism in Theory and Practice* (Ithaca, NY: Cornell University Press, 1996), esp. 117–43; and David Allan, *Commonplace Books and Reading in Georgian England* (Cambridge: Cambridge University Press, 2010), esp. 46–57.

7. Examples include James Patterson, *A Complete Commentary, with Etymological, Explanatory, Critical, and Classical Notes on* Paradise Lost (1744); Zachary Grey, *Critical, Historical, and Explanatory Notes on* Shakespeare (1754), William Huggins, *Annotations on* Orlando Furioso (1757); and Edward Capell, *Notes and Various Readings to* Shakespeare (1779–1780).

8. Gérard Genette, *Paratexts: Thresholds of Interpretation*, trans. Jane E. Lewin (Cambridge: Cambridge University Press, 1997), 337.

9. Genette, *Paratexts*, 1n2.

10. The third edition of Samuel Johnson's *Dictionary* (Dublin: Printed by W. G. Jones for Thomas Ewing, 1768) defines *annotation*; entries for *note* and *commentary* also use the term *annotation*.

11. Important recent studies of eighteenth-century paratexts include James McLaverty, *Pope, Print, and Meaning* (Oxford: Oxford University Press, 2001); Janine Barchas, *Graphic Design, Print Culture, and the Eighteenth-Century Novel* (Cambridge: Cambridge University Press, 2003); Laura Runge and Pat Rogers, eds., *Producing the Eighteenth-Century Book: Writers and Publishers in England, 1650–1800* (Newark: University of Delaware Press, 2009); David A. Brewer, "The Tactility of Authorial Names," *Eighteenth Century* 54, no. 2 (2013): 195–213; Christopher Flint, *The Appearance of Print in Eighteenth-Century Fiction* (Cambridge: Cambridge University Press, 2014); Brad Pasanek and Chad Wellmon, "The Enlightenment Index," *Eighteenth Century* 56, no. 3 (2015): 359–82; and Sandro Jung, *James*

Thomson's The Seasons, *Print Culture, and Visual Interpretation, 1730–1842* (Bethlehem, PA: Lehigh University Press, 2015).

12. For studies of eighteenth-century editing and mock-editing, see Peter Seary, *Lewis Theobald and the Editing of Shakespeare* (Oxford: Clarendon Press, 1990); Margreta de Grazia, *Shakespeare Verbatim: The Reproduction of Authenticity and the 1790 Apparatus* (Oxford: Clarendon Press, 1991); Howard Erskine-Hill, "On Historical Commentary: The Example of Milton and Dryden," in *Presenting Poetry: Composition, Publication, Reception: Essays in Honour of Ian Jack,* ed. Howard Erskine-Hill and Richard A. McCabe (Cambridge: Cambridge University Press, 1995), 52–74; Marcus Walsh, *Shakespeare, Milton, and Eighteenth-Century Literary Editing: The Beginnings of Interpretative Scholarship* (Cambridge: Cambridge University Press, 1997); Edmund G. C. King, "Pope's 1723–25 *Shakespear,* Classical Editing, and Humanistic Reading Practices," *Eighteenth-Century Life* 32, no. 2 (2008): 3–13; Esther Yu, "From Judgement to Interpretation: Eighteenth Century Critics of Milton's *Paradise Lost,*" *Milton Studies* 53 (2012): 181–202; and Walsh, "Swift's *Tale of the Tub* and the Mock Book" and Claude Rawson, "The Mock Edition Revisited: Swift to Mailer," in Bullard and McLaverty, *Jonathan Swift,* 101–18 and 231–67, respectively.

13. For wide-ranging and theoretical studies from other periods, see D. C. Greetham, ed., *The Margins of the Text* (Ann Arbor: University of Michigan Press, 1990); Stephen A. Barney, ed., *Annotation and Its Texts* (Oxford: Oxford University Press, 1991); Evelyn B. Tribble, *Margins and Marginality: The Printed Page in Early Modern England* (Charlottesville: University of Virginia Press, 1993); Helen Smith and Louise Wilson, eds., *Renaissance Paratexts* (Cambridge: Cambridge University Press, 2011); Mary Jane Edwards, "Analyzing the Annotations: Theories and Practices of Explanatory Notes," in *English Past and Present: Selected Papers from the IAUPE Malta Conference in 2010,* ed. Wolfgang Viereck (Frankfurt: Peter Lang, 2012), 205–20; and Jane Griffiths, *Diverting Authorities: Experimental Glossing Practices in Manuscript and Print* (Oxford: Oxford University Press, 2014).

14. For discussions of paratexts in novels, see Barchas, *Graphic Design*; Flint, *Appearance of Print*; and Alex Howard, "The Pains of Attention: Paratextual Reading in *Practical Education* and *Castle Rackrent,*" *Nineteenth-Century Literature* 69, no. 3 (2014): 293–318. For paratexts in historiography, see Grafton, *Footnote.*

15. Analyses of late-century and Romantic annotation include Jacqueline Labbe, "'Transplanted into More Congenial Soil': Footnoting the Self in the Poetry of Charlotte Smith," in *Ma(r)king the Text: The Presentation of Meaning on the Literary Page,* ed. Joe Bray, Miriam Handley, and Anne C. Henry (Aldershot, UK: Ashgate, 2000), 71–86; Dhalia Porter, "Formal Relocations: The Method of Southey's *Thalaba the Destroyer* (1801)," *European Romantic Review* 20, no. 5 (2009): 671–79; Alex Broadhead, "Framing Dialect in the 1800 *Lyrical Ballads*: Wordsworth, Regionalisms, and Footnotes," *Language and Literature* 19, no. 3 (2010): 249–63; Corey E. Andrews, "Footnoted Folklore: Robert Burns's 'Hallowe'en,'" *Studies in Scottish Literature* 37, no. 1 (2013): 24–37; and Elizabeth Edwards, "Footnotes to a Nation: Richard Llwyd's *Beaumaris Bay* (1800)," in *Voice and Context in Eighteenth-Century Verse: Order in Variety,* ed. Joanna Fowler and Allan Ingram (Houndmills, UK: Palgrave Macmillan, 2015), 133–51. An important book-length study that considers annotated poems by Burns, Southey, and Lord Byron is Alex Watson, *Romantic Marginality: Nation and Empire on the Borders of the Page* (London: Pickering and Chatto, 2012).

16. Representative studies include Frank Palmeri, "The Satiric Footnotes of Swift and Gibbon," *Eighteenth Century* 31, no. 3 (1990): 245–62; Peter W. Cosgrove, "Undermining the Text: Edward Gibbon, Alexander Pope, and the Anti-authenticating Footnote," in Barney,

Annotation and Its Texts, 130–51; Grafton, *Footnote*, 94–121; and Claude Rawson, "Heroic Notes: Pope's Epic Idiom Revisited," in *Alexander Pope: Word and World*, Proceedings of the British Academy 91 (Oxford: For the British Academy by Oxford University Press, 1998), 69–110. One exception to this trend is McLaverty, *Pope, Print, and Meaning*, which considers *The Dunciad* alongside Pope's other annotated poems.

17. Genette, *Paratexts*, 333.

18. Thomas Gray to William Mason, September 7, 1757, in *The Correspondence of Thomas Gray*, ed. Paget Toynbee and Leonard Whibley, 3 vols. (Oxford: Clarendon Press, 1935), 2:522.

19. Thomas Gray to James Beattie, February 1, 1768, in Toynbee and Whibley, *Correspondence of Thomas Gray*, 3:1002. For more on the reception and annotation of Gray's odes, see James Mulholland, *Sounding Imperial: Poetic Voice and Politics of Empire, 1730–1820* (Baltimore, MD: Johns Hopkins University Press, 2013), 59–66.

20. Jonathan Swift to Alexander Pope, July 16, 1728, in *The Correspondence of Alexander Pope*, ed. George Sherburn, 5 vols. (Oxford: Oxford University Press), 2:504. For Pope's invitation, see 2:503.

21. *Daily Courant*, June 24, 1709.

22. For Samuel Johnson's collaboration with George Steevens on the notes in his Shakespeare edition (1765), as well as accusations that Johnson's notes plagiarized Thomas Edwards and Edward Capell, see John A. Dussinger, "Johnson's Unacknowledged Debt to Thomas Edwards in the 1765 Edition of Shakespeare," *Philological Quarterly* 95, no. 1 (2016): 45–62.

23. Alexander Pope to William Broome, [1717?], in Sherburn, *Correspondence of Alexander Pope*, 1:394.

24. Hume to Strahan, April 8, 1776, in Greig, *Letters of David Hume*, 2:313.

25. John Dryden to Jacob Tonson, December/January 1695 or 1696, in *The Literary Correspondences of the Tonsons*, ed. Stephen Bernard (Oxford: Oxford University Press, 2015), 121.

26. *Proposals for Printing by Subscription, Miscellaneous Works, in Verse and Prose, of Mr. John Bancks. Adorned with Sculptures, and Illustrated with Notes* (London, 1737).

27. Samuel Johnson, "Life of Pope," in *The Lives of the Most Eminent English Poets*, ed. Roger Lonsdale, 4 vols. (Oxford: Clarendon Press, 2006), 4:74.

28. Robert J. Connors, "The Rhetoric of Citation Systems, Part I: The Development of Annotation Structures from the Renaissance to 1900," *Rhetoric Review* 17, no. 1 (1998): 30.

29. For this anecdote, see Johnson, "Life of Pope," 4:13–14.

30. For the fate of Pope's notes in later and modern editions, see Hopkins's chapter in this volume and Stuart Gillespie, "Translation and Commentary: Pope's *Iliad*," in *Classical Commentaries: Explorations in a Scholarly Genre*, ed. Christina S. Krass and Christopher Stray (Oxford: Oxford University Press, 2016), 309–16.

31. Michael Harris, "Paper Pirates: The Alternative Book Trade in mid-18th Century London," in *Fakes and Frauds: Varieties of Deception in Print & Manuscript*, ed. Robin Myers and Michael Harris (Detroit, MI: Omnigraphics, 1989), 59.

32. William Enfield, *Observations on Literary Property* (London: Printed for Joseph Johnson, 1774), 40.

33. For the 1752 case, see 1 Black. W. 331, 96 Eng. Rep. 184. For a summary of the 1765 case, see *The Cases of the Appellants and Respondents in the Cause of Literary Property, before the House of Lords* (London: Printed for J. Bew et al., 1774), 9.

34. For book-historical studies dealing with these questions, see Andrew Piper, *Dreaming in Books: The Making of the Bibliographic Imagination in the Romantic Age* (Chicago: Univer-

sity of Chicago Press, 2009); James Raven, *Publishing Business in Eighteenth-Century England* (Woodbridge: Boydell Press, 2014); and Sandro Jung and Stephen Colclough, eds., *The History of the Book*, Yearbook of English Studies 45 (Glasgow, UK: Modern Humanities Research Association, 2015).

35. Swift to Pope, July 16, 1728, in Sherburn, *Correspondence of Alexander Pope*, 2:504.

36. Paula McDowell, "Mediating Media Past and Present: Toward a Genealogy of 'Print Culture' and 'Oral Tradition,'" in Siskin and Warner, *This Is Enlightenment*, 239.

37. For a recent discussion of the ancients versus moderns in terms of accessibility and intelligibility, see Henry Power, *Epic into Novel: Henry Fielding, Scriblerian Satire, and the Consumption of Classical Literature* (Oxford: Oxford University Press, 2015).

38. For a discussion of eighteenth-century efforts to balance aesthetic and exchange value, see Jonathan Brody Kramnick, *Making the English Canon: Print-Capitalism and the Cultural Past, 1700–1770* (Cambridge: Cambridge University Press, 1998), 54–104.

39. Alexander Pope to William Warburton, September 20, 1741, in Sherburn, *Correspondence of Alexander Pope*, 4:362.

40. Pope to Warburton, November 27, 1742, in Sherburn, *Correspondence of Alexander Pope*, 4:428.

41. Power, *Epic into Novel*, 109.

42. For discussions of the Enlightenment desire to store comprehensive knowledge and the role of print, see Ann Blair, *Too Much to Know: Managing Scholarly Information before the Modern Age* (New Haven, CT: Yale University Press, 2009); Seth Rudy, *Literature and Encyclopedism in Enlightenment Britain: The Pursuit of Complete Knowledge* (Houndmills, UK: Palgrave Macmillan, 2014); and Chad Wellmon, *Organizing Enlightenment: Information Overload and the Invention of the Modern Research University* (Baltimore, MD: Johns Hopkins University Press, 2015). For sources in ballad editing, see McLane, "Mediating Antiquarians," 252.

43. Blair, *Too Much to Know*, 1.

44. J. C. Stephens, ed., *The Guardian* (Lexington: University of Kentucky Press, 1982), 230.

45. Samuel Richardson to Susanna Highmore, June 4, 1750, in *The Correspondence of Samuel Richardson*, ed. Anna Laetitia Barbauld, 6 vols. (1804; New York: AMS Press, 1966), 2:229.

46. For a discussion of Erasmus Darwin's annotations, see Martin Priestman, *The Poetry of Erasmus Darwin: Enlightened Spaces, Romantic Times* (Aldershot, UK: Ashgate, 2013), 50–52.

47. Walsh, *Shakespeare, Milton, and Eighteenth-Century Literary Editing*, 10.

48. Samuel Butler, *Hudibras*, ed. John Wilders (Oxford: Clarendon Press, 1967), lx. Wilders is describing the annotations of Butler's earliest editor, Zachary Grey. For a criticism of lists of sources, see Thomas Edwards, *The Canons of Criticism, and Glossary, Being a Supplement to Mr. Warburton's Edition of Shakespear*, 3rd ed. (London: Printed for C. Bathurst, 1750), 119.

49. For these competing demands, see Rudy, *Literature and Encyclopedism*.

50. Gray to Beattie, February 1, 1768, in Toynbee and Whibley, *Correspondence of Thomas Gray*, 3:1004.

51. Beattie to Gray, February 1768, in Toynbee and Whibley, *Correspondence of Thomas Gray*, 3:1010.

52. William Warburton to John Knapton, April 25, 1753, in *Pope's Literary Legacy: The Book-Trade Correspondence of William Warburton and John Knapton, 1744–1780*, ed. Donald W. Nichol (Oxford: Oxford Bibliographical Society, 1992), 69.

53. Adam Rounce, "Annotation," in *The Encyclopedia of British Literature 1660–1789*, 3 vols., ed. Gary Day and Jack Lynch (Oxford: Wiley-Blackwell, 2015), 1:55.

54. For the consequences of annotation on note taking by readers, see William H. Sherman, "What Did Renaissance Readers Write in Their Books?," in *Books and Readers in Early Modern England*, ed. Jennifer Andersen and Elizabeth Sauer (Philadelphia: University of Pennsylvania Press, 2001), 123–24.

55. John Smith, *The Printer's Grammar* (London: Printed for the Editor, and Sold by W. Owen . . . and M. Cooper, 1755), 76.

56. For the less-than-positive associations of Restoration and eighteenth-century criticism as "illiterate heckling" and "meanspirited pedantry," see Jack Lynch, "Criticism of Shakespeare," in *Shakespeare in the Eighteenth Century*, ed. Fiona Ritchie and Peter Sabor (Cambridge: Cambridge University Press, 2012), 41.

57. McLaverty, *Pope, Print, and Meaning*, 209.

58. *The Yale Edition of the Works of Samuel Johnson*, ed. W. J. Bate and Albrecht B. Strauss, vol. 4, *The Rambler* (New Haven, CT: Yale University Press, 1969), 111.

59. John Dryden, preface to *Sylvae*, in *The Works of John Dryden*, vol. 3, *Poems 1685–1692*, ed. Earl Miner (Berkeley: University of California Press, 1969), 14.

60. Henry Felton, *A Dissertation on Reading the Classics, and Forming a Just Style* (London: Printed for Jonah Bowyer, 1713), 56–57.

61. [Matthew Concanen], "Of Commentators," in *The Speculatist: A Collection of Letters and Essays, Moral and Political, Serious and Humorous: Upon Various Subjects* (London: Printed by J. Watts, for the Author, 1730), 186–87.

62. Joseph Spence, *Polymetis; or, An Enquiry Concerning the Agreement between the Works of the Roman Poets, and the Remains of the Ancient Artists* (London: Printed for R. Dodsley, 1747), 286–87.

63. Edwards, *Canons of Criticism*, 134.

64. Thomas Gray to Horace Walpole, July 11, 1757, in Toynbee and Whibley, *Correspondence of Thomas Gray*, 2:508.

65. Review of James Grainger, *A Poetical Translation of the Elegies of Tibullus*, in *Critical Review* 6 (December 1758): 476–77.

66. William Shenstone, "On Books and Writers," in *The Works in Verse and Prose, of William Shenstone, Esq* (London: Printed for R. and J. Dodsley, 1764), 273–74.

67. Oliver Goldsmith, *An Enquiry into the Present State of Polite Learning in Europe*, 2nd ed. (London: Printed for J. Dodsley, 1774), 15.

68. Percival Stockdale, *An Inquiry into the Nature, and Genuine Laws of Poetry; Including a Particular Defense of the Writings, and Genius of Mr. Pope* (London: Printed for N. Conant, 1778), 104–5.

69. George Colman, ed., *Q. Horatii Flacci Epistola ad Pisones, de Arte Poetica* (London: T. Cadell, 1783), iii.

70. *Letters of Anna Seward: Written between the Years 1784 and 1807*, 6 vols. (Edinburgh: Printed by George Ramsay . . . for Archibald Constable, 1811), 1:53.

71. *The Literary Correspondence of John Pinkerton, Esq.*, ed. Dawson Turner, 2 vols. (London: Henry Colburn and Richard Bentley, 1830), 1:162–63.

72. Vicesimus Knox, ["On the Use and Abuse of Marginal Notes and Quotations"], in *Winter Evenings; or, Lucubrations on Life and Letters*, 3 vols. (London: Printed for Charles Dilly, 1788), 1:88–91.

73. Vivian Folkenflik, trans., *Major Writings of Madame de Staël* (New York: Columbia University Press, 1987), 67.

74. Francis Hodgson, trans., *The Satires of Juvenal: Translated and Illustrated* (London: Printed by T. Bensley, . . . for Payne and Mackinlay, 1807), iv.

75. *Elia and the Last Essays of Elia*, vol. 2 of *The Works of Charles and Mary Lamb*, ed. E. V. Lucas (London: Methuen, 1903), 174.

76. Leigh Hunt, "My Books," in *The Indicator, and the Companion: A Miscellany for the Fields and the Fire-side* (London: Edward Moxon, 1845), 54.

77. Thomas de Quincey, *The Collected Writings, New and Enlarged Edition*, ed. David Masson, vol. 10 (Edinburgh: Adam and Charles Black, 1890), 165–66.

78. Sherbo, *Johnson on Shakespeare*, 111.

79. For a list of *The Dunciad* imitations, see Richmond P. Bond, "-iad: A Progeny of the *Dunciad*," *PMLA: Publications of the Modern Language Association* 44, no. 4 (1929): 1099–1105.

80. One recent volume on this topic is Kraus and Stray, eds., *Classical Commentaries*.

81. For the beginning of such an inquiry, see Rosie Wyles and Edith Hall, eds., *Women Classical Scholars: Unsealing the Fountain from the Renaissance to Jacqueline de Romilly* (Oxford: Oxford University Press, 2017).

82. Alexander Pope, *The Dunciad*, ed. James Sutherland, 3rd ed., vol. 5 of *The Twickenham Edition of the Poems of Alexander Pope*, ed. John Butt et al. (London: Methuen, 1963), book 1, lines 277–78.

83. For a perspective on the fate of scholarly editing and annotation in the "age of ECCO," see Janine Barchas, "First and Last," *Eighteenth-Century Life* 38, no. 3 (2014): 118–24.

I

GEORGIC ANNOTATION

1

Annotating Georgic Poetry

Karina Williamson and Michael Edson

Georgics appeal to "those who like generous explanatory notes," Juan Pellicer wryly observes.[1] From Pope's *Windsor-Forest* (1713) down to Charlotte Smith's *Beachy Head* (1807), annotation became one of the few regular features of a literary kind conspicuous for its diversity, mutability, and hybrid character. Scholars, though acknowledging the abundance of notes surrounding such poems, have largely omitted annotation from their analyses of georgic verse. There are exceptions: John Chalker has discussed the notes to Richard Jago's *Edge-Hill* (1767); and several recent commentators have remarked on the notes to James Grainger's *The Sugar-Cane* (1764).[2] But the subjects of these analyses have not been properly contextualized in a tradition of original and translated georgics with annotation that extends back to Dryden's translation of Virgil's *Georgics* (1697) or to George Chapman's *Georgicks of Hesiod* (1618). Critics approach *The Sugar-Cane*, for example, with the modern expectation that notes will be brief and self-effacing: labeled as "excessive" and "monstrous," Grainger's notes are claimed to be aggressively prolific, to overthrow the poetry much as the insects, weeds, and slaves threaten to overwhelm the planters described in his poem.[3] But, as this chapter will suggest, Grainger's self-annotations would not have appeared exceptionable alongside John Martyn's 1741 heavily annotated translation of Virgil's *Georgics* or the expansive annotation in other georgics after 1740. Nor would Grainger's contemporaries have detected much tension between the poem and its annotation, notwithstanding the superior share of the page space occupied by the footnotes.

Notes apparently held considerable appeal for readers and poets of the time. John Langhorne, who reviewed *The Sugar-Cane* in 1764, evidently regarded the footnotes as a special attraction. His opinion of Grainger's work as a whole was low ("rather an useful than an entertaining poem"), but he praised the poet for "the liberal and diffusive pains he has taken, in his Notes on this poem, to enlarge the knowledge of the West-Indian botany," adding slyly, "these Notes may, indeed, be considered, both in their medical and botanical capacity, as a very valuable part of the work; and, possibly, there are few parts of it more entertaining."[4] Langhorne's comment raises important questions. For what reasons did georgics accumulate so many notes, and what does this accumulation reveal about the function and understanding of the poetic genre of georgic in the century or so following Dryden's translation of Virgil's *Georgics*? As we will argue, the notes to eighteenth-century georgics serve various functions: they establish a poet's expertise; they evade rules of decorum; and they identify echoes from Virgil and other poets—the purpose of the last being typically to locate such poems in a classical tradition.

The precise mix of goals achieved by the annotation to these poems depends on two additional factors: whether a particular georgic is predominantly didactic or descriptive in character, and whether the annotations are supplied by the poets themselves, as in Grainger's *The Sugar-Cane*, or by later commentators, as in Joseph Warton's 1797 edition of Pope's *Windsor-Forest*. As a review of Charles Dunster's 1791 annotated edition of John Philips's *Cyder* (1708) states, "Where an author is his own commentator, . . . the notes are [more] likely to be kept close to the purpose of direct illustration, than when supplied by another, who cannot . . . think with his author."[5] While it is true to say that editors' notes sometimes approximate authors' own intentions, the categories of authorial and non-authorial annotation nevertheless mark real and important differences in the content and style of notes: this distinction structures the discussion that follows. Authorial notes might appear to be the more significant of the two classes, but non-authorial notes merit attention insofar as they reveal the struggle to define the term *georgic poetry*—as didactic, or descriptive, or both—before the term became established in its modern usage.

One final remark about the problem of genre: the label *georgic*, as used nowadays in relation to poems in English, designates a heterogeneous body of didactic and loco-descriptive texts, often in blank verse, deriving by imitation, adaptation, or modulation from Virgil's *Georgics*.[6] At one end of the spectrum come formal georgics, such as Christopher Smart's *The Hop-Garden* (1752); at the other, come topographical poems like *Windsor-Forest*, philosophical poems like Mark Akenside's *The Pleasures of Imagination* (1744), and poems with an expansive repertoire of subjects, like James Thomson's *The Seasons* (1726–1730). The problem is that the term *georgic* was rarely used before 1800, and then only in reference to poems concerned with rural industry.[7] Before 1800, John Gay's *Rural Sports* (1713) and John Armstrong's *Art of Preserving Health* (1744) were assigned to the category of didactic poetry ("that Class of Poetry which consists in giving plain and direct Instructions to the Reader") while *Windsor-Forest* and the *Seasons* were classed as descriptive poetry (works "intended more to delight, than instruct").[8] Thus it is somewhat misleading to speak of eighteenth-century *georgic*. However, the term cannot be dispensed with entirely, and in this chapter and in table 1.1 below, we classify as *georgic* any poem, on the one hand, identified in the eighteenth century as influenced by the *Georgics*, and on the other, identified by modern scholars as georgic in theme or style.[9] This collocation of poems conceived as "georgic" according to earlier and later definitions parallels the effect of the notes we analyze. After midcentury, the notes to these poems begin to distill a proto-modern concept of "georgic" out of the older categories of didactic and descriptive verse. It is particularly for their role in the invention of the "georgic" that the notes to these poems deserve scrutiny.

AUTHORIAL ANNOTATION IN GEORGICS

Authorial notes in eighteenth-century georgics vary so widely in frequency, length, style, and function that generalization is hazardous. A quantitative approach proves most useful in identifying broad trends. As table 1.1 shows, the practice of annotation began slowly, with few or no notes in georgics until the mid-1740s.[10] From then onward, a conspicuously higher ratio of notes to lines became the norm. Georgic poems with little or no annotation continued to appear throughout the century, though the dominant trend toward increased annotation is clear. Five georgics, Akenside's *The Pleasures of Imagination*, Grainger's *The Sugar-Cane*, William Mason's *The English Garden* (1772–1781), Richard Payne Knight's *The Landscape* (1794), and Smith's *Beachy Head* stand out from the rest because of the amplitude and sophistication of their annotation. Interestingly, Robert Dodsley published five of the earliest heavily annotated georgics: *The Pleasures of Imagination*, Cornelius Arnold's *Commerce* (1751), Nathaniel Weekes's *Barbados* (1754), John Dyer's *The Fleece* (1757), and Dodsley's own *Agriculture* (1753), not to mention *The Sugar-Cane*, which was published in 1764 under the imprint of R. and J. Dodsley following Robert's retirement in 1759. One might speculate that Akenside's success in 1744 awakened Dodsley to the appeal and possible commercial value of annotated poetry and that he consequently urged other authors to follow suit; but the trend toward an increasing number of notes in georgic verse was not limited to any specific poet or publisher. For georgics appearing between 1750 and 1770, the average ratio of notes to lines is 1:34 (see table 1.1), an average all the more impressive when we observe that it includes a poem, James Elphinston's *Education* (1763), with no notes whatsoever.

The catalyst for this increase in annotated georgics may have been the publication of three translations of Virgil's *Georgics* into English: the first in blank verse by Joseph Trapp (1731), the second in prose by John Martyn (1741), and the third in heroic couplets by Joseph Warton (1753), all of them furnished with copious footnotes.[11] Although Dryden's popular translation of the *Georgics* had also been annotated, its notes were printed as endnotes, whereas footnoting became the standard method of authorial annotation in eighteenth-century georgics.[12] As modern scholars recognize, but as eighteenth-century practitioners were also aware, the positioning of notes can be significant. Richard Payne Knight, for example, used both footnotes and endnotes in one of his poems. He explained that he had borrowed passages from Lucretius, "which I should have given at the bottom of the page, did I not rather wish that the whole should be read in its proper order, as a text, upon which I have written a

Table 1.1. Authorial Notes in English Georgics

Date	Author and Title	Notes	Lines	Note-to-Line Ratio
1708	John Philips, *Cyder*	0	1465	
1713	Alexander Pope, *Windsor-Forest*	9	430	1:48
1713	John Gay, *Rural Sports*	0	525	
1717	William Churchill, *October*	21	763	1:36
1720	John Gay, *Rural Sports*	0	443	
1726	James Thomson, *Winter*	1	405	1:405
1727	James Thomson, *Summer*	1	1146	1:1146
1730	James Thomson, *The Seasons*	6	4376	1:729
1730	Stephen Duck, *The Thresher's Labour*	0	283	
1735	William Somervile, *The Chace*	3	2066	1:689
1736	Alexander Pope, *Windsor-Forest*	25	432	1:17
1739	Mary Collier, *The Woman's Labour*	0	246	
1742	William Somervile, *Field Sports*	11	286	1:26
1744	John Armstrong, *The Art of Preserving Health*	7	2063	1:295
1744	Mark Akenside, *The Pleasures of Imagination*	41	2008	1:49
1746	James Thomson, *Winter*	13	1069	1:82
1746	James Thomson, *Summer*	16	1805	1:113
1746	James Thomson, *The Seasons*	34	5422	1:159
1751	Cornelius Arnold, *Commerce*	11	287	1:26
1752	Christopher Smart, *The Hop-Garden*	19	300	1:16
1753	Robert Dodsley, *Agriculture*	26	1518	1:58
1754	Nathaniel Weekes, *Barbados*	21	985	1:47
1757	John Dyer, *The Fleece*	38	2707	1:71
1759	Thomas Marriott, *Female Conduct*	147	4698	1:32
1762	William Falconer, *The Shipwreck*	98	1309	1:13
1763	James Elphinston, *Education*	0	2011	
1764	James Grainger, *The Sugar-Cane*	139	2562	1:18
1764	William Falconer, *The Shipwreck*	115	2333	1:20
1767	Richard Jago, *Edge-Hill*	122	2889	1:23
1767	John Singleton, *A General Description of the West-Indian Islands*	43	2074	1:48
1769	William Falconer, *The Shipwreck*	67	2802	1:41
1772–81	William Mason, *The English Garden*	37	2423	1:65
1774	Nathaniel Tucker, *The Bermudian*	0	332	
1774	Henry James Pye, *Faringdon Hill*	29	1106	1:38
1774–76	Hugh Downman, *Infancy*	0	1655	
1776	John Singleton, *A General Description of the West-Indian Islands*	23	1302	1:57
1777	Anon., *Jamaica: A Poem*	17	408	1:24
1781	George Heriot, *Descriptive Poem of the West Indies*	1	437	1:437
1784	Henry James Pye, *Shooting*	2	688	1:344
1785	William Cowper, *The Task*	1	5185	1:5185
1788	William Crowe, *Lewesdon Hill*	13	477	1:37

Date	Author and Title	Notes	Lines	Note-to-Line Ratio
1791	Erasmus Darwin, *The Botanic Garden*	358	4434	1:12
1791	George Ogilvie, *Carolina; or, the Planter*	11	1492	1:136
1792	Bryan Edwards, *Jamaica*	16	509	1:32
1793	William Wordsworth, *An Evening Walk*	18	446	1:25
1794	Timothy Dwight, *Greenfield Hill*	155	4337	1:28
1794	Richard Payne Knight, *The Landscape*	50	1215	1:24
1799	Luke Booker, *Malvern*	49	1221	1:25
1799	Luke Booker, *The Hop-Garden*	22	703	1:31
1807	Charlotte Smith, *Beachy Head*	64	731	1:11

commentary."[13] The distance of the notes from the text—at the foot of the page, at the back of the book, or in a separate volume—may signal the relative importance of attending to the annotation while reading verse.

The diversity in the content and function of the notes reflects the diversity of georgic poetry itself. The perception of georgics as *didactic* suggests a partial answer to the question posed in the introduction about the motives for such an accumulation of notes in these poems. Didactic poetry was classed as a form of writing that (in Hugh Blair's words) "openly professes its intention of conveying knowledge and instruction." Thus, he continues, it differs, "in the form only, not in the scope and substance, from a philosophical, a moral, or a critical treatise in Prose."[14] Explanatory notes could therefore be regarded as a natural and appropriate extension of the instrumental function of a didactic poem. Early critics, however, valued Virgil's *Georgics* more for its literary allusions than for its practical advice: Addison in 1697 criticized Virgil's predecessor Hesiod for laying on the precepts "so very thick" that the instruction "clog[s] the Poem," and urged English poets to handle technical matters in the Virgilian manner: selectively, indirectly, nonchalantly.[15] But the rise of specialized, science-based disciplines after 1700 led to increased demand that georgics provide experimental proofs and detailed descriptions of natural and technical processes.[16] As Frans de Bruyn explains, the signal moment in this development was the rejection of the *Georgics* as a practical manual by the agriculturalist Jethro Tull in 1733.[17] The title of James Hamilton's 1742 translation, *Virgil's Pastorals Translated into English Prose; as Also His Georgicks, with Such Notes and Reflexions as Make Him Appear to Have Wrote Like an Excellent Farmer*, reflects popular doubts about the efficacy of georgic.[18] The spread of such doubts more or less coincides with the dramatic increase in annotated georgics after 1740. Hamilton's solution to such inadequacy—not to abandon poetry, but to supplement Virgil's poetry with notes—parallels the practice of many English poets in their own poems. Even the notes added by translators of the *Georgics*, such as the 1741 annotations of John Martyn, who was a practicing botanist at Cambridge, respond to the general perception that technical or scientific notes were needed to help georgic remain relevant.

The problem of specialization emerges in the way in which two of the most heavily annotated georgics of the century, Grainger's *The Sugar-Cane* and William Falconer's *The Shipwreck* (1762; 1764; 1769) approach the critical issue in georgic poetics of "*technical words,* or *Terms of Art.*"[19] While vocational jargon, according to Grainger, looks "awkward in poetry," he excuses his use of technical language by referring to his professional identity: "I beg leave to be understood as a physician, and not as a poet."[20] Although Grainger's notes do much more than define terms, his statement is nonetheless revelatory: georgic self-annotation aims to balance detail with dignity, responding to the demand for poets to show technical expertise without violating rules of poetic decorum. Likewise, in his advertisement to *The Shipwreck*, Falconer relates his usage of nautical terminology, and of notes defining those terms, to his status as "a Sailor," an identity "of which he is much more tenacious than of his Character as a Poet."[21] By the 1760s, poets no longer believed, as Addison had in 1697, that any terms of art and practical details that could not be "dressed up" through metaphor and periphrasis were better omitted.[22] Notes were the perfect space for giving technical or scientific information resistant to poetic formulation. Contrary to Samuel Johnson's famous declaration that some "subject[s] . . . cannot be made poetical,"[23] georgic poets seemingly believed that professional and poetical demands could be reconciled by means of annotation. Annotation represents a compromise between Addison's advice that details be omitted so as to avoid "clogged" poetry and John Aikin's radical solution of 1777 to what he also maligns as "clogged" verse: to forgo poetry altogether and to treat the topic in "plain prose."[24]

The variation in the content of notes in both English and transatlantic georgics, from etymology and history to topography, shows, however, that the proliferation of notes was not solely a response to a new culture of specialization. Some poems, such as *The Sugar-Cane*, traded in natural observation and experimental data; many others, such as *Edge-Hill*, supplied primarily geographical and historical information. Poetic category also shaped annotation. The rationale for notes in georgics at the didactic end of the spectrum has already been discussed. What rationale was there for notes in poems of the more descriptive kind? The simplest answer seems to be that annotation was already a convention in loco-descriptive poetry before the eighteenth century began. John Denham's *Coopers-Hill* (1642), acknowledged as a model for *Windsor-Forest*, had eight brief notes giving historical, literary, and local references by the time the so-called authorized edition appeared in 1655; these notes were reprinted in the 1709 edition, probably the one used by Pope.[25] The notes in the 1713 version of *Windsor-Forest* are slightly longer than Denham's but strikingly similar otherwise in frequency and kind. Denham's notes include five references to English monarchs and historical events, one river name, and one reference to a poet, while Pope has six references to monarchs and historical events, one river name, and two references to a poet. Together they seem to have established a pattern for annotation in georgics of the loco-descriptive type that lasted for the rest of the century.[26]

This brings us at last to a general consideration of authorial annotation in English georgics. The first thing to observe is that, though some georgic notes often contain a good deal of scientific information, they are not broadly different in style and method from scholarly annotation in editions of older English poetry by Chaucer (ed. John Urry, 1721), Spenser (ed. John Upton, 1758), and Milton (ed. Thomas Newton, 1752).[27] By adding notes to their own works, poets were, in fact, *editing themselves*. The second observation is that there is a marked tendency for the style of annotation to vary according to which of the two classes, descriptive or didactic, a poem embodied. Of course, even in the eighteenth century the line between didactic and descriptive poetry was blurry, with description often serving a didactic purpose and vice versa. As Pope suggested of *Coopers-Hill*, rural descriptions were often simply vehicles for moral or political instruction: "the Description of Places" can "lead into some Reflection, upon moral Life or political Institution."[28] Likewise, Addison applauded the *Georgics* for making "the dryest of Precepts look like a Description."[29] So, rather than claim that the style of annotation reflects the kind of poem to which it is attached, we should say that the annotation becomes at times a better guide than poetic content to whether a poem was classed as didactic or descriptive.

Some examples will help us consider how notes can both reflect and confer generic identities. To borrow Thomas McFarland's terminology, notes in English georgics may be divided into two main types: *referential* (sourcing quotations, adding classical and historical references, glossing obsolete words and technical terms, and so forth); and *dialogical* (engaging in dialogue with the text, often at considerable length, by explaining, qualifying, reinforcing, or enlarging the argument).[30] While georgics typically carry footnotes of both kinds, there is a marked tendency for some poems to boast a greater share of one of the two kinds of notes. Thus, in descriptive poems annotation usually follows *Windsor-Forest* in giving brief referential footnotes: identifying persons and places mentioned in the text, for example. In didactic poems, on the other hand, the majority of notes are dialogical: qualifying, extending, or elaborating the argument. There are exceptions: among descriptive georgics, William Crowe's *Lewesdon Hill* (1788) is rare in having the lengthy dialogical notes associated with didactic poems. The mixture of referential and dialogical annotation in Weekes's *Barbados*, on the other hand, is an exception that proves the rule, for the first half of the poem, which is mainly descriptive, has only four referential notes; whereas the second half, which is mainly concerned with the cultivation and production of sugar, is conspicuously didactic and is accordingly furnished with copious explanatory notes.[31] Of course, such evidence can be interpreted in the opposite way: *Lewesdon Hill* looks today very much like a descriptive poem, but its extensive dialogical notes may have led early readers to regard the poem as more didactic than its content suggests.[32]

Poets were well aware of the value of notes as rhetorical tools to emphasize, sharpen, or reinforce the main text. Two passages from Akenside's *The Pleasures of Imagination* reveal the strategic interplay of text and footnotes. Early in book 1 the poet claims that he is exploring a new realm in poetry: driven by love of "nature and the muses," he will venture into "secret paths erewhile untrod by man" in the hope of winning poetic laurels, "Where never poet gain'd a wreath before."[33] This passage is virtually a translation of some lines from Lucretius, the Latin original of which is quoted in a footnote. Thus, Robin Dix comments, Akenside stakes his claim to originality in plagiarized lines, "and then point[s] up the plagiarism by a footnote quoting the passage plagiarized."[34] A second example, in book 2, illustrates a point made by Pellicer in reference to *The Sugar-Cane*: that lengthy footnotes invite the reader "to read verse and prose alternately."[35] Akenside shows how this alternation could itself be turned to effect. During a passage of lyrical description of the beauties of nature, which forms part of his concluding account of the benefits of a well-formed imagination (book 2, lines 568–633), Akenside adds a substantial footnote, beginning: "That this account may not appear rather poetically extravagant than just in philosophy, it may be proper to produce the sentiment of one of the greatest, wisest, and best of men on this article." Eventually the best of men is identified as Marcus Aurelius, and a passage from his writings about the influence of "the beauty of universal nature" on the development of philosophical understanding is quoted.[36] Switching back and forth between verse (text) and prose (note) in this case has the double effect of reinforcing the argument by quotation from an illustrious authority and, at the same time, drawing attention to the author's poetry while ostensibly depreciating it.

As part of their broader sensitivity to the rhetorical potential of notes, poets deployed annotation to shape perceptions of generic identity. As in the case of *Lewesdon Hill*, the presence of dialogical notes makes it difficult to classify Crowe's poem as didactic *or* descriptive poetry. The poem looks descriptive, but the dialogical notes lend the poem a greater air of didacticism. The content of notes can also contribute to a poem's categorization and, in fact, anticipate the rise of a third genre bridging the didactic and descriptive that we would recognize as "georgic." As Chalker points out, Jago attaches seven notes to *Edge-Hill* identifying imitations from the *Georgics*. Through such notes "Jago establishes the predominantly Georgic character of his poem."[37] However, since for a modern scholar such as Chalker the georgic status of *Edge-Hill* is never in doubt, he overlooks the degree to which such notes *confer* georgic or didactic status on *Edge-Hill* rather than merely reinforcing it. In 1767, when few would have considered the poem a "georgic," *Edge-Hill* would have appeared as primarily descriptive; as Chalker admits, the imitations of Virgil are so distant that without the notes most of them would pass unnoticed. Thus, by using his footnotes to indicate these supposed imitations from Virgil, Jago confers a greater didactic identity on *Edge-Hill* than it would have otherwise. Moreover, by situating *Edge-Hill* in a Virgilian-georgic tradition, Jago's self-annotations anticipate the practices of non-authorial annotators of georgic verse at the end of the century, practices to which we now turn.

NON-AUTHORIAL ANNOTATION IN GEORGICS

Non-authorial annotations in eighteenth-century georgics share many of the same functions as notes penned by authors: they display expertise and provide technical details, for example. But precisely because they are by individuals other than the author, and are often written decades after a poem's initial publication, they also perform other functions. These include (1) establishing a poem as a "classic" by documenting its imitations of past writings; (2) presenting the poem as a record of a specific time and place; and (3) reinforcing generic cues so that a poem will, in fact, be identified as "georgic" by readers. Table 1.2 shows that non-authorial notes are as plentiful as authorial notes in georgics, but quantitative analysis does not reveal the same trend toward increased density of annotation markedly after 1740.[38] The following section therefore adopts a different approach from the first; it will offer some general observations based on close examination of non-authorial notes to two popular georgics, Pope's *Windsor-Forest* and Philips's *Cyder*.

In *Windsor-Forest*, editors encountered a poem that is unique among eighteenth-century georgics in that it already had several layers of authorial notes; it is also far from typical as "georgic," judged by either modern or eighteenth-century standards, in spite of claims made for its georgic identity in recent studies.[39] It has little technical description of natural phenomena and even less in the way of practical advice on rural occupations. For these reasons, Pope's poem can tell us more about the role and efficacy of notes, especially of non-authorial notes, in helping to make or break genre classifications than, for example, W. Burgh's 1786 notes to Mason's *The English Garden*, a poem with just one layer of authorial notes and whose genre classification was less debatable.[40] *Windsor-Forest* contained annotation from its earliest stages: the manuscript contains seven notes; the first published version of 1713 and that in Pope's 1717 *Works* have nine; and the revision in Pope's 1736 *Works* boasts twenty-five. Whereas the 1717 notes are primarily referential, the fourteen notes added in 1736 are dialogical: they chart the poem's development by listing textual variants that were either revised or omitted in 1713. By 1736, Pope realized that notes "free[d] his poem of certain responsibilities to reveal information." The famous variant referring to "a foreign master's rage" in the note to line 91 (a disparaging reference to William of Orange), enabled Pope to modify the meaning of the poem while taking credit for having the wisdom to omit it.[41] The 1736 notes helped Pope push his anti-Williamite message at the cost of calling attention to the poem's fragmented character; to such an extent that the poem becomes almost anti-georgic in its violation of the principle of coherence declared by Addison to be a hallmark of the georgic kind.[42]

Table 1.2. Authorial and Non-authorial Notes in Selected Georgics

Date	Annotator (Author/Title)	Notes	Lines	Note-to-Line Ratio
1753	William Warburton (Pope, *Windsor-Forest*)	52	432	1:8
1791	Charles Dunster (Philips, *Cyder*)	378	1465	1:4
1794	Gilbert Wakefield (Pope, *Windsor-Forest*)	113	434	1:4
1797	Joseph Warton (Pope, *Windsor-Forest*)	86	434	1:5

With the overall effect of Pope's own annotations in mind, we can now consider the tactics of the first non-authorial annotator of *Windsor-Forest*, William Warburton. Warburton, as the poet's literary executor and editor of the 1751 *Works*, shared Pope's concern about the ability of the reading public to comprehend poetry and sought to preempt misreading by attaching notes that would bridge the cognitive gap between Pope's "compressed, allusive poetry and the new readers."[43] To this end, Warburton adds thirty notes to *Windsor-Forest*, seven of which are attributed to Pope, the other twenty-three being Warburton's own. He also reproduces all but three of the twenty-five notes provided by Pope in 1736.[44] The personal attacks for which Warburton's 1751 apparatus is notorious do not appear in his notes on *Windsor-Forest*[45]; rather, they either identify echoes from Virgil and Ovid or provide additional variants. In a further effort to elevate Pope to "classic" status, Warburton divides his notes into remarks, variations, and imitations in the style of Claude Brossette's "classic" 1717 edition of Boileau, a structure that Pope had adopted for the notes to his *Pastorals* in the 1736 *Works*, and had famously turned to satiric purposes in the *Dunciad Variorum*.

In contrast to Warburton's annotations, the labors of the religious controversialist Gilbert Wakefield (1756–1801) as editor of Pope have received scant attention. This is unfortunate, given that Wakefield is also the first annotator to use his notes to give *Windsor-Forest* a Virgilian or georgic identity. Where Warburton finds six echoes from Virgil and one from Ovid, Wakefield in his 1795 edition identifies thirteen from the *Georgics* and eight from the *Metamorphoses*. As reviewers observed, Wakefield's aim, like Warburton's, is "to recommend Mr. Pope, as an English classic."[46] Wakefield's emphasis on the *Georgics* gives Pope's poem a didactic feel. However, if georgic characteristically finds moral and political lessons in natural phenomena, Wakefield's handling of the political resonances of *Windsor-Forest* undermine this georgic frame. Like Pope in 1736 and Warburton in 1751, Wakefield lists variants at the foot of the page; but, uniquely, Wakefield provides aesthetic justifications for the omission or alteration of lines. About one variant (at line 25) he observes, with typical disdain: "The prosaic vulgar language, and the imperfect rhyme in these verses, justify [its] suppression."[47] He presents Pope's variants as unrelated to the published version and unworthy of attention. Since much of the parallelism between the Norman past and Stuart present in the poem is intensified by the variants, Wakefield's handling of the variant passages diminishes the poem's political didacticism. In his most obvious de-politicizing act as annotator, Wakefield omits two notes from 1736 identifying historical references ("the forest laws" at line 45 and "Richard, 2nd son of William the Conqueror" at line 81). Both of these are retained by Warburton who, unlike Wakefield, seems to have aimed for more balance between exhibiting the poem's historical and political significances, on the one hand, and establishing Pope's classic credentials, on the other.

The notes in Joseph Warton's edition achieve much the same effect as Wakefield's by other means. To the twenty-nine notes of Pope's and nineteen of Warburton's reprinted in 1797, Warton appends thirty-eight annotations of his own. He ignores Wakefield's commentary altogether. Modern scholars see resemblances between Pope's two late-century editors, but to say with the Twickenham editors that "Warton's energies, like those of . . . Wakefield, were mainly directed toward collecting Pope's imitations"[48] is to overlook a central difference in the imitations collected. Wakefield, like Warburton before him, catalogs largely classical imitations. Warton instead prefers to surround Pope with English poets: he points out parallels with Denham and, contrary to all chronology, Thomas Gray. Only four of Warton's notes identify echoes from Virgil, and in two cases, he reproduces Warburton's notes only to controvert them ("Certainly not an imitation of this passage in Virgil"[49]). Where Wakefield adduces echoes from Homer and Virgil in Pope's description of the Thames at lines 329–38,[50] Warton places Pope's river imagery in the tradition of "Spenser, Drayton, and Milton."[51] In seeking to present *Windsor-Forest* as a vernacular "classic," Warton detaches it from a larger tradition of Virgilian poetry.

Of all Pope's editors, Warton historicizes the most relentlessly; in offering lengthy explanations of historical references, he far exceeds the terse, referential annotations of Pope that Warburton and Wakefield adopted. Anecdotes about a legal dispute over William I's proposed tomb, the disposal of the body of William's son, and the building of Windsor Castle—all feature in Warton's notes.[52] Such antiquarian details disconnect *Windsor-Forest* from the political milieu of 1713 and drag the aesthetic down into the dusty realm of historical fact. Where in 1736 the poem and its decontextualized variants possessed a mythic vagueness that blurred Norman past with Stuart present and therefore invited readers to interpret the poem's remarks on William I as applicable to William III, Warton's historical notes make it a good bit harder to read that section of the poem as something other than a representation of Norman tyranny. In addition to detaching *Windsor-Forest* from Virgil's *Georgics*, Warton's annotations, similar to Wakefield's dismissive comments on Pope's variants, work against reading the poem for political lessons.

It is in Warton's edition that the role of non-authorial annotation in shaping generic affiliation emerges most clearly. As Pellicer reflects, without Pope's famous note at line 290 stating that *Windsor-Forest* fractures into two sections, one pastoral and one political, "it is doubtful whether anybody would have suspected [the] existence" of a discontinuity that undermines georgic coherence.[53] But notes can stabilize genre designations, too. Warton's notes to *Windsor-Forest* situate the poem in the context of an evolving and contested concept of "georgic" verse. He takes a cue from the poem: as Pellicer shows, *Windsor-Forest* develops a "generic frame of reference . . . through its engagement with literary models," including its references to *Coopers-Hill* and its closing allusion to Virgil's *Georgics*.[54] But the frame Warton develops is rather different. In addition to omitting some of the Virgilian imitations identified by Warburton, Warton likens *Windsor-Forest* to English descriptive poems today classified as georgics, including Somervile's *Chace*.[55] In the long final note lifted near-verbatim from his own *Essay on the Genius and Writings of Pope* (1756), Warton elaborates on this generic framework:

> Several elegant imitations have been given to this species of local poetry . . . Grongar Hill; the Ruins of Rome; Claremont, by Garth; Kymber, by Mr. Potter; Kensington Gardens; Catharine Hill; Faringdon Hill; Needwood Forest; Lewesdon Hill . . .
>
> Pope, it seems, was of opinion, that descriptive poetry is a composition as absurd as a feast made up of sauces: and I know many other persons that think meanly of it. . . . [I]f the[se] principles lead them to condemn Thomson, they must also condemn the Georgics of Virgil, and the greatest part of the noblest descriptive poem extant; I mean that of Lucretius.[56]

The note signals Warton's desire for *Windsor-Forest* to be viewed as part of a tradition of "local" and "descriptive" verse related to Virgil and Lucretius but best embodied in an English canon of poems—including Thomson's *Seasons*, Crowe's *Lewesdon Hill*, and Henry James Pye's *Faringdon Hill* (1774)—that we recognize as georgics. Whether "georgic" could encompass didactic *and* descriptive verse was still apparently up for debate in 1797, and Warton, holding to the anti-didacticism of the advertisement to his youthful *Odes on Various Subjects* (1746),[57] counteracts the generic cues internal to *Windsor-Forest* and shifts the weight of the "georgic" category toward the descriptive pole. Thus, Warton offers a further answer to a question that we posed earlier: What rationale was there for annotating georgics of the descriptive or topographical sort, including *Windsor-Forest*? At a time when the claim of descriptive verse to membership in the emerging category of georgic (a category primarily defined by didacticism of the Virgilian sort) was in doubt, notes helped both poets and editors to redefine the category more inclusively.

The problem of genre continues to be seen in Charles Dunster's 1791 annotated edition of *Cyder*, a formal georgic originally published without notes. Where Pope's annotators sacrifice topicality in order to situate *Windsor-Forest* in either Virgilian-didactic or English-descriptive traditions, Dunster (1750–1816), in annotating one of the most "local" of English georgics nearly a century later,[58] attempts to retain Philips's political and topographical specificity while also giving the poem both technical efficacy and "classic" status—an impossible task, perhaps, but one showing the host of cultural forces buffeting georgic poetry in the eighteenth century. Dunster, a clergyman known for his notes to Milton's *Paradise Regained* (1795), edits on the assumption that many of "*the works of our English Poets will in another century become in a great measure unintelligible, for want of being accompanied with Notes.*"[59] Accordingly, the footnotes to his edition are crammed with translated excerpts from Greek and Roman texts, which seem to betray a Warburtonian anxiety about the ignorance of the poet's posthumous readers. The sheer quantity of Dunster's notes—378, more than the number of notes attached to Erasmus Darwin's *Botanic Garden* (1791), one of the most densely author-annotated georgics of the era—supports the view that Dunster aimed "to save the antique genre of georgic . . . by supplying [new readers] with the allusive substructure their nonclassical education left them unable to hear."[60]

At least ninety-seven of these 378 notes (25 percent) refer to passages from Milton; at least eighty-one (21 percent) mark imitations or parallels from Virgil (mainly from the *Georgics*); and at least sixty-two (16 percent) refer to texts by classical authors other than Virgil, either offering such texts as influences or using them to explicate Philips's verse.

Dunster's notes offer more than parallel passages. While granting *Cyder* classic status by marking its borrowings from a general literary tradition, Dunster also supplies the poem with the specificity increasingly demanded of georgic verse over the century: both of the historical and topographical kind, as in Warton's notes to *Windsor-Forest*, and of the technical-scientific kind, as in Grainger's self-annotations. Thus his notes identify people, places, and events; provide local history and genealogy related to the poem's Herefordshire setting; and discuss technical matters given perfunctory notice in the poem itself, such as methods of cider making and the layout of a cider mill.[61] In heightening the poem's local character, however, Dunster undercuts the very aesthetic-mythological element that he promotes by identification of classical and Miltonic echoes, reducing Philips's poetic flights to mundane history and factual exactitude. For example, where Philips refers in his opening lines to Herefordshire as "my native soil," Dunster writes: "Though our Author speaks of Herefordshire as his 'native soil,' he was born . . . in Oxfordshire."[62] To Philips's remark on the cider-producing powers of Kentchurch, Dunster replies that the poet stretches the truth, observing, "The Parish of Kentchurch is not particularly noted for its Cider."[63] Such deviations are traced to the poet's ultra-Tory politics. In a note on a reference to a John Mostyn, Dunster reflects: "though the compliments paid to particular persons [in *Cyder*] were probably justified . . . we cannot but trace a violent prejudice of Party governing . . . the Author on public matters."[64] Where Warton's historicizing zeal deprived *Windsor-Forest* of the political resonances it held in 1736, Dunster's contextualizing drive has the opposite effect, reducing stretches of *Cyder* to partisan strategies. Modern scholars might expect this from Philips, who is recognized as a poet-propagandist for Robert Harley and his ministerial circle.[65] But Dunster's notes seem at odds with themselves. In seeking to update *Cyder* for new readers, Dunster's annotations emphasize the outdatedness of the poem's historical and political precepts.

Dunster's criticism of Philips's political message should not be mistaken for a rejection of didacticism. As he observes at one point, *Cyder* "must incontestably rate high as a Didactic Poem; and it may be wondered, that Dr. Blair, in his *Lectures*, should have entirely passed it over."[66] If Dunster aims to make *Cyder* exemplify the "descriptive" side of georgic, he also wants to preserve its "didactic" status, though not its political didacticism. So, like earlier self-annotating poets who added information-laden notes in order to update their poems for an era of specialization, Dunster's footnotes supply the experimental details that *Cyder* omits. It soon becomes clear, however, that knowledge has evolved greatly since 1708, and Dunster's notes detract from the poem's authority without enhancing its utility. Of Philips's statements on tree blight, Dunster observes, "Enquirers have, from repeated observations and experiments, concluded them [i.e., blights] to arise from different causes" than those Philips cites.[67] A paean on the fertilizing properties of snow prompts similar skepticism: "it has been proved from very accurate experiments, that snow contains . . . no nitre."[68] Often these agronomic inexactitudes are attributed to the poet's deference to Virgil. When Philips gives advice on grafting, Dunster states: "Philips seems here to have had in view a passage in the GEORGICS . . . , which experiment has demonstrated to be impracticable."[69] When a stork makes an improbable appearance in Herefordshire, Dunster comments: "our Author has taken this circumstance . . . from Virgil's second GEORGIC, V. 319."[70] Through such notes, Dunster presents *Cyder* as something like a modern georgic, but the demand in 1791 for scientific accuracy in poetry forces him to acknowledge the absurdity of Philips's imitations. His notes, like those to many eighteenth-century georgics, attempt to reconcile competing demands of didactic and descriptive poetry, while also co-opting a specialist terminology and superabundance of technical detail.

CONCLUSION

The foregoing discussion has shown that eighteenth-century georgic verse was more closely tied up with annotation than has been previously observed. The ubiquity of notes in poems such as *The Sugar-Cane*, *The Shipwreck*, and *Edge-Hill* implies the expectation among both readers and poets that such poems both include and require dense annotation. The accretion of notes in later editions of georgics also suggests the centrality of notes in the history of georgic as a poetic genre.[71] Whether notes are dialogical or referential can depend on category—that is, on whether a georgic is more descriptive or didactic. But annotations both reflected and constructed generic categories. From Warburton's 1751 footnote commentary on *Windsor-Forest* to Dunster's 1791 apparatus for *Cyder*, non-authorial notes sought to contain the diverse energies of georgic and assimilate poems to categories defining "georgic" poetry as descriptive, didactic, or a little of both. Such notes patched up the seams and fissures in eighteenth-century notions of genre and in the emerging category of georgic verse. Generic categories are subject to historical change, and therefore the genre assigned to a poem such as *Windsor-Forest*, as we have suggested, depends at a given moment as much on the notes surrounding it as on the internal cues on which modern scholars have traditionally focused—and this is precisely because notes call attention to, or divert attention from, internal markers of genre such as allusions and imitations. Ultimately, where the authorial notes to English georgics of the eighteenth century typically aimed to prevent misreading and modify poems for increasingly technically minded audiences, the non-authorial annotations more often attempted to fit square poems to the round holes of genre categories—didactic, descriptive, local, and Virgilian. Such editorial notes are numerous, yes, but in seeking to impose genre identities they were perhaps something less than "generous."

NOTES

1. Juan Christian Pellicer, "The Georgic," in *A Companion to Eighteenth-Century Poetry*, ed. Christine Gerrard (Oxford: Wiley-Blackwell, 2014), 415.

2. In his *Georgic Tradition in English Poetry* (New York: Columbia University Press, 1935), Dwight L. Durling frequently comments on the abundant notes in these poems, yet attempts no explanation for their presence. For a discussion of Jago's notes, see John Chalker, *The English Georgic: A Study in the Development of a Form* (Baltimore, MD: Johns Hopkins University Press, 1969), 195–99.

3. For Grainger's "excessive" notes, see Beth Fowkes Tobin, *Colonizing Nature: The Tropics in British Arts and Letters, 1760–1820* (Philadelphia: University of Pennsylvania Press, 2005), 45. For his "monstrous" notes, see Michael Ziser, *Environmental Practice and Early American Literature* (Cambridge: Cambridge University Press, 2013), 77. Three studies view Grainger's arrangement of poetry and notes as a print-material correlative for the master-slave, host-parasite, and domestic-wild relationships articulated in the poem: see Carl Plasa, *Slaves to Sweetness: British and Caribbean Literatures of Sugar* (Liverpool: Liverpool University Press, 2009), 21; Ziser, *Environmental Practice*, 80–81; and Britt Rusert, "Plantation Ecologies: The Experimental Plantation in and against James Grainger's *The Sugar-Cane*," *Early American Studies* 13, no. 2 (2015): 341–73.

4. *Monthly Review* 31 (August 1764). Quoted in John Gilmore, *The Poetics of Empire: A Study of James Grainger's* The Sugar-Cane (London: Athlone Press, 2000), 39.

5. *New Monthly Review* 7 (January 1792): 24.

6. For the diversity of georgic, see esp. Alastair Fowler, *Kinds of Literature: An Introduction to the Theory of Genres and Modes* (Cambridge, MA: Harvard University Press, 1982), 202–6; Dustin Griffin, "Redefining Georgic: Cowper's *Task*," *ELH: English Literary History* 57, no. 2 (1990): 865–79; David Fairer, "Persistence, Adaptations and Transformations in Pastoral and Georgic Poetry," in *The Cambridge History of English Literature, 1660–1780*, ed. John J. Richetti (Cambridge: Cambridge University Press, 2005), 259–86; and Courtney Weiss Smith, *Empiricist Devotions: Science, Religion, and Poetry in Early Eighteenth-Century England* (Charlottesville: University of Virginia Press, 2016), 173–210.

7. See, for example, Joseph Trapp on *Cyder*: "As long as the fluctuating State of our Tongue will permit, this *English Georgic* shall infallibly flourish." Trapp, *Lectures on Poetry Read in the Schools of Natural Philosophy at Oxford* (1742; repr., New York: Garland, 1970), 199. Thomas Warton later used the phrase "this old English georgic" to describe Thomas Tusser's *A Hundreth Points of Good Husbandrie* (1557) but also to show how little it conformed to eighteenth-century conceptions of georgic: *The History of English Poetry*, 4 vols. (London: Printed for, and Sold by, J. Dodsley), 3:304–10.

8. For these classifications and the definition of "descriptive" poetry, see *The Art of Poetry on a New Plan*, 2 vols. (London: Printed for J. Newbery, 1762), 1:128. For the definition of "didactic" poetry, see Joseph Addison, "An Essay on the Georgics," in *The Works of John Dryden*, vol. 5, *Poems 1685–1692*, ed. William Frost and Vinton A. Dearing (Berkeley: University of California Press, 1987), 145. See also Joseph Warton, "Reflections on Didactic Poetry," in Christopher Pitt and Joseph Warton, trans., *The Works of Virgil, in Latin and English . . . with Notes on the Whole*, 4 vols. (London: Printed for R. Dodsley, 1753), 1:393–440. Warton illustrates his argument with quotations not only from Virgil but also from John Philips's *Cyder* (1708), William Somervile's *The Chace* (1735), Armstrong's *Art of Preserving Health*, and Akenside's *The Pleasures of Imagination*.

9. Formal imitations of Virgil's *Georgics* include *Cyder* and John Dyer's *The Fleece* (1757). Poems identified in the front matter or in the verse as "georgic" or Virgilian in nature include Somervile's *The Chace*, Grainger's *The Sugar-Cane*, Cornelius Arnold's *Commerce* (1751), and Thomas Marriott's *Female Conduct* (1759). Poems with subtitles indicating their "georgic status" include Gay's *Rural Sports* and Smart's *Hop-Garden*. Poems identified by eighteenth-century critics or reviewers as georgic include *Windsor-Forest*, Thomson's *Seasons*, William Mason's *The English Garden* (1772–1781), and Henry James Pye's *Shooting* (1784). The remainder of the poems in table 1.1 either display structural allusion to the *Georgics* and earlier English georgics, or have been identified as belonging to georgic tradition in modern studies by Durling, Chalker, Pellicer, and others.

10. Charlotte Smith's *Beachy Head* represents an arbitrary stopping point. Annotated georgics continued to appear after *Beachy Head*; see, for example, John Evans, *The Bees* (1806–1813), William Tighe, *Plants* (1808–1811), and James Jennings, *Ornithologia* (1828). For our criteria in assembling table 1.1, see the introduction to this chapter and note 9 above.

11. Joseph Trapp, trans., *The Works of Virgil: Translated into English Blank Verse. With Large Explanatory Notes, and Critical Observations*, 3 vols. (London: Printed for J. Brotherton et al., 1731), 1:91–240; John Martyn, trans., *The Georgicks of Virgil, with an English Translation and Notes* (London: Printed for the Editor, by Richard Reily, 1741); and Pitt and Warton, *Works of Virgil*, 1:167–389.

12. *Georgics*, in *The Works of Virgil Containing His Pastorals, Georgics, and Æneis*, trans. John Dryden (London: Printed for Jacob Tonson, 1697), 103–201. Dryden's "Notes and Observations" appear on pages 675–90. Smith's *Beachy Head*, which uses endnotes, is an exception among later English and American georgics, but it was posthumously edited and published. Smith used footnotes in early editions of her *Elegiac Sonnets*.

13. Richard Payne Knight, preface to *The Progress of Civil Society: A Didactic Poem, in Six Books* (London: Printed by W. Bulmer for G. Nichol, 1796), v.

14. Hugh Blair, *Lectures on Rhetoric and Belles Lettres*, 3 vols. (Dublin: Printed for Messrs. Whitestone et al., 1783): 3:161.

15. Addison, "Essay on the Georgics," 150; cf. Warton's warning against "minute detail," "Reflections on Didactic Poetry," in Pitt and Warton, *The Works of Virgil*, 1:396.

16. For related discussions of georgic's relation to scientific methods, professionalization, and disciplinary specialization, see Kurt Heinzelman, "Roman Georgic in the Georgian Age: A Theory of Romantic Genre," *Texas Studies in Literature and Language* 33, no. 2 (1991): 182–214; Rachael Crawford, *Poetry, Enclosure, and the Vernacular Landscape, 1700–1830* (Cambridge: Cambridge University Press, 2002), 97–99; Kevis Goodman, *Georgic Modernity and British Romanticism: Poetry and the Mediation of History* (Cambridge: Cambridge University Press, 2005), 17–37; and Robert P. Irvine, "Labor and Commerce in Locke and Early Eighteenth-Century English Georgic," *ELH: English Literary History* 76, no. 4 (2009): 963–88.

17. Frans de Bruyn, "Reading Virgil's Georgics as a Scientific Text: The Eighteenth-Century Debate between Jethro Tull and Stephen Switzer," *ELH: English Literary History* 71, no. 3 (2004): 682–85. The relevant work by Jethro Tull is *The Horse-Hoing Husbandry: or, An Essay on the Principles of Tillage and Vegetation* (London: Printed for the Author, and Sold by G. Strahan et al., 1733).

18. James Hamilton, *Virgil's Pastorals Translated into English Prose; as Also His Georgicks, with Such Notes and Reflexions as Make Him Appear to Have Wrote Like an Excellent Farmer* (Edinburgh: Printed by W. Cheyne . . . Sold by J. Traill and G. Crawford, 1742).

19. Trapp, *Lectures on Poetry*, 188.

20. Gilmore, *The Sugar-Cane*, 90.

21. William Falconer, *The Shipwreck. A Poem. In Three Cantos. By a Sailor* (London: Printed by the Author, and Sold by A. Millar, 1762), advertisement. For a detailed discussion of Falconer's notes, see William Jones's chapter in this volume.

22. Addison, "Essay on the Georgics," 146; see also Trapp, *Lectures on Poetry*, 188.

23. James Boswell, *Life of Johnson*, ed. George Birkbeck Hill, 6 vols. (Oxford: Clarendon Press, 1934), 2:453–54.

24. John Aikin, *An Essay on the Application of Natural History to Poetry* (Warrington: Printed for W. Eyres, for J. Johnson, 1777), 58–59.

25. John Denham, *Coopers-Hill. A Poem* (London: Printed by H. Hills, 1709). The first two notes appear as footnotes, the rest in the margin. All notes in earlier editions were marginal, but by 1709 it was becoming standard to print notes at the foot of the page. For identification of the 1655 version as the first "authorized" edition, see Brendan O. Hehir, "'Lost,' 'Authorized,' and 'Pirated' Editions of John Denham's *Coopers Hill*," *PMLA: Publications of the Modern Language Association* 79, no. 3 (1964): 242–53.

26. Pope was already accustomed to adding footnotes: his *Essay on Criticism* had been published in 1711 with notes similar in frequency (nine total) to those in *Windsor-Forest* but consisting entirely of literary references. *An Essay on Man. In Epistles to a Friend. Epistle III* (London: Printed for J. Wilford, 1733), by contrast, had only a solitary note (on page 13).

27. See Marcus Walsh, "Literary Scholarship and the Life of Editing," in *Books and Their Readers in Eighteenth-Century England: New Essays*, ed. Isabel Rivers (London: Leicester University Press, 2001), 191–215.

28. Alexander Pope, *The Iliad of Homer*, ed. Maynard Mack, vol. 8 of *The Twickenham Edition of the Poems of Alexander Pope*, ed. John Butt et al. (London: Methuen, 1967), 261 (l. 466n).

29. Addison, "Essay on the Georgics," 146.

30. Thomas McFarland, "Who Was Benjamin Whichcote? or, The Myth of Annotation," in Stephen A. Barney, ed., *Annotation and Its Texts* (Oxford: Oxford University Press, 1991), 164–65. Shari Benstock treats the two categories as one: see "At the Margin of Discourse: Footnotes in the Fictional Text," *PMLA: Publications of the Modern Language Association* 98, no. 2 (1983): 204.

31. Weekes refers to the work as "Descriptive Poetry," but he also hopes "that a due Regard might be paid to the Advice he recommends." Nathaniel Weekes, preface to *Barbados A Poem*. (London: Printed for R. and J. Dodsley, 1754), v, xii.

32. Imitation and influence also affect the number and type of notes. Somervile's *The Chace* is exceptional among fully didactic georgics in having only three short notes, all referential, but this poem was the earliest formal georgic to have any notes at all. The paucity of notes in Pye's 1784 *Shooting* (in contrast to his *Faringdon Hill*, 1774) may be accounted for by the fact that he took *The Chace* as his model: Henry James Pye, *Shooting, a Poem* (London: J. Davis, 1784), lines 19–24.

33. Mark Akenside, *The Pleasures of Imagination: A Poem in Three Books* [2nd ed.] (London, 1744), 1:lines 45–55.

34. Robin Dix, *The Literary Career of Mark Akenside* (Madison, NJ: Fairleigh Dickinson University Press, 2006), 112–13.

35. Pellicer, "The Georgic," 414.

36. Akenside, *The Pleasures of Imagination*, 102n.

37. Chalker, *English Georgic*, 199.

38. Other georgics with non-authorial notes that could have been listed in table 1.2 include W. Burgh's additions to William Mason, *The English Garden: A Poem. In Four Books*, new ed. (Dublin: Printed by P. Byrne, 1786); John Stanier Clarke's apparatus to *The Shipwreck, a Poem by William Falconer . . . the Text Illustrated by Additional Notes* (London: Printed for William Miller, 1804); and John Smythe Memes's notes to *The Task* in *The Works of William Cowper with . . . Notes*, 2nd ed., 3 vols. (Edinburgh: Fraser, 1835), 3:167–306. The "notes" column in table 1.2 lists the cumulative number of notes, both authorial and non-authorial, for each poem or edition. In addition to the 342 footnotes accompanying the text, Dunster also offers "Additions to the Notes" at the end of his volume. Although some of Dunster's thirty-six endnotes supplement earlier footnotes, they have been counted as discrete notes.

39. For discussions of *Windsor-Forest* as a georgic, see Juan Christian Pellicer, "Corkscrew or Cathedral? The Politics of Alexander Pope's *Windsor-Forest* and the Dynamics of Literary Kind," *Huntington Library Quarterly* 71, no. 3 (2008): 453–88; and Pat Rogers, *Pope and the Destiny of the Stuarts* (Oxford: Oxford University Press, 2005).

40. See the review of Mason's *The English Garden* in *Gentleman's Magazine* 47 (September 1777): 449–50. The reviewer begins by hailing the poem as "didactic" but, at the end, identifies the poem as a "Georgic."

41. James McLaverty, *Pope, Print, and Meaning* (Oxford: Oxford University Press, 2001), 232, 236.

42. Scott M. Cleary, "Slouching toward Augusta: Alexander Pope's 1736 'Windsor Forest,'" *SEL: Studies in English Literature* 50, no. 3 (2010): 645–63, esp. 659–60.

43. Elise F. Knapp, "Community Property: The Case for Warburton's 1751 Edition of Pope," *SEL: Studies in English Literature* 26, no. 3 (1986): 456.

44. The three notes from 1736 that Warburton fails to reproduce are textual variants— "perhaps," Pat Rogers posits, "to present the poet in the most flattering . . . light." See Rogers, *Pope and the Destiny of the Stuarts*, 82.

45. Robert M. Ryley, *William Warburton* (Boston: Twayne, 1984), 80, 88.

46. *British Critic* 4 (December 1794): 590.

47. *The Works of Alexander Pope*, ed. Gilbert Wakefield (Warrington: Printed for the Author by W. Eyres, 1794), 67n.

48. Alexander Pope, *Pastoral Poetry and An Essay on Criticism*, ed. E. Audra and Aubrey Williams, vol. 1 of *The Twickenham Edition of the Poems of Alexander Pope*, ed. John Butt et al. (London: Methuen, 1961), viii.

49. *The Works of Alexander Pope*, ed. Joseph Warton, 9 vols. (London: Printed for B. Law et al., 1797), 1:118n.

50. Wakefield, *Works of Alexander Pope*, 91n.

51. Warton, *Works of Alexander Pope*, 1:133n.

52. Ibid., 115n, 116n, 130n.

53. Pellicer, "Dynamics of Literary Kind," 457.

54. Ibid., 488.

55. Warton, *Works of Alexander Pope*, 1:117n.

56. Ibid., 1:139n. The long note that Warton attaches to the end of *Windsor-Forest* is lifted from pages 50–51 of his *Essay* as reprinted in vol. 1 of Adam Rounce, ed., *Alexander Pope and His Critics* (New York: Routledge, 2004).

57. In the advertisement, Warton expresses his belief that "the fashion of moralizing in verse has been carried too far." See Joseph Warton, *Odes on Various Subjects* (London: Printed for R. Dodsley, 1746).

58. See Pat Rogers, "John Philips, Pope, and Political Georgic," *Modern Language Quarterly* 66, no. 4 (2005): 419.

59. John Philips, *Cider, a Poem in Two Books*, ed. Charles Dunster (London: Printed by George Stafford, for T. Cadell, 1791), [v].

60. Heinzelman, "Roman Georgic in the Georgian Age," 203.

61. For the notes on the cider mill and cider making, see Dunster, *Cider*, 104–6n, 112–13n.

62. Dunster, *Cider*, 3n.

63. Ibid., 9n.

64. Ibid., 3n.

65. See Juan Christian Pellicer, "Celebrating Queen Anne and the Union of 1707 in Great Britain's First Georgic," *Journal for Eighteenth-Century Studies* 37, no. 2 (2014): 217–27.

66. Dunster, *Cider*, 172n.

67. Ibid., 100n.

68. Ibid., 117n.

69. Ibid., 32n.

70. Ibid., 42n.

71. For a discussion of how notes and paratexts shape perceptions of generic identity, see David Duff, *Romanticism and the Uses of Genre* (Oxford: Oxford University Press, 2009), passim.

2

William Falconer's *The Shipwreck* and the Birth of the *Dictionary of the Marine*

William Jones

In October 1749, a British merchant ship left the port of Candia (Heraklion) in Crete bound for Venice.[1] A few days later, driven north by a southerly gale, the ship was wrecked on the rocky headland of Cape Sounion, near Athens, with the loss of all hands except for three survivors. One of these was the second mate, William Falconer (1732–1770), who in 1762 was to publish his account of this catastrophic voyage, *The Shipwreck. A Poem. In Three Cantos. By a Sailor.*[2] The poem is a narrative of a voyage, and uniquely in English poetry, it is dense with technical detail of the rigging and handling of an ocean-going ship, which even to Falconer's contemporaries would have been obscure. It is also a narrative with a dramatic climax, and as such it enjoyed wide appeal at a time when voyage and shipwreck were popular literary topics.[3]

The poem is distinctive in a number of ways; for the purposes of this chapter, I will focus on two of these distinguishing features. First, *The Shipwreck* relates the progress of the voyage with a high proportion of "tarpaulin" technical sea language and, for this reason, adds to the text an equally large measure of explanatory notes. Falconer's annotations establish his expertise and provide technical instruction to young sailors. Second, Falconer defines his poem in relation to a prose work of nautical reference, first to the absence or inadequacy of any such work, which justifies Falconer's definitional notes, and later, in the third edition of 1769, to Falconer's own effort to supply that missing reference work, the *Universal Dictionary of the Marine* (1769), which remained the standard nautical dictionary until the end of the days of sail.[4] This chapter will show that the *Dictionary* grew directly from the annotation to *The Shipwreck*, and that both works demonstrate aspects of Falconer's distinctive character: poet, sea-scientist, and lexicographer. Furthermore, the development of the notes over the three authorial editions (1762, 1764, 1769; hereafter referred to as *Shipwreck* A, B, and C) exhibit Falconer's effort to reach new readers and to adapt specialist knowledge to poetry.

REVIEWS OF *SHIPWRECK* A
AND FALCONER'S EARLY WRITING

The Shipwreck is little regarded today. No editions of Falconer's poetry appeared after 1900, until my edition in 2003.[5] Similarly, since the end of commercial and naval sailing vessels, the *Dictionary of the Marine* has only been reprinted as a historical source.[6] This obscurity is in contrast to the considerable popularity Falconer enjoyed during his lifetime, a popularity that long outlasted his death in 1770. Many post-humous editions of the poem were published, ranging from cheap pocket reprints to lavish editions illustrated by eminent artists, including Nicholas Pocock, Richard Westall, and Birket Foster.[7] Only in the late Victorian period, with the decline both of the sailing ship and of popular taste for eighteenth-century verse, did *The Ship-wreck* disappear from public view, but not until the poem had seen over 150 editions and earned inclusion in all the major anthologies and poetry collections from Samuel Johnson's *Works of the English Poets* (1779–1781) onward.[8] Falconer was warmly praised by greater poets—William Blake, Robert Burns, Samuel Taylor Coleridge, and Lord Byron among them.[9] Posthumous editions of *The Shipwreck* tended to ab-breviate Falconer's large annotations, though in James Stanier Clarke's 1804 edition the notes were expanded.[10]

The Shipwreck was published in late May 1762, by Andrew Millar, in quarto, and with two fold-out plates engraved by Thomas Kitchin: "A Chart of the Ship's Path from Candia to Cape Colonne" and "Elevation of a Merchant-Ship." Priced at 5s, *Shipwreck* A is a relatively expensive volume, compared, say, to James Thomson's *The Castle of Indolence* (1748), a quarto of approximately the same length that sold for 3s. Oliver Goldsmith's *The Traveller* (1764) and *The Deserted Village* (1770), again both published in quarto, were priced, respectively, at 1s. 6d. and 2s., but they are very much shorter than *The Shipwreck* and it must be remembered that Falconer's poem was printed on "a fine medium paper" and contained the fold-out engrav-ings.[11] And in any case, the poem was "printed for the Author," and Falconer would have computed the price carefully given that he was taking the risk. His calculation appears to have been justified: all copies had been sold by 1764, "notwithstanding the high price."[12]

The annotation to the poem is extensive. Many of his ninety-eight notes are brief dictionary-style definitions of nautical terms: "Bows are the round parts in the fore-end of a Ship that meet and close in the Stem or Prow" (A.1.197n).[13] Others define and interpret, often revealing Falconer's didactic intentions: "A-weather, the reason of putting the helm a-weather, or to the side next the wind, is to make the Ship veer before it, when it blows so hard that she cannot bear her side to it any longer" (A.2.33n). Falconer also prefaces *Shipwreck* A with a justification of the annotations.

The advertisement links Falconer's annotations to his dual identity as a poet *and* a sailor, which is to say, to his concern about the suitability of technical matters to poetry:

> The Author of this Poem thinks it necessary to acquaint the Public, that it was not his first Intention to swell the Work with so many Notes: to avoid which he proposed to refer his Readers to any of the modern Dictionaries, which he might find most proper for explaining the sea-phrases, occasionally mentioned in the Poem: but upon strict Examination, finding most of them deficient in the technical Terms expressed there, he could not recommend them, without forfeiting his claim to the Capacity assumed in the Title Page, of which he is much more tenacious than of his Character as a Poet. (advertisement to *Shipwreck* A)

As the advertisement suggests, Falconer was anxious about how his notes would be received. However, the great number of notes included show he was more concerned with the necessity of annotation or, more precisely, of explanation, which, as he tells us, he had hoped to be satisfied by reference to "modern dictionaries." This remark, and his professed dissatisfaction with published reference works, reveals his exacting standards—so exacting that, in the absence of a good dictionary, Falconer is willing to risk displeasing readers rather than forego the technical terminology and accompanying annotations. The advertisement links this unstinting commitment to technical detail to Falconer's professional identity: he is more a "Sailor" than a "Poet."

Falconer's insistence that his annotations confirm his status as sailor reflects a larger debate. Since 1697, when Joseph Addison discouraged introducing "terms of art" into poetry, poets had been wary of including in georgic verse the sort of technical descriptions found in *The Shipwreck*. For Pope and Addison, poets should "deliver what is abstruse of it self in such easy Language as may be understood by ordinary Readers" or avoid discussing it altogether.[14] Falconer, of course, is not alone in employing the didactic-technical discourse of a specific art or profession; this was to be found in the work of other poets such as Christopher Smart's *The Hop Garden* (1752) or John Dyer's *The Fleece* (1757). Samuel Johnson's ridicule of James Grainger is a well-known example of the reception awaiting poets who employed technical terminology without also maintaining an elevated style. According to James Boswell, Grainger's reading of his own plantation georgic *The Sugar-Cane* (1764) was severely interrupted by Johnson's laughter at the line: "Now, Muse, let's sing of *rats*," leading Grainger to substitute the periphrastic "whisker'd vermin race."[15] In distinguishing his nautical from his poetical identity, Falconer thus shares the concern of other georgic poets: the tension between expert exposition and poetical style. Grainger, for example, in his own preface to *The Sugar-Cane* equally claims to "beg leave to be understood as a physician, and not as a poet."[16]

Concern about the suitableness of technical terms intensified in the mid-eighteenth century as increasing scientism and specialization generated more technical information. Farming and other traditional subjects for georgic poetry became more complex in their procedures than a poem for "ordinary" or general readers could reasonably admit. Doubts spread about the capacity for georgic poetry to fulfill its didactic function, and notes were sometimes added in order to supplement georgic instruction.[17] Technical processes were instead associated with an increasing array of prose reference works, including encyclopedias and guides such as Ephraim Chambers's *Cyclopædia* (1728), Stephen Switzer's *Practical Husbandman* (1733), and Malachy Postlethwayt's *Universal Dictionary of Trade and Commerce* (1751).[18] At least for one early reviewer of *The Shipwreck*, however, despite making much of Falconer as self-taught and of humble origins, and of the seafaring life as far from conducive to that of a poet, a specialist idiom is not totally inimical to poetry:

> It has been frequently observed, that true genius will surmount every obstacle which opposes its exertion. The very poetical and interesting performance before us, is a striking proof of this observation. How unfavourable soever the situation of a *Seaman* may be thought to the *Poet*, certain it is the two characters are not incompatible: for none but an able Sailor could give so didactic an account, and so accurate a description of the voyage and catastrophe here related; and none but a particular favourite of the Muses could have embellished both with equal harmony of numbers and strength of imagery.[19]

Born in February 1732 to a family living in the poor Edinburgh district of Nether Bow, given limited schooling, and sent as an apprentice around 1746 into the treacherous North Sea coal trade (at least based on internal evidence from *The Shipwreck*; see C.1. 260–73), Falconer had indeed faced "every obstacle" in becoming a poet.[20] Taking a cue from Falconer's advertisement, the reviewer presents seamanship and poetry as distinct fields, though subsequent references in the same review to Falconer as a "nautical Poet" and a "poetical Sailor" question these divisions. Other reviewers were less ambivalent. In a brief, condescending notice in the *Critical Review*, Falconer's superior status as a sailor is made clear:

> This poem . . . is a very extraordinary performance, and so truly didactic, that a man by studying the piece may become a tolerable sailor. Not that we would insinuate that it has no other merit. No—it abounds with poetical flights, though they are a little irregular; and notwithstanding many incorrectnesses, which ought to be excused on account of the author's education and occupation, it contains a great number of pathetic touches, which will not fail to interest the reader of sensibility.
>
> We therefore warmly recommend it to the public as a very curious original, which, we hope, will entitle the author to preferment in the service.[21]

Citing Falconer's "occupation" as the cause for the poem's errors and irregularities, and implying that the poem will advance the author in the navy, the reviewer presents the roles of sailor-specialist and poet-amateur as distinct and declares the sailor as making up the greater share of Falconer's identity. As these reviews show, there was no consensus in 1762 that poetry and technical information were mutually exclusive, yet Falconer nonetheless sought to preempt any objections to his sea-phrases by identifying himself as a specialist rather than a poet-generalist.

By all appearances, Falconer himself saw poetry and technical instruction as compatible. Prior to the publication of *Shipwreck* A, Falconer had demonstrated his skills as a writer both in the appearance of poetical pieces in journals and in a surviving manuscript logbook that records voyages between the West Indies and North America and London in 1760 and 1761. The ship is the *Vestal*, and Falconer has now risen to the rank of chief mate. The log is characterized by fastidiousness: hours, speed in knots, and wind directions are minutely recorded; this entry is from February 20, 1760 (in reference to compass variation between magnetic and true north): "Magnetical Amplitude and true Amplitude equally correspond, therefore no Variation." The log also contains reflections on each day: "Continuance of temperate and mild weather, serene & unclouded Hemisphere attended with a gentle breeze."[22] In addition to anticipating the factual exactitude of the annotations to *The Shipwreck*, these entries reveal Falconer's confidence in the suitability to poetry of subjects more typical to technical prose genres such as logbooks. As well as the only substantial surviving manuscript in Falconer's hand, the log book gains importance for containing drafts of Falconer's shorter poems, indicating that verse composition was very much in Falconer's mind by 1760 and that to him poetry and the technical genres were not distinct.[23]

ANNOTATION TO *SHIPWRECK* A

Falconer's belief in the compatibility of poetry and technical instruction informs the annotation to *Shipwreck* A. As will be clear from table 2.1, which identifies the various kinds of annotations in the three authorial editions of *The Shipwreck*, nearly all the notes to *Shipwreck* A are of the nautical or technical sort—those primarily intended for sailors. The technical footnotes have great variety in themselves ranging from simple definitions to detailed discussions of ship maneuvers. The poem is remarkable for its density of nautical terms of art and, therefore, for the frequency of its annotation, as the following excerpt demonstrates:

> Around the sail, the gasketts[g] are convey'd,
> And rolling-tackles[h] to the cap[i] belay'd;
> The yards, to point the wind, by some, are brac'd;
> Some, to send down top-gallant-yards[j], are plac'd:
> Some, trav'llers up the weather-back-stays[m], send;
> At each mast-head, the top-ropes[n], others bend;
> The parrels[o], lifts[p], and clue-lines soon are gone,
> Topp'd[q], and unrigg'd, they down the back-stays run. (A.2.94–101)

This is the only poetical text on this (quarto) page; the remainder is taken up with nine footnotes glossing the words marked with superscript letters. Some of the notes offer definitions: "Gasketts are platted ropes to wrap round the sails, which is called furling them" (A.2.94n). Others offer advice on good practice: "It is usual to send down the top-gallant-yards at the approach of a storm, to ease the mast-heads: they are the highest yards that are rigged in a Ship" (A.2.97n). Novice sailors would find both kinds of notes informative.

Despite Falconer's focus on educating sailors, his 1762 notes often inadvertently target non-specialists as much as the "gentleman of the sea." As table 2.2 shows, many of the notes in *Shipwreck* A might be most appreciated by general readers. The first two columns identify notes that define terms or specify practices for sailors. The third column lists notes of definition or description primarily aimed at land-based readers. The fourth column indicates notes of a non-nautical kind, including the geographical, historical, literary, and etymological notes (see table 2.1) that will increase in proportion in the two subsequent editions. There is inevitably some overlap between these distinctions, but overall they give a more nuanced analysis of the annotation. Some short definitions of terms give the kind of technical detail that only a sailor would need or wish to know, for example, "cat-harpings are ropes which draw in the shrouds parallel to the yard, that the yard may the more easily be braced sharp" (A.3.386n). Other definitions are so basic that it is hard to imagine any sailor needing such information. For example, yards are defined as "long round pieces of timber tapering to each end; their uses are to extend the sails across the masts" (A.1.198n). Such a definition would appeal to general readers. The audience for still other of Falconer's annotations is uncertain. One note that remains unchanged across the three editions of *The Shipwreck* is that on the usage of "timoneer" ("from Timon, Ital. the Helm") for helmsman (A.2.40n), a note later included in Falconer's *Dictionary*, where it is derived from the French *timonier*. He is clearly fond of this term, despite it not being in common "tarpaulin" usage. Ultimately, the variations within the 1762 notes appear to reflect a compromise with rules of decorum. While the nautical terms may be inappropriate to the poem and inaccessible to ordinary readers, Falconer compensates by phrasing his notes in such simple language that they can be appreciated by a general audience.

Of the notes addressed to mariners, most range from the short definition of a technical term to larger discussion and instruction on professional practice. An example is the note on "fore stay sail":

> Vulgarly so called, but properly the fore-topmast-stay-sail, is a three-cornered sail that runs upon the fore-top-mast-stay over the bowsprit: its use is to command the fore-part of the Ship, as the mizen commands the hinder or after-part, and balance each other: thus if a Ship wants to cling the wind with her side, the mizen is set and the stay-sail down; and if she wants to veer, the stay-sail is hoisted and the mizen brail'd up, &c. (A.2.52n)

The exactness shown here is typical of the annotation aimed at seafarers and displays Falconer's advocacy of nautical practices based on sound principles rather than custom. The multiplication of specialist terms (bowsprit, mizen, brail), terms rarely defined on the same page but instead explained at intervals across the poem according to the occasions afforded by the narrative, is representative of many of Falconer's

Table 2.1. Types of Notes in *The Shipwreck*

Shipwreck A	Nautical/ Technical	General Description	Geographical	Historical	Literary	Etymological	Total
canto 1	16						16
canto 2	76		1				77
canto 3	5						5
Total	97		1				98

Shipwreck B	Nautical/ Technical	General Description	Geographical	Historical	Literary	Etymological	Total
canto 1	18		2				20
canto 2	83		1			1	85
canto 3	6	1	1		2		10
Total	107	1	4		2	1	115

Shipwreck C	Nautical/ Technical	General Description	Geographical	Historical	Literary	Etymological	Total
canto 1	6		1	1	1		9
canto 2	49					1	50
canto 3	7				1		8
Total	62		1	1	2	1	67

Chapter 2

Table 2.2. Specialist and Non-specialist Notes in *The Shipwreck*

Footnotes to Shipwreck A	Nautical Definition (Sailors)	Nautical Practice (Sailors)	Nautical (General Public)	Other/ Non-Nautical	Total
canto 1	2	1	13	0	16
canto 2	10	21	45	1	77
canto 3	1	2	2	0	5
Total	13	24	60	1	98

Footnotes to Shipwreck B	Nautical Definition (Sailors)	Nautical Practice (Sailors)	Nautical (General Public)	Other/ Non-Nautical	Total
canto 1	3	0	15	2	20
canto 2	10	22	50	3	85
canto 3	1	1	4	4	10
Total	14	23	69	9	115

Footnotes to Shipwreck C	Nautical Definition (Sailors)	Nautical Practice (Sailors)	Nautical (General Public)	Other/ Non-Nautical	Total
canto 1	0	1	5	3	9
canto 2	2	8	39	1	50
canto 3	0	1	4	3	8
Total	2	10	48	7	67

1762 annotations. From the first edition, his notes can be seen to chafe against the restrictions of their own format. One might argue that the poem's narrative is at times written as if to give Falconer an opportunity for using and defining nautical terms: the voyage proceeds from flat calm to destructive tempest, with the annotation keeping pace and thus producing a "manual" of seamanship in these evolving and changing conditions. But no narrative could give occasion for the annotation of every term and maneuver a sailor needed to know. Each element of rigging and ship handling is interconnected with numerous other elements, and such interconnections do not lend themselves to the artificial isolation and dispersal of explanation associated with notes. Longer annotations can offset this fragmentation, and Falconer did write some lengthy notes in *Shipwreck* B. But in *Shipwreck* A, which contains just six notes (of ninety-eight) exceeding four lines, Falconer avoids them, as if sensitive to how over-long annotations would violate his uneasy truce with generalist laws of decorum, a truce depending on his defining specialist terms in simple and concise ways.

In 1762, Falconer's solution to the shortcomings of the note was cross-referencing. The note on "head-rope," for instance, informs the readers to "See Bolt-rope, p. 29" (A.2.79n). Such cross-references have an interesting effect. They tend to emancipate notes from the poem's plot, at times presenting the annotations as a quasi-independent text. For example, readers who encounter the term "chain" in the poem and follow the asterisk to the foot of the page do not return quickly to the main text (A.1.253n). The note on "chain" confronts them with additional cross-references, to "gunnels" and "shrouds," both terms that are discussed in the annotations to other passages of the poem (A.1.359n, A.2.149n). Readers who pursue these references are confronted in turn by further references: the note of "shrouds," for example, directs readers to the note on "lannyards" (A.2.383n). For readers who follow the cross-references out to their furthest extent, the fragmentary notes are reconstituted as a somewhat more complete explanation of rigging and procedure. That is, the footnotes become a self-enclosed reference system, a system reminiscent of the articles in the same kind of nautical dictionary to which Falconer had hoped to refer his readers. This is not to claim that in 1762 Falconer was planning his *Dictionary* or was drafting entries in his footnotes. Rather, he was addressing an organizational problem by adopting a method in his notes that imitated the non-narrative organization of the dictionary.

ANNOTATION TO *SHIPWRECK* B

In 1764, a much enlarged revised edition of *The Shipwreck* appeared, in octavo format, with the fold-out plates, at half the original price of 5s. Previously published texts with large alterations or new annotation were sometimes seen from the perspective of copyright as new works, and Falconer was wise enough to realize this, given that his apparent knowledge of the book trade had led his old navy friend John McMurray (later Murray) to invite Falconer in 1768 to join McMurray's fledgling printing house.[24] However, we do not know if Falconer issued *Shipwreck* B in order to demand additional payment from his publisher, as had been demanded from Millar by Thomson for enlarged versions of *The Seasons*. The impetus for the edition of 1764 appears rather to have been Falconer's desire to reach new audiences. The advertisement provides Falconer's own perspective on his reception: in addition to intensifying his 1762 rebuke of current marine dictionaries, which now includes "a silly inadequate performance that has lately appeared by a Sea-Officer," Falconer identifies the first edition, though having sold out ("notwithstanding the high price, and the singularity of the subject") as so expensive as to have deterred "inferior officers of the sea from purchasing it." In fact, the great majority of the readers of *Shipwreck* A proved not to be seafarers, but the general public: "the gentlemen of the sea, for whose entertainment it was chiefly calculated, have hardly made one tenth of the purchasers." Falconer had misjudged his audience, and as a result of "repeated requests" from these officers, his poem "has been printed now in a smaller Edition" (advertisement to *Shipwreck* B).

This preponderance of non-seafaring readers had a major influence on the revisions to the second edition of the poem. Despite shifting from quarto to octavo and halving the price in order to attract a naval audience, Falconer in *Shipwreck* B aims explicitly at the general readers that *Shipwreck* A had unexpectedly received. The revision is highly detailed: almost every line is modified, and there are substantial additions. The officers are now given names, characters, and histories: Albert the captain is experienced and wise; the first mate, now named Rodmond, is a diehard traditionalist from the North Sea colliers (the trade in which Falconer served his apprenticeship) and representative of the deep conservatism among seafarers that Falconer sought to counter in his writings. The third mate, Arion, aptly named from the classical myth of the young poet saved from shipwreck, is the personification of Falconer himself—the young man with an organized and inquiring mind, eager to develop himself as a sea-scientist. This differentiation of the characters of the officers provides Falconer with alternate voices in debating good seamanship as the storm worsens. All these additional aspects of the poem, which almost doubled its length, were intended for Falconer's newly discovered wider readership.

The most substantial addition to the poem is the insertion of an entirely new subplot—a doomed love affair between Anna, the captain's daughter, and the son of the ship's owner, Palemon. Sent to sea to separate him from Albert's daughter, Palemon is tragically caught up in the loss of the ship. This pathetic and moral element changes the balance of the poem from the first version, in which the ship is very much the central "character": the final scene in *Shipwreck* A is of the wreck; in the later versions, it is of the death of young Palemon. The pathos of this ending is reinforced by the addition to this revised version of an "Occasional Elegy" lamenting the unrecorded fate of the crew in the style of Thomas Gray's *Elegy Written in a Country Churchyard* (1751).[25] More explicit literary references are added as well. *Shipwreck* B refers to Orpheus, Aeneas, Daedalus, and Leonidas, among various other literary and historical personages, most of whom do not receive annotation.

In modifying the poem to the taste of general readers, Falconer seeks to improve the lot of his fellow mariners, drawing public attention to the hardships and heroic sacrifice of the merchant marine. Among the hardships to which Falconer calls attention is the scourge of "wrecking," or the plundering of stranded vessels by local inhabitants, sometimes with violence to the crews. Despite legislation this practice was common in some parts of England, and Falconer expresses his strong disgust at the "foul reproach and scandal of our land" in a speech by the captain to the crew (C.2.858). Also in keeping with his humane concern for the livelihood of merchant seafarers, Falconer focuses in another note on the "veteran sailor's . . . safe retreat" of Greenwich Hospital (B.1.406n).[26] Where *Shipwreck* A could be characterized as a poetical "sailor's yarn," with the focus falling squarely on the ship's voyage and the climax involving the violent wreck, *Shipwreck* B is more at odds with itself, introducing a sentimental element while increasing the amount of nautical language in Falconer's continuing effort to instruct sailors.

The extensive revisions to the text in both *Shipwreck* B and C are mirrored in changes to the annotation. Falconer adds notes identifying newly inserted allusions to Milton, Shakespeare, and Ovid (B.3.85n and C.1.52n). Such references tell us about Falconer's reading, and suggest that his newfound popularity led him to locate his own work in a context of a literary canon. New geographical and historical notes identifying events and places such as Sounion, Panama, and the siege of Candia also appear. The technical notes, though increased in number, are often given a more general appeal and sometimes include information that would have been obvious even to novice sailors. Thus the note on "Bow," quoted above, now adds: "this word is pronounced like the bough of a tree" (B.1.650n). The note defining "stay-sails" (A.1.226n) acquires in the revised second version a domestic simile: "Stay-sails are three-cornered sails, which are hoisted up on the stays, as a curtain runs on its rod" (B.1.678n), an explanation much extended and targeted at non-specialists ("land-readers") in a subsequent note on the operation of staysails:

> I am sufficiently sensible of the difficulty of explaining this operation to a land-reader, as there is no method to explain one term of art, but by some others, which is still leading the mind into greater labyrinths, as the ideas become more complex: I shall, however, attempt to make it intelligible by a familiar object. Suppose a curtain extended on a rod with a row of holes parallel to its upper part, and a weight of lead stretching out the bottom of it, if a line is passed thro the holes in the parallel row, and then over the top of the curtain alternately, it is easy to conceive, that by drawing this line tight, it will draw up a great part of it: but that the line may not strain the upper ridge of the curtain, it must be passed thro the rings, which are more able to sustain the weight that hangs at the bottom. Note, *the reason of mentioning a piece of lead being hung below, is to perform the same operation that the force of wind does on a sail.* (B.2.218n)

This long note anticipates Falconer's tendency in the *Dictionary* to explain at length and to link his definitions to larger discussions of physical laws of nature. This specific note indicates his awareness as early as 1764 of a problem that will lead him to compile his *Dictionary*: since in discussing a complex topic one technical term begets others, a single note typically opens "labyrinths" of detail that defy the very expectation of a note as a concise tool for explanation.

Falconer's didactic impulses persist and intensify despite the shift in his anticipated readership. A note on the term "mizen" (B.2.75n) indicates Falconer's continuing preoccupation with accuracy, albeit an exactitude perhaps more suitable to sailors than non-specialists. In the 1764 revision, this note itself acquires a footnote, including a cross-reference to a further long note on the physical forces operating on sails (B.2.633n). Nor is Falconer's personal voice lost. In the note on "sheets," for example, he displays a slightly testy exasperation with the misuse of nautical terminology:

> It is necessary in this place to remark that the sheets, which are universally mistaken by the English poets and their readers, for the sails themselves, are no other than the ropes, used to extend the *clues*, or lower-corners of the sails to which they are attached. (C.2.163n)

In another note, he expresses impatience with the deep traditionalism of his profession. As the weather worsens and the officers "dispute" the safest course of action, Falconer turns to satire:

> This is particularly mentioned here, not because there was or could be any dispute at such a time between the master of a ship and his chief-mate, as the former can always command the latter; but to expose the obstinacy of a number of our veteran officers, who would rather risk every thing than forego their ancient rules, altho many of them are in the highest degree equally absurd and dangerous. It is undoubtedly to the wonderful sagacity of these connoisseurs that we owe the truly English sea-maxims, of avoiding to whistle in a storm, because it will increase the wind; of whistling on the wind in a calm: of nailing horse-shoes on the mast, to prevent the power of witches: of nailing a fair wind to the starboard cat-head. (B.2.177n)

The sarcastic treatment of nautical superstition in *Shipwreck* B furthers Falconer's aim of educating young seamen in the latest scientific principles of their craft.

Falconer's lexicographical agenda is more pronounced in *Shipwreck* B. Writing at a time of shifting terminology, including the giving way of "larboard" to "port" as the term specifying the left hand side of the ship when facing forward, Falconer's lexicographical instincts are on display when he explains such terminological niceties: "the left side of the ship is called port in steering, that the helmsman may not mistake larboard for starboard, when the pilot calls" (B.3.59n).[27] While the number of cross-referenced notes in *Shipwreck* B remains steady, there is an increase both in the total number of notes (from 98 to 115) and in the number of notes over four lines long (from six to nineteen). One very long note, introduced in 1764 and repeated with variation in the edition of 1769, is in the form of a substantial essay of the encyclopedic kind later found in the *Dictionary of the Marine* (B.2.633n; C.2.908n). Some one thousand words long, the note discusses the maneuvers of *trying* and *scudding*, both extreme measures to save a ship in a dangerous gale: to *try* is to heave the ship to with the aim of preventing too much forward movement if there is a lack of "sea room." *Scudding* is a desperate resort when the ship, weakened by the force of the waves on the hull, is forced to turn and run headlong downwind, with little ability to steer a course to avoid danger. Here, Falconer's professional and encyclopedic desire for comprehensive detail transforms a note—in effect independent of the poem for any reader who reads it all the way through—into a dictionary entry. Notes such as this betray a tension between Falconer's provision of technical instruction as well as general explanation, a tension that will lead him to turn from technical annotation to the compilation of his *Dictionary of the Marine*. The notes to a poem increasingly aimed at a general readership cannot accommodate the expansive explanations needed to educate young sailors. Where in 1762 Falconer's apparent regard for decorum made him wary of extended annotations, the longer notes of 1764 suggest his waning tolerance for the instructional limits of an annotated georgic. For the sake of instruction, he pushes the limits both of poetry and of poetic decorum.

The revisions in *Shipwreck* B held ramifications for Falconer's identity. The *Critical Review*, which, as discussed earlier in the chapter, had linked the failings of the first edition to Falconer's occupation, praises *Shipwreck* B for having "fully removed these objections" through additions so numerous "that it almost new-models the poem."[28] For this reviewer, Falconer in *Shipwreck* B has become equal parts sailor and poet, despite his increasing both the technical language and notes. By contrast, the *Monthly Review*, which had lauded Falconer for embracing both identities in the 1762 version, withdraws its praise. After voicing doubts that "our sea-faring Poet hath improved his piece" by enlarging it, the reviewer identifies Falconer as "a greater Master of the nautical than of the poetical art"—despite his having outfitted the latest version with literary allusions and sentimental scenes.[29] Since both reviewers again pass over Falconer's notes without comment, their fluctuating estimates of his identity appear to have little to do with the technical terms and explanatory notes. Instead, his identity as sailor-specialist or poet-generalist depended more on the balance between the technical and narrative-sentimental aspects of the poem. This may explain Falconer's choice to amplify his literary elements at the same time he extended the notes.

THE TRIUMPH OF ANNOTATION: *AN UNIVERSAL DICTIONARY OF THE MARINE* AND *SHIPWRECK* C

The third and final revised edition of *The Shipwreck*, the first on which the author's name appeared, was published on November 25, 1769, after Falconer had sailed as a passenger on the frigate *Aurora*. Falconer's destination was India, where he would have taken a position with the East India Company—had the ship arrived. After calling at Cape Town around Christmas on its way into the Indian Ocean, the *Aurora* was never heard of again. After searches, it was presumed lost—probably in the hazardous Mozambique Channel.[30] In the year before, Falconer had completed the *Universal Dictionary of the Marine*, which was published in March. There are indications that the *Dictionary* absorbed Falconer's energies and his 1769 revision of *The Shipwreck* was hurried: for example, the last 200 lines remain, most uncharacteristically, unaltered from 1764. The revision of the annotation to *Shipwreck* C is also less intensive. Falconer's focus in 1769 was on pruning the notes, a task that often involved rewriting the poem so as to eliminate sea-terms that would require annotation. The sixty-seven notes in *Shipwreck* C reflect a considerable reduction from the 115 notes in *Shipwreck* B, though the decrease reflects partly Falconer's combination of notes that had appeared separately in 1764.

While it is difficult to generalize the differences between *Shipwreck* B and C, the changes reflect Falconer's concurrent work on his *Dictionary*. The textual revisions are thorough, but not structural. In 1769, Falconer creates a more harmonious synthesis of the various elements in the poem: for example, the plight of the unhappy

lovers Palemon and Anna is, in *Shipwreck* C, told to Arion by Palemon while awaiting a fair wind to sail, thus integrating and dramatizing this pathetic story. Many sea
terms are replaced, even to the extent of substituting "left" or "front" for "port" or
"bow." Such changes continue his effort from 1764 to make the poem appealing to
general readers—but with a difference. Where in 1764 the addition of a sentimental
plot accompanied an expansion of the technical language, Falconer's reduction in
1769 of such language and its accompanying annotation signals a retreat from his
earlier goal both to edify young sailors *and* to entertain general readers. This is not
to be unexpected: even in *Shipwreck* B, where Falconer's terminology and annotation
reached their height, a professional sailor would have recognized that the lessons on
nautical procedures therein were too scattered, and too incomplete, for the poem
to be adequately didactic. Cross-referencing and long notes offset the dispersion
of information associated with notes only to a degree. His work on the *Dictionary*,
which afforded unrestricted space for complete discussion of maneuvers, would have
further impressed on Falconer the limitations of poetry for the elaboration of sea
procedures. Only a non-specialist could declare, as had the *Critical Review* in 1762,
that by studying *The Shipwreck* one "may become a tolerable sailor." Falconer knew
that more was required.

Falconer's trajectory altered a good deal after *Shipwreck* B, and these alterations
appear to have shaped his handling of notes in *Shipwreck* C. From 1766 to 1768,
Falconer held a number of administrative positions in the Royal Navy, and with his
mind dominated by nautical matters, the sea-scientist finally overthrows his competing identity of the poet.[31] This shift was apparent as early as the much enlarged notes
to *Shipwreck* B, which indicated Falconer's growing encyclopedism, his desire in his
notes to offer not merely a stopgap in the absence of a work of nautical reference,
as in 1762, but to supply *in extenso* this missing treatment of nautical terms and
precepts. The first step on this path was a now-obscure encyclopedic work: *A New
General Dictionary of Arts and Sciences; or, Compleat System of Universal Knowledge*
(1766–1767), to which Falconer contributed articles on "Naval and Marine Affairs,
and Naval Architecture." Other contributors to this work included James Scott
(poetry and theology), Charles Green (mathematics), and James Meader (botany).[32]
Rushed and incomplete, the *New General Dictionary* is a strange volume: some
articles are full and learned; others are brief and perfunctory. Falconer's selection of
subjects is curious: there are numerous short entries on minor nautical technicalities,
while important subjects are omitted.[33] Such haphazard entries betray the volume's
claims to "universal" knowledge, but the project nonetheless gave Falconer experience in using a scheme of knowledge organization beyond the annotated poem.

Showing his characteristic meticulousness, Falconer's contributions to the *New
General Dictionary* look back to his annotations and forward to his own *Dictionary*.
His articles are substantial, well illustrated, and cross-referenced: that on "fleet" (a
company of ships of war, or merchantmen, or both"), for instance, is long and illustrated with two engraved plates. Occasional glimpses are given of Falconer's own
experience: under "Corposant" (*"ignis fatuus* often seen about the decks or rigging of

a ship . . . in a violent storm") he notes, "we have seen three of these at once in such a situation ourselves." Falconer's articles clarify his view of the relation between poetic annotation and prose reference. For example, the entry on "Chesstree" ("a piece of wood . . . bolted to the ship's side") is cross-referenced to his own note in his 1764 poem ("Shipwreck, p51 in the Notes" [B.2.130n]). As late as 1767, the poem and its notes continue in Falconer's mind to carry the same authority as a work of prose reference and are thus worthy of cross-referencing. Interestingly, some of Falconer's articles in the *New General Dictionary* are identical to entries in the *Universal Dictionary of the Marine*, suggesting that Falconer's work on the *New General Dictionary* is either a preparatory exercise for the *Dictionary*, or the two were in preparation at the same time (the subscription proposal for the *Dictionary* appeared in 1768).[34]

Beyond whetting his encyclopedic appetite, Falconer's work on the *New General Dictionary* gave him a template for the comprehensive treatment of nautical knowledge realized in his monumental *Universal Dictionary of the Marine*. In a move indicative of Falconer's understanding of his annotated poem as a building block toward this prose work of reference, he picks up in his preface to the *Dictionary* where the 1762 and 1764 advertisements to *The Shipwreck* left off: with the now-familiar attack on the existing marine dictionaries, but this time revealing their names and authors. These are all well-known precursors of Falconer, including Henry Manwayring's *Sea-Man's Dictionary* (1644) and Thomas Blanckley's *Naval Expositor* (1750).[35] The *Dictionary* was well received and rapidly became the standard work on the subject. Numerous later editions were published, including in 1815 a much revised and extended edition by Dr. William Burney.[36] The *Dictionary* shows all Falconer's characteristic qualities as a lexicographer: the articles are methodically ordered, cross-referenced, and fastidiously compiled. They range from brief definitions to substantial essays: that on "Naval Architecture," for example, is a thorough exposition of the theory, principles, and current state of the subject. The *Dictionary* is also illustrated by plates, which, as Falconer hastens to add in his preface, are "more numerous, useful, and correct, than what has hitherto appeared in any work of the kind."

The articles in the *Dictionary* improve upon the annotations accompanying Falconer's poetry. Falconer is writing in an "age of dictionaries," as Johnson observed in 1754, and his *Dictionary* adopts the formatting and temperament of contemporary reference works.[37] Unlike the annotations to *The Shipwreck*, which do not permit quick retrieval of information because readers must search the narrative for the relevant occasion for explanation of a term or tactic, the topics in the *Dictionary* are presented in alphabetical order, an organization adopted by most other dictionaries and encyclopedias of the era. Further, the great length of the entries, a length again consistent with other contemporary reference works, offers discussion of naval procedures with more complexity than the necessarily selective and compressed annotations to *Shipwreck* A, B, and C. Falconer also echoes Johnson's practice in his *Dictionary* of 1755, for example, in providing etymologies for his "most material expressions." Falconer adds French equivalent terms in order to "understand their pilots, when we may have occasion for their assistance" (preface to the *Dictionary*).

True also to Johnsonian lexicographical practice as well as his own satirical turn, Falconer enjoys moments of levity. His definition of "retreat" reads: "The order or disposition in which a fleet of French men of war decline engagement, or fly from a pursuing enemy." To this he adds a note: "candour and impartiality obliges us to confess their superior dexterity in this movement."

The annotations in *Shipwreck* C reflect both Falconer's work on the *Dictionary of the Marine* and his shift from poetic annotation to prose as the preferred vehicle for his encyclopedic ambitions. Not only does Falconer remove technical terms and their corresponding notes, he also simplifies many of the remaining annotations. Consider once again his note on the term "mizen." In 1764, the note reads: "The mizen is a large sail bent to the mizen-mast, of an oblong figure, only that the upper-end of it is peaked or sloped: it is commonly reckoned one of the courses, which are mail-sail, fore-sail, mizen, and fore-stay-sail; but chiefly the main-sail and fore-sail" (B.2.75n). Here, Falconer's desire for comprehensiveness escapes his control, his explanation raising more questions or terms than it answers or defines. The topic is too complex, too interconnected with other processes, to abide the constraints of the note. By contrast, the considerably abbreviated note on "mizen" in *Shipwreck* C reads: "The mizen is a large sail of an oblong figure extended upon the mizen-mast" (C.2.162n). The changes here and elsewhere mark a shift from the procedural to the definitional. Consider the differences between the 1764 and 1769 versions of the note on "a-weather." As quoted above, the 1764 note focuses on the "reason of putting the helm a-weather" (B.2.82n). The 1769 note reads: "The helm is said to be *a-weather* when the bar by which it is managed is turned to the side of the ship next the wind" (C.2.169n). Where in 1764 Falconer skips defining "a-weather" in eagerness to describe the handling of the ship, in 1769 he simply defines "a-weather." Such changes are more than another instance of Falconer simplifying his notes for general readers, though of course such readers would have appreciated the more direct nature of the notes in 1769. These changes reflect Falconer's new sense that complicated procedural matters cannot be accommodated in footnotes, and that such specialist explanations of ship handling must be saved for more capacious treatment elsewhere.

What made Falconer's reduction of his 1769 notes possible was his confidence in the existence of that "elsewhere": his own *Dictionary of the Marine*. Falconer offloads much of the procedural instruction of the 1764 notes into his *Dictionary*. Consider Falconer's reworking of the previously discussed long note at the end of canto 2 on *trying* and *scudding* (C.2.908n). Most of the language from the 1764 note (B.2.628n) remains in 1769, though in 1769 the note is expanded and presented as an excerpt from the *Dictionary* ("I have quoted a part of the explanation of those articles as they appear in the *Dictionary of the Marine*"). Again suggesting that his poetic annotations formed the basis for the *Dictionary*, Falconer incorporates most of his 1764 note in his *Dictionary* entry for "tack": in effect, the note from *Shipwreck* B is exported and embedded in a larger dictionary entry, only then for the entry to be excerpted and placed back into *Shipwreck* C. This is the only instance in *Shipwreck* C where one of the extended, procedural annotations from *Shipwreck* B is retained (the dispute between the captain and first mate at B.2.177n is dropped), and it is relevant that Falconer re-presents this note as an excerpt. By doing so, he draws a distinction between poetic annotation and prose reference. Unlike dictionary entries, notes are short, definitional, and omit detailed procedural discussions. He also distinguishes general from specialist knowledge. Non-specialists require the sort of definitions seen throughout *Shipwreck* C, but because this note details a sea procedure, Falconer identifies it as separate, as an excerpt from a reference work and therefore as specialized in nature. More than evidence of his recognition of the affordances of a prose reference work, the reduced annotations in *Shipwreck* C reflect Falconer's evolving eighteenth-century understanding of a split between general and specialist knowledge. All along Falconer was "more tenacious" of his identity as sailor "than of his Character as a Poet," and it was his increasing awareness of the difference between a poet-generalist and a sea-specialist that, ultimately, prompted his turn to lexicography.

CONCLUSION

Today Falconer is better known among maritime historians for his *Dictionary* than he is among literary scholars for his poetry. He would probably be content to be so remembered. Nevertheless, it is worth noting that on the title page of all editions of the *Dictionary* the author's name is given as "By WILLIAM FALCONER, AUTHOR of THE SHIPWRECK," which implies the links between Falconer's lexicographic and poetic achievements. In the 1762 edition of *The Shipwreck*, he is a sailor, driven by a powerful impulse not only to tell his story but to educate both young seafarers in their craft and also the wider reading public on the realities and hardships of the merchant marine. His initial dissatisfaction with marine dictionaries leads him, apparently against expectations, to provide his own annotation to his poem. Guided by Falconer's growing encyclopedic impulse, the annotation develops into a very large apparatus of explanatory notes by the 1764 edition. Thenceforward Falconer's energies begin to turn to the exposition of sea-science through lexicography, and Falconer the experienced annotator begins to separate from the poet. By the end of his life, Falconer is more or less wholly committed to lexicography.

Falconer's shift from poetry to lexicography responds to developments of his time. In a midcentury culture of increasing scientism and specialization, poetry was no longer the inevitable vehicle for didactic ambitions. Although intended as a supplement to heighten the comprehensiveness of poetry, annotations were an implicit acknowledgment that poetry alone could not organize information or teach practices in the same detail associated with dictionaries and technical guidebooks. And notes by their very nature were limited in the complexity and completeness of their explanations. At first, Falconer was not concerned with the instructional limits of the annotated poem; but as he increased his technical instruction in *Shipwreck* B, his changes to the notes indicate a growing awareness, if not a frustration, with the constraints of the note format. Through his 1766–1767 contributions to the *Dictionary of Arts and Sciences*, Falconer experimented with a more capacious, non-narrative structure that further exposed the limitations of the annotated poem, a structure he later used to great effect in his 1769 *Universal Dictionary of the Marine*. The reduction of the number and extent of the notes in *Shipwreck* C indicate Falconer's alertness to the limitations of the annotated poem, limitations that also informed his understanding of the difference between lay and specialist knowledge.

Nonetheless it is clear that Falconer regarded annotation as central, not marginal, to his literary objectives. In explaining the need for annotation in the advertisement to *Shipwreck* A, Falconer tellingly describes his intention to "swell the Work," rather than simply add extraneous or optional apparatus. The annotation reveals the character of the expert seafarer, and as the advertisement asserts, a character of which Falconer is "much more tenacious than of his Character as a Poet." It might be excessive to claim that Falconer is consciously redefining the georgic genre, but *The Shipwreck*, by embedding a nautical dictionary at the foot of the page, crosses boundaries of genre and form (georgic poem, prose dictionary) in a manner unique in eighteenth-century poetry. This unique character of Falconer the poet—perhaps deriving from his separation from the literary mainstream owing to his background and the detached working life of the mariner—is complemented by his distinctive qualities as annotator. From the first appearance of his major poem in 1762, he signals his concern for annotation as a core element in his work. The annotation is a critical and inseparable element in the poem. In the revised and enlarged *Shipwreck* B, the annotation is expanded and consciously shaped for a wider readership. The *Dictionary* is an extension of this poetic annotation. In this it can be claimed that Falconer is rare, if not unique, among poets in that annotation replaces poetry as his first preoccupation.

NOTES

1. I would like to thank Juan Pellicer, Michael F. Suarez SJ, James Sambrook, and Bridget Keegan for their assistance with and feedback on this chapter.

2. William Falconer, *The Shipwreck. A Poem. In Three Cantos. By a Sailor* (London: Printed by the Author, and Sold by A. Millar, 1762). Hereafter referred to in the text as *Shipwreck* A.

3. Important critical discussions of Falconer and his poetry include M. K. Joseph, "William Falconer," *Studies in Philology* 48 (1950): 72–101; G. P. Landow, *Shipwrecks and Castaways, Images of Crisis: Literary Iconology, 1750 to the Present* (Boston: Routledge & Kegan Paul, 1982), 75–84; Bridget Keegan, *British Labouring-Class Nature Poetry, 1730–1837* (Houndmills, UK: Palgrave Macmillan, 2008), 122–37; Siobhan Carroll, *An Empire of Air and Water: Uncolonizable Space in the British Imagination, 1750–1850* (Philadelphia: University of Pennsylvania Press, 2015), 84–92; and Janet Sorensen, *Strange Vernaculars: How Eighteenth-Century Slang, Cant, Provincial Languages, and Nautical Jargon Became English* (Princeton, NJ: Princeton University Press, 2017), 262–71.

4. William Falconer, *An Universal Dictionary of the Marine; or, A Copious Explanation of the Technical Terms and Phrases Employed in the Construction Equipment, Furniture, Machinery,*

Movements, and Military Operations of a Ship . . . by William Falconer, Author of The Shipwreck (London: Printed for T. Cadell, 1769).

5. William R. Jones, *A Critical Edition of the Poetical Works of William Falconer* (Lewiston, NY: Edwin Mellen, 2003).

6. The *Dictionary* was reprinted several times until 1789. Later marine lexicographers—Admiral W. H. Smyth, for example—used Falconer as a major source, though by the date of Smyth's 1867 *Sailor's Word-Book*, the art and science of the sea were rapidly changing (William Burney's 1815 revision of the *Dictionary* contains an early use of the term "steam-boat"). The opening of the Suez Canal in 1869 is commonly regarded as a key date in the transfer from sail to steam. The *Dictionary* has been reprinted in facsimile in modern times (1970, 2006) and an abbreviated edition, *The Old Wooden Walls* (ed. Claude Gill) was published in 1930.

7. For details about these illustrations, see Jones, *Poetical Works of William Falconer*, 24, 32–33, 38–39.

8. For a list of the collections containing Falconer's poem, see William St. Clair, *The Reading Nation in the Romantic Period* (Cambridge: Cambridge University Press, 2004), 525–34.

9. See the introductory section titled "Falconer's Reputation" in Jones, *Poetical Works of William Falconer*, 13–32.

10. *The Shipwreck, a Poem by William Falconer a Sailor: The Text Illustrated by Additional Notes*, ed. James Stanier Clarke (London: Printed for William Miller, 1804). *The Poetical Works of William Falconer* (London: Printed for C. Cooke, 1796), for example, a volume in Charles Cooke's popular pocket British poets series, contains sixty-one notes, six notes fewer than were in the third edition of 1769 and fifty-four fewer than the second edition of 1764.

11. For the advertisement of *Shipwreck* A in the *Public Advertiser*, May 15, 1762, see Jones, *Poetical Works of William Falconer*, 59.

12. [William Falconer], *The Shipwreck. By a Sailor. A New Edition, Corrected and Enlarged* (London: Printed for A. Millar, 1764), advertisement. Hereafter referred to in the text as *Shipwreck* B.

13. All references to *The Shipwreck* in this chapter will be cited parenthetically in the text and follow this convention: the initial letter (A, B, C) indicates the edition (1762, 1764, 1769); the first number (1, 2, 3) indicates the canto; and the second number indicates the line(s). Thus C.1.260–73 refers to lines 260–73 of canto 1 in the third (1769) edition.

14. Donald F. Bond, ed., *The Spectator*, 5 vols. (Oxford: Clarendon Press, 1965), 3:63.

15. For Boswell's anecdote, see James Boswell, *Life of Johnson*, ed. George Birkbeck Hill, 6 vols. (Oxford: Clarendon Press, 1934), 2:453–54.

16. James Grainger, *The Sugar-Cane, A Poem* (London: Printed for R. and J. Dodsley, 1764), vii.

17. For these doubts, see Frans de Bruyn, "Reading Virgil's Georgics as a Scientific Text: The Eighteenth-Century Debate between Jethro Tull and Stephen Switzer," *ELH: English Literary History* 71, no. 3 (2004): 682–85.

18. For a discussion of increasing specialization and the eighteenth-century flourishing of dictionaries and other reference works, see Richard Yeo, *Encyclopaedic Visions: Scientific Dictionaries and Enlightenment Culture* (Cambridge: Cambridge University Press, 2001).

19. *Monthly Review* 27 (September 1762): 197.

20. Jones, *Poetical Works of William Falconer*, 1–2. William Falconer, *The Shipwreck . . . The Third Edition, Corrected* (London: Printed for T. Cadell, 1769). Hereafter referred to in the text as *Shipwreck* C.

21. *Critical Review* 13 (May 1762): 440.

22. Log entry for February 27, 1760. National Maritime Museum, Greenwich, UK. NMS Barker MSS BRK/13.

23. The manuscript includes drafts of several poems, including the lyric published as "Written at Sea; by the Author of the Shipwreck" in *St. James' Magazine* 1 (October 1762): 110–12. See Jones, *Poetical Works of William Falconer*, 330, 471.

24. William Zachs, ed. *The First John Murray and the Late Eighteenth-Century London Book Trade with a Checklist of His Publications* (Oxford: For the British Academy by Oxford University Press, 1998), 19–20. For annotations as a way of circumventing copyright rules, see Michael Harris, "Paper Pirates: The Alternative Book Trade in mid-18th Century London," in *Fakes and Frauds: Varieties of Deception in Print & Manuscript*, ed. Robin Myers and Michael Harris (Detroit, MI: Omnigraphics, 1989), 59.

25. The "Occasional Elegy" was introduced in *Shipwreck* B and repeated with some variations in *Shipwreck* C.

26. The printed numeration in the *Shipwreck* B text identifies the allusion to Greenwich Hospital as in line 405. In fact, the line numbering is off by one, so the correct line number (406) has been cited in the text.

27. Despite the obvious potential confusion of "larboard" and "starboard," especially in the noise of wind and rigging, it is an example of the traditionalism of the seafaring profession that it was not until 1844 that the term *port* was officially adopted by the Royal Navy. *Admiralty Order* 22 (November 1844) states that "it is their Lordships direction that the word 'Larboard' shall no longer be used."

28. *Critical Review* 17 (April 1764): 294.

29. *Monthly Review* 30 (May 1764): 395–96. Overall, reviews of *Shipwreck* B were favorable, finding the Palemon and Anna plot "pathetic and affecting." Nonetheless the reviewers felt the moving of the catastrophe from the wreck to the death of Palemon "diverts the attention from the more genuine and manly distress of the poem" (398).

30. The fate of the *Aurora* became a matter of considerable public disquiet, owing to the presence on board of East India Company commissioners. There were repeated searches made by the *Morse* East Indiaman, but without success. News from the Indian Ocean traveled slowly, and Falconer's wife was still receiving his wages in April 1771. The *Gentleman's Magazine* for this month (April 1771) reports the growing concern that the ship has been lost (237). The *Aurora* had sailed from Cape Town on December 27, 1769. There was an unofficial report of another East Indiaman seeing the *Aurora* at Madagascar in April 1770. Given the likelihood the ship was lost in the Mozambique Channel, it is almost certain that Falconer died in 1770, not 1769, as all previous writers have assumed.

31. See Jones, *Poetical Works of William Falconer*, 7–10.

32. James Scott et al., *A New General Dictionary of Arts and Sciences; or, Compleat System of Universal Knowledge*, 2 vols. (London, 1766–1767).

33. Substantial articles not included in Falconer's *Dictionary* are "Anchorage," "Shipbuilding," "Latitude," and "Longitude." For a substantial article in both publications, though different in composition, see "Mast."

34. *Proposal for Printing by Subscription, an Universal Dictionary of the Marine . . . by William Falconer* (London: Printed for T. Cadell, 1768).

35. Sir Henry Manwayring, *The Sea-Mans Dictionary; or, An Exposition and Demonstration of All the Parts and Things Belonging to a Shippe: Together with an Explanation of All the Termes and Phrases Used in the Practique of Navigation* (London: Printed by G. M. for John Bellamy, 1644); Thomas Blanckley, *A Naval Expositor, Shewing and Explaining the Words and Terms of*

Art Belonging to the Parts, Qualities, and Proportions of Building, Rigging, Furnishing, & Fitting a Ship for Sea (London: Printed by E. Owen, 1750).

36. *A New Universal Dictionary of the Marine . . . Originally Compiled by William Falconer,* ed. William Burney (London: Printed for T. Cadell, 1815).

37. Johnson to Samuel Richardson, March 28, 1754, in *Letters of Samuel Johnson,* ed. Bruce Redford, 5 vols. (Princeton, NJ: Princeton University Press, 1992–1995), 1:79.

II

NATIONALISM, ANTIQUARIANISM, AND ANNOTATION

3

The Afterlife of Annotation

How Robert of Gloucester Became
the Founding Father of English Poetry

Jeff Strabone

The eighteenth-century reader knew nothing of *Beowulf* or *Sir Gawain and the Green Knight*. Touched by only a handful of antiquarians over the centuries, they remained lonely, unique manuscripts hidden away in the Cotton Library. Both were printed for the first time in the nineteenth century, as were most other Old and Middle English texts that we now take for granted as the start of the English canon. What the eighteenth century had instead was the Chronicle of Robert of Gloucester.

Although forgotten today, the thirteenth-century Chronicle was one of scant few pre-Chaucerian English poems available in print at the time. It was first published in 1724 in an edition by Thomas Hearne (1678–1735), whose copious paratextual apparatus instructed readers to recognize not the Chronicle's literary merits but, rather, its value as historical evidence. This was normal: archaic English texts were typically printed in the sixteenth and seventeenth centuries for the ammunition they provided to ecclesiastical and political debates about the church, the law, the powers of the sovereign, and not for the nation to admire its oldest literary remains. But over the course of the eighteenth century, the function and meaning of archaic poetic manuscripts changed. With the emergence of Romantic ideas of the nation and its native cultural origins, Old and Middle English poetry came to be valued for a new set of reasons: to demonstrate the antiquity of a national literature and to inspire new poets to recall the genius of the ancient bards.[1]

This chapter is not about Robert or his Chronicle. It is about how the eighteenth century edited, annotated, read, and misread it, and ultimately used it as part of an emerging Romantic narrative of literary history that imagined the roots of the modern nation stretching back to a bardic era of poetry and song. It is about annotation and the afterlife of annotation: how the authority bestowed on a text by one editor's annotations transfers to other texts that borrow its authority in their own annotations, sometimes for wildly different purposes.

The Chronicle is an illustration of a wider change beginning in the eighteenth century whereby early English poetry in manuscript came to be read in a new light in print. What had been the preserve of a handful of antiquarians became, thanks to print circulation, available to anyone who cared to purchase or borrow a copy. Once in print, however, it is fair game for all. It can support any number of arguments, particularly if, as we will see, an influential reader egregiously misreads it. As the Chronicle moved from being an annotated printed text to being an annotation to other printed texts, it was transformed into an important work of literature, and Robert came to be seen, for a time, as the founder of English poetry. Despite the classical frame that Hearne had put around the Chronicle—literally, as his annotating voice was in Latin—subsequent editors of other texts used it to corroborate the bardic narrative of literary history that emerged in the second half of the eighteenth century.

I will illustrate this transformation in the function of archaic poetry by, first, exploring the intellectual underpinnings of Hearne's work on the Chronicle: how he used preface, footnotes, glossary, and visual elements like typefaces and alphabets—everything from Runic to blackletter—to situate the text as an object, not of literature, but of history. Hearne was a transitional figure: although obsessed with all things medieval, he was the last gasp of a neoclassical order as well. The second half of the chapter will trace the Chronicle's evolution through other hands: from Samuel Johnson, who called Robert the founder of rhyme; to Thomas Percy, who folded him into his bardic narrative of literary history and spread misunderstanding about Anglo-Saxon prosody; to Samuel Taylor Coleridge, whose *Christabel* meter uncannily resembles Percy's misrepresentation of the Chronicle and who elevated Robert to his highest point of importance. What had been a historical document to the classically trained antiquarian became to the Romantic era a poem that underpinned the ballad tradition and marked the beginning of the English nation. Annotation played a crucial part in transforming the function of early English poetry in the eighteenth century.

BARDIC MEDIATION AND THE NEW NATIONALISM

I use the term *bardic mediation* to describe the distinct way that late eighteenth-century antiquarians and poets revived archaic poetry in new forms. Archaic (and faux-archaic) texts, ballads included, became the foundation of a new model of literary history that traced the modern nation's cultural origins further back in time to indigenous bardic cultures of song and poetry, real or imagined. The methods, agendas, and paratextual apparatus of these new endeavors moved definitively away from Elizabethan and seventeenth-century obsessions with ecclesiastical conflicts and also away from Augustan-era contempt for England's Saxon remains. The bardic model marked a national turn away from neoclassical identifications with Augustan Rome and toward the native medieval. In short, the English came to see themselves as descendants of bards and barbarians, and, for the first time, they thought that was good.

In calling these practices bardic, I am indebted to Katie Trumpener's *Bardic Nationalism* (1997), which broke new ground on something that had previously been hiding in plain sight: the central figure of the bard in Romantic culture.[2] Although Trumpener limited the scope of the bardic to cultural nationalism on the Celtic periphery, the English were, I argue, as invested in reinventing their nation according to the bardic narrative of literary history as were the other nations of the British Isles.

The concept of mediation I borrow chiefly from two places. One is Celeste Langan and Maureen N. McLane's insistence that the eighteenth century's theoretical awareness of the media of poetry—orality, manuscript, print, paratext—is historicizable and that it helped shape the discipline of literary study as well as the composition of new poems.[3] The other is Clifford Siskin and William Warner's idea of the history of mediation. They define mediation in the literal sense of the word: anything "in between."[4] A history of mediation is thus an account of how, in a given period and place, content in one form was put into another form, as when, say, oral ballads were transcribed and edited in print. One thing that makes a movement or period distinct from others is that it tends to work on certain clusters of preexisting content in historically distinct ways. Romanticism, for instance, can be distinguished by the peculiar ways that it engaged and repurposed medieval poetry and ballads into print editions and new poems.

Finally, this chapter is motivated by a question left unanswered by Benedict Anderson in *Imagined Communities* (1983), still the most influential account of the rise of modern nationalism. Anderson famously argued that nations are historically young but imagine themselves primordially old.[5] Yet he did not work out *how* the archaicization of the nation occurs. I argue that in England, Scotland, Wales, and elsewhere, print editions of archaic poetry played this role: antiquarians dug up arcane, archaic texts and—despite gaps of several centuries in which many of these texts went unread—reframed them, with lengthy prefaces and ostentatiously learned footnotes, as the ancient literary roots of the nation. As English antiquarians pushed further and further past Chaucer in time, the nation's founding originary genius got older—and less legible to a modern audience.

THE DISGRACE OF ANTIQUARIANISM

At the start of the eighteenth century, few welcomed the return of early English poetry. We tend to forget how invested the English literati were in their identifications with the classical world of ancient Rome and how little they wanted to be reminded of their Northern, Gothic origins. It is important to remember that, before the eighteenth century's bardic turn, the English regarded the medieval era chiefly as a time of shameful barbarism that few cared to revisit. Jonathan Swift was not alone in 1710 in fretting about the "natural Tendency towards relapsing into Barbarity" by letting the English language slip back to its Northern origins.[6] It was not only the contents of early English culture that attracted scorn but also the work of the antiquarians to bring it back, and even the antiquarians themselves. William Warburton in 1727 was explicit about not wanting England's barbarous forebears dredged up:

> Every Monkish Tale, and Lye, and Miracle, and Ballad, are rescued from their Dust and Worms, to proclaim the Poverty of our Forefathers; whose Nakedness, it seems, their pious Posterity take great Pleasure to pry into: For of all those Writings given us by the *Learned Oxford Antiquary*, there is not one that is not a Disgrace to Letters; most of them are so to common Sense, and some even to human Nature. Yet how set out! how trick'd! how adorned! how extolled![7]

Whether or not Warburton had Hearne specifically in mind as the nameless Oxford antiquarian, he certainly objected to the prefaces and annotations that adorned the printed editions of the impoverished forefathers' literary remains.

Alexander Pope's satire *The Dunciad* (1729) ridicules Hearne by name even before the poem begins—in an annotation on the spelling of the poem's title. Here Scriblerus, the poem's annotating voice, mocks him as "the exact Mr. *Tho. Hearne*; who, if any word occur that to him and all mankind is evidently wrong, yet keeps he it in the Text with due reverence, and only remarks in the Margin, *sic M.S.*"[8] The mock footnotes that annotate Hearne's appearance later in the poem suggest that Pope felt, as Warburton did, that reviving features of archaic English was a ridiculous endeavor. In book 3, Elkanah Settle, the father dunce, speaks to Lewis Theobald, the son dunce, in lines of mock-antique diction:

> 'But who is he, in closet close y-pent,
> Of sober face, with learned dust besprent?
> Right well mine eyes arede the myster wight,
> On parchment scraps y-fed, and Wormius hight.
> To future ages may thy dulness last,
> As thou preserv'st the dulness of the past!'[9]

As Pope's annotations to the passage reveal, certain words (*arede*, *hight*) were taken straight from Hearne's edition of the Chronicle. Pope dug deep into Hearne's glossary and picked out some of the longest glosses that he then incorporated as verbatim excerpts (still long!) in *The Dunciad*'s footnotes, as if Hearne's pedantry were self-evidently risible. Thus we find a mock footnote quoting an über-serious gloss to a medieval Chronicle. However unfunny Hearne's glosses may be in his own edition, the very same words are turned to comic effect as footnotes to Pope's satire. In *The Dunciad* at least, it is the main text that frames the reading of the footnote.

The substance of Pope's mockery is not only that Hearne's glosses are overly long or that antiquarians are fusty types who prefer the company of parchments to people. After one of the excerpts from Hearne's glossary, Scriblerus's voice returns to gloss the gloss:

> I do herein agree with Mr. *H*. Little is it of avail to object that such words are become *unintelligible*. Since they are *Truly English*, Men *ought* to understand them; and such as

are for *Uniformity* should think all alterations in a Language, *strange, abominable,* and *unwarrantable.* Rightly therefore, I say again, hath our Poet used ancient words, and poured them forth, as a precious ointment, upon good old *Wormius* in this place. SCRIBLERUS.[10]

Keeping in mind that the satirical agreement means actual disagreement, we can see that Pope mocked Hearne's project not just for his overly copious paratextual tendencies but also because of what Hearne was reviving: linguistic relics from the English language's barbarous past that many in the 1720s did not care to claim as their own. Robert's Chronicle represented, for those ashamed of the Gothic roots of England, the national return of the repressed.

ROBERT WHO?

About Robert himself we know very little. He flourished, if that's the word for it, from c. 1260 to c. 1300 and may have been a monk in Gloucester. The Chronicle's internal evidence tells us nothing about him but does indicate intimate knowledge of Gloucester and Oxford in the 1260s. John Stow, an Elizabethan antiquarian, was the first to refer to its author as "Robert of Gloster," but we have no idea what evidence Stow based his belief on.[11] Today we believe the Chronicle to be the work of at least two authors, neither of whose names we know.

Unlike its nominal author, the Chronicle has left behind many traces and enjoyed a good two centuries of prestige. Two versions of the Chronicle survive in a total of fourteen medieval manuscripts, plus two prose adaptations from the fifteenth century. The longer version of the verse Chronicle is approximately 12,000 lines long and reaches the year 1270; the shorter has about 10,000 lines and ends in 1272. It adapts content from a range of sources, most substantially Geoffrey of Monmouth, Henry of Huntingdon, and Layamon.[12]

Metrically, the Chronicle is written in iambic hexameter couplets with variable line lengths, as we see from its first eight lines in Hearne's edition:

> Engelond ys a wel god lond, ich wene of eche lond best,
> Y set in þe ende of þe world, as al in þe West.
> Þe see goþ hym al a boute, he stont as an yle.
> Here fon heo durre þe lasse doute, but hit be þorw gýle
> Of fol of þe selue lond, as me haþ y seye wyle.
> From Souþ to Norþ he ys long eiʒte hondred mýle:
> And foure hondred myle brod from Est to West to wende,
> A mýdde þo lond as yt be, and noʒt as by þe on ende.[13]

Although we cannot always be sure what counted as a syllable in late thirteenth-century Gloucestershire, these lines appear to vary between eleven syllables (line 6) and fourteen (line 8) while the most common length, appropriately for hexameter verse, is twelve. More important, for our purposes, than the poem's actual formal and metrical features is how they were understood, and misunderstood, in the eighteenth century.

The Chronicle in its entirety has only appeared in two published editions: Hearne's in 1724, reprinted in 1810[14]; and edited anew by William Aldis Wright as part of the Rolls Series in 1887. Compared to the eighteenth century when it stood almost alone as an example of pre-Chaucerian verse in print, the Chronicle's star had faded badly by the late Victorian era. Wright's judgment is harsh: he found nearly no value in it as history, and "As literature, it is as worthless as twelve thousand lines of verse without one spark of poetry can be."[15] Of course, by the time Wright wrote, a wide range of Old and Middle English poems had arrived in print to outshine the Chronicle. There was at least one flattering comment, however indirect, in Wright's edition. Volumes in the Rolls Series began with a statement by the Master of the Rolls: according to the Treasury Minute of February 9, 1857, the series was an "important national object."[16] Alas, the phrase was not a remark on the Chronicle; it was the paratextual afterglow from a government bureaucrat's praise of the series as a whole thirty years earlier.

THE MAN WHO LOVED MANUSCRIPTS

Whatever readers made of the Chronicle on its first appearance in print, the credit, or blame, for publishing it belongs to Thomas Hearne, an Oxford antiquarian who lived up to Arnaldo Momigliano's famous description: "The antiquary was a connoisseur and an enthusiast; his world was static, his ideal was the collection. Whether he was a dilettante or a professor, he lived to classify."[17] Hearne's devotion to textual accuracy is still praised by scholars today, although he appeared totally uninterested in producing interpretive insights about the manuscripts he published.[18] All he seemed to want from them was to find them and to share them with the world through print. He so loved discovering manuscripts that he composed a prayer thanking God for them: "I continually meet with most signal instances of this Thy Providence, and one act yesterday when I unexpectedly met with three old MSS for which in a particular manner I return my thanks."[19] Biographical accounts tend to portray Hearne as a vicious, petty disputant who perceived slights everywhere and held on to grudges forever.[20] He rose to second librarian at the Bodleian in 1712 but was permanently locked out in 1716 for refusing to take the Hanoverian oaths. He nevertheless refused to let go of his keys even after they changed the locks.[21]

While Hearne may have been indiscriminate in selecting the many manuscripts he published, the Chronicle seems to have held a special place in his affections. The fragments that had been edited by earlier antiquarians did not satisfy him. The dream of editing the entire work had occupied his attention since youth. Indeed, it may have been a case of antiquarian love at first sight: "yet I can testify thus much for my self, that, when I first saw a MS. of this Author (which was when I was even a young Undergraduate) in the Bodleian Library, being one of the first MSS. I ever perus'd there, I was wonderfully delighted with it, and could not but often signify, that I was not at all pleas'd with those, that insinuated, that there was enough of him already published to gratify any curious Reader."[22] There is an inescapable erotic connotation to Hearne's confession as he takes the position of defending his love from the insults of a disrespectful world. While fragments of Robert were more than enough for others, Hearne needed to have it all.

Of greater interest to us than Hearne's bibliophilia is the paratextual interventions of his two-volume edition of the Chronicle. The edition marks a halfway point in the way that medieval English material was recovered, reframed, and revived: it has a foot on each side of a historical divide. On one hand, Hearne embraced a work of medieval verse and used it to date the start of a national English poetry at least a century before Chaucer—unusual positions to take at the time. Yet the way that he framed the Chronicle predated the bardic narrative that generations of antiquarians and other literati after him were beginning to adopt in Scotland and soon more generally across Great Britain.[23] Although Hearne was drawn to the medieval world, he was at the same time no less a classicist than his detractors. Consequently, he presented Robert in classical attire. Dressing barbarous Middle English content in classical garb made for an odd sight, as we will see shortly. It was a bit like trying to drape a toga on a Viking or a Saxon peasant.

For someone averse to interpretation, Hearne had no trouble stuffing the work with paratext to instruct his audience, sometimes by visual means, how they were to understand the text. My treatment of his paratextual apparatus will focus on two aspects: the content of the preface; and the print appearance of the Chronicle, including the typefaces and languages of the footnotes. The size of the edition's parts speaks to the scale of Hearne's efforts: an 84-page preface, 571 heavily annotated pages for the Chronicle, 40 pages of appendices, 132 pages of glossary, 49 pages of index. The pages devoted to the text of the Chronicle are divided into 464 pages from a manuscript in the Harley Library (BL MS Harley 201), followed by 127 pages of the continuation of the Chronicle in a manuscript from the Cotton Library, but the copious footnotes account for at least a quarter of the length.[24] The longest note runs over two and a half pages in length from page 519 to 522; the two pages in between are all one ongoing annotation with not a single line of the Chronicle on either one. All this long note consists of, like the overwhelming majority of the notes, is material from an alternative manuscript of the Chronicle with occasional reference to other authorities. Hearne's annotations are stunningly devoid of interpretive commentary, yet he is instructing his audience how to understand this document by other means.

Before tackling the preface's framing of the Chronicle, let's first digress for a moment. Digression is an essential feature of Hearne's preface. The preface's many excursions, some wholly unrelated to the Chronicle, complicate Gérard Genette's famous definition of what paratext does to a text: that its purpose is to "surround it and extend it, precisely in order to *present* it, in the usual sense of this verb but also in the strongest sense: to *make present*, to ensure the text's presence in the world, its 'reception' and consumption in the form (nowadays, at least) of a book."[25] Instead, the Chronicle often becomes absent as the preface takes us through the cabinet of

Hearne's curious mind. His antiquarian way of thinking seems to find all old things equally arresting: he devotes pages to, among other things, woodcuts in sixteenth-century Bibles, the burial of Mercian queen Æthelflæd in 920 CE, and the worship of wells among the Saxons (1:xix, xxxvi, xlvii). While he may be flexing his editorial authority by displaying the range of his mastery, we can also discern a flattening approach to knowledge whereby all facts are equal and, synchronically, fly free of narrative or argument. Then every so often he catches himself: "Now to return to Robert of Gloucester, as he was an Antiquary, as well as an Historian, so here are interspers'd divers Remarks, that properly belong to the business of an Antiquary" (1:xxxiv). The business of an antiquary, as Hearne understood it, was a circuitous business indeed.

Now to return to Robert of Gloucester ourselves, Hearne stresses throughout the preface that Robert was "one of the first Rank in our old Historians," not that he was a poet (1:lii). The Chronicle's value is always expressed in historical terms rather than literary, even when Hearne discusses its poetry. Where others have found the Chronicle overly derivative of Geoffrey of Monmouth's twelfth-century *Historia Regum Britanniae*, Hearne finds the relationship between the two texts an indication of Robert's skill and reliability: "By comparing Robert of Gloucester with him [Geoffrey], the Reader will soon perceive, what a faithfull Historian Robert was, when he took care to be very exact in what he extracted from him" (1:xvi). Given Hearne's exacting standards, he may have seen his own reflection in the Chronicle. So careful was Robert that Hearne praises him for not letting poetry get in the way of the historian's work: in "his unaffected way of relating matter of Fact in Rhythm, our Author is to be commended, as a true Picture of Antiquity" (1:li). What Hearne fails to see is that poetic form and meter can also have historical value.

The Chronicle's other great value, according to Hearne, is as a guide to Anglo-Saxon, although, as we have seen, there was little appreciation of older forms of the language in the early 1700s. Hearne does not treat the poetry as part of a continuous national literary tradition from which modern poets might draw inspiration but rather as a source book for learning an older form of the English language:

> But now of all Books of this kind, I know none hardly so valuable as this Chronicle of Robert of Gloucester, and upon that account, were there no other reason, it is very proper to be read over and considered by all such as are willing to be acquainted with the old Saxon Tongue, a Language which even the vulgar are very fond of talking of, though they are perfectly ignorant of it. (1:xi–xii)

Why one would want to learn Saxon is less clear. Knowing the origins of place names is one reason Hearne offers. Literary value is not, nor is tapping into the national genius in its originary archaic form.

Poetry has an alternative use for Hearne: as prosodic evidence to help him distinguish between what was the original content in the various surviving manuscripts of the Chronicle and what was added by later scribes (which earlier antiquarians had failed to detect). He describes the meter and formal features of the Chronicle's poetry in order to demonstrate his methods and skills as an editor. When he finds what was to him clearly non-Robert content "intermix'd" in his main manuscript of the Chronicle, he takes great care in separating the authentic from the inauthentic: "I have left out much the greatest part of it, and confin'd my self to the genuine Work of Robert of Gloucester, which, however, I have carefully compar'd with this MS. of the Heralds Office, and taken notice of what I thought proper" (1:liii). He is able to place different samples of verse in their historical periods by recognizing rhythms, line lengths, and other metrical features. And he flatters his readers that they would see what he has seen:

> The Reader will perceive at first sight, that these Rhythms are much shorter than those of Robert of Gloucester. And indeed in this very MS. in the Body of the Book, is also a great Number of other Rhythms, that are also shorter than Robert's, I mean such as relate to Richard the First; (which nevertheless are erroneously ascrib'd by Dr. Fuller to Robert of Gloucester:) but then I have quite omitted all these, partly because they are (in many respects) strangely Romantick, and partly because they are of the same kind with those that were printed by Wynkyn de Worde in the Year 1528. (1:lv–lvi)

Hearne has no trouble spotting inauthentic intrusions even when "The Author, [of the interpolated lines] took a great deal of pains in new modelling Robert of Gloucester, and in adapting every Thing to his own Scheme" (1:liv). Given the dearth of knowledge about medieval prosody at the time, Hearne's analysis is an achievement, which he flaunts to raise himself above his antiquarian predecessors. To give another twist to Genette, we might say that the paratext makes the *editor* present.

On the Chronicle's poetry as poetry, Hearne is silent even when he elevates Robert above Chaucer in the English canon. He positions Robert as the founder of the nation in classical terms: "But he (and not Chaucer, as Dr. Thomas Fuller, and some others would have it,) is the Ennius of the English Nation, and he is, on that account, to be as much respected, as even Ennius himself was among the Romans, and I have good reason to think, that he will be so by Friends to our Antiquities, and our old History" (1:l).[26] The invocation of Ennius, founder of Roman poetry, has to be seen as a double-edged sword. It is a move both for and against medieval poetry.

On the one hand, Hearne has raised a text of thirteenth-century verse to a position previously only allowed Chaucer. This may seem like a small matter, but it is, in fact, an important push into a then-shrouded period of English literature that had to overcome ignorance and prejudice before it would be accepted as legitimate. It is thus an incremental step toward accepting even older texts into an emerging canon of medieval literature that, in the nineteenth century, would swell the history of English literature to over a millennium: Chaucer to Dryden is a 300-year span; *Beowulf* to Wordsworth is a thousand.

On the other hand, it is also a turn away from all that was poetically distinct about the Chronicle. The move to understand a medieval text in classical terms is a move away from appreciating the rough, rugged, uncouth qualities of medieval expression. It is a perspective that invites us not to admire the peculiar idiosyncrasies of a poetic voice from a relatively unknown period of England's past but, rather, to locate Robert in a classical pantheon: more of a marble bust in a museum than a poet whose writerly spirit might still speak to us.

For Hearne, what redeems the barbarous expressions of medieval voices is not our ability to appreciate their uniqueness, let alone the formal properties of their poetry. It is their value as history. Speaking of his source texts, Robert apologizes for their barbarity: "For tho' the Pictures are but rude, yet there are many things in them, that will be of use to curious Men, as even our Saxon Coyns are, notwithstanding the Barbarousness of them. . . . We ought not, therefore, to reject old Pictures of this kind upon account of their Rudeness" (1:xvii). Valuing poetry just for the pictures it gives us of history renders it nothing more than a medium for seeing something other than poetry; it is not an appreciation of how, say, poetic form might also reveal the past. He instructs us to value the Chronicle *despite* its barbarity, not because of it. The rude simplicity of medieval poetry is something that would remain unappreciated until the emergence of Romanticism and the bardic mode of mediation associated with Thomas Percy and others. If Hearne's goal was to establish the first poet of the nation for historical purposes, his edition of the Chronicle accomplishes that in its preface, long before the poem itself begins. Next we will see how Hearne visually contained the barbarism of the Chronicle's text on the page.

THE VISUAL WORK OF PARATEXTS

Hearne's edition of the Chronicle, coming at the vanguard of acceptability for pre-Chaucerian verse, uses visual means in a way that betrays his era's anxieties about the untamed primitivism of the medieval. Throughout the edition, multiple languages, typefaces, and even alphabets are combined in unusual ways that reflect the uncertain status of medieval content in the early eighteenth century. Blackletter, roman, and italic typefaces run together in sentences that also incorporate modern English, Anglo-Saxon, and Runic alphabets.[27] Strangest of all may be that Hearne's annotating voice for the pages of the Chronicle's text is Latin, yet when he annotates a short modern text in the appendix, he does so in English. Why use Latin to annotate a Middle English text and, in the same volume, use modern English for his other annotations and editorial compositions? The answers may lie in the need to contain and legitimate the rude, rough beast of medieval poetry, its hour come round at last. The classicist imposition of Latin reflects, I argue, the anxieties about medieval culture as it emerged into view after a centuries-long sleep.

The first thing one notices about Hearne's text of the Chronicle is that all 571 pages of it have been printed in blackletter typeface. He explains his anachronistic decision this way: "this Chronicle of Robert of Gloucester is the very first intire Book, that was ever printed in this Kingdom (it may be, in the whole World) in the manner I have done it, that is, in the black Letter, with a mixture of some Saxon Characters, which is the very Garb that was in vogue in the Author's time" (1:lxxxiv–lxxxv). Blackletter may have been in vogue in England in 1274, when Robert was alive, but it was certainly out of fashion in 1724 when the Chronicle reached print.[28] Whether Hearne's edition is actually the first printed book to combine Saxon characters with blackletter type is less interesting than his desire to use obsolete characters from the Anglo-Saxon alphabet in a modern edition in the first place: thorn (þ) and the Insular G (ȝ, which Hearne preferred to yogh). It would be like present-day writers using the long S when spelling Gloucefter.[29] The appearance of these letters amid blackletter type does not make the book easier to read, and it was certainly no way to win over a skeptical early eighteenth-century audience.

Pleasing the audience seems the furthest thing from Hearne's mind in his thinking about the volume's visual features. It is not that he was unaware of the hurdles he faced:

> I am very sensible, that the Obsoleteness of the Language will deterr [*sic*] many from Reading this very usefull Historian . . . . As it is a Reproach to us, that the Saxon Language should be so forgot, as to have but few (comparatively speaking) that are able to read it; so 'tis a greater Reproach, that the black Letter, which was the Character so much in use in our Grandfathers days, should be now (as it were) disus'd and rejected, especially when we know, the best Editions of our English Bible and Common Prayer (to say nothing of other Books) are printed in it. (1:lxxxv)

Aside from providing a glossary, Hearne's edition is quite stubborn, defiant even, in *not* assisting the reader in comprehending the text. The annotations, packed with textual variations also in blackletter, provide no interpretive or historical help. In fact, he seems to have made the book deliberately harder for anyone but an antiquarian like himself to enjoy. His reproach extends to the entire nation for forgetting its past.

Beyond the Middle English language and blackletter type of the Chronicle's text, the volume abounds in other typefaces and languages, sometimes in strange combinations. In the preface (figure 3.1), for instance, Hearne quotes several lines of a Saxon source—using the Saxon alphabet—as if its meaning were plain as day to his readers (1:xxxvi):

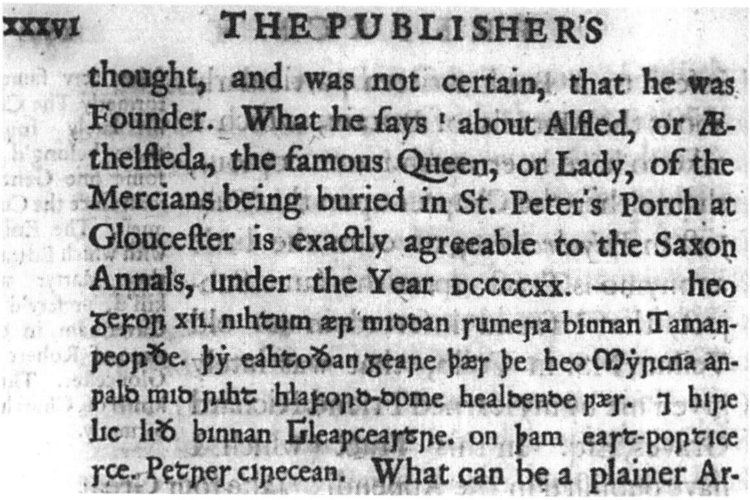
xxxvi THE PUBLISHER'S

thought, and was not certain, that he was Founder. What he ſays ¹ about Alfled, or Æthelfleda, the famous Queen, or Lady, of the Mercians being buried in St. Peter's Porch at Glouceſter is exactly agreeable to the Saxon Annals, under the Year DCCCCXX. —— heo ȝefor xii. nihtum ær miððan sumera binnan Tamanpeorðe. þy eahtoðan ȝeare þæs þe heo Myrcna anpald mid rihte hlaford-dome healdende pæs. ⁊ hire lic liȝð binnan Gleapceastre. on þam east-portice sce. Petres cirecean. What can be a plainer Ar-

Figure 3.1.
Thomas Hearne, ed., Robert of Gloucester's Chronicle, 2 vols. (Oxford: Printed at the Theater, 1724), 1:xxxvi.

In some places (figure 3.2), the full range of typefaces and alphabets converge in a few lines, as in his glossary entry for "leue" (2:665):

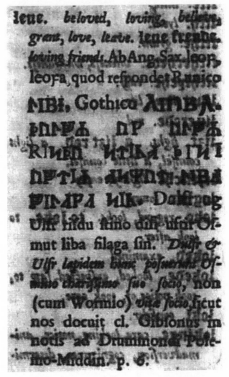

Figure 3.2.
Glossary entry, Thomas Hearne, ed., Robert of Gloucester's Chronicle, 2 vols. (Oxford: Printed at the Theater, 1724), 2:665.

The glossed word appears in blackletter, followed by the modern English definition in italic type and the etymological root in Anglo-Saxon characters, with lexicographical comments in Latin, followed by something in Runic, and so on.

I don't believe the gloss is a typographical demonstration that leue, or love, transcends all languages. Rather, this polyglotly motley dress tries simultaneously to pay visual homage to the Chronicle as an ancient document from a pre-print era while situating it in an international, multilingual world of scholarship in the present. It is, to borrow Warburton's derisive phrase, tricked out with the full weight of Hearne's antiquarian learning, although it is doubtful that he understood Runic.[30] What any reader would recognize is the extent of learning brought to bear on the edition, even in languages and alphabets totally inscrutable to an eighteenth-century audience.

Finally, let us turn to the most curious visual feature of the edition: the footnotes in Latin at the bottom of the Chronicle text's pages. As noted, the footnotes to the text chiefly record manuscript variants, in blackletter, while Hearne's own annotating voice appears in roman-type Latin. While this may seem unremarkable, it was not Hearne's practice when annotating modern texts. One of the last sections of the edition is an appendix of six short texts with varying degrees of connection to the project. One of them, a letter by Hearne himself on the work of Chaucer, is, like Hearne's preface, a text written in modern English. This text he annotates not in Latin but in English. There he writes in a footnote: "This may be seen in the Complaint he made to his empty Purse, which Mr. *Speght* found ten times larger in Mr. *Stow*'s MS. than in the Print" (2:605). Yet every time Hearne speaks in a footnote to the Chronicle, he writes in Latin. For instance: "𝕴𝖓 𝖙𝖗𝖆𝖛𝖆𝖎𝖑 𝖆𝖘 𝖍𝖊 𝖜𝖆𝖘 𝖇𝖔𝖗𝖊, 𝖍𝖎𝖘 𝖒𝖔𝖉𝖊𝖗 𝖜𝖆𝖘 𝖕𝖔 𝖉𝖊𝖉 *Ar.* è regione vero (in margine) manu recentiori, 𝖍𝖎𝖘 𝖒𝖔𝖙𝖍𝖊𝖗 𝖉𝖞𝖊𝖉 𝖎𝖓 𝖈𝖍𝖎𝖑𝖉𝖊 𝖇𝖊𝖉𝖊" (1:11). The italicized Latin reads: *but in the margin in a later hand.* (The "*Ar.*" is Hearne's abbreviation for one of the manuscripts he used.) Why would Hearne only speak to us in Latin when he annotates the Chronicle's Middle English and not otherwise?

I read this typographical relationship as the visual framing of primitive, barbarous matter made tame by a classically learned antiquarian. If we recall the hostility toward England's supposedly barbarous medieval era, the use of Latin to annotate the Chronicle makes sense as a means of containment and legitimation. Hearne's contemporaries worried about England relapsing into the barbarity from which it had, in their minds, triumphantly lifted itself. The Latin voice of classical civilization is here, on the page, to accompany the reader's journey into a rude, unpolished era. It also insulates the editor from accusations of barbarism on his part: he may love medieval history, but he hasn't gone totally primitive on us. The barbarity of the past has been brought back under the light of scholarship: contained, curated, civilized, tamed.

Hearne's edition of the Chronicle was an early instance of publishing an archaic English manuscript not as part of political and ecclesiastical debates but because it was poetry, however historically he insisted it be read. The medieval barbarism that caused early eighteenth-century readers anxiety was legitimated by Hearne's editorial hand: his insistence on the Chronicle's value as history, his reassuring Latin voice in the footnotes, his equating Robert of Gloucester to Ennius of ancient Rome. The paratextual features of his edition do this work, sometimes by elements that we do not typically think of as paratextual, like alphabets and typefaces.

Hearne's classicist treatment of medieval poetry was soon to give way to a new approach. The rest of the chapter will show the afterlife of Hearne's paratextual work. Once he had put this relic of ancient English poetry into circulation, a new mode of mediation emerged, one that related Robert not to the founder of Roman literature but to the lost bards who were now imagined to have founded English literature. In the second half of the century, barbarous archaic poetry would be appreciated not *despite* its barbarism but *because* of it. The Chronicle would develop new literary-historical uses and become attached to new meanings and connections. It would break away from Hearne's classical framing and take on a bardic Romantic cast instead.

THE BARDICIZATION OF ROBERT OF GLOUCESTER

The next important appearance of the Chronicle is Samuel Johnson's *Dictionary* of 1755, which acts as a midpoint between Hearne's classical perspective and the bardic framing that would soon follow. In the *Dictionary*, the Chronicle serves two purposes: as a source for lexicography and as a turning point in a long narrative of national literary history. Johnson plucked a few citations from both the Chronicle and Hearne's glossary.[31] North of the Tweed, John Jamieson did likewise in his Johnsonian-scale dictionary of Scots in 1808.[32] What had been a self-evident object of ridicule to Pope soon became a standard source of lexicographic authority.

Besides the occasional definition, Johnson gave a key role to the Chronicle in his essay "The History of the English Language," part of the *Dictionary*'s paratextual apparatus. There a 202-line excerpt of the Chronicle takes its place in a historical sequence of excerpts from literary texts produced in England beginning with Alfred's ninth-century Anglo-Saxon imitation of Boethius. Like Hearne, Johnson frames Robert's Chronicle as a major event, but the terms used to describe the event are much different:

> Hitherto the language used in this island, however different in successive time, may be called *Saxon*; nor can it be expected, from the nature of things gradually changing, that any time can be assigned, when the *Saxon* may be said to cease, and the *English* to commence. *Robert of Gloucester* however, who is placed by the criticks in the thirteenth century, seems to have used a kind of intermediate diction, neither *Saxon* nor *English*; in his work therefore we see the transition exhibited, and, as he is the first of our writers in rhyme, of whom any large work remains, a more extensive quotation is extracted.[33]

Where Hearne reached back to Rome to situate Robert, Johnson locates him in a national continuum and privileges poetic elements in his account: Robert is the first English poet to use rhyme. For Johnson, Robert is the turning point in language and poetry by which the Saxon and the Norman were joined: he thus marks the birth of the modern nation. Johnson is far more concerned with the Chronicle as literature than Hearne was, but it still functions more as a historical marker on the way to something else than as a literary text to inspire poets interested in reviving antique voices and forms.

Later eighteenth-century figures would favor the rude effusions and wild passions from the nation's barbarous past that so vexed their predecessors, and Robert would be fit into the new bardic narrative of literary history. The stigma of medieval barbarism was transformed in the Romantic era into a store of rude originary genius whose loss was to be regretted. Thomas Percy's ballad collection *Reliques of Ancient English Poetry* (1765), one of the most prefaced, headnoted, and footnoted productions of the eighteenth century, gave the bardic turn its most influential statement. The *Reliques* popularized a new mode of mediating archaic poetry that transformed its use and function: classical antiquarian framings of historical value gave way to assessments of literary value and calls to living poets to revive the bardic spirits of their ancestors. In the case of the Chronicle in particular, Percy's gross misreading of its meter became the basis of an erroneous theory of Anglo-Saxon prosody that took decades to debunk and may have influenced a key Romantic poem by Coleridge.

A common feature of projects like Percy's *Reliques* is the admission that their archaic contents were, in fact, rude and barbarous. That recognition is then accompanied by copious paratextual matter meant to cultivate the reader's patriotic taste for rude content from the nation's past. Rudeness was now becoming a polite aesthetic value. Percy's preface tells his readers how to appreciate it:

> In a polished age, like the present, I am sensible that many of these reliques of antiquity will require great allowances to be made for them. Yet have they, for the most part, a pleasing simplicity, and many artless graces, which in the opinion of no mean Critics have been thought to compensate for the want of higher beauties, and, if they do not dazzle the imagination, are frequently found to interest the heart.[34]

There is simultaneously a note of lament for what has been lost: this barbarous material is full of raw effusions of feeling that seemed inaccessible in the eighteenth century. The promise of collections like the *Reliques* is that, through them, the reader can connect not just with the cultural origins of the nation but with pools of feeling that have dried up in the modern world. In place of an Augustan cultural history that looked to ancient Rome as the source and the measure of English civilization, a new construction took its place, one that looked instead to the primitive simplicity of the nation's medieval past.

Percy turns directly to the Chronicle in an essay-length headnote in volume 2 of the *Reliques* that accompanies the ballad "The Complaint of Conscience." The headnote has its own title: "On the Alliterative Metre, without Rhyme, in Pierce Plowman's Visions." That the Chronicle, four decades later, wound up as an annotation to a ballad, the most popular of poetic forms, would surely have scandalized Hearne had he been alive to see it. Here Percy tries to unravel the mysteries of the accentual meter and alliterative verse of the Anglo-Saxons at a time when there were virtually no examples available in print and when no one understood their prosody. To those, like him, "who are desirous to recover the laws of the ancient Saxon Poesy, usually given up as inexplicable," he has a hunch to follow: "I am of opinion that they will find what they seek in the Metre of Pierce Plowman (*q*)." Footnote (*q*) tantalizingly says: "(*q*) And in that of Robert of Gloucester."[35] The authority of the Chronicle that Hearne painstakingly built up in his edition is about to be used to support a theory of prosody that is totally wrong.

Percy next describes, somewhat speculatively, the historical overtaking of alliteration by rhyme, a turn of which the Chronicle is an example. Alliteration, he says, was "swallowed up and lost in our common Burlesque Alexandrine, or Anapestic verse (*r*)." Then in footnote (*r*), he says of Robert's verse that it is anapestic and that it was modeled on Anglo-Saxon poetry: "Consisting of four Anapests ˘ ˘ ‒ in which the Accent rests upon every third syllable. This kind of Verse . . . was early applied by Robert of Gloucester to serious subjects. That writer's metre, like this of

Langland's, is formed on the Saxon models."³⁶ Footnote (*t*) goes into more detail: "(*t*) Thus our poets use this verse indifferently with 12, 11, and even 10 syllables. For though regularly it consists of 4 Anapests or twelve syllables, yet they frequently retrench a syllable from the first or third Anapest."³⁷ Percy's claim is thus that Robert's Chronicle is anapestic and that the earlier Anglo-Saxon poetry on which it was based was similarly anapestic.³⁸ Hearne could not imagine a poem's formal features, as opposed to its verbal content, bearing historical value. Percy, on the other hand, dares to find in the Chronicle's meter a latent history of poetry.

Despite being wildly wrong, Percy's theory hung around and was not explicitly debunked until Hales and Furnivall's new edition of Percy's sources in 1858. They alert the reader specifically about Percy's essay on alliterative meter: "The reader must be warned against three extraordinary misstatements in this essay, following close upon one another near the end of it. These are (1) that Robert of Gloucester wrote in anapæstic verse, whereas he wrote in the long Alexandrine verse, containing (when perfect) six *Returns*."³⁹ This matters because Coleridge was, in the meanwhile, a reader of Percy's *Reliques*: he took the name Christabel directly from Percy's ballad "Sir Cauline" and may have been influenced by his misreading of the Chronicle's meter as well.

Coleridge's metrical variations in his experimental poem *Christabel*, published in 1816, resemble the principle described by Percy in the annotations to his essay on alliterative meter. In the unpublished draft version of the poem's preface, Coleridge described its meter this way: "substituting anapest or dactyl followed by a trochee instead of two Iambics, either in the first or latter half of the verse & sometimes of giving four anapests, sometimes four trochees, instead of the four Iambics—in brief, having no other *law* of metre, except that of confining myself to four *strokes*, or accentuated syllables." He goes on to say of it that "our oldest Writers in the most barbarous ages adopt it."⁴⁰ It is hard to imagine where besides Percy's annotations Coleridge would have gotten the wrongheaded idea that England's oldest poets ever wrote variably anapestic verse like that of *Christabel*. There thus appears to be a line of erroneous prosodic influence from Robert of Gloucester's Chronicle to Coleridge's *Christabel* that runs through Percy's use of the Chronicle in his footnotes.

Robert of Gloucester reached his peak of importance just two years after the publication of *Christabel* in a lecture on literature at the London Philosophical Society on Fleet Street on February 3, 1818. The speaker was Coleridge. In his lecture series, he attempted to bring all of the strands that led to English poetry together into a coherent literary-historical narrative beginning with the "Union" or "collision" of the Romans' "stern and austere habits" with the "more indefinite and imaginative Superstitions of the Gothic Nations."⁴¹ The barbarous Northern spirit was no longer an existential threat to modern English civilization, as it was for Swift, but instead a key component that went into forming the national genius. Robert of Gloucester, in all his glorious rudeness, now marked the start of an English literary continuity that Coleridge himself carried on in his poetry and which he narrativized as a literary historian:

If we take the Roman at the one extreme, and the Teutonic Languages i.e. the Norse, Danish, Swedish, and German, as modifications of the Gothic, at the other, as the two rings or staples of a Chain, the chain will commence at the Roman end with the Romance or Romantic, or the language in which the Troubadours or Love-singers of Provence and the neighboring districts wrote or sang: and at the other end, namely the German, it ends with the English from 1280, the date when Robert of Gloucester finished his Chronicle in rhyme, to 1380, in which year the Canterbury Tales of Chaucer were first made public.[42]

According to Coleridge, who appears to have known the Chronicle only from secondary sources, all of European history converges in the union of Roman and Gothic cultures. That union reached its resolution in the century of English poetry initiated by Robert of Gloucester and closed by Chaucer. No one would think so highly of the Chronicle again.

When Hearne annotated Robert of Gloucester's Chronicle for his 1724 edition, he used the full range of paratextual devices to frame it in specifically classicist terms as a historical document. If, as Josephine M. Guy and Ian Small have said, the premise of annotation is to promote some readings of a text at the expense of others,[43] then the missing element in the way we typically think about annotations and other paratexts is time. Hearne invested a largely unknown text with the authority of his learning. People read it, invoked it, and made new annotations citing it because of his efforts. But the meaning and function of the Chronicle became something totally different over time.

In the century that followed, the authority that Hearne had invested in the Chronicle was redirected to new purposes: its significance as a historical document was overtaken by its character as a poem, one whose importance steadily rose in the Romantic era. A medieval chronicle that had served as evidence for antiquarian curiosities found its place in a bardic literary-historical narrative of the origins of the nation, and the birth of the English nation was thus pushed further back in historical time. And the same was happening with other newly edited archaic texts across all the nations of Great Britain and Ireland. The bardic turn—the mediating of native archaic poetry as part of a narrative of national literary history that begins with primitive medieval spirits sadly lost—is the start of the construction of our modern national literary canons and of the historicist model of literary history that still holds sway today.

In 1815, Grímur Jónsson Thorkelin published the first edition of *Beowulf*. In 1839, Frederic Madden published *Sir Gawain and the Green Knight* for the first time. Many more Old and Middle English poems followed to crowd out Robert's Chronicle, which soon resumed its place in obscurity. This happened because other texts were annotated by editors who proclaimed *them* as the founding texts of a nation now proudly descended from Anglo-Saxons and Vikings. The outcome was not just a demonstration of the antiquity of a national literature but the production of new poems inspired by newly printed old ones: from Coleridge's *Christabel* to Tennyson's *Battle of Brunanburh* to, more recently, Seamus Heaney's translations of Henryson's

The Testament of Cresseid and, of course, *Beowulf.* New poems with old features were not what Hearne had in mind, but they are nevertheless a legacy of his urge to annotate medieval texts—a legacy that, in unforeseen ways, has had a long afterlife.

NOTES

1. On eighteenth-century Scottish efforts to edit the Middle Scots poets into a canon of national literature, see Thomas Van der Goten's chapter in this volume.

2. Katie Trumpener, *Bardic Nationalism: The Romantic Novel and the British Empire* (Princeton, NJ: Princeton University Press, 1997).

3. Celeste Langan and Maureen N. McLane, "The Medium of Romantic Poetry," in *The Cambridge Companion to British Romantic Poetry*, ed. James Chandler and Maureen N. McLane (Cambridge: Cambridge University Press, 2008); Maureen N. McLane, *Balladeering, Minstrelsy, and the Making of British Romantic Poetry* (Cambridge: Cambridge University Press, 2008).

4. Clifford Siskin and William Warner, "This Is Enlightenment: An Invitation in the Form of an Argument," in *This Is Enlightenment*, ed. Clifford Siskin and William Warner (Chicago: University of Chicago Press, 2010), 5.

5. Benedict Anderson calls this the paradox of "the objective modernity of nations to the historian's eye vs. their subjective antiquity in the eyes of nationalists." Benedict Anderson, *Imagined Communities: Reflections on the Origin and Spread of Nationalism*, 3rd ed. (London: Verso, 2006), 5.

6. Jonathan Swift, *The Tatler* 230 (September 26–28, 1710), in *The Lucubrations of Isaac Bickerstaff Esq; Revised and Corrected by the Author*, 4 vols. (London: Printed: [*sic*] And sold by *Charles Lillie . . .* and *John Morphew . . .* , 1710–1711), 4:181.

7. William Warburton, *A Critical and Philosophical Enquiry into the Causes of Prodigies and Miracles, as Related by Historians* (London: Printed for Thomas Corbett, 1727), 64.

8. Alexander Pope, *The Dunciad*, ed. James Sutherland, 3rd ed., vol. 5 of *The Twickenham Edition of the Poems of Alexander Pope*, ed. John Butt et al. (London: Methuen, 1963), 59.

9. Pope, *The Dunciad*, 170–72 (book 3, lines 181–86).

10. Pope, *The Dunciad*, 171.

11. Edward Donald Kennedy, "Gloucester, Robert of (*fl. c.*1260–*c.*1300)," *Oxford Dictionary of National Biography*; William Aldis Wright, preface to *The Metrical Chronicle of Robert of Gloucester*, 2 vols. (London: Eyre and Spottiswoode, 1887), 1:v.

12. Kennedy, "Gloucester, Robert of (*fl. c.*1260–*c.*1300)"; Wright, *The Metrical Chronicle of Robert of Gloucester*, 1:xv–xvi.

13. Thomas Hearne, ed., *Robert of Gloucester's Chronicle. Transcrib'd, and Now First Publish'd, from a MS. in the Harleyan Library by Thomas Hearne, M.A.*, 2 vols. (Oxford: Printed at the Theater, 1724), 1:1.

14. *Robert of Gloucester's Chronicle*, vols. 1–2 of *The Works of Thomas Hearne, M.A.* (London: Printed for Samuel Bagster, 1810).

15. Wright, *The Metrical Chronicle of Robert of Gloucester*, 1:xl.

16. "The Chronicles and Memorials of Great Britain and Ireland during the Middle Ages," in Wright, *The Metrical Chronicle of Robert of Gloucester*, n.p.

17. Arnaldo Momigliano, "Ancient History and the Antiquarian," *Journal of the Warburg and Courtauld Institutes* 13, nos. 3–4 (1950): 311.

18. "His accuracy, judged by the most rigid modern standards, was as extraordinary as his memory was excellent." David C. Douglas, *English Scholars 1660–1730*, 2nd ed. (London: Eyre & Spottiswoode, 1951), 191. "The achievement of Hearne is difficult to over-estimate: . . . the accuracy of his text might rightly be envied by a modern editor." Anne Hudson, "Robert of Gloucester and the Antiquaries, 1550–1800," *Notes & Queries*, n.s. 16, no. 9 (September 1969): 331.

19. Quoted in Douglas, *English Scholars*, 180.

20. Harmsen's recent biography of Hearne is a more sympathetic exception. Theodor Harmsen, *Antiquarianism in the Augustan Age: Thomas Hearne 1678–1735* (Oxford: Peter Lang, 2000).

21. Kennedy, "Gloucester, Robert of (*fl. c*.1260–*c*.1300)"; Douglas, *English Scholars*, chap. 9.

22. Hearne, preface to *Robert of Gloucester's Chronicle*, 1:x. Hearne had thought about publishing it for years but waited until he found a manuscript whose quality suited his exacting standards; see 1:lii. Subsequent references to Hearne's preface and edition are cited parenthetically in the text.

23. Allan Ramsay had recast the Middle Scots poets as "these good old *Bards*" who had defended the nation's culture from foreign encroachment, in an edition called *The Ever Green*, also published in 1724. Allan Ramsay, *The Ever Green, Being a Collection of Scots Poems, Wrote by the Ingenious before 1600*, 2 vols. (Edinburgh: Printed by Mr. Thomas Ruddiman for the Publisher, 1724), 1:vii. In the 1760s, Evan Evans and Thomas Percy would do the same for Wales and England, respectively.

24. A page of Hearne's edition with no annotation has 28 lines of verse. The full 12,000 lines run 571 pages; 12,000 lines divided by 571 pages yields an average of 21 lines per page (i.e., 75 percent Chronicle, 25 percent footnotes). Alternatively, 28 lines per page with no annotation would run only 428 pages. The footnotes thus occupy the equivalent of approximately 143 pages.

25. Gérard Genette, *Paratexts: Thresholds of Interpretation*, trans. Jane E. Lewin (Cambridge: Cambridge University Press, 1997), 1. Despite Genette's limitation that "the editorial note . . . falls outside the definition of the paratext" (337), I join the widespread critical practice, post-Genette, of referring to editorial notes as paratext. Then again, we could consider the book the work of Hearne rather than of Robert, as the publishers of the 1810 reprinting did by calling the Chronicle volumes 1 and 2 of *The Works of Thomas Hearne, M.A.*

26. Thomas Fuller (1607/8–1661) was a clergyman and historian of the Church of England.

27. The first Anglo-Saxon type was commissioned by John Day and underwritten by Archbishop of Canterbury Matthew Parker for the 1566 publication of texts by Ælfric of Eynsham (c. 950–c. 1010). Eleanor N. Adams, *Old English Scholarship in England 1566–1800*, Yale Studies in English no. 55 (New Haven, CT: Yale University Press, 1917), 157–58. Franciscus Junius had used Runic type in his 1665 edition of the Codex Argenteus, published in Dordrecht. This and other exotic types he bequeathed to Oxford in 1677. On the history of runic type, see Robert W. Rix, "Runes and Roman: Germanic Literacy and the Significance of Runic Writing," *Textual Cultures* 6, no. 1 (2011): 114–44.

28. The 1810 reprinting of the 1724 edition used roman type rather than blackletter but held on to Hearne's thorn and Insular G.

29. Genette considers typefaces only as a feature of the peritext, which is the publisher's domain. Genette, *Paratexts*, 34. Hearne's mixing of typefaces and alphabets opens up additional possibilities for theorizing about paratexts.

30. Douglas believed Hearne did not know Anglo-Saxon either, although the only evidence he offers is that Hearne printed an edition of the Old English poem "The Battle of Maldon" as if it were prose and not verse. Douglas, *English Scholars*, 192. Given that the rules of Anglo-Saxon prosody were not understood by anyone until the nineteenth century, this error is hardly conclusive.

31. Samuel Johnson, *Johnson on the English Language*, ed. Gwin J. Kolb and Robert DeMaria Jr., vol. 18 of *The Yale Edition of the Works of Samuel Johnson*, ed. W. J. Bate et al. (New Haven, CT: Yale University Press, 2005), 163n.

32. John Jamieson, *An Etymological Dictionary of the Scottish Language*, 2 vols. (Edinburgh: Printed at the University Press; for W. Creech et al., 1808).

33. Johnson, *Johnson on the English Language*, 162.

34. Thomas Percy, preface to *Reliques of Ancient English Poetry*, 4th ed., 4 vols. (London: Printed by John Nichols, for R. and C. Rivington, 1794), 1:xiv.

35. Percy, *Reliques of Ancient English Poetry*, 2:280, 281.

36. Ibid., 2:281.

37. Ibid., 2:282.

38. Percy expanded his paratextual matter with each new edition of the *Reliques*. The anapestic reading of the Chronicle first appears in the 1767 second edition.

39. John W. Hales and Frederick J. Furnivall, eds., *Bishop Percy's Folio Manuscript. Ballads and Romances*, 3 vols. (London: N. Trübner, 1867–1868), 3:xxxixn1.

40. Samuel Taylor Coleridge, "On the Metre of *Christabel*," in *Shorter Works and Fragment*, ed. H. J. Jackson and J. R. de J. Jackson, vol. 11 of *The Collected Works of Samuel Taylor Coleridge*, ed. Kathleen Coburn (Princeton, NJ: Princeton University Press, 1995), 442. In this and the other Coleridge quotations to follow, I have omitted Coleridge's canceled words. Perhaps covering his tracks, Coleridge described the meter as "new" in the published preface to the poem.

41. Samuel Taylor Coleridge, Lecture 1, in *Lectures 1808–1819: On Literature*, ed. R. A. Foakes, vol. 5 of *The Collected Works of Samuel Taylor Coleridge*, ed. Kathleen Coburn (Princeton, NJ: Princeton University Press, 1987), book 2:50, 48.

42. Coleridge, Lecture 3, *Lectures 1808–1819: On Literature*, book 2:89–90.

43. Josephine M. Guy and Ian Small, *Politics and Value in English Studies: A Discipline in Crisis?* (Cambridge: Cambridge University Press, 1993), 152.

4

Topographical Annotation in Thomas Percy's *The Hermit of Warkworth* and John Pinkerton's *The Bruce*

Thomas Van der Goten

When Thomas Percy wrote to his fellow antiquary George Paton on February 9, 1769, about a collection of Scottish songs and ballads, he wished it had been accompanied "with a few historical or topographical Notes" to assist the reader.[1] Spelling this comment out in his letter, Percy provided an outline of what he considered to be the four possible kinds of antiquarian notes. The first kind covered the identity of the author as well as the antiquity of the songs or ballads, while the second was meant to explain the "History or Story referred to." The third kind, to which he devoted considerable attention, Percy envisioned as intended to "inform us in South-Britain, where the particular Scene or Place lies" that is mentioned in the poems. Fourth, Percy listed the miscellaneous kind, "either explanatory, or Digressive: particularly to illustrate any Allusions to the old Manners, Customs, Opinions, or Idioms of the ancient Scotch Nation."[2] Concentrating on the first two as well as the last of Percy's four categories, scholarship on eighteenth-century antiquarianism has always recognized the utility of notes for the authentication, explication, and contextualization of ancient texts. Yet it has understood this usefulness in exclusively interpretative terms, fixed on gathering the necessary information to support the reader in establishing the text's meaning.[3] Recent studies on eighteenth-century textual editing have maintained that the literary and historical scholarship employed in annotation serves a similar interpretative purpose.[4] One element consistently overlooked by this sort of hermeneutic reasoning, however, is the role annotation plays in actively constructing rather than merely supporting a specific narrative of antiquity.

This chapter will focus on the third annotative kind Percy itemized, the topographical note, and will argue that in antiquarian literature of this period the landscape is read as a charged and meaningfully inscribed surface that can be used, like a historical document, to make a locality legible and culturally significant. According to Percy's example in the letter, unknown or unspecified areas could be designated by association with a particular building or architectural site—in his case, the ancient Abbey of Melrose near the Tweed. Providing an examination of Thomas Percy's *The Hermit of Warkworth* (1771) and John Pinkerton's *The Bruce* (1790), this chapter will explore the ways in which the material culture of the past is mediated, through topographical annotation, to promote a cultural-patriotic vision of British antiquity. This chapter seeks to make sense of annotation as a tool for the creation of a topography of British landmarks that make up a repertoire of cultural artifacts. In doing so, this chapter will contribute to an understanding of eighteenth-century conceptualizations of the local, regional, and national in antiquarian annotation.[5]

Eighteenth-century antiquarianism has in recent scholarship remained, in Susan Manning's terms, the "shadow-history" of Britain, "created through antiquarian collections of artefacts, tales, songs, myths and legends of the nation."[6] Radically opposed to the synthetic, progressive narratives of eighteenth-century formal histories, antiquarianism manifested itself most conspicuously in annotation. It drew its discourse of peripheral nominalism literally in the margins of eighteenth-century historiography.[7] Yet, as Maureen McLane has observed, in antiquarian literature these "marginal spaces," in fact, became "central."[8] This interchange between the marginal and the central in turn energized further tensions, between the discursive and the medial, between geographical centers and fringes, between cultural particularism and cultural nationalism. Featuring not just in ballads and songs, these tensions, as Katie Trumpener has demonstrated, were also embodied in the new prose literatures of the late eighteenth century—including sentimental, historical, picaresque, and Gothic fiction.[9] Equally important, in many of these eighteenth-century texts, as in *The Hermit* and much of *The Bruce*, the action is situated around the border between England and Scotland. On the one hand, this was simply due to the rich history of violent conflict in the area, attested by the Percy-Douglas ballads and their intriguing system of border laws, feudal demesnes, and warring English and Scottish lords. Yet, on the other hand, neither side of the border area was considered a national region, nor was the border seen as a rigid divide between two nations; rather, it formed a contested space that challenged the very concept of what constitutes a nation.[10] In the topographical annotation of the poetry celebrating this region, these intensely fraught spaces were transformed into a repertoire of monuments of culture that could then underpin a spatially inflected heritage and sense of uniqueness. For it is precisely in the margins of antiquarian literature that the margins of "North" and "South-Britain," to use Percy's words, were being defined.

INSCRIBING NORTHUMBRIA
IN *THE HERMIT OF WARKWORTH*

On May 21, 1771, Thomas Percy's (1729–1811) efforts in antiquarian studies as chaplain to the Duke of Northumberland and his family culminated in the publication of *The Hermit of Warkworth: A Northumberland Ballad in Three Fits or Cantos.*[11]

A tale of love and loss, *The Hermit* deals with the story of young Henry Percy, the son of "Hotspur," second Earl of Northumberland, and Eleanor, daughter to Ralph Neville, first Earl of Westmoreland, as well as with the tragic romance of Sir Bertram and Isabel, the former ending in marriage, the latter ending in death and solitude. The title's generic tags and the wealth of paratextual material supporting the poem contrast starkly with its reception as a simplistic piece of verse. To a great extent, the anecdote of Samuel Johnson's extempore lampooning of its rhymes has eclipsed any noteworthy afterlife the poem may have enjoyed.[12] Although it was positively reviewed by the *Critical Review* and the *Gentleman's Magazine* as a pure and unaffected ballad in the old style, the *Monthly Review*, generally negative, suggested Percy remove "fits" from the title, as it was found an improper word in a modern poem.[13] For Percy, however, the generic term *fit* carried significant weight as an indicator of his ambition to furnish a properly historicized ballad. As the headnote to *The Hermit* reveals, "FIT was the word used by the old Minstrels to signify a PART or DIVISION of their Historical Songs." Readers who could check up on the note's cross-reference to the *Reliques of Ancient English Poetry* would discover that *fit* was an indicator both of the performative setting historically accompanying ancient ballad-singing and of the groatsworth, or individual monetary value, of the ballad's various subdivisions.[14] It is evident from this deliberate partitioning into fits that Percy's claims to minstrelsy were matched by his claims to historicity. Yet the usage of *fit* was not the only historicizing mechanism Percy introduced; his annotation proved ideologically as significant as any other paratext. Since the ballad introduced the names of many historical figures who are all in some way related to one another, some assistance in the form of documentary footnotes would no doubt have been desirable to many eighteenth-century readers. Nevertheless, only two aspects of the ballad were consistently annotated: the names of the Percy ancestry and the sites of the Northumberland region.

The indication in the title of a division into "three fits or cantos" actually obscures the existence of a fourth narrative layer, "The Hermit's Tale," which is embedded in the story of Henry and Eleanor. As soon as Henry and Eleanor, lost during a storm at Warkworth, are reunited by the hermit, they decide to get married at the Chapel of the Hermitage. On entering the chapel, "the wondering pair" (*Hermit*, 18) are so enchanted by the solemnity of the tomb and statues that they urge their companion to relate the history of the place. "The Hermit's Tale," like the chapel enshrined by the vault, is enclosed by the frame narrative of the two lovers but forms the actual core of Percy's ballad. At their request, the hermit unfolds the story of Sir Bertram, old Lord Percy's friend and companion-in-arms, and his fair maid Isabel, who dwelt at Widdrington Castle "about five miles south of Warkworth," as a footnote indicates. In an attempt to persuade the maid to consent to marry Bertram, Lord Percy organizes a feast at "Alnwick's princely hall" during which "the great atchievements" (*Hermit*, 20) of the Percy race are sung by minstrels.

In this part of the ballad, Percy's self-fashioning as Northumbrian minstrel is most noticeable. Unlike any other passage in the ballad, the minstrels' song is accompanied by three long and detailed footnotes that trace the Percy name back to the

Norman conquest of England and then to the barons who oversaw the ratification of the Magna Carta. The song sits oddly with the overarching tale of the hermit, and the notes only add to the digressive nature of this gloss on Percy's ancestry. Moreover, as the song is suddenly interrupted by the entrance of Isabel's servant, who introduces the quest Bertram has to complete before earning the right to marry, the genealogical overview seems an even more strained interruption of the romance of Sir Bertram and his maiden. Embedded within the various guises in which the speaker appears in the narrative framework (Poet/Hermit/Minstrel), the genealogy of the Percy name is a tribute not so much to the medieval protagonists of *The Hermit* as to Bishop Percy's patron, Hugh Percy, the first Duke of Northumberland.

On the face of it, the footnotes reflect the research Percy conducted at Alnwick Castle, when he was working on the Northumberland household book.[15] At the same time, however, he revived a form of ancient minstrelsy that allowed him to show that he, too, could offer a noble family's lineage in verse. Mimicking the register and imaginative powers of the ancient bards he used to edit and emend for the *Reliques*, Percy manifested the same "mimetic desire" Trumpener has identified in the poetry of Macpherson and Chatterton, who equally sought to identify themselves with Ossian and Rowley.[16] At another crucial moment in the ballad, the minstrelsy motif reemerges. When Bertram sets out to look for the abducted Isabel, he dresses up as a minstrel in order to gain access to the castle where she is held captive. His brother, who had accompanied Bertram in his quest, eventually rescues her, himself dressed "in highland garb" (*Hermit*, 37). In stressing these sartorial transformations, Percy imitated the story of King Alfred's disguised intrusion into the Danish camp, which had featured in the "Essay on the Ancient Minstrels in England" in the second edition of his *Reliques* (1767). At the climax of a confusion ending first in fratricide and then in the accidental slaying of Isabel, the tale unveils the true identity of the hapless Bertram as none other than the hermit himself, who after this calamity withdrew into solitary existence. A double move by Percy to insert the conventional ballad motif of cross-dressing while also announcing the fatal denouement of the ballad, the disclosure of the hermit's identity makes him at once hero and minstrel, at once sung about and singing. Percy, in his capacity as Warkworth balladeer, identifies with the hermit, both as mediator between past and present and as chronicler of the Northumberland family, himself singing in fits for the Alnwick nobility and secretly coveting affiliation as their namesake.[17]

A second element of major importance in *The Hermit* is related to the references to Northumberland indicated in the title and reinforced by the footnotes in the poem. Percy's intention was to celebrate the Percy name and its history as a Northumberland family by attaching it to the architectural remains of the area, most notably the Warkworth hermitage. In this respect, Percy's ballad serves as a reiteration of his dedication of the *Reliques* to the Duchess of Northumberland and his sanctioning of her family's rightful claim to their property. In dedicating his publication to the countess, Percy had the order of the poems reversed, which placed "Chevy-Chase," formerly in the third volume, together with "The Battle of Otterbourn" at the head of the first volume.[18] These two poems deal explicitly with the Percy branch and their struggles against the Scottish Douglases. The final pieces of the first book—"Edom O'Gordon" and the "Elegy on Henry Fourth Earl of Northumberland" (written by John Skelton, who was patronized by Henry Algernon Percy)—were two poems whose topography of border locales is as important as their position in the volume. By analogy, Percy placed another three such pieces in the third book, making sure that the first volume as a whole was characterized by Northumbriana while negotiating the relationship between the Percy name and the Northumberland region.[19] Similarly, once he had taken up his position as chaplain in 1765, Percy produced *A Letter Describing the Ride to Hulne Abbey from Alnwick in Northumberland*, an epistle that betrays his particular attraction to Hulne Park, which was later routinely circulated among visitors as a local guidebook.[20] Gradually, however, his fascination with the Hulne area waned. By the beginning of the next decade, he had turned his attention completely to the Warkworth estate.

From the paratextual supplements to *The Hermit* such as the advertisement and the endnotes, it is as if Percy merely wanted to interrogate and correct several misconceptions about the Warkworth locus. In the advertisement, he gave a descriptive account of the castle and hermitage, declaring, "What slight traditions are scattered through the country concerning the origin and foundation of this Hermitage, Tomb, &c. are delivered to the Reader in the following rhimes." From the discrepancies between what the place was commonly thought to be and what the architecture and sculptures reveal, Percy asserted that the extant "appearances . . . strongly confirm the account given in the following poem, and plainly prove that the HERMIT of WARKWORTH was not the same person that founded BRINKBURN Priory in the twelfth century, but rather one of the BERTRAM family, who lived at a later period." The physical, petrous evidence here functions in the same affirmative way as the extract from a Northumberland chronicle Percy introduced in the endnote, yet he applied this method to his ballad as well.

Like the Anglo-Scottish border ballads Percy included in his *Reliques*, *The Hermit* is a poem of travel and violence as much as one of love, and the Northumbrian localities featuring in the ballad are accentuated by a number of footnotes. At his father's death, young Henry Percy was sent abroad to be brought up by the Regent of Scotland, Robert Stuart, Duke of Albany. On his return, he wanted to see the lands and castle that were his by hereditary right. He arrived, in the guise of a forester, at "noble NEVILLE's house" (*Hermit*, 9), or, as the footnote specifies, at Raby Castle, the residence of the Earl of Westmoreland in the bishopric of Durham, where he also met the earl's daughter, Eleanor. Despite the animosity between their families, the two fall in love and flee to Scotland, but conveniently end up at Warkworth. Their marriage is performed by a friar from "COQUET Isle," a little island near Warkworth where, the note explains, "are still seen the ruins of a Cell, which belonged to the Benedictine monks of Tinemouth-Abbey" (*Hermit*, 15). Similarly, "The Hermit's Tale" is one of border harassment, abduction, and pursuit, clearly in line with the Percy-Douglas ballads featuring in the *Reliques*.[21] In an attempt to earn the helmet and, subsequently, Isabel's love, Bertram and his companions ride out to meet a band of Scottish raiders who were pillaging the land. In the battle that ensues, Bertram is severely wounded but rescued by Lord Percy and carried to Warkworth Castle to recover. At the end of the second fit, Percy supplies an endnote—marked as in his *Reliques* by three asterisks—which identifies Warkworth Castle as "a fortress belonging to the English, and of great note in ancient times, [which] stood on the southern bank of the river Tweed, a little to the east of Tiviotdale, and not far from Kelso. It is now intirely destroyed" (*Hermit*, 28). The closing remark is essential. For a place like this to be remembered, it has to be recovered through the antiquary's notes. Percy's ballad recuperates the vestigial castle as a symbol of medieval conflict while his annotated page invokes it as a material remnant. The ruin is appropriated as a token of ancient culture and national identity, though its symbolism is less important than the locality in which it is found. If the ruin is "the material remnant of cultural memory,"[22] then the footnote identifying and historicizing that ruin has an identical function: it performs an act of collective memory in the guise of more conventional—that is, explanatory—historical inquiry. Consequently, Percy's body of notes is not a tool for interpretation but a mnemonic device that mediates the cultural landscape of the Northumbrian past.

Much of the ballad's imagery is focused on inscription, carving, and engraving as acts of rehabilitating the foundational narrative of the second Lord Percy in a Northumberland locale. A growing antiquarian interest in non-linguistic, material culture in this period resulted in an expanded use of the metaphorics of inscription—on manuscripts, ancient artifacts, and, by extension, the landscape.[23] Comparable to the lack of any remaining trace of Warkworth Castle, the hermit's cell "is now in ruins," as the endnote at the conclusion of the first fit reveals. The chapel of the hermitage, on the other hand, "cut in the solid rock, is still very intire and perfect" (*Hermit*, 12). In fact, most of the references in *The Hermit* pertain to the inscribing and carving out of stone. "Deep-hewn within a craggy cliff" the hermitage lies, its "shapely steps, / All cut with nicest skill" (*Hermit*, 16). As the hermit relates at the end of his story, he was granted the hermitage with the approval of his friend Lord Percy, and at the very spot where the lovers are united in matrimony, he "carv'd her [Isabel's] beauteous form, / And scoop'd this holy cave" (*Hermit*, 44). In contrast to the dismemberment topos of many eighteenth-century ballads, Warkworth's confined locality is a hallowed ground where the hermit unites the two lovers and where Percy underlines the authenticating powers of the landscape.[24] The tomb and effigies of Isabel and the angel, mentioned in the preface, appear as cut "All in the living stone," a testament of which is provided by a footnote informing the reader that they may still be admired today. Among these figures crafted in "goodly sculpture" is also an escutcheon and "a sacred Text" to be found, carved above the doors of the chapel, which "Invites to godly fear" (*Hermit*, 17). In the postscript Percy added, this inscription is spelled out: "It will perhaps gratify the curious Reader to be informed, that from a word or two formerly legible over one of the Chapel Doors, it is believed that the Text there inscribed was the Latin verse of the Psalmist, which is in our Translation, My Tears

HAVE BEEN MY MEAT DAY AND NIGHT" (*Hermit*, 48). Hardly surviving in legible state, the inscription operates like the vestige of Warkworth Castle, made legible through the antiquary's careful emendation. All of the imagery and rhetorical commonplaces in the ballad contribute to the composite notion of inscription Percy introduces, a notion that considers the editorial apparatus of preface, postscript, and annotation as equal to the memorializing function of statues and monuments.[25]

THE LANDSCAPE AS
HISTORICAL AND CULTURAL-PATRIOTIC RECORD

By shifting scholarly attention to a physical rather than oral medium of transmission, a manuscript, epigraph, or printed ballad collection, Percy also argued for a literary-antiquarian recovery of the landscape as a matrix for cultural patriotism. As scholars such as Nick Groom and Robert Rix have recently demonstrated, Percy emphasized a scribal, bibliographic culture in his work, a mediality he read consistently "in terms of national myths—of the spatialization of culture."[26] Almost all of the notes in *The Hermit* refer to the spatial dimensions of Northern England and summon the landscape textually as a testimonial of the authenticity of Percy's account. Especially in the aftermath of the Ossian controversy and the critical response to his own collection of ancient ballads, Percy modulated the way in which he handled his source material at the level of mediation and discourse. Whereas eighteenth-century ballad collections such as the *Reliques* were characterized by an elaborate editorial apparatus, that apparatus was focused predominantly on the protocols of citing manuscript variants, circuits of transmission, and networks of correspondents who had somehow contributed to the collection.[27] But Percy's *The Hermit of Warkworth*, an eighteenth-century pastiche of the type of ancient ballad usually featuring in such collections, does not derive its authenticity from fellow ballad collectors or their transcriptions of oral poetry. Rather, its legitimacy is extracted from the monumental landmarks it invokes and revisits, a process Trumpener describes in terms of a slippage from bardic landscape to antiquarian text, which witnesses authors retransmitting past traces back onto the landscape from whence they were originally drawn.[28] This reciprocal movement unearths the fragments of an environment particularly fraught with meaning and relays them back through annotation as synecdoches of the historical and cultural moment that produced them. The medial appropriation of the sculptured effigies in the chapel of Percy's *Hermit* represents the way in which a surface or locality could be revived through the annotation of a poetic composition, enlivening the figures on the tomb as well as those populating the footnotes.

Buttressing their objects of inquiry with the material remnants of the past provided antiquarians like Percy with an opportunity to counter any suspicions about the authenticity of their sources. Unlike the obscure folio manuscript Percy snatched from the fire, the topographical heritage of Britain could not so easily be dismissed by hotheaded critics like Joseph Ritson, who had gone out of his way to expose Percy as an imposter.[29] Instead, antiquarianism presents itself as grounded in a locality that functions as a historical record that can be verified by visiting the sites themselves. Not only Percy's advertisement and postscript to *The Hermit* but the majority of his notes inform the reader that certain ruins "are still seen" in the area, underpinning his prefatory claims that the poem is no mere fiction.

The addition to the 1782 edition of *The Hermit* of an excerpt from Francis Grose's report on a tour he took around the area reinforces this idea of invoking place through paratext. Presented as an extract from a letter, the endnote shows Grose visiting the Warkworth hermitage while using the Percy ballad as a kind of poetic guidebook. Grose, from whose six-volume *Antiquities of England and Wales* (1773–1787) the postscript was taken, was attuned to the popular tales of myth and magic attached to the different localities of Britain. In what he depicts as a "most romantic ride" from Warkworth Castle down to the hermitage, he notes the fine condition of the estate, with special attention to its "apartments, all of them hollowed in the solid Rock, and hanging over the river in the most picturesque manner imaginable, with a covering of ancient hoary Trees, Reliques of the venerable Woods, in which this fine solitude was anciently embowered."[30] Although Grose's positive comments on *The Hermit* were surely valued in their own right, there is another reason why Percy included them at the end of his ballad. In appropriating Grose's report of the area in his endnotes, Percy adopted a discourse that was not only authenticating or explanatory but resolutely dialogical as well. Grose's emphasis on the antiquity of the trees as "Reliques" of a venerable past is mustered by Percy as a retort to Thomas Pennant's unfavorable account of the Alnwick estate in his 1771 *Tour in Scotland*: "At *Alnwick*, a small town, the traveller is disappointed with the situation and environs of the castle, the residence of the *Percies*, the antient Earls of *Northumberland*. You look in vain for any marks of the grandeur of the feudal age."[31] Even more offensive to Percy was Johnson's take on these comments, famously reiterating Pennant's calling the gardens at Alnwick *trim*, when Percy insisted the duke had planted many trees there in order to promote the unsophisticated appearance of the place.[32] With *The Hermit*'s endorsing an artless primitivism and its paratextual matter reaffirming the relevance of Warkworth, Percy proposed an alternative Northumberland site to admire, one adorned with "ancient hoary Trees, Reliques of the venerable Woods," true picturesque icons of the past.

Alternating between the poetic text, the note referring to a picturesque description, and the exterior landscape ultimately happened via a set of mental, typographical, and material cues that guided the reader.[33] Reading this intermedial, three-way relationship evidently required a degree of cultural literacy that could conjoin various discursive, empiricist, and experiential modes. After minute descriptions of all the vaults and niches in the hermitage, Grose's note continues: "In this delightful solitude, so beautiful in itself, and so venerable for its antiquity, you will judge with what pleasure I perused the very amusing and interesting Tale of the Hermit of Warkworth: having the whole Scene before me, and fancying I was present at the Hermit's tender relation."[34] This, then, was the founding premise of antiquarian poetry: to turn the affective, historically inscribed landscape into a kind of collective property and to invite the reader to experience and interiorize the localities made public through the notes by acts of socialization.

SCOTLAND, CANONIZATION, AND TOPOGRAPHY IN THE WORK OF JOHN PINKERTON

In constructing a landscape made up of British cultural artifacts such as castles and chapels, antiquarian annotation absorbed the institutional bodies of the late eighteenth century—including geographical surveys, military surveillance operations, and archaeological sketches—and adopted their processes of topography and toponymy.[35] The creation of that landscape on the basis of sites and objects of historical and cultural value inevitably entailed matters of transmission. For how could a region's geographical legacy be made tangible, experienced, or exchanged? How was the antiquary to be instrumental in facilitating the mediation of a cultural-nationalist inheritance through print? How could annotated poetry be used as a mechanism for the transcription and transmission of cultural memory? By virtue of their multifaceted and multimedial nature, moreover, antiquarian publications were products of complex negotiations between several agents in the publishing industry, who collaborated to accommodate the editions with packaging devices, including complex apparatuses of notes as well as maps, tables, and illustrations.[36] In a manner altogether different from manuscripts held in libraries, which, in their highly privatized and jealously guarded setting of possession and permission, could never be considered a form of property held collectively by the public or the nation, the landscape of Britain could be made legible through the medium of print. Even though both were considered elite territory, the differences in accessibility and dispersion were certainly not negligible.

While incorporating the protocols of empirical inquiry, antiquarian annotation was at the same time the product of institutions, like the literary and antiquarian societies of London and Edinburgh, that continued to embed their scientific findings in a rhetoric of cultural nationalism.[37] In Scotland, the professionalization and formalization of antiquarianism in the 1780s and 1790s was epitomized by the chartering of the societies of Edinburgh and Perth.[38] Among the founding figures of these societies was David Steuart Erskine, eleventh Earl of Buchan (1742–1829), who was particularly successful as a catalyst in commissioning a program of Scotch cultural patriotism.[39] He proposed to register a complete, statistical survey of Scotland and labored continuously to preserve and chart Scotland's own unique relics. Because a specifically Scottish canon did not exist, however, Scots went looking for their own monuments. Not only comprising the manuscripts of the *makars* tucked away in their libraries, these monuments were also to be found in the Scottish landscape with its many castles, churches, and statues. In the late 1770s and 1780s, as Sandro Jung has recently indicated, print-cultural developments in Scotland in particular were increasingly seen as fundamental in the construction of a Scottish identity. "Scottish book illustrations and topographical prints were increasingly conceived of as media through which Scottish literary texts, authors, landscapes, and monuments could be celebrated."[40] This cultural vision of Scottishness rested on the belief that geographical thinking was an important epistemological prerequisite. Topographical annotation, correspondingly, enacted this idea in antiquarian literature.

A few suggestions toward assembling a Scottish literary canon had already been made by English literati such as Percy and Thomas Warton, but they were far from systematic or comprehensive. Percy had been working for some time on the Maitland Folio MS, held at the Pepysian Library in Cambridge, when he discovered the Bannatyne MS in the Advocate's Library in Edinburgh in 1772. "I wish we had correct and neat editions of all the best old Scottish Poets," he wrote to Paton in October 1772, "but it is an undertaking that requires some little consideration. I should be glad to concur towards it in any shape."[41] Almost as gingerly as Percy, Warton concluded at the end of his section on Scots poetry in *The History of English Poetry* (1774) "that a well-executed history of the Scotch poetry from the thirteenth century, would be a valuable accession to the general history of Britain." Yet in spite of "much curious and instructive information" both ample and readily accessible, the subject "has never yet been uniformly examined in its full extent."[42] Whatever the shape of the prospective editions of Scottish poets Percy and Warton would "concur towards," it would take a Scotsman to accomplish that task. John Pinkerton (1758–1826), who was born and educated in Edinburgh but moved to London after his father's death, would spend at least two decades studying and publishing on ancient Scottish history and literature, not impeded like Percy and Warton by the obligations of a clerical or academic profession.[43] Recognizing some of his own vigor in Pinkerton's scholarly pursuits,[44] Percy informed Pinkerton of the Maitland MS, provided him with copies of poems and notes, and introduced him to prominent figures in the field such as Warton, who took pleasure from Pinkerton's 1783 *Select Scottish Ballads*, "both Text and Notes."[45] Soon, Pinkerton was focusing on creating a full-scale translation of Scottish manuscript pieces into print, bridging the London and Edinburgh book markets, and launching one of the first sustained attempts at constructing a Scottish literary canon.

Within a few years, Pinkerton's archival activities intensified as his attention fell on other, more uniquely Scottish literary treasures, including but not restricted to the Bannatyne manuscript. The fruit of Pinkerton's labor, most notably his persistence in obtaining permission to make transcripts from the Maitland Folio and Quarto manuscripts, was published on December 15, 1786, as *Ancient Scotish Poems, Never before in Print*. The elaborate title page advertised the edition as espousing the qualities of novelty and authority, and it presented an abundance of unprecedented archival material for the first time in print.[46] The first 150 pages of the 328-page first volume are taken up by paratextual material, including a preface, an essay "on the origin of Scotish poetry," and a list of "all the Scotish poets; with brief remarks," and at the end, there is one page of "Fac-similes *of the Folio MS.*" Almost half of the second volume consists of endnotes, an appendix, a glossary, and another table of contents, as well as a section on passages and words "*not understood*" and some additions and corrections. As Pinkerton's biographer Patrick O'Flaherty has observed, *Ancient Scotish Poems* "was not so much a history of Middle Scots literature as a call to action, combining inquiry into the lives of the poets, discussion of the texts in print, brief assessments of each writer's work, and a plan for 'new editions' of the seven poets, 'in which labour much remains to be done.'"[47] To some extent, this overload of scholarly accoutrements obscured the fact that the edition contained Scots pieces of genuine poetic merit and is one reason why it did not attract a large readership. But what the paratextual information reveals instead is Pinkerton's conception of the publication of the Maitland MS as a thoroughly Scottish nationalist undertaking. His plans for editions of the greatest Scottish poets, already outlined in a letter to Percy of November 19, 1785, all dealt with the charting of Scottish history and literature, and would continue to occupy him for at least another seven years.

Concluding the second volume of *Ancient Scotish Poems* were proposals for the publication by subscription of *Vitae Antiquae Sanctorum* (published in 1789), an edition of the lives of the Scottish saints that was as much a map of Scotland's ecclesiastical topography. "A Life of a Saint may be regarded as a religious novel," Pinkerton had written earlier in 1789 in his *Enquiry into the History of Scotland*, "in which, tho the miracles be fiction, the geography and history are always real."[48] Earlier, Pinkerton had asked Paton and Buchan for "a small map, or bird's-eye view, of the whole island of Icolmkill," better known in its Gaelic form as Iona, which ultimately featured as an engraving on the title page of *Vitae* in 1789.[49] The subscription venture was a disaster. While John Nichols printed the work and oversaw the subscription details in London, Pinkerton's liaisons in Scotland were William Creech in Edinburgh and, as the prospectus stated, "one capital bookseller in *Glasgow, Perth*, and *Aberdeen*."[50] According to Pinkerton, the chief cause for the *Vitae*'s failure lay with Creech's unreliability and his having "lost" the list of Scottish subscribers.[51] Although, as Richard Sher has shown, he was certainly not alone in his low esteem of Creech, it is likely that Pinkerton had slighted too many influential Scottish patrons in order to reach the intended 100 subscribers.[52] It is also possible that his misconception or deliberate misrepresentation of the Picts as Goths, as in his equally unsuccessful *Enquiry*, had been too controversial for a wide readership to stomach.[53]

THE BRUCE: ANNOTATED HISTORY IN VERSE

In the eventful year 1789, Pinkerton was focused on getting another work into print, in addition to his *Enquiry* and *Vitae*: an edition of John Barbour's fourteenth-century epic romance, *The Bruce*.[54] Pinkerton had started inquiring about extant manuscripts as early as 1785.[55] On March 16, 1789, he wrote to the Earl of Buchan to inform him that "Barbour is in the press,—one volume printed: two others remain; and it will not be out till next winter. It is finely printed by Hughes, and to be ornamented with plates."[56] He had been occupied with Barbour, he said, "as a relaxation from historical pursuits," but he had actually been commissioned by the publishing firm of the Morisons of Perth to produce an annotated edition of *The Bruce* for their "Select Scotish Poets" series.[57] On July 30, 1787, in a letter to Buchan, Pinkerton had expressed his gladness in hearing that Barbour was about to be published in the Morison series—alongside *The Works of James I, King of Scotland* (1786) and *Select Works of Gawin Douglass* (1787)—and ensured he would "with pleasure give a Preface, Life of the Author, Notes and Glossary, as I promised, to Messrs. Morison."[58] However, *The Bruce* was eventually published, not by the Morisons, but by George Nichol.

On numerous occasions, Pinkerton expressed his desire to assist his readers with lucid editing and a supportive apparatus. He shared the Morisons' view on catering to the improvement of "the cultural literacy of Scotland, specifically [knowledge of] the topography of the country."[59] Writing to Buchan in July 1787 about the proposed Morison edition of *The Bruce*, he added instructions regarding spelling and punctuation. Although the manuscript was to be published *literatim*, as he called it, Pinkerton realized that retaining certain odd, archaic spellings "would spoil the sale of the book," so they had to be adjusted. Furthermore, *The Bruce* was to be divided into twenty books, each containing a prefatory argument "which will very much relieve and assist the reader."[60] As Jeremy Smith has observed, the Scots "Buke" for "Book" in the heading "shows an attempt by Pinkerton to offer readers an authentic experience."[61] Pinkerton's attempts to reproduce "Scotishness," Smith points out, were "designed to flag the antique setting of the work in ways which would appeal to a contemporary reader," and comprised linguistic features, the reproduction of Robert's coin on page 3, as well as "the romantic and/or 'sentimental' depiction on the title-page not of a battle but of the tearful leave-taking of Bruce and his queen when she and her ladies were sent for safety to Kildrummy Castle."[62] Of the four pillars of antiquarian editing discussed in the letter to Buchan—preface, life, notes, and glossary—the notes were given precedence, at least in terms of printing order. "The printer must begin with the poetry and notes," Pinkerton instructed. "The Preface, Life, and Glossary, I shall prepare, but must have the whole work printed off and sent me before I send them; that I may refer to pages, &c." Comparing his method to Thomas Tyrwhitt's in his 1775 edition of Chaucer, Pinkerton understood the notes at the bottom of the page not, like David Hume saw endnotes, as a distraction, but as intended to "relieve the reader in so long and uniform a poem."[63] Rather than being simply inferior to the main text because of its subordinate position at the bottom of the page, the antiquarian footnote functioned, according to Pinkerton, as a cog in a larger chain of paratextual paraphernalia. He understood that it would determine the way in which his readers would be exposed to this exemplar of literary antiquity.

Revealing his understanding of bibliographical uniformity as commercially attractive, the four editorial components Pinkerton mentioned to Buchan were all retained in his edition of *The Bruce*. As he had already provided a biography of Barbour in his *Ancient Scotish Poems*, he integrated a shortened version of it in the preface to *The Bruce*. The emphasis of this preface is squarely on the convergence of poetry and history in the early literature of "most nations" (*Bruce*, 1:v), and on the figure of the poet as historian and chronicler. Barbour is "an excellent Naevius" who merits comparison with Dante, Chaucer, or "any other early poet of the present nations in Europe" (*Bruce*, 1:xvii, x). The most significant message the preface conveys, however, revolves around the value of *The Bruce* as a historical romance—part real, part fiction. Pinkerton had already divulged in his *Ancient Scotish Poems* that "this Romance is just such a one as the Iliad; that is, a Poem founded on real facts, but embellished in many parts with fiction."[64] When the word *Romanys* appears in *The Bruce* for the first time, Pinkerton annotates it with an exposition of the origin of the term (as "a narration of facts in *romance*, or the *vulgar tongue*") and contemporary misuse of it. "Barbour begins, ver. 8, &c. with telling us, that his narration is *suthfast*, or true: and the reader needs only peruse *Dalrymple's Annals*, to see the veracity of most, if not all of it" (*Bruce*, 1:21). In this footnote, Pinkerton establishes the poem's credentials as an accurate historical account by virtue of its being a romance in his understanding of the genre. Since Lord Hailes turned to *The Bruce* as "a constant authority" for his rigorous *Annals of Scotland* (1776–1779), it is not surprising, according to Pinkerton, that the facts take up the best part of the work. Assessment by invocation of Lord Hailes's authority confirms Pinkerton's earlier statement that "this venerable writer is, in fact, not only the first existent poet, but the first existent historian of Scotland."[65] As in the example Pinkerton gave in the preface to *The Bruce* of a 1775 Spanish collection of poems by Tomás Antonio Sánchez, the prefatory letter of which was supplemented "with long notes by the editor, forming almost a history of Spanish poetry preceding the year 1400" (*Bruce*, vi), annotated poetry can function as historiography in both text and notes.

This peculiar conjunction of fact with fiction is what distinguishes *The Bruce* from that other Scottish classic, Blind Hary's *Wallace*. Comparison with *Wallace* spills over into the notes, many of which are modally as subversive as they are supportive. Early on in "Buke I," for instance, the introduction of James Douglas is glossed by a note on William Douglas, James's father, who was the first to join Wallace, but whose failure at Falkirk terminated their campaign against the English. As a consequence, the footnote reads, Wallace's progress was over "in a twelve-month, or so; and Henry's poem on him is but the history of two years, while this of Barbour embraces twenty-four" (*Bruce*, 1:15). The footnote thus performs a dual function as it is both a historical digression on the Douglas family and a clever marketing strategy that settles comparison between the two texts strongly in favor of *The Bruce*. In another footnote, appearing in "Buke VIII" when James Douglas and his men approach Lanark, Pinkerton appropriates the material remnants of the Scottish medieval landscape and transforms them into the equivalent of a historical source. At the appearance of Lanark castle, of which now no ruin remains, "its scite [*sic*] being now a bowling-green and garden," Pinkerton explains that this was the place where Wallace's wife was murdered, "which seems the first cause which incited him to arms." Generally, as Pinkerton stresses continuously, "Henry the minstrel is no authority, his work being an absurd romance; tho' in this instance he accords with history, and with tradition, a large cave in Cartland Craigs near Lanark, where Henry says that Wallace lurked, being called Wallace's Cave to this day. It is remarkable that Sir D. Dalrymple should have omitted this important circumstance" (*Bruce*, 2:20). In contrast to a privileged aristocrat like Dalrymple, Pinkerton recognized that annotation, in addition to performing multiple acts of authentication, explanation, and historicization, could negotiate medially diverse sources that were collectively accessible. For him, topography, like etymology and the history of place names, was what joined the history and poetry of a nation—and he was not the only one to think so.[66] When the Earl of Buchan decided to have the 1488 manuscript of "Henry the minstrel's *Metrical History of Wallace*" transcribed for inclusion in "Select Scotish Poets," the Morisons promptly "engaged some of the gentlemen of the Literary Society there to accompany the proposed edition with historical and topographical notes."[67]

INSCRIPTION, ETYMOLOGY, AND TOPOGRAPHY IN *THE BRUCE*

Increasingly in the eighteenth century, antiquarians recognized the value of etymology and place names as significant historical records.[68] Like Wallace's Cave, the diverse loci of the British landscape were inscribed with textual or linguistic signs as traces of their historical provenance. In the case of Scottish place names, the question of their Gothic or Celtic origin remained a bone of contention for many antiquarians. Categorically rejecting the possibility of any Irish or, more broadly, Celtic traces in the etymology of Scotland's localities, Pinkerton used the annotative medium in his most outspokenly racist work, his *Dissertation on the Origin and Progress of the Scythians or Goths* (1787), to substantiate that claim. Yet examples of this technique are manifold in *The Bruce* as well. At Robert's arrival in Dumfries in book 2, prior to the moment when he murders John Comyn in front of the altar of the Greyfriars, Pinkerton intervenes to rectify a common but mistaken assumption. "Edinburgh is erroneously thought the *Castrum Puellarum*, as it was thought the *Castra Alata*, tho' the later be Inverness" and Dumfries the "celebrated *Castrum Puellarum*" instead. "Nothing can be more risible than to see Irish etymologists tell us, that *Dun Edin*, the Irish name of Edinburgh, implies *Castra Alata*" (*Bruce*, 1:34). Further on, when glossing Aberdeen, Pinkerton notes that "Scotish names in *Aber* are ridiculously supposed Welch; but they abound in Germany" (*Bruce*, 1:56). His professed expertise in Gothic etymology and toponymy forms a stark contrast with his disdain for Irish topography. When Robert's younger brother Edward, Earl of Carrick, journeys to Ireland in book 14, Pinkerton conveniently admits that he is "not sufficiently versed in Irish topography to trace accurately Edward's progress in Ireland" (*Bruce*, 2:178), a shortcoming he can pass over lightly, as "[o]ur poet's geography of Ireland is very imperfect" as well (*Bruce*, 3:40). Regardless of his biased and, at times, racist predisposition, Pinkerton made the study of the landscape and its names a resolutely cultural practice, defining a localized identity and verifying the authenticity of his source by submitting it to spatial scrutiny.[69] Notions of inscription abound in *The Bruce*, whether in the form of an interiorization of Scottish architectural monuments into the notes or of a projection of poetic mythmaking onto various nodes in the landscape. When no trace but the "bowling-green and garden" remains, antiquarian literature presents itself as a reconstruction and contextualizes itself, through annotation, as a product of examination and recovery. At the beginning of the second book, when Douglas meets up with the Bruce for his coronation at Scone Palace (Scone, Pinkerton notes, is a typically Gothic name, occurring frequently in Scandinavia, too), the footnote, in fact, devotes far less attention to Scone Palace than to the neighboring Forteviot, the "chief palace of our Pikish [i.e., Pictish] monarchs" (*Bruce*, 1:39).[70] Though preceding Scone in antiquity and venerability, the Forteviot site is nonetheless unexplored. "It is a pity that the fate and remains of the palace of Forteviot are not investigated," Pinkerton exclaims in the note. "Perhaps curious antiquities may be found buried there. A work on the history and antiquities of Perthshire would be very acceptable" (*Bruce*, 1:39). In Pinkerton's view, and like Percy's in *The Hermit*, antiquarian literature counters this erasure by re-inscribing the landscape meaningfully and retransmitting it via the notes' recuperative and discursive functions.

In this respect, the note is like the fragment in the sense established by Elizabeth Harries and Jung, suggesting a "framework of authenticity" to which it belongs and forming a synecdoche from which the reader has to derive a more unifying whole.[71] In Groom's words, "the antique object becomes merely a signifier of the past. It has no functional value, even when it purports to: it is exclusively mythological" and, it should be added, metonymical, as it only acquires meaning in relation to the whole and in comparison with other objects.[72] Connecting the castles inscribed textually by the notes to *The Bruce*, the reader establishes a trajectory that not merely follows Bruce's medieval odyssey but draws up a literary map based on Scotland's most emblematic landmarks. As Evan Gottlieb and Juliet Shields have remarked, such delineation "usually acknowledges that the area in question is always implicitly subordinated to a larger geopolitical entity, and must be understood synecdochally as part of a whole."[73] Annotative assembly of such iconic Scottish places as the cities of Dumfries (*Bruce*, 1:34), Edinburgh (1:34; 2:85), Perth (1:39), and Aberdeen (1:56), as well as the castles of Kildrummy (1:77), Turnberry (1:131), Bothwell (2:3), and Stirling (2:104) designates linguistically and demarcates locally those areas that stand in for the nation, and so creates a Scottish nation out of its own material-cultural heritage.

One way of turning the "rust and ruins, and worn-out dates, and half-obliterated inscriptions" of this heritage into consumer items appealing to a wide readership was by invoking other media that described the picturesque qualities of Scotland's landscape.[74] Such publications as Pennant's *Tour in Scotland*, Charles Cordiner's *Antiquities & Scenery of the North of Scotland* (1780), and Adam de Cardonnel's *Picturesque Antiquities of Scotland* (1788) enjoyed great popularity because of their illustrations. These ranged from head- and tail-pieces to large vignettes and full-page plates. On occasion, Pinkerton inserted allusions to these works in his notes, inviting his readers to "see a description" of a site or building in Barbour's poem. At the end of book 3, for example, when the island of "*Rauchryne*" [i.e., Rathlin] appears at line 680, a footnote promptly recommends the reader to "[s]ee a description of this iland [*sic*], and Bruce's castle, in Hamilton's Observations on the North of Ireland" (*Bruce*, 1:90). More often than not an illustration existed in print, as in the case of "Dunstafnage on the western shore of Lorn, a strong castle, and the residence of the chief. See a description and view of it in Mr. Pennant's Tour" (*Bruce*, 2:63). In tandem with illustrations of the kind also provided by Francis Grose, annotation thus offered the possibility of textualizing a canon of antiquities visualized elsewhere.

The reason why antiquarians would invest such energy in establishing links with illustrated literature is that they understood themselves as constructing as much as illuminating and historicizing a landscape. Albeit unavoidably discursive to some extent, the medium of topographical annotation should rather be understood as a commodifying device akin to the topographical plate. Offering scaled-down versions of a physical environment, the notes provide consumers with bite-size building blocks from which to draw a map of cultural monuments that are somehow emblematic of a community or nation. Whether placed at the foot of the page or thrown to the back of a volume or even issued separately, the note becomes a commodity in itself, valued as such by purchasers and marketed conspicuously on the title pages of antiquarian publications.[75] Through the mediation of the printed note, the ancient edifice in its natural setting becomes acculturated as a commodified object. "The very act of localizing and particularizing place," as Penny Fielding has written in the context of river poetry, "renders it discursive, socialized, and produced."[76] Annotation thus turns the landscape into a culturally charged space and shapes reader response by turning mimetic representations of its most iconic aspects into commodities.

FROM MARGINAL TO CENTRAL

Couched in terms of a movement from outside to inside, margin to center, the antiquarian annotation of poetic texts often mirrored the eighteenth-century transition from the external, peripheral realm of the Celtic fringe to the realm of the museums and collections at the heart of the metropolitan centers of Great Britain. In search of the relics of the past, the eighteenth-century antiquarian went on a real and armchair pilgrimage through the countryside in order to extrapolate from it a new literary-cultural landscape. Both *The Hermit* and *The Bruce*, as well as their notes, embody this journey through the local and metropolitan geography of North Britain. Though Percy was associated with such "Anglican and Tory apologists" as Samuel Johnson and Thomas Warton, and shared the assumption that the nation-state finds its "sanctioned cultural expression in Scripture, law, history, and a canon of published great works by known authors," it is impossible to ignore his vesting cultural legitimacy in the regional and parochial dimensions of Northumberland.[77] In publishing *The Bruce*, Pinkerton reconfirmed the Scottish compulsion of, in Gerard Carruthers and Liam McIlvanney's terms, "'writing back' . . . to the centre" of civilizations, cultures, and literatures.[78] With his edition of *The Bruce*, Pinkerton "wrote" a momentous chapter in the history of Scotland's struggle for independence "back" to the center of Scottish culture. Not only did it bring a foundationally Scottish text back to the focus of attention, it was also a petition for granting the Older Scots language a central position in a newly conceived and uniquely Scottish identity.

Antiquarian annotation does not pretend to solve the hermeneutic difficulties raised by the discovery and mediation of historically distant material. Rather, antiquarian notes are synecdochal expressions of the collaborative networks of scholars, collectors, and correspondents, situating the iconic monuments of the past in miniature narratives, the rhetoric of which echoes the cultural patriotism of the respective families, institutions, and societies that endorsed such projects. Percy used the Warkworth site to translate a reality of distance and dislocation into a methodically historicized myth of love and local heritage. With *The Hermit*, he welded his scholarly interest in Northumberland with his loyalty to the duke and his family. For Pinkerton, a compound notion of topography and print was essential in authenticating and then mediating a patriotic vision of the Scottish nation as demarcated, both historically and geographically, and in facilitating the creation of a Scottish literary canon. "I must confess," he wrote in his *Scotish Poems Reprinted from Scarce Editions*, dedicated to the Earl of Buchan, "that the neglect of our antiquities was one great argument with me to enter that thorny field; and that it appears to me a kind of patriotism for a man to attempt to supply any branch of his native literature, which is particularly deficient."[79] Pinkerton acknowledged the importance of print culture in the formation of cultural and national identities, but in doing so he qualified the distinction between notes as signs of the production of literary texts on the one hand, and as signs of their consumption on the other. Annotation was therefore valued by producers and purchasers alike, as a commodity in the burgeoning markets for printed poetry, antiquarian scholarship, and the tourist trade. In addition to its more commonly accepted procedures of citation and authentication, the annotation of antiquarianism ultimately gained particular qualities, too, as a tool for spatially inflected thinking about regional and national identities.

NOTES

1. *The Percy Letters: The Correspondence of Thomas Percy and George Paton*, ed. A. F. Falconer (New Haven, CT: Yale University Press, 1961), 20.
2. Falconer, *Percy Letters*, 21.
3. The classic thesis is Arnaldo Momigliano, "Ancient History and the Antiquarian," *Journal of the Warburg and Courtauld Institutes* 13, nos. 3–4 (1950): 285–315, which emphasized the static distinction between collection and interpretation in antiquarian studies.

4. Marcus Walsh, "Literary Scholarship and the Life of Editing," in *Books and Their Readers in Eighteenth-Century England: New Essays*, ed. Isabel Rivers (London: Continuum, 2001), 191–215. Ian Small and Marcus Walsh distinguish between two approaches, one that believed in an objective, determinate edition and one that believed in the indeterminacy of the text and its meaning. Ian Small and Marcus Walsh, eds., *The Theory and Practice of Text-Editing: Essays in Honour of James T. Boulton* (Cambridge: Cambridge University Press, 1991), 10, 162.

5. This chapter has benefited greatly from Sandro Jung, "'A Scotch Poetical Library': James Thomson's *The Seasons*, the Morisons' 'Select Scottish Poets' Series and the Construction of a Scottish Poetic Canon," *Journal of the Edinburgh Bibliographical Society* 9 (2014): 9–41. I have adopted his argument that "a canon based on antiquity and value was seen to underpin specific claims to nationhood and national distinctness" (17) and have expanded it to include notions of topography. For a similar reading of canon building as a patriotic act, see Thomas F. Bonnell, *The Most Disreputable Trade: Publishing the Classics of English Poetry 1765–1810* (Oxford: Oxford University Press, 2008), 331–32.

6. Susan Manning, "Post-Union Scotland and the Scottish Idiom of Britishness," in *The Edinburgh History of Scottish Literature*, vol. 2, *Enlightenment, Britain and Empire (1707–1918)*, ed. Susan Manning, Murray Pittock, and Thomas Owen Clancy (Edinburgh: Edinburgh University Press, 2007), 48.

7. Susan Manning, "Antiquarianism, the Scottish Science of Man, and the Emergence of Modern Disciplinarity," in *Scotland and the Borders of Romanticism*, ed. Leith Davis et al. (Cambridge: Cambridge University Press, 2004), 66–67.

8. Maureen N. McLane, "Mediating Antiquarians in Britain, 1760–1830: The Invention of Oral Tradition; or, Close Reading before Coleridge," in *This Is Enlightenment*, ed. Clifford Siskin and William Warner (Chicago: University of Chicago Press, 2010), 248.

9. Katie Trumpener, *Bardic Nationalism: The Romantic Novel and the British Empire* (Princeton, NJ: Princeton University Press, 1997), 16, 107.

10. Penny Fielding, *Scotland and the Fictions of Geography: North Britain 1760–1830* (Cambridge: Cambridge University Press, 2008), chap. 3. See also Maureen N. McLane, *Balladeering, Minstrelsy, and the Making of British Romantic Poetry* (Cambridge: Cambridge University Press, 2008), 97–103. According to McLane, the border area instead "connotes more specifically a Scottish region" (98).

11. Printed for Thomas Davies and Samuel Leacroft in London. Subsequent references are cited parenthetically in the text as *Hermit*.

12. Bertram H. Davis, *Thomas Percy: A Scholar-Cleric in the Age of Johnson* (Philadelphia: University of Pennsylvania Press, 1989), 181–82, 208.

13. *Critical Review* 31 (May 1771): 390–95; *Gentleman's Magazine* 41 (August 1771): 363–66; *Monthly Review* 45 (August 1771): 103.

14. Thomas Percy, comp., *Reliques of Ancient English Poetry: Consisting of Old Heroic Ballads, Songs, and Other Pieces of Our Earlier Poets*, 2nd ed., 3 vols. (London: Printed for James Dodsley, 1767), 2:166–67, 397–98.

15. Davis, *Thomas Percy*, 178–79, 187, 216–17.

16. Trumpener, *Bardic Nationalism*, 119.

17. Davis, *Thomas Percy*, 217–19.

18. Nick Groom, *The Making of Percy's Reliques* (Oxford: Oxford University Press, 1999), 223.

19. Davis, *Thomas Percy*, 216–17; Groom, *The Making of Percy's Reliques*, 103.

20. Davis, *Thomas Percy*, 143.

21. The *Critical Review* went as far as calling *The Hermit* a "rival [to] the most celebrated model of the English ballad"—that is, "Chevy-Chase"—a comparison Percy would have taken as a high compliment (31:395).

22. Sandro Jung, *The Fragmentary Poetic: Eighteenth-Century Uses of an Experimental Mode* (Bethlehem, PA: Lehigh University Press, 2009), 124.

23. Fielding, *Scotland and the Fictions of Geography*, chap. 4.

24. Groom points to the tropes of mutilation and fragmentation frequently recurring in ballads and argues that this ruined condition is a prerequisite for them to be perceived as "reliques" (Groom, *The Making of Percy's* Reliques, 49–51).

25. For a similar argument, see Christine Baatz's study on the use of typography and design in the *Reliques*, "'A Strange Collection of Trash'? The Re-evaluation of Medieval Literature in Thomas Percy's *Reliques of Ancient English Poetry* (1765)," in *Anthologies of British Poetry: Critical Perspectives from Literary and Cultural Studies*, ed. Barbara Korte, Ralf Schneider, and Stefanie Lethbridge (Amsterdam: Rodopi, 2000), 105–24.

26. Groom, *The Making of Percy's* Reliques, 103. For a recent study arguing for Percy's scribal emphasis in response to Ossian, see Robert Rix, "Thomas Percy's Antiquarian Alternative to Ossian," *Journal of Folklore Research* 46, no. 2 (2009): 197–229.

27. McLane, "Mediating Antiquarians in Britain," 248. Elsewhere, McLane has argued persuasively that the ballad collection, which she perceives as a genre in its own right, used annotation as a means to verify as well as remember the multifarious elements in the collaborative balladeering venture (McLane, *Balladeering*, 44–82).

28. Trumpener, *Bardic Nationalism*, 105, 113.

29. Ritson did not believe Percy was indeed in possession of such a manuscript. For a sympathetic biography of Ritson, see Bertrand H. Bronson, *Joseph Ritson: Scholar-at-Arms*, 2 vols. (Berkeley: University of California Press, 1938).

30. Thomas Percy, ed., *The Hermit of Warkworth, a Northumberland Ballad. In Three Fits or Cantos. A New Edition with Additions* (London: Printed for Thomas Evans, 1782), 52.

31. Thomas Pennant, *A Tour in Scotland. MDCCLXIX* (Chester: Printed by John Monk, 1771), 31.

32. Davis, *Thomas Percy*, 224–27.

33. I have modeled my reading of this triangular, medial relationship on Sandro Jung, "William Shenstone's Poetry: The Leasowes and the Intermediality of Reading and Architectural Design," *Journal for Eighteenth-Century Studies* 37, no. 1 (2014), 53–77.

34. Percy, *The Hermit of Warkworth* (1782 ed.), 55.

35. Trumpener, *Bardic Nationalism*, 25–26; Charles W. J. Withers, *Geography, Science and National Identity: Scotland since 1520* (Cambridge: Cambridge University Press, 2001); Noah Heringman, *Sciences of Antiquity: Romantic Antiquarianism, Natural History, and Knowledge Work* (Oxford: Oxford University Press, 2013).

36. For a recent discussion of book illustration in Scotland, see Sandro Jung, "Thomson, Macpherson, Ramsay, and the Making and Marketing of Illustrated Scottish Literary Editions in the 1790s," *PBSA: Papers of the Bibliographical Society of America* 109, no. 1 (2015), 5–61.

37. See Manning, "Antiquarianism," 60–64. Recent scholarship has increasingly focused on political institutions and learned societies financially and ideologically supporting antiquarian inquiry. See Rosemary Sweet, *Antiquaries: The Discovery of the Past in Eighteenth-Century Britain* (London: Hambledon and London, 2004), chap. 3.

38. Valentina Bold, "Eighteenth-Century Antiquarianism," in *The Edinburgh Companion to Scottish Traditional Literatures*, ed. Sarah Dunnigan and Suzanne Gilbert (Edinburgh: Edinburgh University Press, 2013), 91–93.

39. See esp. Jung, "'A Scotch Poetical Library.'" For Buchan's rhetoric as articulated in annotation, see Michael Edson, "Scotland, the Earl of Buchan, and Stockdale's 1793 Commentary to *The Seasons*," *Studies in the Literary Imagination* 46 (2013): 91–113.

40. Jung, "Thomson, MacPherson, Ramsay," 57.

41. *Letters from Bishop Percy, &c. to George Paton* (Edinburgh: Printed for John Stevenson, 1830), 17.

42. Thomas Warton, *The History of English Poetry*, 4 vols. (London: Printed for, and Sold by, J. Dodsley, 1774), 2:334.

43. Patrick O'Flaherty, *Scotland's Pariah: The Life and Work of John Pinkerton, 1758–1826* (Toronto: University of Toronto Press, 2015), 25–26.

44. *The Percy Letters: The Correspondence of Thomas Percy & John Pinkerton*, ed. Harriet Harvey Wood (New Haven, CT: Yale University Press, 1985), 41.

45. *The Correspondence of Thomas Warton*, ed. David Fairer (Athens: University of Georgia Press, 1995), 490.

46. *Ancient Scotish Poems, Never before in Print. But Now Published from the MS. Collections of Sir Richard Maitland, of Lethington, Knight, Lord Privy Seal of Scotland, and a Senator of the College of Justice. Comprising Pieces Written from about 1420 till 1586. With Large Notes, and a Glossary*, 2 vols. (London: Printed for Charles Dilly, 1786). McLane draws attention to Pinkerton's emphasis on the aristocratic name in the title (McLane, *Balladeering*, 49).

47. O'Flaherty, *Scotland's Pariah*, 37.

48. John Pinkerton, *An Enquiry into the History of Scotland: Preceding the Reign of Malcom III. or the Year 1056. Including the Authentic History of that Period* (London: Printed for George Nichol, 1789), 1:60.

49. *The Literary Correspondence of John Pinkerton, Esq.*, ed. Dawson Turner, 2 vols. (London: Henry Colburn and Richard Bentley, 1830), 1:121, 186, and 197.

50. *Ancient Scotish Poems*, 2:555.

51. Turner, *Correspondence of John Pinkerton*, 1:176–77.

52. Sher mentions Robert Burns and William Smellie (Richard B. Sher, *The Enlightenment and the Book: Scottish Authors and their Publishers in Eighteenth-Century Britain, Ireland, and America* [Chicago: The University of Chicago Press, 2006], 432–3). For the subscription proposal, see Turner, *Correspondence of John Pinkerton*, 1:165–66.

53. For Pinkerton's offence to Lord Hailes, see Turner, *Correspondence of John Pinkerton*, 1:107–108, and to Paton, 187–88. Buchan spoke of a "violent disgust" among his countrymen in reaction to Pinkerton's *Enquiry* (Turner, *Correspondence of John Pinkerton*, 1:235–36). See also O'Flaherty, *Scotland's Pariah*, 54–58.

54. Eventually published as *The Bruce; or, The History of Robert I. King of Scotland. Written in Scotish Verse by John Barbour. The First Genuine Edition, Published from a MS. Dated 1489; with Notes and a Glossary*, 3 vols. (London: Printed for George Nichol, 1790). Subsequent references are cited parenthetically in the text as *Bruce* with volume and page number.

55. He had also written to Lord Hailes and Buchan for transcripts of Barbour's *Bruce* (Turner, *Correspondence of John Pinkerton*, 1:95, 102), as well as to Beattie regarding the same and other Scottish works in the Aberdeen libraries (Turner, *Correspondence of John Pinkerton*, 1:81).

56. Turner, *Correspondence of John Pinkerton*, 1:214.

57. Ibid., 1:197. For a detailed examination of the Morison series, see Jung, "'A Scotch Poetical Library,'" 11–20; for the place of the Anglo-Scot James Thomson in this canon, see also Sandro Jung, *James Thomson's The Seasons, Print Culture, and Visual Interpretation: 1730–1842* (Bethlehem, PA: Lehigh University Press, 2015), 88–94.

58. Turner, *Correspondence of John Pinkerton*, 1:157.

59. Sandro Jung, "Thomson, Macpherson, Ramsay," 57.

60. Turner, *Correspondence of John Pinkerton*, 1:158.

61. Jeremy Smith, "Textual Afterlives: Barbour's *Bruce* and Hary's *Wallace*," in *Scots: Studies in Its Literature and Language*, ed. John M. Kirk and Iseabail Macleod (Amsterdam: Rodopi, 2013), 49.

62. Smith, "Textual Afterlives," 50.

63. Turner, *Correspondence of John Pinkerton*, 1:162. Anthony Grafton, *The Footnote: A Curious History* (Cambridge, MA: Harvard University Press, 1997), 101–3.

64. *Ancient Scotish Poems*, lxxxi.

65. Ibid., lxxxi.

66. For a comparable case in which archaic poetry is valued primarily for its history rather than its aesthetic qualities, see Jeff Strabone's discussion of Thomas Hearne in the present volume.

67. Turner, *Correspondence of John Pinkerton*, 1:246.

68. See Fielding, *Scotland and the Fictions of Geography*, chap. 4.

69. Sweet reveals how the fabrication of a Celtic or, in Pinkerton's case, Gothic past implied a reliance on antiquarian and institutional authorities as well as on spatial dimensions in order to create a Scottish national history (Sweet, *Antiquaries*, 139).

70. In his *Enquiry* of 1789, Pinkerton had explained that a *Fors*, not to be confused with a *Ford*, is some sort of "place of strength" almost exclusively to be found in Scotland (1:153).

71. Elizabeth W. Harries, *The Unfinished Manner: Essays on the Fragment in the Later Eighteenth Century* (Charlottesville: University Press of Virginia, 1994); Jung, *Fragmentary Poetic*, 15–16. The symbolic, biblical, and Christian overtones of the fragmentary and the "relic" are explored by Harries, *The Unfinished Manner*, 48–51, and Trumpener, *Bardic Nationalism*, 28.

72. Groom, *The Making of Percy's Reliques*, 34–35.

73. Evan Gottlieb and Juliet Shields, *Representing Place in British Literature and Culture, 1660–1830: From Local to Global* (Aldershot, UK: Ashgate, 2013), 3.

74. Quotation taken from a review of Francis Grose's *Antiquities* in the *Monthly Review* 52 (March 1775): 238.

75. Endnotes are most obviously detachable from the main body of the text. As Percy noted in the letter to Paton, the printer or binder not infrequently had the last say in where the notes were to be placed (February 9, 1769 [Falconer, *Percy Letters*, 20–21]). In his advertisement to his 1782 *Observations on the Three Volumes of the History of English Poetry* (London: Printed for John Stockdale), for instance, Joseph Ritson declared that his remarks on Warton's history, printed in the same size, "are extremely proper to be bound up with that celebrated work, to which they will be found a very useful Appendix."

76. Penny Fielding, "Usurpt by Cyclops": Rivers, Industry, and Environment in Eighteenth-Century Poetry," in Gottlieb and Shields, *Representing Place*, 151.

77. Marilyn Butler, "Antiquarianism (Popular)," in *An Oxford Companion to the Romantic Age: British Culture, 1776–1832*, ed. Iain McCalman (Oxford: Oxford University Press, 2001), 330.

78. Gerard Carruthers and Liam McIlvanney, *The Cambridge Companion to Scottish Literature* (Cambridge: Cambridge University Press, 2012), 3. For a discussion of *The Bruce* as a propagandistic piece of Scottish proto–nation building, see Gerard Carruthers, *Scottish Literature* (Edinburgh: Edinburgh University Press, 2009), 30–33.

79. John Pinkerton, *Scotish Poems Reprinted from Scarce Editions*, 3 vols. (London: Printed by and for J. Nichols, 1792), 1:x.

5

Marginal Imprints

Robert Southey's Notes to *Madoc*

Alex Watson

In a letter responding to the reviewer and translator William Taylor's criticisms of the peculiar medieval Welsh and Aztec conquest epic *Madoc* (1805), Robert Southey, the poem's author, avowed:

> You will see my Hippogryff touch at Hindostan—fly back to Scandinavia & then carry me among the Fire worshipers of Istakhar. You will see him take a peep at the Jews, a flight to Japan, & an excursion among the Saints & Martyrs of Catholicism.[1]

Here Southey (1774–1843) likens the act of writing poetic epics to the experience of riding the legendary creature with the front quarters of an eagle and the hind quarters of a horse featured in Ludovico Ariosto's 1532 mock-heroic epic *Orlando Furioso*. Southey's allusion to "Hindostan" refers to his prospective "Hindu" epic *The Curse of Kehama* (1810), but he also projects eventually unwritten works based on Catholic, Japanese, Jewish, Scandinavian, and Zoroastrian traditions. Southey's comparison of his ambitions to being carried by a bizarre creature born of a mating between a griffin and a filly foregrounds his delight in unruly juxtaposition and culture clash, as well as his promiscuous use of a wide range of genres: journalism, poetry, prose, and travel writing. The quotation reveals the extent to which Southey regarded writing epics as an intertextual journey, in which the task of researching these historically and geographically distant societies and belief systems on which his poems were based represented a form of imaginative flight. Indeed, this consideration is highlighted by his allusion to "the fire worshippers of Isktakhar." Southey mostly likely read about these people in William Beckford's 1782 Oriental Gothic novel *Vathek*, who himself found out about them from the French jeweler and traveler Jean Chardin.[2] Moreover, by imagining himself as Ariosto's wandering knight Ruggiero, Southey portrays his own scrutiny of esoteric tomes and musty volumes as a chivalric quest.

Yet Southey's flippancy, and the parodic status of the subject of his allusion, reveal an awareness of the quixotic aspects of what he described elsewhere as his attempt to display "all the more prominent and poetical forms of mythology which have [emerged] at any time . . . among mankind, by making each the groundwork of an heroic poem."[3]

As this quotation shows, Southey's treatment of these places and religions as virtually interchangeable resources of poetic inspiration betrays a somewhat myopic attitude that overlooks their historical richness and philosophical complexity. The miscellaneousness of Southey's selection betrays an addiction to cultural accumulation at the expense of reflecting on or attempting to synthesize the materials collected. Instead his desire to "take a peep" at such cultures implies both fascination for and fear of them. Southey's confidence in his own intellectual stealth is particularly significant when we consider his notorious political transfiguration, from the controversial Jacobin of the 1790s to the establishment Tory he had become by 1810. Viewed from this angle, the mobility of which Southey boasts represents a form of evasiveness: he seems to believe that he can experiment with a variety of cultural perspectives and ideological viewpoints and then shove them aside and return to his original starting point. Southey's proclamation of his own maneuverability, therefore, reveals two, perhaps fatal, naiveties: a belief that he can evade capture and not be held to account for the standpoints he occupies; and a conviction that he can expose himself to alterity without being altered in the process. The former belief was controverted by events such as the surreptitious republication in 1817 of Southey's radical 1794 play *Wat Tyler*, which highlighted the conservative poet laureate's apostasy. The latter was confounded by Southey's shocked and hostile response to the foreign cultures with which he experimented; in particular, his experience of living in Portugal, which he visited three times for long periods between 1795 and 1800, visits that incited a long-lasting antipathy toward Roman Catholicism.

I have dwelled on this particular quotation at length because it illustrates concerns central to this chapter. In particular, the quotation's concept of "flight"—both in terms of a journey to a foreign land, and of an escape from a prior situation or previous self—can help us understand something central about how, in his 1805 poetic epic *Madoc* and its extensive endnotes, Southey began to reposition himself from the radical of the 1790s to the pro-imperialist conservative he would become. In the verse of this idiosyncratic piece, Southey retells the legend of Madoc, the Welsh prince who escaped dynastic conflict by sailing to South America and establishing a colony in Mexico. In his copious endnotes, Southey displays an exotic compendium of extracts from volumes of Portuguese poetry, histories of American Indians, Welsh druids, and South American conquistadors as well as travel accounts of Canada, China, the West Indies, and the South Sea Islands.

As I will show, the complicated and sometimes fraught relationship between the notes and the text of the poem enact a complex process of identity formation. In the endnotes, Southey presents his textual journey as an avid consumer and arranger of the foreign worlds and anterior perspectives he discovered in printed books. Southey's annotations can therefore be regarded as textual imprints, imprints with which we can trace his voyage from the radical he was in the last years of the eighteenth century to the conservative poetic and political identity that would define him as a man of letters in the nineteenth century. In the next section, I will sketch the critical history of the poem before examining how the Southey of 1805 attempts to use his paratexts to politically reposition himself. In the following parts, I investigate how Southey's representation of, first, medieval Wales and, second, Aztec South America is complicated by the relationship between note and text. I will suggest that Southey's movement toward a new conservative persona marks a broader transition in the dominant mode of elite British literary culture, from eighteenth-century enlightenment cosmopolitanism to nineteenth-century Romantic imperialism.

ON THE TRAIL OF THE
WHITE ELEPHANT: SOUTHEY'S MOBILITY

Recent critical discussions of *Madoc* have traced how the poem documents Southey's political transformation. For instance, Lynda Pratt describes *Madoc* as "a complex poem, one whose shifts (from radicalism to enlightenment toleration, to conversion narrative) reflect the ideological and intellectual conflicts that beset its author."[4] In particular, such scholars have revealed how *Madoc*'s disequilibrium mirrors Southey's changing feelings about his and Samuel Taylor Coleridge's "Pantisocracy" scheme: their failed plan in the 1790s to establish an egalitarian community, first, beside the Susquehanna River in Pennsylvania and, second, in Wales. For example, according to Carol Bolton, "much of the interest in reading *Madoc* comes from tracing the faint outline of Southey's egalitarian society behind the imperialist project that *Madoc* institutes."[5] Most of all, critics have highlighted the difficulty of characterizing Southey in any straightforward way, even suggesting that his work's evasiveness and complexity characterizes an age besotted with—yet repelled by—the foreign and unfamiliar. Pratt suggests, "this lack of fixity, the ability both to blur and to blend, lies at the very heart of Southey's writings, making him both an instigator and an embodiment of a Romantic period culture beset by ambiguity and ambivalence, a world in which the familiar coexisted with the bizarre."[6]

For many critics, however, the difficulty and boredom of following this outlandish and disconcerting poem is wholly out of proportion to the rewards of doing so. Nigel Leask, for instance, memorably describes it as "one of the most spectacular white elephants of English Romanticism."[7] He casts the poem as an example of what Susan Stewart calls a "distressed genre": an archaic form undergoing transformation in a literary culture experiencing fundamental changes in production and reception.[8] In this sense, Southey's use of annotation to mediate his poetic project suggests a self-conscious historical distance, a feeling that epic is no longer a spontaneous cultural production expressing the life and worldview of the poet's society but has become a mode from a distant past requiring mediation. In their persistent disruption of the verse, the notes could thereby be said to register the fragmentation of the epic form, as industrial capitalism and enlightenment values transformed the religious, superstitious, and feudal society from which the genre emerged and undermined the vatic, orphic authority of the epic voice. Nonetheless "distress" implies not only new historical and economic pressures but also psychological anxieties. In this manner, Southey's fractured text mirrors his own psychological and political anxieties about the viability of his earlier radicalism and the rights and wrongs of his political transition.

Critics of Southey's own time tended to cast him as having attempted a peculiar generic and ideological hybrid with an epic ambition that backfired. In the *Monthly Review*, John Ferriar pictured Southey "mounted on a strange animal, something between a rough Welsh poney and a Peruvian sheep, whose utmost capriole [caper or leap] only tends to land him in the mud."[9] Like Southey's own description of riding the hippogriff, Ferriar's bathetic comment portrays a poet who has allowed his imagination to run away with him. In spite of *Madoc*'s eccentricity and enormousness, the poem did gain flamboyant acclaim from some critics. The *Imperial Review* even labeled it "certainly the second heroic production in the English language" after Milton's *Paradise Lost* (1667).[10] Most critics, however, derided the poem's peculiarity. Ferriar disparaged Southey's unusual character names such as the "jaw-dislocating *Ayayaca*."[11] Such complaints reveal how Southey's incorporation of foreign, unfamiliar elements stimulated a visceral sense of disruption in readers and critics. Reviewers also objected to the poem's Gothic goriness, which they regarded as so excessive as to become absurd. The *Eclectic Review* explained:

> We have piles of skulls—skulls for drinking bowls—beads of human hearts incased with gold, and hung round the necks of chief and heroes. One of his heroes, Coanocotzin, hangs up the skeleton of his enemy, a neighbouring prince, and makes it hold a lamp, in the hall where he sups and revels. Others of his heroes strip off the skins of the slain, and dance before us, as they wear them, all dropping with blood. Others make their drums out of them.[12]

As we will see, Southey's preoccupation with such partial objects in *Madoc* mirrors both the poem's disintegrating form and his own fragmentation and reformulation. On the one hand, the gruesome act of flaying one's enemies and refashioning the remaining skin into a torch parallels Southey's compulsive habit of peeling away passages from exotic esoterica and attempting to intertwine them into his own fractious, annotated epics. On the other, this revolting practice echoes Southey's own experience of identity transformation, as his former radicalism disintegrated and he reconstructed himself into the conservative controversialist he would remain for the rest of his life.

While writing the poem, Southey often declared it to be his masterpiece, exclaiming "*Madoc* is to be the pillar of my reputation."[13] However, at other moments, Southey's towering confidence disintegrated into sand, and he remonstrated elsewhere that "the subject is bad, it was chosen too soon, & has been too long in hand."[14] Southey, then, had a schizophrenic attitude toward *Madoc*, regarding it sometimes as his magnum opus and at others as a poem contaminated or divided by aesthetic deformities and generic impurities. Although he had begun the poem as early as 1789, he completed the first version in 1799. In this early variant, Southey represents resistance to Anglo-Saxon rule as an anticolonial struggle, using the Middle Ages to link the radical cause to a broader tradition of British liberty, in the same way as he does in his other major radical works of the 1790s, *Wat Tyler* and *Joan of Arc* (1796). The rendition that was eventually published, which he revised between 1802 and 1804, adopts a more conservative, pro-imperialist standpoint, and bears the marks of his extensive research into Welsh and Spanish-American history, as I will show later in this chapter. The endnotes are one of the main results of Southey's scholarly labors and form a skeleton around which Southey wraps the narrative of the poem. Southey has often been mocked for what H. N. Fairchild described as his "method of writing his poems to fit his footnotes,"[15] but, as we will see, his practice helps us to better understand the nature of his intellectual and political development.

Southey articulates the movement between his anticolonial self of 1799 and the more pro-imperialist figure of 1804 in many of the 1805 volume's paratexts. The first epigraph, "Omne solum forti patria" (as Leask has it, "any ground is home for a brave man")[16] links the earlier version's pantisocratic utopianism to a broader imperial agenda. In a further, self-penned epigraph located prominently at the frontispiece to the volume, Southey emphasizes the parallels between his and Madoc's experiences:

> COME, LISTEN TO A TALE OF TIMES OF OLD!
> COME, FOR YE KNOW ME! I AM HE WHO SUNG
> THE MAID OF ARC; & I AM HE WHO FRAMED
> OF THALABA THE WILD & WONDEROUS SONG.
> COME, LISTEN TO MY LAY, & YE SHALL HEAR
> HOW MADOC FROM THE SHORES OF BRITAIN SPREAD
> THE ADVENTUROUS SAIL, EXPLORED THE OCEAN WAYS,
> AND QUELLED BARBARIAN POWER, & OVERTHREW
> THE BLOODY ALTARS OF IDOLATRY,
> AND PLANTED IN ITS FANES TRIUMPHANTLY
> THE CROSS OF CHRIST. COME, LISTEN TO MY LAY![17]

Southey here may be seeking to advertise the book to prospective readers and promote himself as a serious author, but what is particularly interesting is the way in which this invocation establishes an implicit link between the poet and his protagonist. Just as Madoc escaped his original identity, and explored foreign, alternative ideas before reaffirming aggressively his own Christianity, so Southey experimented with radicalism in *Joan of Arc* and even perhaps Islam in the 1801 "Muslim" epic *Thalaba the Destroyer* before returning to the Christian, imperialist values he attempts to assert in *Madoc*. The character Madoc's circular voyage is also a metaphor for Southey's own physical, literary, and political journeyings: his flirtation with and rejection of pantisocracy in favor of imperialism; his travels around Portugal that led to a lifelong hostility toward Roman Catholicism; his lengthy exploration of various exotic and antiquarian tomes before his consolidation of their contents into the text before the reader; and his own initial experimentation with radical, deist ideas before his turn to Anglican conservatism.

"BRITON WITH BRITON IN UNNATURAL WAR": TWELFTH-CENTURY WALES IN *MADOC'S* NOTES

As we have seen, if *Madoc* could be said to be a pro-imperialist text, the particular na-ture of the imperialism Southey espouses in it is highly unusual, not to say internally unstable. The poem begins with the figure of Madoc returning from a naval voyage to South America, the events of which he narrates in books 5 and 6 of the poem. The Wales to which he returns is one virtually ripped apart by conflicts between the Welsh and the Anglo-Saxons. The aged Urien laments to Madoc on his return: "Oh, if my dear old master saw the wreck / And scattering of his house! . . . that princely race! / The beautiful band of brethren that there were!" (book 1, lines 84–86). The spectacle of what another character described as "Briton with Briton in unnatural war" (book 3, line 80) not only provokes Madoc to leave Wales for South America, but, more important, echoes Southey's own political and psychological disintegra-tion. Southey's annotations accentuate this atmosphere of danger and lawlessness. In one, for example, Southey prints an extract from John Wynn's account of fifteenth- and early sixteenth-century Wales, *The History of the Gwedir Family* (1770), that describes the rudimentary justice system operating in Wales at the time: "It was the manner of those days, that the murtherer only, and he that gave the death's-wound, should fly, which was called in Welch Llawrudd, which is a red-hand, because he had blouded his hands. The accessories and abetters to the murtherers were never hearkened after [*sic*]" (276). Such descriptions of rough justice in a society marked by criminal anarchy have an equivocal effect. In one sense, Southey thereby locates the Wales of the time in a Whiggish teleology in which Wales's Union with England represents a necessary step in the civilizing process. In another, Southey undermines the Union and the legal system it helped develop by revealing their violent, illegiti-mate origins. Southey thereby places the reader in a state of cognitive dissonance, requiring them at once to look forward to the British state's seeming transcendence of such apparently "local" conflicts within a broader centralized state legal apparatus and glance backward to the violence and domination that brought this structure into being. In a third sense, the murderer's quick flight parallels Southey's own declared talent for exfiltration. Yet the image of a murderer having the blood of their victim marked on their hands suggests the difficulty of escaping the consequences of one's actions. In this way, Southey's notes speak against the poet's assertion of human flex-ibility, implying instead that the past cannot be so easily eluded.

In the sections set in twelfth-century Wales, Robert Southey relies most heavily on the Whiggish, Unionist William Warrington's 1786 *History of Wales* to ward off anti-English perspectives. Nonetheless, Southey is by no means uncritical even of Warrington. In the verse, for instance, Southey compares Madoc's anxiety about the reverse culture shock he may experience on returning to the Wales he left a while before to "the lights / Which there upon Aberfraw's royal walls / Are waving with the wind" (book 1, lines 42–44). In his accompanying annotation, Southey describes how "the palace of Gwynedd, or North Wales. Rhodri Mawr" was moved from "Caer Seiont in Arvon, near the present town of Caernarvon" via "Dyganwy" to its present location (276). He then cites Warrington's comment that "'it is strange . . . that he [King Alfred] should desert a country where every mountain was a natural fortress, and, in times of such difficulty and danger, should make choice of a residence so exposed and defenceless.'" However, Southey asserts that "this very danger may have been his motive" (276). By making such critical interventions, Southey aligns his scholarship with the skeptical, source-based approach of such enlightenment historians as Edward Gibbon.[18] These comments act also as records of Southey's own intellectual and geographical peregrinations, tracing the particular landscapes in which the poem is set. He informs us in the same note that "a barn now stands upon the site of the palace, in which there are stones that, by their better workmanship, appear to have belonged to the original building" (276). By revealing how political events continue to restructure the landscape, Southey undermines the ostensive Unionist position of his text, drawing attention to Britain's geopolitical fluidity.

Southey's annotations cast a critical gaze on the military and political machinations by which the English crown colonized Wales. Madoc's lamentation that "my father's son. . . . / He wed the Saxon . . . the Plantaganet!" (book 1, lines 105–106) prompts Southey to corroborate Madoc's ululation in the margins, with the assertion that "this marriage was in fact one of the means whereby Henry [III] succeeded for a time in breaking the independent spirit of the Welsh" (276). In such comments, Southey not only asserts the distinctiveness of Welsh identity but also the ultimately ineffectual nature of English attempts to destroy it. Further annotations highlight the cruelty and barbarity of Henry's attacks on Wales. For example, Southey prints an extract from Raphael Holinshed's 1577 *Chronicles of England, Scotland and Ireland*, a comprehensive description of English history used as a source by Shakespeare, in which Holinshed records how Henry "'did justice on the sons of Rhys, and also on the sons and daughters of other noblemen . . . causing the eyes of the young striplings to be pecked out of their heads, and their noses to be cut off or slit; and the eares [*sic*] of the young gentlewomen to be stuffed'" (278). What is especially striking about such comments is how the English methods of punishment at that time parallel those of the Aztecs Madoc later encounters. As we will see, such forms of retribution compel Madoc to begin his colonial campaign against them. It is possible that Southey is deploying such parallelism deliberately, as a means of giving a clearer psychological rationale for Madoc's later reaction. However, the effect of such notes is to confuse the text's ideological position, allowing the poem both to avow imperialism at the same time to highlight its brutality and illegitimacy.

Those quotations taken from those scholars of a more radical, proto-nationalist disposition tend to focus on less overtly political topics, such as religious beliefs and practices or material history. For instance, he quotes from Edward Williams, known as Iolo Morganwg (1747–1826): a poet, antiquarian, collector, and literary forger who developed an elaborate Druid mysticism based on manuscripts he produced, as well as founding the Gorsedd, a community of Welsh poets, at a ceremony on June 21, 1792, in Primrose Hill, London.[19] Southey quotes, for example, Williams's account of "the Bardic system, as laid down in the Triads of *Bardism*," which describes "'three Circles of Existence: the Circle of Infinity, where there is nothing but God, of living or dead, and none but God can traverse it; the Circle of Inchoation, where all things are by Nature derived from Death . . . this Circle hath been traversed by man; and the Circle of Happiness, where all things spring from Life'" (279). Southey is perhaps considering other historical models of the poetic vocation in order to reflect on his own efforts to develop a literary career. Yet Southey's quotation of such extracts nevertheless has a peculiar and disconcerting effect. On the one hand, he presents Druidic traditions as primitive relics of a bygone age. On the other, he exoticizes Welsh bardism and, in so doing, imbues the belief systems half-transcribed and half-invented by such figures as Williams with a poetic allure that strengthens the appeal of their more radical approach to Welsh tradition and history.

In most cases, when Southey does present information derived from those Welsh antiquarians of a more radical, proto-nationalist disposition, Southey seeks to undermine them by interposing ironic, almost churlish commentary. For instance, in one annotation he nicknames the Welsh antiquarian and grammarian William Owen Pughe "Caradog"—a play on Caradoc Vriechvras, the semi-legendary ancestor of the Welsh Kings and Knights of the Round Table. In this example, the character Urien's pleas to Madoc to "bear with thy brother" (book 1, line 167)—a fictionalized version of the Prince of Gwynedd Dafydd ab Owain Gwynedd—prompts an endnote in which Southey contests Urien's plea, instead highlighting Dafydd's "cruelty and untractable spirit" and describing him as "killing and putting out the eyes of those who were not subservient to his will, after the *manner of the English!*" (276). The irony of Southey's undercutting of Urien's entreaty is compounded by the poet's haughty reiteration of Pughe's description of English violence. Yet Southey's attempt to dismiss Pughe's concerns through mockery is undermined by the gruesome history that he reveals to the reader. In jarring contrast with Southey's playful jeering, the note nonetheless attests to English colonial violence. While the Southey of 1802–1804 seeks to erase the reality of both English imperialism and his former political beliefs, their imprints nonetheless remain on the margins of his text. Or if we were to put it in Southey's melodramatic, murderous mode: one can pull out the eyes of enemies or even murder them, but one can never rid oneself of the stench of the corpse.

"KILL ALL THAT YOU CAN":
SOUTH AMERICA IN *MADOC'S* NOTES

In those annotations accompanying the passages set in South America, Southey protects against perspectives of the Spanish conquest more sympathetic to the indigenous population by only presenting the perspective of the colonizer and by providing passages that describe gruesome native South American practices. As Leask has pointed out, the greater sympathy Southey shows for imperialism in the version of the poem Southey made between 1802 and 1804 was partly the result of the poet's reading of sixteenth-century Spanish accounts of the conquest of South America when researching his projected "History of Portugal" in the Royal Library at Lisbon in 1800.[20] Southey quotes extensively the Spanish conquistador Bernal Diaz del Castillo's 1632 *True History of the Conquest of New Spain*, a bellicose account of the conquest of Mexico written in the sixteenth century but only printed and translated into English a few years before *Madoc's* publication by Maurice Keatinge in 1800. Southey includes Castillo's descriptions of "The Great Cu of Mexico" with its foundations of "Gold and jewels . . . and human blood" (287), and enthuses in a further annotation that "the account in Bernal Diaz" of native Mexican "midnight sacrifice, performed by torch-light, and in the sight of the Spanish army, is truly terrific" (288). By presenting Diaz's descriptions and highlighting their intense, frightening qualities, Southey emphasizes the brutality of the native Mexicans rather than their Spanish conquerors. But what is particularly noticeable is Southey's enthusiastic attitude toward such writings, as if by reading them exclusively for their lurid, shocking aspects he can remove himself from their reference to an actual lived place and past and present them instead as titillating grotesque artifacts of an evil civilization.

Frequently, Southey also quotes the sixteenth-century Sevillian historian Francisco López de Gómara's *The Pleasant Historie of the Conquest of the Weast India, Now Called New Spayne* (1578). For instance, Southey prints Gómara's macabre description of the custom of "stuff[ing] the skin of the royal, or noble prisoner, and suspend[ing] it as a trophy." Southey claims "Gomorra's account of this custom is a dreadful picture of the most barbarous superstition which ever yet disgraced mankind" (288). Southey's disparaging comments may condemn the native South Americans, but they also disguise unconvincingly his fascination with such grisly customs. Importantly, these shocking practices are revealed only after Southey prints in earlier annotations Gómara's far more complimentary description of the initial reception of the Spanish, in which the Aztecs "'came with smiling countenance, and presented unto them divers kinde of floures and sundry fruites'" (286). This passage accompanies Southey's verse's description of the idyllic "imperial city" of Aztlan, with "Her garden groves, and stately palaces, / Her temples mountain size, her thousand roofs" (book 6, lines 126–28) in which Madoc finds to his horror the dead body of the former king Tepollomi "Stood up against the wall, by devilish art / Preserved; and from this black and shriveled hand / The steady lamp hung down (book 6, lines 250–52). Both annotation and verse tell an analogous story, in which a foreign society is presented initially as an idyll of Rousseavian noble primitivism or Orientalist idealization reminiscent of Coleridge's *Kubla Khan* (1797/1816), only to be revealed to disguise a hidden inhumanity. Witnessing this clandestine cruelty strips Western observers of their initial optimistic illusions and leads them to realize the need to assert Christian values and political control over the region. In the verse, Madoc's discovery of "the dead Tepollomi" (book 6, line 249) causes him to turn against the Aztlan king, contending "I know thy power, and thou shalt then know mine" (book 6, line 264). Whereas the main text describes this process of conversion metaphorically, via Madoc's narrative, the endnotes take the reader on a similar journey of initial intoxication or seduction, followed by shock, rejection, and then resolution—an immunizing procedure of exposure that poisons to protect against the foreign non-Christian Other.

Although Southey's notes about South America are generally more pugnacious than those concerning Wales, many are still double-edged. For instance, the final endnote is an additional quotation from Diaz's *True History* that reads: "kill all that you can, said the Tlascallans to [Hernán] Cortes; the young that they may not bear arms, the old that they may not give counsel" (353). The "Tlascallans" or Tlaxcalans were pre-Hispanic inhabitants who allied themselves with the Spanish to defeat the Aztecs. Southey may intend the note to display the barbarity of the native South Americans; but the effect is to show the cruelty and cunning of the Spanish conquest. Importantly, Southey places the note alongside Aztlan's King Yuhidthiton's warning, following Madoc's successful annexation of Aztlan, that the Aztec people will nonetheless resist Welsh incursions: "If blind to your own welfare, ye persist / Woe to ye, wretches!" (book 24, lines 91–92). In the verse, Southey appears to reject Yuhidthiton's admonition, and he portrays Madoc informing the Aztec monarch that "by force we won your City . . . / By force we will maintain it" (book 24, 98–99). Yet the annotation reveals a more anxious sense of vulnerability. In particular, the endnote challenges the verse's idealized representation of Madoc as a Christian conqueror or a "deliverer" (book 24, line 24) who has brought "redemption" (book 24, line 14) to the city via subjugation and religious, legal, and linguistic union with Erillyab, the Aztec queen. In contrast with the verse's proselytizing perspective, the endnote confronts the reader with the genocidal pathology underlying Southey's imperial project. According to Leask, in the 1802–1804 version of the poem, Southey "appropriated . . . counter-reformation Catholic triumphalism . . . to inject new energy into the discourse of nineteenth-century British imperialism."[21] Yet Southey's notes' constant inventorying of battles between the Spanish and the native South Americans, as well as his descriptions of destroyed temples and captured Incans, allow the reader to infer an alternative perspective in which the Spanish are aggressors not saviors.

CONCLUSION: THE RETURN OF THE HIPPOGRIFF

In his eccentric 1836 prose collection, *The Doctor*, Southey resurrects the motif of mythical equestrianism as a metaphor for poetic creativity, describing a reverie he experienced after going to sleep:

> it was that in the visions of the night I mounted Nobs. Tell me not of Ariosto's hip-pogriff. . . . Tell me not even of Pegasus! I have ridden him many a time; by day and night have I ridden him; high and low, far and wide, round the earth, and about it, and over it, and under it . . . I have been on him when he has glided through the sky with wings outstretched and motionless, like a kite or a summer cloud; I have bestrode him when he went up like a bittern, with a strong spiral flight, round, round and round, and upward, upward, upward, circling and rising still; and again when he has gone full sail or full fly, with his tail as straight as a comet behind him. But for a hobby or a night horse, Pegasus is nothing to Nobs.[22]

Southey's description of exchanging the grandiose delights of Pegasus for the more prosaic pleasures of Nobs echoes his transition from his ambitious, cosmopolitan, radical youth to his humbler, shrewder, more conservative adulthood. Southey's giddily enthusiastic description of Pegasus's flamboyant pirouettes and corkscrewing leaps reveal his nostalgia for the personal metamorphoses and ideological fervor he experienced in the 1790s. In contrast, he views his current state of stability with fondness but also a sense of regret and even illegitimacy or charlatanry: a hobby horse, after all, is a costumed actor in British folk tradition. Such passages reveal the extent to which an undercurrent of self-reproach continued to permeate the writing of the later conservative Southey.

As we have seen, from his early critical reception onward, Southey has been ac-cused of being incoherent. Bolton has suggested that Southey's later support for imperialism lacked both consistency and nuance, claiming:

> Southey should not be seen as advocating a systematic, structured approach to colonisa-tion. He simply believed that colonial expansion would generally benefit indigenous populations abroad, as well as providing commercial opportunities for British citizens, whose own country was in danger of being over-populated and over-industrialised.[23]

And, for Leask, Southey's sympathy for the Spanish "Spiritual Conquest" of Mexico is held in check by the poet's disdain for Roman Catholicism and his suspicion of Cortés's devotion to the Spanish crown and frequent brutality toward the indigenous people:

> Southey's "sympathy for the devil" here may well have been prompted by his struggle to accommodate the Spanish conquest into his ideological programme for British Chris-tian imperialism. . . . [T]he character of the historical Cortes seems to have offended Southey's deeper republican instincts, leading him to sympathise with his vanquished Indian foes.[24]

However, one criticism we might make of both scholars is that they assume that the poem *should* have an ideological coherence and then criticize it when this particular white elephant evades them. In particular, they tend to see radicalism and conservatism as if they were preexisting identities that Southey could select and switch. However, as Kevin Gilmartin points out:

> The political application of "conservative" was for the most part a later nineteenth-century development, anticipated in the 1810s by Robert Southey and others, but not decisively claimed by the Tory party until a *Quarterly Review* article of 1830. "Counterrevolutionary" was similarly emerging in the period, again with assistance from Southey.[25]

Such fluidity did not simply apply to political identities, but also to geo-cultural ones. According to Lauren Benton, at this time nations and empires "did not cover space evenly but composed a fabric that was full of holes, stitched together out of pieces, a tangle of strings."[26] The poem's apparent disjointedness or inconsistency may in part be because Southey is actively attempting to forge new forms of political and geopolitical identity. Indeed, this sense of open-endedness is encouraged by Southey's use of endnotes. While the headnote provides a coherent interpretative and contextual frame for the text, and the footnote interrupts it with asides, the endnote extends the text, enabling the reader to amble further across new textual territories, without compelling them to integrate this textual journey into a coherent interpretation or experience of the text.

However, there is a broader systematic pattern in Southey's imperial ideology. Throughout *Madoc*, the same narrative recurs; colonization compels the colonized to escape and found a new colony where those they colonize are prompted to do the same ad infinitum. The experience of moving and encountering another people first places the colonizer's original religious beliefs and cultural identities in question but, ultimately, reaffirms them, enabling them to live according to their original ideas with real conviction. The process of transforming from colonized rebel to colonizing master is defended as one that grants maturity to an individual and stability to a society. As we have seen, this narrative echoes Southey's own personal and political transition. However, while Southey struggles to present a coherent new identity as a pro-imperial conservative, this identity is itself haunted by his prior radical self, and the contradictions in the ideology he has adopted resurface in the margins.

At the same time as creating new ideological structures, Southey is also pioneering new literary forms. In their irony and incongruity, Southey's notes recall the clergyman Samuel Henley's annotations for Beckford's *Vathek* (1786). And their archness and dedication to scrutinizing primary sources is reminiscent of Edward Gibbon's notes for *The History of the Decline and Fall of the Roman Empire* (1776–1788). Yet, in their weight of antiquarian and ethnographic detail, Southey's endnotes point forward to the annotations featured in the bestselling "Oriental epics" of Lord Byron and the antiquarian epics and historical novels of Sir Walter Scott. Byron's and Scott's works were crucial in promoting imperial and nationalist ideologies throughout the globe. In Southey's and these two poets' works, the dialectic between note and text replicates the relationship between imperial and national margins in the period, as agrarian communities both in and outside Britain were absorbed into the industrial capitalist nation-state. Just as the notes in *Madoc* both support and, in subtle ways, subvert the poem's imperial and nationalist principles, so marginalized localities, from Wales to Mexico, existed in a complex relationship to structures of power, both reinforcing and potentially undermining. Indeed, the fracture created by annotation registers a broader sense of fragmentation, by disrupting the flow of the reading process and call attention to the artificial and illusory manner in which the story's image of reality and implicit ideological standpoints have been constructed. *Madoc*, therefore, provides us a compelling example of how the emergence of romantic nationalism from the earlier enlightenment cosmopolitanism generated an abject remainder, in which the new geopolitical identities that were being established continued to be haunted by the more hybrid and interwoven identities and communities that they superseded.

In Southey's efforts in 1804 to rework a poem he had begun in the heady revolutionary year of 1789 and revised intermittently in the intervening period, he created a text that is not only strange and heterogeneous but permeated by an underlying sense of political and colonial guilt. The interstitial position of the margins enables Southey both to refute and revisit his origins, presenting an archive not only of Spanish or English conquest but also of the poet's past. Attention to such apparently marginal details, therefore, reveals an image of the former poet laureate more complex that the fustian, Casaubonian caricature, in which, as his early twentieth-century biographer William Haller claimed, "all his reading was done . . . not to enlarge his own spirit, but merely to confirm his preconceptions about life, and to condemn what disagreed with them."[27] Instead, Southey's rapacious reading caused a personal revolution, in which the ulterior voices and ideas he attempted hastily to consume were initially endorsed before ultimately being rejected. Yet their traces remain at the margins of Southey's texts and the poet's psyche. Investigating Southey's textual, political, and psychological fissures reveals a richer picture of the poet, in which the radical ideals of his younger Southey remain traumatic imprints on the reactionary, antiquarian, yet market-savvy figure Southey would become.

NOTES

1. Robert Southey to William Taylor, November 14, 1805, *The Collected Letters of Robert Southey: Part Three: 1804–1809*, ed. Carol Bolton and Tim Fulford, *Romantic Circles*, accessed April 14, 2015, http://www.rc.umd.edu/editions/southey_letters/Part_Three/HTML/letterEEd.26.1119.html.

2. The derivation of this motif from Jean Chardin via William Beckford is suggested by the fact that each of these writers locate the Zoroastrians mistakenly in Istakhar, when, in fact, they were based in the more Southern city of Persepolis. See William Beckford, *"Vathek," with The Episodes of "Vathek,"* ed. Kenneth W. Graham (Peterborough, ON: Broadview Press, 2001), 75n.

3. Quoted in Mark Storey, *Robert Southey: A Life* (Oxford: Oxford University Press, 1997), 8.

4. Lynda Pratt, introduction to *Robert Southey: Poetical Works 1793–1810*, vol. 2, *Madoc*, ed. Lynda Pratt with Carol Bolton and Paul Jarman (London: Pickering and Chatto, 2004), 2:xxvi.

5. Carol Bolton, *Writing the Empire: Robert Southey and Romantic Colonialism* (London: Pickering and Chatto, 2007), 77.

6. Lynda Pratt, introduction to *Robert Southey and the Contexts of English Romanticism*, ed. Lynda Pratt (Aldershot, UK: Ashgate, 2006), xxviii.

7. Nigel Leask, "Southey's *Madoc*: Reimagining the Conquest of America," in Pratt, *Robert Southey and the Contexts*, 133.

8. Susan Stewart, "Notes on Distressed Genres," *Journal of American Folklore* 104, no. 411 (1991): 5–31.

9. *Monthly Review* 48 (October 1805), repr. in *Robert Southey: The Critical Heritage*, ed. Lionel Madden (London: Routledge, 1972), 104.

10. *Imperial Review* 5 (November 1805), repr. in Madden, *The Critical Heritage*, 105.

11. Ibid., 103.

12. *Eclectic Review* 1 (December 1805), repr. in Madden, *The Critical* Heritage, 106.

13. Robert Southey to Grosvenor Charles Bedford, October 1–10, 1795, *The Collected Letters of Robert Southey: Part One: 1791–1797*, ed. Lynda Pratt, Romantic Circles, accessed March 12, 2015, http://www.rc.umd.edu/editions/southey_letters/Part_One/HTML/letter-EEd.26.136.html.

14. Robert Southey to Joseph Cottle, August 25, 1805, *Collected Letters . . . Part Three*, accessed March 9, 2015, http://www.rc.umd.edu/editions/southey_letters/Part_Three/HTML/letterEEd.26.1097.html.

15. H. N. Fairchild, *The Noble Savage: A Study in Romantic Naturalism* (New York: Columbia University Press, 1928), 205.

16. Quoted in Leask, "Southey's *Madoc*," 137.

17. Pratt, *Robert Southey: Poetical Works*, 2:8. Subsequent references to *Madoc* are cited parenthetically in the text. Quotations from the poem will be cited by book and line number; quotations from the notes will be cited by page number.

18. For more details, see Anthony Grafton, *The Footnote: A Curious History* (Cambridge, MA: Harvard University Press, 1999), 97–106.

19. See Prys Morgan, "Williams, Edward (1747–1826)," *Oxford Dictionary of National Biography*.

20. See Leask, "Southey's *Madoc*," 144.

21. Ibid.

22. Robert Southey, *The Doctor, &c.*, 2 vols. (New York: Harper and Brothers, 1836), 1:25–26.

23. Carol Bolton, "'Green Savannahs' or 'Savage Lands': Wordsworth's and Southey's Romantic America," in Pratt, *Robert Southey and the Contexts*, 131.

24. Leask, "Southey's *Madoc*," 150.

25. Kevin Gilmartin, *Writing against Revolution: Literary Conservatism in Britain, 1790–1832* (Cambridge: Cambridge University Press, 2007), 11.

26. Lauren Benton, *A Search for Sovereignty: Law and Geography in European Empires, 1400–1900* (Cambridge: Cambridge University Press, 2010), 2.

27. William Haller, *The Early Life of Robert Southey, 1774–1803* (New York: Columbia University Press, 1917), 258.

III

VARIETIES OF ANNOTATION

6

A Translator's Annotation

Alexander Pope's Observations on His *Iliad*

David Hopkins

The earliest editions of Alexander Pope's translation of Homer's *Iliad* were accompanied by a substantial body of paratextual material: a preface by Pope himself; an "*Essay* on the Life, Writings, *and* Learning of Homer" by the poet's friend Thomas Parnell; a "Poetical Index" of characters, speeches, descriptions, similes, and versification, together with thematic indexes of "Persons and Things" and "Arts and Sciences"; maps of Greece and the plain of Troy; and extensive and detailed notes, or Observations, integrally related to the text of the translation itself by lemmas and line numberings.[1] The Observations incorporated a detailed account of the "Catalogue of the Ships" (book 2), an "Essay on Homer's Battels" (book 4), and a full description and discussion, complete with engraved plate borrowed from the French scholar Jean Boivin, of the Shield of Achilles (book 18). In the quarto and folio editions of 1715–1720, the Observations were printed at the end of each book of Homer's poem, and they occupy almost as many pages (in closer line spacing) as the text itself. In the duodecimo editions published in Pope's lifetime (1720, 1732, 1736, 1743), they were transferred to the foot of the page. But from the late eighteenth century onward, it became customary either to omit Pope's notes entirely, to present only a selection from them, or to replace them with notes by a later editor. It was only in the twentieth century that Pope's Observations were reprinted in their entirety, first as part of the eleven-volume Twickenham edition of Pope's complete poetry (1939–1969), then in Steven Shankman's stand-alone Penguin English Poets edition of the *Iliad* translation (1996).

Both these editions are now difficult to access outside major libraries.[2] There is, therefore, at present, no readily available edition of Pope's translation that presents the whole work as Pope originally designed it. This situation, I will argue, has made an important contribution to the widespread neglect and misunderstanding of one of the major English literary texts of the eighteenth century.

Pope's *Iliad* is today a sadly neglected work. Though one of the most admired and widely read poems of its day, continuously in print from its first appearance until well into the twentieth century, it is nowadays regularly bypassed in university courses in favor of material of far inferior merit and has few general readers. Pope's Homer is not represented in any of the most widely used student anthologies, and the modern scholarship that has done much to explain and defend the principles that informed Pope's endeavor does not appear to have permeated, to any great extent, the larger literary consciousness.[3] Pope's translation is, as a consequence, regularly described in general literary histories and reference books in terms that have changed little since the days of Leslie Stephen and Matthew Arnold, when Pope's reputation was at its lowest ebb. The classical scholar Richard Bentley's reported remark—"A very pretty poem, Mr Pope, but you mustn't call it Homer"[4]—is still regularly trotted out as if it represented the last word on Pope's translation. Modern handbook accounts do little to question the Victorian charges that Pope had distorted Homer beyond recognition to accord with his own age's demand for "good sense" and "correctness,"[5] and had "elevate[d] . . . the bard by high-heeled shoes and a full-bottomed wig" more appropriate to his own times than to the eighth century BCE.[6] One twentieth-century poet (Peter Levi) has described Pope's version as "Homer in Silver Gilt." Another (Norman Nicholson) has written that the "glittering decoration" of Pope's translation "often makes his minor figures seem like pieces of painted china" and his animals no more realistic than "heraldic beasts on an embroidered flag."[7] In such accounts, Pope's *Iliad* is portrayed as a translation fundamentally similar in spirit and intention to Antoine Houdar de la Motte's à la mode French *Iliad* of 1701–1714, which had substantially abridged and sanitized Homer to accord with contemporary French conceptions of decorum and gentlemanliness.[8]

Such accusations, indeed, were sometimes expressed in Pope's own day. One early poetic response, for example, alleged of Pope's treatment of Homer that "He smoothes him o'er, and gives him grace and ease, / And makes him *fine,* —the *Beaus* and *Belles* to please."[9] Antiphaus ("The Hater of Dazzle"), one of the characters in Joseph Spence's dialogic *Essay on Pope's* Odyssey (1726–1727), expressed his "distaste" at the "*glitterings* and *elevation*" that he has encountered in Pope's Homer translations.[10] And Samuel Johnson noted that "it has been objected by some . . . that Pope's version of Homer is not Homerical; that it exhibits no resemblance of the original and characteristick manner of the Father of Poetry, as it wants his awful simplicity, his artless grandeur, his unaffected majesty."[11] "Homer," Johnson conceded, "doubtless owes to his translator many *Ovidian* graces not exactly suitable to his character."[12]

But Johnson also argued that, though Pope's felt need to make Homer "graceful" had "lost him some of his sublimity,"[13] this did not ultimately detract from the supreme value of his translation. Pope's *Iliad* was, Johnson affirmed, "the noblest version of poetry which the world has ever seen" and a "poetical wonder . . . a performance which no age or nation can pretend to equal."[14] Pope's addition of un-Homeric "graces" was excusable since, despite their presence, nothing essentially

Homeric had, in his version, been "taken away." And the notes that he had included with his version had made an important contribution to the other abundant pleasures that his translation had to offer:

> The copious notes with which the version is accompanied, and by which it is recommended to many readers, though they were undoubtedly written to swell the volumes,[15] ought not to pass without praise: commentaries which attract the reader by the pleasure of perusal have not often appeared; the notes of others are read to clear difficulties, those of Pope to vary entertainment.[16]

The reasons for the present neglect of, and misconceptions about, Pope's *Iliad* among non-specialist readers are too complex to be fully investigated here. But a careful reading of Pope's translation alongside his Observations shows clearly that Pope had a far more sophisticated and historically aware conception of his activity than many modern accounts allow. Pope's Observations show that, *pace* Bentley, Pope understood only too well that he could not possibly, at least in any simple way, "call" his version "Homer." No rendering of an ancient author, Pope realized, can ever teleport us directly into a past culture, or offer us direct and unmediated access to an ancient text. All translations must involve and display a complex process of dialogue and negotiation between the translator and his source. A version of Homer must, of necessity, involve a simultaneous recognition of Homer's familiarity and of his "otherness." Thus, in Pope's translation and Observations, as one recent scholar has put it, "transmission of the original goes hand-in-hand with the acknowledgement of difference: differences which are linguistic and cultural and which flow from the heightened self-consciousness generated in the act of translation."[17]

POPE, HOMER, AND NATURE

The larger aesthetic assumptions that inform Pope's translation and commentary on the *Iliad*, and his sense of the principal qualities that characterize Homer's poem— and which it must therefore be a translator's first priority to convey to his readers— are set out eloquently in his preface to the translation and in the *Essay on Criticism* (1711), published four years before the first installment of his *Iliad*. Homer's poetry, Pope declares in his preface, is characterized above all by an "unequal'd Fire and Rapture, which is so forcible . . . that no Man of a true Poetical Spirit is Master of himself when he reads him":

> What he writes is of the most animated Nature imaginable; every thing moves, every thing lives, and is put in Action. If a Council be call'd, or a Battle fought, you are not coldly inform'd of what was said or done as from a third Person; the Reader is hurry'd out of himself by the Force of the Poet's Imagination, and turns in one place to a Hearer, in another to a Spectator. The Course of his Verses resembles that of the Army he describes, . . . *They pour along like a Fire that sweeps the whole Earth before it.*[18]

Such "fire" is also present—albeit in a muted, intermittent, or strenuously controlled form—in other poets (Virgil, Lucan, Statius, Milton, Shakespeare), but "in *Homer*, and in him only, it burns every where clearly, and every where irresistibly" (*TE*, 7:5). Homer's imagined personages, Pope asserts, are more sharply characterized and more aptly differentiated in their mode of speech than those of any other writer. His depiction of the Olympian gods gives an "Importance and Dignity" to the action of his poem (*TE*, 7:7). His imagery and similes are more bold, vivid, and imaginatively fertile than those of any other poet: "There are in him more daring Figures and Metaphors than in any good Author whatever. An Arrow is *impatient* to be on the Wing, a Weapon *thirsts* to drink the Blood of an Enemy, and the like" (*TE*, 7:10). Homer's readers are, for all these reasons, profoundly *involved* in his presentation of his action. But such involvement is in no way incompatible with a sense of disorientation that we feel at first when reading such an ancient poem:

> When we read *Homer*, we ought to reflect that we are reading the most ancient Author in the Heathen World; and those who consider him in this Light, will double their Pleasure in the Perusal of him. Let them think they are growing acquainted with Nations and People that are now no more; that they are stepping almost three thousand Years back into the remotest Antiquity, and entertaining themselves with a clear and surprizing Vision of Things no where else to be found, the only true mirror of that ancient World. By this means alone their greatest Obstacles will vanish; and what usually creates their Dislike, will become a Satisfaction. (*TE*, 7:14)

Our consciousness of the historical remoteness of Homer will, Pope suggests, enable us to overcome potential obstacles encountered when reading the *Iliad*, such as the presence of repeated epithets and the allegedly "low and mean Expressions" that have been frequently objected to by those of "a false Delicacy and Refinement" (*TE*, 7:16).

Homer is able to confront us simultaneously with the sense of alienation and familiarity, since the "Nature" that is the subject of his poetry is not merely the world of everyday life but what Samuel Johnson was later to call General Nature, "the truth and reality *in* everyday life, a truth and reality we are blind to until the great writer shocks us into perceiving it."[19] This transcendent Nature, however, Pope realized, can only be communicated through a host of contingent particularities. For, like his poetic master, John Dryden, Pope was fully aware of the paradox that, though "mankind" may ultimately be "ever the same, and nothing lost out of Nature" (a necessary faith if the past is to be considered intelligible at all), "everything is altered" by the processes of historical and cultural change.[20]

Pope's "Nature" is the mysterious entity that is the "*Source*, and *End*, and *Test*" of all true art (*Essay on Criticism*, line 73). It is the force that brings art into being in the first place; it is the true subject of art; and it is the means whereby the truth of art is recognized and judged by its readers. Like the "informing Soul" that animates the body with "Spirits" and "Vigour," and which is seen "in th' *Effects*" while remaining "*It self unseen*" (*Essay*, lines 76–79), its presence in a work of literature provokes in the reader a spark of acknowledgment and a feeling of inevitable "rightness": "*Something*, whose Truth convinc'd at Sight we find, / That gives us back the Image of our Mind" (*Essay*, lines 299–300). So vivid and inclusive, Pope thinks, was Homer's capacity to produce such effects that when Virgil, intent on writing "A Work t' outlast Immortal *Rome*," eventually came to study Homer carefully, "*Nature* and *Homer* were, he found, the *same*" (*Essay*, lines 131, 135). Homer, Pope suggests, had captured Nature so compellingly and comprehensively that, in his work, Nature and Art seemed to Virgil to be identical and inseparable. This was, above all, what made Homer such a perpetual resource for later poets, a "copious Nursery which contains the Seeds and first Productions of every kind, out of which those who follow'd him have but selected some particular Plants, each according to his Fancy, to cultivate and beautify" (*TE*, 7:3). For this reason, the student of Homer will inevitably be drawn to the later poems that have grown from the seeds planted by his work. Later poets' use of Homeric material will, indeed, provide a kind of creative commentary on his work, more useful in some respects—and certainly more pleasurable—than that of scholars. In a letter to a friend, Pope declared himself to be "one, who values the Authority of one true Poet above that of twenty Critics or Commentatours."[21] And, as we will see, he frequently followed his own advice in consulting the poetry of "the *Mantuan Muse*" (Virgil) as the most illuminating of all "*Comment*[s]" (commentaries) on Homer (*Essay*, line 129).

POPE AND THE SCHOLARS

But Pope's conviction that it is poets rather than scholars who are ultimately best equipped to bring out Homer's abiding interest should not lead us to assume that he was neglectful of the many ways in which a communication of Homeric "Nature" and of the "fire and rapture" of his verse to modern readers would be dependent on a command of scholarly detail. Pope's claim was not that scholarship can be ignored but that scholarship not informed by a poet's empathetic insight into the "spirit" that animates the *Iliad* can easily lose touch with the very features that make Homer worth reading in the first place and, thus, degenerate into mere pedantry. At the very beginning of his Observations, he expresses his reservations about existing Homeric scholarship, and he sets out the ways in which his own Homeric commentary will be significantly different from those that preceded it:

> It is something strange that of all the Commentators upon *Homer*, there is hardly one whose principal Design is to illustrate the Poetical Beauties of the Author. They are Voluminous in explaining those Sciences which he made but subservient to his Poetry, and sparing only upon that Art which constitutes his Character. This has been occasion'd by the Ostentation of Men who had more Reading than Taste, and were fonder of showing their Variety of Learning in all Kinds, than their single Understanding in Poetry. Hence it comes to pass that their Remarks are rather Philosophical, Historical, Geographical, Allegorical, or in short rather any thing than Critical and Poetical. Even the

Grammarians, tho' their whole Business and Use be only to render the Words of an Author intelligible, are strangely touch'd with the Pride of doing something more than they ought. . . .

The chief Design of the following Notes is to comment upon *Homer* as a Poet. (1/ Introductory Note)

Pope's reservations about existing Homeric scholarship, and his emphasis on "Homer as a Poet," are, however, accompanied by frank acknowledgment of his debts to the scholarly tradition, particularly to the commentaries of Eustathius, the twelfth-century bishop of Thessalonica, and to the annotated prose translation by the contemporary French scholar Madame Anne Dacier.[22] He has also read carefully, albeit by no means uncritically, the earlier English renderings of Homer by Chapman, Hobbes, John Ogilby, and others. In in a letter to his friend Thomas Parnell, he lists yet more of his "sources": the editions of Homer by Spondanus (Jean de Sponde) and Joshua Barnes; the French translation by the abbé de la Valterie; and the miscellaneous writings on Homer of Leo Allatius, Gisbertus Cuperus, J. C. Scaliger, Macrobius, and Aulus Gellius.[23] But he is insistent on the constant obligation "to make something out of a hundred Pedants that is not Pedantical" (1/Introductory Note). Writing to one of his assistants, William Broome, who supplied him with translated extracts from Eustathius, Pope insisted:

> Be so kind to take this method: translate such notes only as concern the beauties or art of the author—none geographical, historical, or grammatical—unless some occur very important to the sense, and none of the poetical history. What are allegorical, if obvious and ingenious, abstract; if far-fetched, omit; but leave out none of the art or contrivance of the poet, or beauties, it being on account of these alone that I put you to this trouble.[24]

But, while insisting on the need to foreground "poetical" considerations, Pope is also aware of his obligation to ground his celebration of Homer's finest poetic moments in solid evidence and argument, rather than merely enthusiastic effusion. "Madame *Dacier*," he admits, "has made a farther Attempt than her Predecessors to discover the Beauties of the Poet," and "her Remarks all together are the most judicious Collection extant of the scatter'd Observations of the Ancients and Moderns." Her preface, moreover, is "excellent, and her Translation equally careful and elegant." But her specifically critical remarks are often too general, offering "general Praises and Exclamations instead of Reasons" (*TE*, 7:82–83). It is such "Reasons" that Pope seeks to provide in his Observations.

Pope's emphasis on the need for "poetical" commentary might prompt initial surprise at the substantial presence in his Observations of annotation that might seem to fall squarely into his rejected categories of the "historical," "grammatical," "philosophical," and "geographical." For a large number of Pope's notes are devoted to the detailed exposition of "antiquities"—of the circumstances in Homer's imagined world that are vital, if his narrative drift, and thus the force of his poetical vision, is to be properly experienced and understood by modern readers.

POPE AND THE HOMERIC WORLD

In his Observations, Pope expatiates at length on the mores of Homeric society. In book 1, he declares (1/600), Homer has provided us with the fullest extant description of an ancient sacrifice, the details of which Dryden (misled by Chapman) has seriously misrepresented in his translation: Dryden's sacrificers, Pope observes, eat the sacrificial meat, a procedure absolutely forbidden in the ancient world.[25] Elsewhere Pope comments on other features of Homeric social practices, conduct, and beliefs: the custom of warriors to shave their forelocks to prevent them being seized by the enemy (2/649); the swearing of solemn oaths (3/341); the delivery of prayers standing, rather than, as in Hebrew religion, kneeling (5/498); the need for respectful treatment of heralds (7/331); the handling of dead bodies and burial (5/361, 6/335, 7/399, 19/30, 19/209, 23/166); the importance in Homeric society of hospitality (6/267); the treatment of wives, mistresses, and bastards (5/92); the details of battle tactics (4/336 and the "Essay on Homer's Battels," 5/284, 5/353, 13/177, 14/442); the conduct of plowing (10/419), mowing (11/89), reaping (18/645) and horse-shoeing (11/197); the measurement of time (11/119); types of dancing (13/797); bathing customs (14/10); female dress (14/203, 22/600); tripods (9/159, 18/440), oracles (16/285), and beliefs about ghosts (23/92); the structure of tents (24/553) and fortifications (10/73); dining customs (7/387, 9/271–72); medicine (11/636); and the use of mules and oxen in funeral processions (7/507). Pope also comments on the distinctive social positions, hierarchies, and codes of conduct on which Homer's narrative depends: the legal basis of Agamemnon's seizure of Briseis (1/172), the precise nature and limits of Agamemnon's power—a power quite different from that of the absolute monarchs of Pope's own day (2/243)—the role of kings in performing sacrifices (3/364), the heroic ideals that prompt Homeric warriors to fight in the first place (12/371), the propriety of seizing an enemy's arms in battle, but not of mere pillaging (13/339). Pope is at pains to clarify those instances in which Homer differentiates the mores of his own time from those of the past age that he is imagining (7/520). Trumpets, for example, were used in Homer's time but not at Troy (3/3, 18/259). But the use of chariots depicted in the *Iliad* represents the practice of a heroic past rather than that of Homer's day (4/336). And in the feast offered by Achilles to the ambassadors, Homer is also depicting past rather than present "manners" (9/271).

I have discussed elsewhere Pope's scrupulous attentiveness to the temporal and spatial elements of Homer's narrative.[26] In the arguments to each book of his translation, in the "Essay on Homer's Battels," and in the map that he provided of the Trojan plain, he displays a detailed, almost novelistic, fascination with the minutiae of Homer's imagined scenario: the number and position of each army; the direction, speed, and timing of each military maneuver; the disposition of the Greek ships and positioning of their fortifications. Pope notes exactly where and when each event occurs, and he has a clear sense of the time taken over each action. Pope would, one imagines, have been quite prepared "to stand 'a stiff cross-examination'" on the geography of the Trojan plain and the movements and conduct of Homer's combat-ants.[27] His interest in this regard is fully supported in specific notes. A precise imag-ining of Homer's action, Pope declares (10/182, 14/1), is dependent on an accurate awareness of the location of each battle (11/217, 11/476, 15/472) and its timing (10/298). The reader also needs to know the numbers of warriors involved. Pope is particular (2/586) in listing all the contingents involved on the Greek side—an exactness, he says, not observed by any previous translator except Ogilby (2/906). Pope notes (2/155) the exact size of the Trojan army, correcting the suggestion of the fifteenth-century commentator Politian that the fifty thousand Trojan troops mentioned at the end of book 8 does not include the Trojan auxiliaries: the totality of the Trojan army is thus, he says, smaller than Politian had supposed. He describes (8/270, 14/39) the precise positioning of the Greek ships and the exact distribution of the Trojan army (12/99). He scrupulously notes (24/427) the timing and route of the journey that Priam makes to Achilles's tent to ransom the dead Hector's body. Homer's unparalleled capacity to involve the reader, Pope clearly believes, is inextri-cable from the detailed sense that he provides of the circumstances surrounding each incident in his narrative.

POPE AND HOMERIC LANGUAGE

If Pope is exact in his recording of Homeric mores and actions, he is equally scrupu-lous about details of Homeric expression, and about the rhetorical skill that Homer displays in the speeches of his characters. Some of Pope's earliest critics were eager to stress the limitations of the poet's knowledge of Greek.[28] Pope himself was conscious of his "imperfectness" in the Greek language, and he was aware of the attacks on his translations that his limitations in this regard would be likely to provoke.[29] Such criticisms have persisted to our own day. Joseph Levine, for example, has confidently dismissed Pope's erudition as "illusory," his Greek as "uncertain," and his scholarship as "nonexistent."[30] Pope, it must certainly be acknowledged, did not possess the kind of knowledge of Greek that would have enabled him, like Bentley, to expose the fraudulent attribution of the *Epistles of Phalaris* or, like Joshua Barnes, to produce a full-dress scholarly edition of Homer's text. But Samuel Johnson—hardly himself an indulgent witness in matters of scholarship—offers a judiciously positive account of Pope's qualifications as a Homeric translator,[31] and Pope's Twickenham editors, after a thorough survey of the relevant evidence, conclude that "Pope's understanding of Greek emerges as sufficient for his purpose."[32]

Perhaps partly out of anxiety not to be thought ignorant of, or inattentive to, the niceties of Homeric Greek, Pope devotes many of his notes to specifically linguistic and textual matters. On several occasions (2/485, 8/679, 9/586, 13/543, 16/113), he discusses variant readings in Homer's text, sometimes defending, and sometimes rejecting as spurious lines that had been included by various scholars and editors. Elsewhere, he comments on, and sometimes attempts to mirror in his version, the mimetic effects of Homer's verse, noting, for example, the melancholy flow of the lines describing Chryses's state of mind (2/47) and of Homer's verbal imitations of the sound of a breaking sword (3/447); of "Blood running in a long Trace" (4/177); of the fleeing Dolon's sudden loss of swiftness (10/444); of the "broken Pantings" of a dying warrior (13/720); of roaring waters (13/1005); of Achilles's labor in fighting the river (21/263); of the progress of the mules bearing the body of Patroclus (23/141); and of the "languishing" movement of a horse's luxurious bathing (6/656). On other occasions (1/41, 1/86, 1/413, 3/83, 5/261, 9/268, 16/288, 21/276, 22/167, 24/816), Pope clarifies the often contested meaning of particular Homeric words and phrases, and their bearing on the action at hand. He is also fully attentive to Homer's stylistic peculiarities. He will only, he says (1/117, 8/707), preserve Homer's repeated epithets in his version when they move beyond the merely routine and formulaic, to say something of specific relevance to the action. Thus (1/767) the description of Juno as "white armed" is retained, since, though it has been "used by *Homer* several times before in this Book" (and not translated by Pope on those occasions) "the Action she is here describ'd in, of extending her Arm to the Cup, gives it an occasion of displaying its Beauties, and in a manner demands the Epithet." On another occasion (1/478), Pope comments on Homer's repetitions, "one of those Faults which has with most Justice been objected to our Author," and defines the circumstances in which they are acceptable—for example, "where Messages are deliver'd in the Words they were received"—and those in which they seem merely "tedious." Milton's close imitation of Homer's repetitions is partly cited in their defense. Elsewhere (9/648) Pope homes in on what he perceives as a stylistic oddity in Homer, a "little Affectation" that—interestingly, in the light of the remark of Johnson's quoted above, and of his own extensive borrowings from Ovid when rendering Achilles's fight with the river in book 21[33]—he says one is more likely to find in Ovid than in Homer. He observes (13/353) that Homer's dialogue seems occasionally so colloquial that it resembles "Chit-chat." But on another occasion (4/352), he issues a general and salutary warning about the problems of determining the exact meaning and tone of *any* expression in a language as old, and as lacking in parallels, as Homer's.

POPE AND HOMERIC CHARACTERIZATION

Pope's concern with Homer's imagined world and with the details of his language is inseparable from his responsiveness to Homer's characterization. His *Observations* introduce each of Homer's characters on his or her first appearance, and they describe the main traits of each personage that are sustained throughout the poem's lengthy narrative. Pope thus provides elegant and pointed character sketches of Nestor (1/339), Agamemnon (2/93, 2/568, 11/headnote), Thersites (2/255), Menelaus (2/711, 3/278), Paris (3/37, 3/86, 3/551, 6/390), Hector (3/53), Priam (3/211), Diomedes (5/1), Aeneas (5/212, 13/578), Andromache (6/524), Ajax (11/591),

Idomeneus (13/278), Sarpedon (16/512, 16/605), and Hecuba (22/114). These are supplemented by detailed comments—often drawing on the ancient discussions by Dionysius of Halicarnassus and Quintilian—on the distinctive rhetoric and style of speech given by Homer to each of his characters. Pope is particularly attentive to the mellifluous persuasiveness and digressive garrulousness—sometimes perhaps exercised to a fault (11/800)—of Nestor (3/271, 7/145, 9/73), to the plain and orderly "*Laconick*" style of Menelaus, and the measured and cautious manner of Ulysses (3/135). He also notes Homer's telling use of silences in spoken exchanges (5/848), and he describes the developing dynamic of each speaker's utterances, for example, in the gradual "warming" of Achilles's speech as he addresses the ambassadors (9/406) and its subsequent cooling down (9/713).

It is in his discussion of the figure of Achilles that Pope's treatment of Homer's more challenging characterization is perhaps to be seen to its fullest and best advantage. Pope relays the moralistic interpretation of the *Iliad* offered by critic René Le Bossu as a warning "[t]hat a Misunderstanding between Princes is the Ruin of their own States,"[34] and he notes (20/541) that Achilles is proposed by Homer "not as a Pattern for Imitation" since "the Moral" that Homer "design'd the Reader should draw from [the *Iliad*], is, that we should avoid Anger, since it is ever pernicious in the Event." But the main emphasis of his commentary, as of the translation that it supports, is far less straightforwardly censorious than such a moralistic summary might seem to imply. Pope's main stress—fully in accord with his larger appreciation of Homer's distinctive genius—is not so much on moral condemnation as on the Greek poet's portrayal of Achilles as an awesome and inexorable force of Nature, possessed of a *mênis* that is far more than any mere "Wrath," and which will only ever subside because Nature itself "cannot support Anger eternally" (16/headnote).[35] Near the beginning of his commentary, Pope addresses the question directly, warning his readers that they should not misunderstand and, thus, feel "shock" at the actions that Achilles will shortly perform:

> We should know that the Poet rather study'd Nature than Perfection in the laying down his Characters. He resolv'd to sing the Consequences of Anger; . . . And thus we must take his *Achilles*, not as a mere heroick dispassion'd Character, but as compounded of Courage and Anger; one who finds himself almost invincible, and assumes an uncontroul'd Carriage upon the Self-consciousness of his Worth; whose high Strain of Honour will not suffer him to betray his Friends or fight against them, even when he thinks they have affronted him; but whose inexorable Resentment will not let him hearken to any terms of Accommodation. These are the Lights and Shades of his Character, which *Homer* has heighten'd and darken'd in Extreams; because on the one side Valour is the darling Quality of Epic Poetry, and on the other, Anger the particular Subject of this Poem. When Characters thus mix'd are well conducted, tho' they be not morally beautiful quite through, they conduce more to the end, and are still Poetically perfect. (1/155)

Pope reminds us on several occasions (e.g., 1/464, 9/532) of Achilles's choice of brief glory, followed by certain death, over a long life of obscure ease. Our memories of this crucial life decision are made to weigh upon us with particular intensity in the episode in book 21 that depicts Achilles's encounter, after his return to the battle, with Lycaon. Lycaon, a son of Priam and previously Achilles's captive, makes a ritual supplication for mercy, "amass[ing]," Pope says, many "moving Arguments" in an attempt to persuade Achilles to spare him. Achilles, however, "is immoveable, his Resentment makes him deaf to Entreaties" (21/84) and he kills Lycaon in a way that seems to show him at his most barbarously cruel, throwing his victim's corpse into the water and hoping that the fish will "surround" his "bloated Corse, and suck [his] goary Wound" (21.135–36). Pope comments:

> I must confess I could have wish'd *Achilles* had spared him: There are so many Circum-stances that speak in his Favour, that he deserv'd his Life, had he not ask'd it in Terms a little too abject.

But then Pope's commentary pointedly changes tack:

> There is an Air of Greatness in the Conclusion of the Speech of *Achilles*, which strikes me very much: He speaks very unconcernedly of his own Death, and upbraids his Enemy for asking Life so earnestly, a Life that was of so much less Importance than his own. (21/84)

In Pope's translation, Achilles's speech to Lycaon contains the following lines:

> Die then, my Friend! what boots it to deplore?
> The great, the good *Patroclus* is no more!
> He, far thy Better, was fore-doom'd to die,
> "And thou, dost thou, bewail Mortality?" (21.115–18)

Achilles's argument here, Pope realizes, resembles a passage in Lucretius (*De Rerum Natura*, 3:1042–52), in which the poet is admonishing mankind for bewailing a mortality that they share with the philosopher Epicurus, Lucretius's hero, and, in his view, someone whose life is worth far more than that of most men. Lucretius's lines were, in fact, a direct imitation (via Ennius)[36] of Homer's. In his translation, Pope borrows from Lucretius—in Dryden's 1685 translation, indicating the presence of the quotation with inverted commas[37]—the lines that Lucretius had himself bor-rowed from Homer. In doing so, he is simultaneously registering and capitalizing on one of those occasions in which a later poet has "cultivated" a "Seed" from the copious Homeric "Nursery." Achilles's actions here are clearly far removed from the *ataraxia* (freedom from disabling emotion) recommended by Lucretius. But the hero's clear-sighted acknowledgment of the inexorable laws that govern nature are imbued by Pope with the powerful, albeit unpalatable, wisdom of the Roman phi-losopher-poet. Several commentators have stressed the ways in which the language and ethos of Pope's *Homer* is in some ways closer to the more dignified, elevated, and measured epic decorum of Virgil than to Homer's earthier, more swift-moving, and more violent epic mode.[38] Here, however, Pope's presentation is in no way softened by Virgilian *dignitas*. At a moment when Achilles seems at his most extreme distance from the "polite" ideals of the eighteenth century, Pope is able to pay tribute to his "Air of Greatness" and to his ability to speak "unconcernedly" of his own certain fate. Here we are certainly light years away from Homer in "high-heeled shoes and a full-bottomed wig."

POPE AND HOMERIC COMPASSION

As well as demonstrating an unexpectedly positive responsiveness to such violent moments, Pope is equally appreciative of the tender and compassionate aspects of Homeric "Nature" that, as he points out (22/628), counterpoint the poem's main action. He writes, for example, with a particularly warm eloquence about Homer's use of telling details to animate the last parting of Hector and Andromache:

> There never was a finer Piece of Painting than this. *Hector* extends his Arms to embrace his Child; the Child affrighted at the glittering of his Helmet and the shaking of the Plume, shrinks backward to the Breast of his Nurse; *Hector* unbraces his Helmet, lays it on the Ground, takes the Infant in his Arms, lifts him towards Heaven, and offers a Prayer for him to the Gods: then returns him to the Mother *Andromache*, who receives him with a Smile of Pleasure, but at the same instant the Fears for her Husband make her burst into Tears. All these are but small Circumstances, but so artfully chosen, that every Reader immediately feels the force of them, and represents the whole in the utmost Liveliness to his Imagination. This alone might be a Confutation of that false Criticism some have fallen into, who affirm that a Poet ought only to collect the great and noble Particulars in his Paintings. But it is in the Images of Things as in the Characters of Persons; where a small Action, or even a small Circumstance of an Action, lets us more into the Knowledge and Comprehension of them, than the material and principal Parts themselves. . . . There is a vast difference betwixt a *small* Circumstance and a *trivial* one, and the smallest become important if they are well chosen, and not confused. (6/595)[39]

Pope's sympathy with Homer's more tender and pathetic imaginings is perhaps most sustainedly displayed in his response to Homer's treatment of Helen. Pope's notes to book 3 amply support the presentation of Helen in his translation as a suffering victim, fully and repentantly conscious of the suffering and destruction that her actions have caused, but impotent in the face of Venus's designs upon her. "The Reader," Pope notes, "has naturally an Aversion to this pernicious Beauty, and is apt enough to wonder at the *Greeks* for endeavouring to recover her at such an Expence":

> But her amiable Behaviour here, the secret Wishes that rise in favour of her rightful Lord, her Tenderness for her Parents and Relations, the Relentings of her Soul for the Mischiefs her Beauty had been the Cause of, the Confusion she appears in, the veiling of her Face and dropping a Tear, are Particulars so beautifully natural, as to make every Reader no less than *Menelaus* himself, inclin'd to forgive her at least, if not to love her. (3/165)

Such a general impression, Pope observes, is confirmed by the reaction of the Trojan counsellors, old men "who had suffer'd all the Calamities of a tedious War" who "seeing the only Cause of it approaching towards them, are struck with her Charms, and cry out, *No wonder!* &c." (3/203). It is also confirmed by Priam, who "encourages [Helen] by attributing the Misfortunes of the War to the Gods alone, and not to her Fault" (3/211):

> No Crime of thine our present Suff'rings draws,
> Not Thou, but Heav'ns disposing Will, the Cause:
> The Gods these Armies and this Force employ,
> The hostile Gods conspire the Fate of *Troy.* (3.215–18)[40]

POPE AND HOMERIC RELIGION

Pope's understanding of Helen's quintessentially Homeric predicament—the victim of Fate or the gods, but with an unshakeable feeling of responsibility for her actions[41]—is closely intertwined with his larger sense, expressed in both his translation and notes, of the theology that informs Homer's poem. Pope has sometimes been charged with bringing Homer's Olympian Gods into too close proximity to the beliefs of his own religion. In his account of Pope's handling of the quarrel between Jupiter and Juno in book 1, for example, H. A. Mason observes that Pope "effaces Homer . . . and makes Zeus speak to Hera as the Hebrew God might have addressed Milton's Lucifer":

> "What *is,* that *ought* to be"—could there be a greater anachronism than that? It summarizes Pope's whole procedure. That, he felt, was how God ought to speak, must speak, and therefore that is what Homer must have said, or, at least, must have meant to say.[42]

Pope certainly colors his descriptions of the Olympians at times with terms derived from his own religion. But he is also extremely concerned at various places in his notes to differentiate Homer's theology from his own. This can be seen in his treatment of allegorical interpretations of Homer, and of the similarities between Homeric and biblical lore and narrative that had been such a prominent feature of Madame Dacier's commentary. Pope, to be sure, quotes in his Observations many of the allegorical interpretations of Homer that had been offered by Eustathius and others, usually to defend Homer against his detractors. Some of these (e.g., 4/585, 7/327, 12/15, 21/447), he accepts in their broad outline—though often more for what might be called their larger suggestiveness than from any insistence on the necessity of a strictly allegorical reading—while others (e.g., 1/514, 11/773, 18/461) he dismisses as downright far-fetched and fanciful. Others, again, he cites noncommittally, offering them, it seems, merely for the reader's disinterested contemplation. As far as biblical parallels are concerned, Pope draws regularly on Madame Dacier for passages that depict Hebrew mores, artifacts, and behavior in ways that parallel those described by Homer. He also admits some of Dacier's parallels between Homeric and Hebrew divinity, and he makes a number of similar suggestions of his own—for example (12/9), that human existence in both Homer and scripture is short-lived without divine help, and (13/102) that the face of divinity cannot be looked at directly by men. But Pope insists firmly on the danger of pursuing such analogies too far and, particularly, on the danger of Dacier's suggestion that Homer's religion can be directly identified with, or was even derived from, that of the Bible. Commenting (8/95) on Dacier's likening of Jupiter's declaring himself against the Greeks by thunder and lightning to the conduct of the Hebrew God of Samuel 1 and Psalm 18, Pope reflects on the apparent similarities between Homeric and biblical depictions of divine inconsistency but concludes:

> I must confess, that in comparing Passages of the sacred Books with our Author one ought to use a great deal of Caution and Respect. If there are some Places in Scripture that in Compliance to human Understanding represent the Deity as acting by Motives like those of Men; there are infinitely more that shew him as he is, all Perfection, Justice, and Beneficence; whereas in *Homer* the general Tenor of the Poem represents *Jupiter* as a Being subject to Passion, Inequality, and Imperfection. I think M. *Dacier* has carry'd these Comparisons too far, and is too zealous to defend him upon every occasion in the Points of Theology and Doctrine.

Pope uses many of his notes to clarify the distinctive nature of Homeric theology and its effect on the human action of the poem. Homer's Jupiter, he maintains, certainly anticipates monotheism in important respects. Homer, Pope declares, had a "Belief of one supreme, omnipotent God, whom he introduces with a Majesty and Superiority worthy the great Ruler of the Universe" (8/35). His promises are always honest and effective (1/61), and Pope defends him on two occasions (2/9, 4/18) against potential charges of deceit and perjury. On several occasions, Pope meditates on the precise powers of Jupiter. At the very beginning of the Observations (1/8), he attempts to make sense of Homer's puzzling theology and view of free will. Plutarch, he reports, interprets Homer's *Dios boulê* ("the will of God"; *Iliad* 1.5), as referring not to Jupiter but to Fate, since it would not be "consistent with the Goodness of the supreme Being, or *Jupiter*, to contrive or practise any Evil against Men." Eustathius, on the other hand, makes Jupiter's "will" here "refer to the Promise which *Jupiter* gave to *Thetis*, that he would honour her Son by siding with *Troy* while he should be absent." Pope proposes a third possibility: that Fate has decreed the destruction of Troy, and that Jupiter fulfilled that decree by providing the means whereby it might come to pass. But, he points out, Homer makes clear in book 16 that Jove *can*, at least in theory, countermand the decrees of Fate, since he designs to save his son Sarpedon, even though the Fates have decreed his death (16/535). And the opening of the *Odyssey* shows that Homer believes in human free will, since the destruction of Odysseus's colleagues is here attributed to their own folly. Jupiter's foreknowledge of future events, Pope argues in a long note (15/67), is rendered by Homer in a manner that in no way compromises our sustained interest in how the events of his narrative will work out. But Homer's gods, he insists, should not be in any simple way assimilated to Christian theology. Though, as Pope notes, Milton has drawn on the passage describing Nature's "Tokens of Joy at the Performance of the nuptial Rites" of Jupiter and Juno for his Adam's and Eve's lovemaking both before and after the Fall, drawing on the very "Turn" and "Cadence" of Homer's verse to convey the "beauty" of the scene, and though Pope himself renders the scene with evident relish, we should not, Pope insists, forget that Homer's episode, viewed from the point of view of his own religion, is "an impious Fiction" (14/395). Homer's heaven, moreover, is characterized by the same dissent and anger that are to be seen on earth (1/694). And the combat between his deities is often marked by insults and violence. Unless there is some allegorical significance in the relevant passages, Pope declares— and allegory, he insists, is flawed if its purpose cannot be easily fathomed—Homer sometimes properly deserves "the Censure past upon him by the Ancients, that as he rais'd the Characters of his Men up to the Gods, so he sunk those of Gods down to Men" (21/566).

SIMILES AND "LOW TERMS"

Many of the earliest and most persistent criticisms of Homer focused on the poet's conduct of his similes, and particularly on his comparisons of heroic action with "low" or "indecorous" occupations or phenomena. Homer, in the judgement of the early scholiasts, was often guilty of *aprepeia* (violations of decorum) that seriously marred the dignity of his epics. And such criticisms are paralleled in a lengthy tradition of Homeric commentary stretching from Xenophanes, Plato, and Zoilus in antiquity, through the Renaissance humanists Scaliger and Marco Vida, to the French *modernes* of the seventeenth century.[43] Later commentary has viewed Homer's homely touches more favorably and has criticized Pope for giving us an *Iliad* that has been inappropriately "improved" in a decorous and "polite" direction. In the two chapters devoted to the similes in *To Homer through Pope*, Mason pays tribute to some aspects of Pope's responses to his Greek original but, ultimately, judges Pope both to have expected from Homer's similes a tighter degree of correspondence between tenor and vehicle than they, in fact, possess, and to have had a narrower concept of Nature than Homer's. Pope, Mason argues, was therefore unwilling to follow the Greek poet in his uncensorious comparisons of his heroes to brutal and savage animals. Pope, Mason also maintains, "seizes every opportunity . . . to make the hero more heroic"[44] and, in line with the general Virgilian tendency of his translation, regularly departs from Homer to see his comparisons through more orderly and decorous spectacles provided by Virgil's imitations.

One example selected by Mason is the description of the actions of Menelaus in book 17, when, stirred up by Minerva, he rushes to defend the body of Patroclus from the Trojans. On this simile, Pope comments:

> It is literally in the *Greek, she inspir'd the Hero with the Boldness of a Fly.* There is no Impropriety in the Comparison, this Animal being of all others the most persevering in its Attacks, and the most difficult to be beaten off: The Occasion also of the Comparison being the resolute Persistance of *Menelaus* about the dead Body, renders it still the more just. But our present Idea of the Fly is indeed very low, as taken from the Littleness and Insignificancy of this Creature. However, since there is really no Meanness in it, there ought to be none in expressing it; and I have done my best in the Translation to keep up the Dignity of my Author. (17/642)

Mason thinks that such comments represent such a clear case of Pope's "desperate . . . need to raise the author's dignity," that "commentary" is "superfluous."[45] But let us consider Pope's rendering of the simile a little more closely:

> So burns the vengeful Hornet (Soul all o'er)
> Repuls'd in vain, and thirsty still of Gore;
> (Bold Son of Air and Heat) on angry Wings
> Untam'd, untir'd, he turns, attacks, and stings:
> Fir'd with like Ardour fierce *Atrides* flew,
> And sent his Soul with ev'ry Lance he threw. (17.642–47)

Pope's note makes clear that his substitution of "hornet" for Homer's "fly" is (*pace* Mason) not effected to enhance Menelaus's stature. The intention of Homer's simile, Pope argues, was to stress the "resolute persistence" of Menelaus in the fighting around the body of Patroclus and the fact that he is "persevering in [his] attacks," like a fly, "the most difficult [of "animals"] to be beaten off." Homer's simile does not work so well for English readers because "our present idea of the fly [i.e., that prevailing in England in 1720] is indeed very low, as taken from the littleness and insignificance of this creature." Here "low" clearly means not "vulgar" or "gross," but "unimportant" or "tiresome, rather than seriously threatening." A hornet, Pope thinks, is the English insect that conveys most powerfully the noxious, aggressive, bloodthirsty, and unyielding nature of Menelaus's behavior. (The standard modern commentary on the *Iliad* confirms that Homer is primarily thinking of the "bold persistence" and "longing for blood" of his flies.)[46] Thus, when Pope says that his substitution of "hornet" for "fly" was designed to "keep up the dignity of [his] author," his suggestion is not that his comparison will make Homer's hero more "dignified," but that the substitution will bring out, in terms intelligible to his English readers, the serious point of Homer's comparison.

Pope does, indeed, as both Pamela Poynter Schwandt and Robin Sowerby have confirmed, sometimes draw on Virgil's imitations of Homeric similes to make Homer's comparisons more orderly and coherent, and less digressive, and to give them a greater point-by-point correspondence.[47] But both critics have also shown that his interventions are often motivated less by a snobbish or fashion-conscious desire to eliminate Homer's "low" or "vulgar" elements than by an attempt to maintain a cogent connection between Homer's local observations and his larger themes. In his discussion of the comparison of Greek warriors to flies around milk pails, for example, Pope's prime consideration is not on the "lowness" of the simile in itself but with the discrepancy between the image and those that precede it (2/552). Pope's solution is, therefore, not to eliminate the comparison but to reorder the sequence of images and to "heighten the Expression" (and then only marginally, from "flies" to "insects") "so as to render the Disparity less observable." And in the same Observation, Pope notes, with apparent approval, Milton's "close" copying of Homer in such "humble Comparisons." Pope, moreover, as Schwandt shows,[48] by no means always avoids "low" terms if he thinks they are fully appropriate to the occasion on which they are employed. When, as in the passage depicting the fighting around Patroclus's body, warriors are again compared to flies swarming around a milk pail, Pope does not hesitate, this time, to translate Homer's "flies" as "flies" (16.781). Similarly, when Homer likens the Trojan counselors (3.201) to "grasshoppers" (cicadas), Pope again follows the Homeric comparison exactly. And when the Trojans fleeing from Achilles into the river are compared with locusts fleeing from a burning field, Pope, once again, relays the "locust" image intact (21.14).

Many of Pope's notes, moreover, defend Homer's similes directly, sometimes by pointing out a precision of appropriateness that, because of changes in mores, or unfamiliarities of locale or circumstance, modern readers might miss, and sometimes by arguing that the salient words had less demeaning overtones than their most obvious equivalents in modern English, and therefore would have produced a different, and less incongruous, effect on their original audience. In several places (2/111, 2/534, 3/7, 3/37, 4/170, 4/478, 7/71, 8/371, 13/191, 16/194), Pope defends Homer's similes against their detractors by detailed analyses, spelling out their precise point-by-point appropriateness at length or (conversely) by arguing that Homer sometimes allows the reader freedoms precluded by over-tight correspondences. Elsewhere, he reminds his readers of felicities in Homer's figurative language that are dependent on phenomena with which modern readers might not be familiar. The aptness of Homer's comparison of troops about to enter battle with storm clouds about to break is likely, Pope says (5/641), to be undervalued if readers are not acquainted with weather conditions in mountainous regions. Elsewhere (14/21), he suggests that readers are likely to misunderstand Homer's evocation of the fluctuations of Nestor's mind if they have not experienced the swelling ebb and flow of a calm at sea. In other places, our appreciation is enhanced by knowledge of the times that Homer depicted or in which he wrote. Homer's comparison of battle scenes to particularities of "rural Life," such as threshing and mowing, is not to be taken as demeaning, since "in early Times, before Politeness had rais'd the Esteem of Arts subservient to Luxury, above those necessary to the Subsistence of Mankind, Agriculture was the Employment of Persons of the greatest Esteem and Distinction" (13/739). Pope explicitly defends several of Homer's similes referring specifically to "the meanest and smallest things in Nature." Homer's comparison of the Myrmidons to wasps, for example, is made "not on account of their Strength and Bravery but of their Heat and Resentment." His comparison of soldiers to flies is designed to stress "their busy Industry and Perseverance about a dead Body; not diminishing his Heroes by the Size of these small Animals, but raising his Comparisons from certain Properties inherent in them, which deserve our Observation" (16/314). The "humble" comparison of Pallas's protection of Menelaus to a mother protecting her sleeping child from a fly (or a hornet)[49] is defended (4/163) both for its precise appropriateness and its sublimity of religious implication:

> The Care of the Goddess, the unsuspecting Security of *Menelaus*, the Ease with which she diverts the Danger, and the Danger itself, are all included in this short Compass. To which it may be added, that if the Providence of heavenly Powers to their Creatures is exprest by the Love of a Mother to her Child, if Men in regard to them are but as heedless sleeping Infants, and if those Dangers which may seem great to us, are by them as easily warded off as the Simile implies; there will appear something sublime in this Conception, however little or low the Image may be thought at first sight in respect to a Heroe. A higher Comparison would but have tended to lessen the Disparity between the Gods and Man, and the Justness of the Simile had been lost, as well as the Grandeur of the Sentiment.

Pope, to be sure, on occasion believes that to follow Homer's "low terms" directly would be simply unacceptable to his eighteenth-century readers. He cannot, he says, find any graceful English equivalents for Ulysses's felt cap (10/309), for Iris's bitter reproach ("*kuon adëes*"; "audacious dog"; 8/522), for the young Achilles's vomiting wine over his tutor, Phoenix (9/612), or for Hector's supposedly "scandalous" epithet (*thêluterai*)[50] for the Trojan women (8/648). In one of the most famous of his notes in book 11, Pope considers Homer's comparison of the retreating Ajax to an ass. He cites André Dacier's observation that "'[t]he Name of that Animal was not then converted into a Term of Reproach, but it was a Beast upon which Kings and Princes might be seen with Dignity,'" and Madame Dacier's insistence that Homer's main focus is not (as la Motte had suggested in his translation) on the "obstinate Gluttony" of the ass but on its "Patience . . . Obstinacy, and Strength," and continues:

> To judge rightly of Comparisons, we are not to examine if the Subject from when they are deriv'd be great of little, noble or familiar; but we are principally to consider if the Image produc'd be clear and lively, if the Poet has the Skill to dignify it by poetical Words, and if it perfectly paints the thing it is intended to represent.

"However, upon the whole," Pope continues,

> a Translator owes so much to the Taste of the Age in which he lives, as not to make too great a Complement to a former; and this induced me to omit the mention of the word *Ass* in the Translation.

But Pope's note ends with a lengthy translation of a passage from Boileau's "Remarks on Longinus," in which the French critic had argued that terms that may seem "elegant" or "noble" in Greek may not have the same resonance if replaced by their most obvious equivalents in other languages:

> Thus the word *Asinus* in *Latin*, and *Ass* in *English*, are the vilest imaginable, but that which signifies the same Animal in *Greek* and *Hebrew*, is of Dignity enough to be employed on the most magnificent Occasions. (11/668)

Pope's omission of Homer's "ass" is, therefore, not an objection to humble words per se but to his conviction that the English word, in this particular context, will jar on his readers, and produce an effect far from Homer's original intentions.

But, if Pope does sometimes omit details in Homer that might seem merely "mean" to his readers, his usual tactic—as, for example, at 7/270, where he adopts the translation "Armourer" for "Leather-dresser," when both are equally possible renderings of the Greek—is to find terms that are both faithful to Homer's meaning and simultaneously acceptable to more "polite" tastes. And though, as we have seen, he reshapes and reorders some of his similes along Virgilian lines, praises the intrinsic beauty of many of Virgil's Homeric echoes, and invokes the authority of some of Virgil's interpretations of Homer to support his own readings (3/7, 4/478, 4/502), he also frequently comments on the inferiority of Virgil's imitations to their Homeric originals—or their use for very different purposes than Homer's (2/111, 4/170, 5/116, 5/1054, 6/652, 8/371, 10/301, 13/43, 13/191, 14/264). Elsewhere—as in the lengthy note on the funeral games at the end of book 23—he juxtaposes Homer's and Virgil's treatment of similar material in order to bring out the characteristic strengths of both, rather than to set either above the other.

CONCLUSION

Pope's Observations on his *Iliad* clearly confirm his devotion to communicating Homer's poetic "fire" and "force" and to involving his readers in every detail of the Greek poet's constantly "animated" action. They also show that Pope's engagement with Homer was more sophisticated, more diverse in its responsiveness, less predictable in its conclusions, and more historically attuned than the crude and complacent "accommodation" of Homer to "polite" eighteenth-century tastes still described in many accounts. Pope's Observations record a subtle and ever-developing transhistorical dialogue, in which the English poet both acknowledges his great predecessor's (sometimes disturbing) otherness and simultaneously confirms Homer's ability to speak powerfully and irresistibly across time.

Even some admirers of Pope's translation, however, have maintained that his recreation of the *Iliad*, for all its virtues, offers an experience significantly narrower in its linguistic range and less comprehensive in its imaginative sympathies than Homer's original. Like Shakespeare, such critics have argued, Homer could command a capacious range of diction, from the sublime and lofty to the plain and earthy, and could modulate rapidly and effortlessly between such extremes. Pope, they have suggested, conscious of the need at all costs to avoid prosaic "flatness," generally renders Homer's text at a more consistent level of stylistic elevation than is found in the Greek. He thus misses the "just pitch" of the Homeric style.

Such arguments may have some measure of truth. But they also may underestimate the difficulty of achieving any degree of certainty about the effects of diction, tone, and register in a language as ancient and unparalleled as Homer's. Colin Burrow has observed that while "Homer is hard not to read as a unified and intelligible author" it is nevertheless "difficult to avoid feeling at the same time that the Homeric poems are, to some degree, falling apart." Burrow cites Pope's Observations as one among many instances of later writers' attempts to "hold Homer together" and "to impose a consistent sense" on his narratives.[51] It is perhaps more difficult than is sometimes supposed to determine at any point whether Pope's translation and commentary are trammeling Homer's poetic flights, or giving the *Iliad* a conceptual coherence and linguistic consistency that it actually lacks in the original. Be that as it may, what seems certain is that no other English translation of Homer has been able to recreate the narrative of the *Iliad* in as poetically compelling and satisfying a way as Pope's. When compared with his version, all the other English "Homers" have seemed (like Chapman's) quaint, wayward, and eccentric, or (like Hobbes's and Ogilby's) lame and awkward, or (like Cowper's) stiff and stilted, or (like Lattimore's) literal minded and prosaic.[52] Only Pope has produced a version that is both a consistently and intelligently focused response to Homer's original and, in the words of George Steiner, "a masterpiece in its own right and an epic which, as far as English goes, comes second only to Milton."[53] The eloquent and often moving Observations that accompany Pope's translation form an integral part of the sustained celebration of Homer's "poetic fire" that is so vividly and consistently embodied in the translation itself.

NOTES

1. I am grateful to Sandra Hopkins, Charles Martindale, Tom Mason, and Paul Hammond for their helpful comments on a draft of this chapter.

2. *The Twickenham Edition of the Poems of Alexander Pope*, ed. John Butt et al., 11 vols. (London: Methuen, 1939–1969; henceforth *TE*) has long since been out of print. Penguin has discontinued Shankman's edition, and though a reprint is now available (Eugene, OR: Wipf & Stock, 2009), it is beyond the price range of many ordinary readers.

3. See, particularly, the extensive introduction in *TE*, 7:xxv–ccxlix; Howard Clarke, *Homer's Readers: A Historical Introduction to the* Iliad *and the* Odyssey (Newark: University of Delaware Press, 1981), 135–40; Paul Davis, *Translation and the Poet's Life: The Ethics of Translating in English Culture, 1646–1726* (Oxford: Oxford University Press, 2008), chap. 4; David Hopkins, *Conversing with Antiquity: English Poets and the Classics, from Shakespeare to*

Pope (Oxford: Oxford University Press, 2010), chaps. 10–12; David Hopkins, "Homer," in *The Oxford History of Classical Reception in English Literature*, vol. 3, *1660–1790*, ed. David Hopkins and Charles Martindale (Oxford: Oxford University Press, 2012), 165–95; Douglas Knight, *Pope and the Heroic Tradition: A Critical Study of his* Iliad (New Haven, CT: Yale University Press, 1951); G. F. Parker, "'Talking Scripture out of Church': Parson Adams and the Practicality of Translation," *Translation and Literature* 14, no. 2 (2005): 179–95; G. F. Parker, "Classic Simplicity," in *Translation and the Classic: Identity as Change in the History of Culture*, ed. Alexandra Lianeri and Vanda Zajko (Oxford: Oxford University Press, 2008), 227–42; Matthew Reynolds, *The Poetry of Translation: From Chaucer & Petrarch to Homer & Logue* (Oxford: Oxford University Press, 2011), chaps. 19 and 20; Felicity Rosslyn, "The Making of Pope's Translation of the *Iliad*" (PhD diss., University of Cambridge, 1978); Felicity Rosslyn, "Pope on the Subject of Old Age: The *Iliad* Translation, Books XXII–XXIV," in *The Art of Alexander Pope*, ed. Howard Erskine-Hill and Anne Smith (London: Vision Press, 1979), 119–31; Felicity Rosslyn, "'Awed by Reason': Pope on Achilles," *Cambridge Quarterly* 9 (1980): 189–202; Felicity Rosslyn, "Heroic Couplet Translation—a Unique Solution?," in *Translating Literature*, ed. Susan Bassnett (Cambridge: Boydell and Brewer, 1997), 41–63; Pamela Poynter Schwandt, "Pope's Transformation of Homer's Similes," *Studies in Philology* 76, no. 4 (1979): 387–417; Steven Shankman, *Pope's* Iliad: *Homer in the Age of Passion* (Princeton, NJ: Princeton University Press, 1983); Robin Sowerby, "The Augustan *Odyssey*," *Translation and Literature* 4, no. 2 (1995): 157–82; Robin Sowerby, "The Decorum of Pope's *Iliad*," *Translation and Literature* 13, no. 1 (2004): 49–79; Robin Sowerby, *The Augustan Art of Poetry: Augustan Translation of the Classics* (Oxford: Oxford University Press, 2006). H. A. Mason's *To Homer through Pope: An Introduction to Homer's* Iliad *and Pope's Translation* (London: Chatto and Windus, 1972), though in some ways one of the most stimulating accounts of Pope's Homer, is declaredly more concerned to use the translation as a "way in" to Homer himself, rather than to assess the merits of Pope's version per se. The closer we approach Homer through Pope, Mason suggests, "the more aware we are of the respects in which Pope is unhelpful" (177). In "Translation and Commentary: Pope's *Iliad*," in *Classical Commentaries: Explorations in a Scholarly Genre*, ed. Christina S. Kraus and Christopher Stray (Oxford: Oxford University Press, 2016), Stuart Gillespie considers Pope's relation to the traditions of commentary on both classical and English authors.

   4. For variants of this anecdote, see Samuel Johnson, *Lives of the Most Eminent English Poets*, ed. Roger Lonsdale, 4 vols. (Oxford: Clarendon Press, 2006), 4:314n285. For other early critical responses, see Johnson, *Lives of the Most Eminent English Poets*, 4:333–34n349. It might be noted that, since *pretty* is a stronger word in eighteenth-century English than it is nowadays (see the *Oxford English Dictionary*, definition A.1.a–b). Bentley's remark (if accurately reported) isn't necessarily as unqualifiedly adverse as a modern reader might suppose.

   5. Leslie Stephen, *A History of English Thought in the Eighteenth Century*, 3rd ed., 2 vols. (London: Smith, Elder, 1902), 2:353–57; Leslie Stephen, *English Literature and Society in the Eighteenth Century* (London: Duckworth, 1904), 88.

   6. Cf. Leslie Stephen, *Alexander Pope* (London: Macmillan, 1880), 74. In his lectures *On Translating Homer* (1861), Arnold had found Pope's version culpably overintellectualized and wanting in conveying what he took to be the key principal qualities of Homer's art: rapidity, plainness, directness, and nobility. See Matthew Arnold, *On the Classical Tradition*, ed. R. H. Super (Ann Arbor: University of Michigan Press, 1960).

   7. Peter Levi, "Homer in Silver-Gilt," *TLS*, January 5, 1973; Norman Nicholson, *William Cowper* (London: John Lehmann, 1951), 150–51.

8. On this translation, see Noémi Hepp, *Homère en France au XVIIe siècle* (Paris: Klincks-ieck, 1968), 661–88; Kirsti Simonsuuri, *Homer's Original Genius: Eighteenth-Century Notions of the Early Greek Epic (1688–1798)* (Cambridge: Cambridge University Press, 1979), chap. 3; Richard Morton, *Examining Changes in the Eighteenth-Century Translations of Homer's* Iliad *by Anne Dacier and Houdar de la Motte* (Lewiston, NY: Mellen Press, 2003).

9. Bezaleel Morrice, *Three Satires* (London: Printed for J. Roberts, 1719), 8. For similar comments, see Johnson, *Lives of the Most Eminent English Poets*, 4:333–34.

10. Joseph Spence, *An Essay on Pope's* Odyssey (London: Printed for James and J. Knapton et al., 1726–1727), 2–3. For a discussion of Spence's dialogic approach, see Sowerby, "Augustan *Odyssey.*"

11. Johnson, *Lives of the Most Eminent English Poets*, 4:73.

12. Ibid., 4:74.

13. Ibid., 4:74.

14. Ibid., 4:17, 72–73.

15. Johnson's suggestion (for which see also Johnson, *Lives of the Most Eminent English Poets*, 4:15) is supported by David Foxon's account of the need for notes to fill out the instalments of the subscription edition. See David Foxon, *Pope and the Early Eighteenth-Century Book Trade*, ed. James McLaverty (Oxford: Clarendon Press, 1991), 51.

16. Johnson, *Lives of the Most Eminent English Poets*, 4:74.

17. Parker, "'Talking Scripture out of Church,'" 181–82.

18. *TE*, 7:4. All quotations from Pope are from *TE*. References for quotations from the preface are hereafter given in text by volume and page. Reference to the text and notes of Pope's translation are given in text by line or book- and line numbers, in the style 1.1 for the text of the translation, and 1/1 for notes. In my own text, I follow Pope's use of Latin equivalents for the names of Homer's gods and human characters. For the implications of Pope's "fire" image, see Reynolds, *Poetry of Translation*, chap. 19.

19. H. A. Mason, *Humanism and Poetry in the Early Tudor Period* (London: Methuen, 1959), 15.

20. John Dryden, preface to *Fables, Ancient and Modern*, in *The Poems of John Dryden*, ed. Paul Hammond and David Hopkins, 5 vols. (New York: Pearson/Longman, 1995–2005), 5:76. For the paradox, compare Clifford Geertz: "the significant works of the human imagination . . . speak with equal power to the consoling piety that we are all like to one another and to the worrying suspicion that we are not" (*Local Knowledge: Further Essays in Interpretive Anthropology* [London: Fontana Press, 1993], 42).

21. Alexander Pope to Ralph Bridges, April 5, 1708, in *The Correspondence of Alexander Pope*, ed. George Sherburn, 5 vols. (Oxford: Clarendon Press, 1956), 1:44.

22. On Pope's complex relations with Madame Dacier, see Howard D. Weinbrot, "'What Must the World Think of Me?': Pope, Madame Dacier, and Homer—the Anatomy of a Quarrel," in *Eighteenth-Century Contexts: Historical Inquiries in Honor of Phillip Harth*, ed. Howard D. Weinbrot, Peter J. Schakel, and Stephen E. Karian (Madison: University of Wisconsin Press, 2001), 183–206.

23. Alexander Pope to Thomas Parnell, in Sherburn, *Correspondence of Alexander Pope*, 1:225. For further information on Pope's sources in his notes, see *TE*, and Hans-Joachim Zimmermann, *Alexander Popes Noten zu Homer* (Heidelberg: Carl Winter Universitätsverlag, 1966). For the sources of the translation itself, see *The Iliad of Homer. Translated by Alexander Pope, Esq., a New Edition, with Additional Notes, Critical and Illustrative*, ed. Gilbert Wake-

field, 6 vols. (London: For T. Longman et al., 1796); *TE*, 7:cvii–clxiii; 10:appendix F; Rosslyn, "Making of Pope's Translation," passim.

24. Alexander Pope to William Broome, November 29, 1714, in Sherburn, *Correspondence of Alexander Pope*, 1:270.

25. Pope also criticized Thomas Tickell's translation on these grounds: see Felicity Rosslyn, "Pope's Annotations to Tickell's *Iliad* Book One," *Review of English Studies* 30, no. 117 (1979): 52–53. Pope's friend John Arbuthnot praised Pope for the scrupulousness of his rendering of "*ancient Ceremonies and Rites*, &c.": see John Arbuthnot to Alexander Pope, July 9, 1715, in Sherburn, *Correspondence of Alexander Pope*, 1:305.

26. See "Pope's Trojan Geography," in Hopkins, *Conversing with Antiquity*, 270–92.

27. Mrs. Brookenham in *The Awkward Age*. See *The Notebooks of Henry James*, ed. F. O. Matthiessen and Kenneth B. Murdock (Oxford: Oxford University Press, 1947), 193.

28. See *TE*, 7:lxxxi–cvii; Johnson, *Lives of the Most Eminent English Poets*, 4:259–60. Pope, as a Roman Catholic, had been denied the kind of school and university education experienced, for example, by his great predecessor Dryden.

29. See Pope to Bridges in 1708, quoted by Johnson (*Lives of the Most Eminent English Poets*, 4:438 = Sherburn, *Correspondence of Alexander Pope*, 1:43–45), and Alexander Pope to John Caryll, May 1, 1714, in Sherburn, *Correspondence of Alexander Pope*, 1:220.

30. Joseph M. Levine, *The Battle of the Books: History and Literature in the Augustan Age* (Ithaca, NY: Cornell University Press, 1991), 195.

31. Johnson, *Lives, of the Most Eminent English Poets*, 4:14–17

32. *TE*, 7:lxxxviii.

33. See Rosslyn, "Making of Pope's Translation," 80–81; Rosslyn, "Heroic Couplet Translation," 52–59.

34. See Pope's summary of Le Bossu, appended to his translation of Homer's *Odyssey*, *TE*, 9:6.

35. On Pope's positive appreciation of Homer's Achilles, see Clarke, *Homer's Readers*, 136–40; Rosslyn, "'Awed by Reason'"; and Sowerby, "Decorum of Pope's *Iliad*," 62–79.

36. See Rosslyn, "Making of Pope's Translation," 118.

37. "Lucretius: Against the Fear of Death," in Hammond and Hopkins, *The Poems of John Dryden*, 2:328 (lines 237–39).

38. On this subject, see particularly Mason, *To Homer through Pope*; Rosslyn, "Making of Pope's Translation"; and Sowerby, *Augustan Art of Poetry*.

39. For an appreciative near-contemporary appreciation of Pope's translation of this episode, see Sir Thomas Fitzosborne [William Melmoth], *Letters on Several Subjects* (London: Printed for R. Dodsley, 1748), 189–90.

40. Pope's contemporary George Sewell responded warmly to the poet's presentation of Helen, describing her as a "guilty, lovely Dame, / Worthy to set another World on Flame." See "To Mr Pope on His Poems and Translations," in *A New Collection of Original Poems* (London: Printed for J. Pemberton and J. Peele, 1720), 62.

41. See Albin Lesky, "Motivation by Gods and Men," trans. H. M. Harvey, in *Homer: Critical Assessments*, ed. Irene J. F. de Jong, 4 vols. (London: Routledge, 1999), 2:384–403. Bernard Williams, *Shame and Necessity* (Berkeley: University of California Press, 1993), passim.

42. Mason, *To Homer through Pope*, 54.

43. See Clarke, *Homer's Readers*, chap. 3; on early responses, see M. Van der Valk, *Researches on the Text and Scholia of the* Iliad, 2 vols. (Leiden: E. J. Brill, 1963–1964), passim, and Nigel Wilson, "Scholiasts and Commentators," *Greek, Roman, and Byzantine Studies* 47 (2007): 61;

on the Renaissance humanists, see Robin Sowerby, "Early Humanist Failure with Homer," *International Journal of the Classical Tradition* 4, no. 1 (1997): 37–63, 165–94; on the French *modernes*, see Hepp, *Homère en France*, 521–90, 629–755; Levine, *Battle of the Books*, chap. 4.

44. Mason, *To Homer through Pope*, 79, 88.

45. Ibid., 100–101.

46. *The Iliad: A Commentary*, vol. 5, *Books 17–20*, ed. Mark W. Edwards (Cambridge: Cambridge University Press, 1991), 117–18.

47. See Sowerby, *Augustan Art of Poetry*; Sowerby, "Decorum of Pope's *Iliad*"; and Schwandt, "Pope's Transformation of Homer's Similes."

48. Schwandt, "Pope's Transformation of Homer's Similes," 410.

49. "Hornet" appears in Pope's lemma to the Observation. In his *Dictionary*, Johnson defines "hornet" as "a very large strong stinging fly."

50. The English translation of Dacier by Ozell, Broome, and Oldisworth, consulted by Pope, takes the epithet to refer to female sexual appetites, and thus to be "very dishonourable to the Ladies" (*The Iliad of Homer, Translated from the Greek into Blank Verse, by Mr. Ozell, Mr. Broom, and Mr. Oldisworth, to which Are Added a Preface, the* Life of Homer, *and Notes by Madam Dacier*, 2nd ed., 2 vols. [London: Printed for Bernard Lintot, 1714], 2:214). The English translators obviously regarded the matter as so scandalous that their (English) explanation is disguised in Greek characters. The standard modern commentary passes over the epithet with no further comment than that it is "presumably" designed "to emphasize the functional differentiations of age and sex'" (*The Iliad: A Commentary*, vol. 2, *Books 5–8*, ed. G. S. Kirk [Cambridge: Cambridge University Press, 1990], 337).

51. Colin Burrow, *Epic Romance: Homer to Milton* (Oxford: Clarendon Press, 1993), 11–12.

52. For some pointed criticisms to such effect, see Mason, *To Homer through Pope*, 179–206; Parker, "'Talking Scripture out of Church,'" 186–87; David Ricks, "On Looking into the First Paperback of Pope's Homer," *Classics Ireland* 4 (1997): 97–120; Rosslyn, "The Making of Pope's Translation," 39–74, 97–102; Rosslyn, "Heroic Couplet Translation"; Sowerby, *Augustan Art of Poetry*, 336–52; Donald Carne-Ross, "A Mistaken Ambition of Exactness: Richmond Lattimore's *Odyssey*," in *Classics and Translation: Essays by D. S. Carne-Ross*, ed. Kenneth Haynes (Lewisburg, PA: Bucknell University Press, 2010), 123–51.

53. George Steiner, "Lessons of Falling Darkness," *TLS*, November 19, 1982.

7

Allusion and Quotation in Chaucerian Annotation, 1687–1798

Tom Mason

The diversity of allusion, the plenitude of curious matters treated, the unnecessary elaboration, and the apparent digressive impertinence of many eighteenth-century annotations on Chaucer's poetry, as on that of others, make it impossible to summarize (and sometimes even to guess at) the procedures that gave them form. This chapter is concerned with one particular species of note, one that was frequently represented or repeated, for example, in William Dodd's *The Beauties of Shakespear* (1752). Commenting on Hamlet's suggestion (act 4, scene 4) that "Looking before and after" is an expression of, and a precondition for, God-given reason, Dodd (1729–1777) turned to a predecessor in annotation:

> This, says Mr. *Theobald*, is an expression purely Homeric;
> Αμα προσσω και οπισσω
> Λευσσει—
> Turns on all hands its deep-discerning eyes;
> Sees what *befell*, and what may yet *befall*:
> Concludes from both, and best provides for all.
>
> *Pope*, B. 3. 150

> And again,
> Ο γαρ οιος ορα προσσω και οπισσω
> Skill'd to discern the *future* by the *past*.
>
> *Pope*, B. 18. 294
>
> The short scholiast on the last passage, gives us a comment, that very aptly explains our author's phrase: "For it is the part of an understanding man to connect the reflection of events to come with such as are past, and so to foresee what shall follow." This is as our author phrases it, *looking before and after*.[1]

Dodd, like many other annotators, was in general footnote-dialogue, as it were, with other footnotes in other books by other minds. Here he was openly borrowing from the seventh volume of Lewis Theobald's *The Works of Shakespeare* (1733).[2] Dodd's contribution was to translate the comment from the "short scholiast" on Homer, and, in support of Theobald's austerely un-glossed Greek quotations and references ("*Iliad.* γ. ver. 109, *Iliad.* ς. ver. 250"), to add quotations from and references to Alexander Pope's version of Homer.

The modern quotations enlarge the scope of what Theobald and Dodd might imply by "an expression purely Homeric"[3]; it is not clear if the implication is that Shakespeare *borrowed* Homer's thought, or if Shakespeare's hitting on a similar notion is to be taken as a sign that his (or Hamlet's) wisdom is *qualitatively* "Homeric" (in describing the essential constituents of human wisdom, Shakespeare and Homer have been, by Theobald and by Dodd, found the same). Dodd quoted Pope's *Iliad* from the moment when Menelaus, before the duel with Paris in book 3, calls for the agreement of the "deep-discerning Eyes" of Priam's wise old age that see "what *befell*, and what may yet *befall*," and the description of Hector's wise but disregarded friend Polydamas, "Skill'd to discern the *Future* by the *past*."[4] Ancient and modern wisdoms are presented together, the oldest poem in the newest form.[5] The Dodd-Theobald procedure is peculiarly transchronological: they are using the paraphrase of a "scholiast" on *Homer* to gloss a thought of *Shakespeare's*. By quoting from Pope, Dodd is, in effect, looking at the same time both before and after Shakespeare, justifying the phrase in his title where he proclaims that he provides as illustrations to Shakespeare "*similar* passages from *ancient* and *modern* authors" (italics mine). Dodd is as interested (and assumes his readers will be similarly interested) in passages that predate Shakespeare (and may be considered as sources or analogues) and in those that are merely analogous, or that present Shakespeare's thoughts as reflected in the works of later writers—or, being vaguely "similar," subserve some altogether indeterminate function.

A similar set of procedures can be seen in a note that Dodd reproduces from Samuel Johnson's *Miscellaneous Observations on the Tragedy of Macbeth* (1745), comparing Macbeth's fears as he goes to murder Duncan with a short night piece from one of Dryden's plays. Johnson paraphrased Macbeth's apprehension: "Now o'er one half the world / Nature seems dead": "That is, *over our hemisphere* all *action and motion seem to have ceased.*" He regards the image as "perhaps, the most striking that poetry can produce." For Johnson, it is a testimony to the force of the image that it should have been "adopted by *Dryden* in his *Conquest of* Mexico": "All things are hush'd as nature's self lay dead." Johnson cites the passage from Dryden as a further illustration of the force of the image, a force revealed in its having been borrowed and transformed. The reader is offered an opportunity to meditate, here and now, on the power of a poetical image to work to differing ends: "These lines, though so well known, I have transcribed, that the contrast between them and this passage of *Shakespear*, may be most accurately observed.—Night is described by two great poets." Johnson's word *observed* suggests some detachment, but what Johnson (and

Dodd) promise is a comparison of different experiences: "He that reads *Dryden*, finds himself lull'd with serenity, and dispos'd to solitude and contemplation: he that peruses *Shakespear*, looks round alarmed, and starts to find himself alone."[6]

Most important, the juxtaposition of the passages from Shakespeare and Dryden attempts a demonstration of the (related but differing) powers of "two great poets." Given that Thomas Rymer had in 1674 exhaustively and minutely demonstrated (over thirteen pages) the superiority of Dryden's passage to all that the ancient and modern literatures had to offer, Johnson's contention was perhaps that both writers were aggrandized by such juxtaposition.[7] As Shakespeare was shown (by Theobald) to be Homeric, so Dryden was shown (by Johnson) to be Shakespearian.[8]

Johnson assumes that both experiences will be pleasurable for readers, rather as he considered that Pope's "copious" notes to the *Iliad* "attract the reader by the pleasure of perusal" and "vary entertainment."[9] It was presumably both to vary the entertainment and to praise great poets that Pope referred to Chaucer in his "Observation" on the felling of forests for the funeral of Patroclus described in book 23 of his *Iliad*:

> This Description of felling the Forests, so excellent as it is, is comprehended in a few Lines, which has left room for a larger and more particular one in *Statius*, one of the best (I think) in that Author . . . . I the rather cite this fine Passage, because I find it copied by two of the greatest Poets of our own Nation, *Chaucer* and *Spencer*. The first in the *Assembly of Fowls*, the second in his *Fairy Queen*. lib. I.[10]

Pope points to the poetic quality of the passage in Homer, but also to its brevity, and the room left, as it were, for productive expansion. Statius, who had seized the opportunity, is quoted at length, but that quotation is, in turn, offered for further comparison with passages from English poets. Pope quotes Spenser at length, leaving it up to his reader to discover to what degree Spenser was following Chaucer. The reader is offered a comparison across time: Pope's modern version of Homer's ancient text, and its reflection both in the Latin of Statius and in two English elaborations. The offer seems to be similar to that presented by Johnson when comparing night pieces: to enjoy the relations between the greatest poets. There may also be the hint of a parallel between analogous ancient and modern literary histories, and some critical challenge to prevailing tastes hidden beneath Pope's quiet claim that Chaucer and Spenser are "two of the greatest Poets of our own Nation."

LANGUAGE AND PROSODY: SPENSER AND DRYDEN

Such critical linking between poets is evident (though in different ways and to markedly different degrees) in all the editions of Chaucer current in the eighteenth century: Thomas Speght (1687); Dryden (1700); John Urry (1721); Thomas Morell (1737); and Thomas Tyrwhitt (1775).[11] "Similar" passages from ancient and modern authors are interlaced with the concerns more strongly marked in editions of Chaucer than in those of most other English poets: the glossing of old words, the identification of old objects and customs, and observations on Chaucer's metrical intentions.

All the editions are closely interconnected, by incorporation or in contradiction. *The Works of Our Ancient, Learned, & Excellent English Poet, Jeffrey Chaucer* (London, 1687) was a reprint of the edition of 1602 by Thomas Speght (d. 1621), which had included much material from Speght's edition of 1598.[12] All Speght's texts were in circulation in the eighteenth-century; it was the 1598 text that was most used by Dryden and Pope.[13]

One of the purposes of Speght's edition was to place Chaucer with Homer. In the edition of 1598, the testimony of "Mr. *Ascham*" is cited (c.iii.r) as calling Chaucer "*English Homer*" and as valuing Chaucer's "Authority of as high Estimation as ever he did either Sophocles or Euripides in Greek." A poem "Of the Animadversions upon Chaucer," printed (av) before the "Life" in 1602 and 1687, praises "[t]he helpful Notes explaining *Chaucer's* Mind" supposedly contained in the volume, but in fact most of the "Corrections of some faults, and Annotations upon some places" that had been printed in 1598 were absorbed into the list of "[t]he Old and Obscure Words in *Chaucer* explained" in 1602. Several of the notes in the earlier edition particularize the relation between Homer and Chaucer. Of the dialogue between "ire" and "resoun" that takes place in Theseus's mind in the "Knight's Tale," issuing in a condemnation of merciless kings ("Fie upon a Lord that will haue no mercy &c."), Speght's annotation observes, "He blameth a prince that will rule by rigour, and not by discretion and gentlenes" citing Homer, who is again adduced ("in the 19. of the Iliads") as having given the precept "Carrie a gentle heart within thee" to a king.[14] In the edition of 1602, Theseus's speech is marked with a manicule (fol.5), and in 1687 with an asterisk of approbation (16).

As well as looking back to Homer, the edition of 1598 had looked forward in presenting Edmund Spenser as Chaucer's (then living) modern embodiment. The prefatory letter from Francis Beaumont, "to his very loving and assured good friend, Mr. Thomas Speght," puts a case that may have seemed hopelessly behind the times in 1687:

> But so pure were *Chaucer's* Words in his days, as *Lidgate*, that learned Man, calleth him, The Loadstar of the *English* Language; and so good they are in our days, as Mr. *Spencer* . . . hath adorned his Stile with . . . Beauty and Gravity . . . and his much frequenting of *Chaucer's* ancient Words, with his excellent imitation of divers Places in him, is not the least help that hath made him reach so high, as many learned men do think, that no Poet, either *French* or *Italian*, deserves a second place under him.[15]

At the end of "The Life of Our Learned *English* Poet, Geffrey Chaucer" (b3v), particular attention is drawn to Spenser's completion of the "Squires Tale," "which he had not done, had he not felt (as he saith) the Infusion of *Chaucer's* own sweet Spirit surviving within him."

Chaucer's fathering of Spenser, and Chaucer's analogous position in English poetry to that of Homer in the Greek, are powerful notions in the preface to Dryden's

Fables, Ancient and Modern (1700): "we have our lineal descents and clans, as well as other families: Spenser more than once insinuates that the soul of Chaucer was transfused into his body; and that he was begotten by him two hundred years after his decease."[16] *Fables* was not, strictly speaking, an edition of Chaucer, although it was sometimes treated as such by some later editors. Three Canterbury Tales are represented in free translations, together with a version of *The Flower and the Leaf,* which was generally assumed to be Chaucer's and had been printed for the first time in 1598. The volume concluded with a (repunctuated but unannotated) text of the four Chaucerian poems, presenting the text of Speght's earliest edition in modern type (for the first time). Included in the preface, alongside the famous critical account in which Chaucer is held "in the same degree of veneration as the Grecians held Homer,"[17] were several editorial considerations: some (scattered) emendatory and metrical comments, observations on Chaucer's sources, and several engagements with Speght's comments and annotations.

The challenge to future editors and critics of Chaucer was the following (for the time, remarkable) confessional assertion of Dryden's:

> I prefer in our countryman, far above all his other stories, the noble poem of Palamon and Arcite, which is of the Epic kind, and perhaps not much inferior to the *Ilias* or the *Æneis*. The story is more pleasing than either of them, the manners as perfect, the diction as poetical, the Learning as deep and various.[18]

Where in all Speght's editions the culminating modern critical authority had been Spenser (and Sidney), the "Testimonies of Learned Men concerning *Chaucer* and His Works" in John Urry's edition of *The Works of Geoffrey Chaucer* (1721) concludes with two extracts from "Mr. *Dryden* in the Preface to His Fables."[19]

Despite this endorsement, Urry (1666–1715) himself may have wanted to counteract Dryden's views of Chaucer's prosody by restoring him "*to his feet again*" (Urry, i2ᵛ). Urry had died before the work was finished; the volume was the product of a research team, as it were, being completed largely by the brothers Timothy and William Thomas, Timothy composing the "Preface," and (with his brother perhaps) compiling the "Glossary."[20] It was the young poet and antiquarian John Dart (d. 1730), however, who wrote the "Life of Geoffrey Chaucer" in this edition, and who treats Dryden most clearly as the presiding authority: "There is a wild Beauty in his Works, which comes nearer the Descriptions of *Homer*, than any other that followed him: . . . Mr. *Dryden*, than whom there was no better Judge of the Beauties of *Homer* and *Virgil*, positively asserts that he exceeded the latter, and stands in competition with the former" (Urry, e2v).

For Dart, the highest praise that can be given to Chaucer's language is to point to its adoption by the later poet: "His Language . . . in some places . . . is to this day so smooth, concise and beautiful, that even Mr. *Dryden* would not attempt to alter it, but has copied some of his Verses almost *literatim*" (Urry, fr). At the same time, Dart reflected Dryden's rejection of Speght's prosody (itself recorded in Urry's "Testimonies"): "I cannot go so far as he who published the last Edition of him; for he would make us believe the Fault is in our Ears, and that there were really Ten Syllables in a Verse where we find but Nine." Dryden's conclusion had been based on the unevenness in Speght's texts, including texts of many poems not now attributed to Chaucer (and that no one has ever been able to scan), and alluding to those who had transcribed the Chaucerian poems: "Equality of Numbers in every Verse which we call *Heroick*, was either not known, or not always practised in *Chaucer*'s Age" (Urry, iv).

So it is that Dart wrote of Chaucer's lines that even "nice discerning Persons would find it difficult, with all their straining and working, to spin out some of his Verses into a measure of ten Syllables" and that Chaucer "was not altogether regardles of his Numbers; but his thoughts were more intent upon solid sense than gingle" (Urry, fr). A footnote attached to this passage instructs the reader to "See *Misse-metre* in the Gloss." That note, however, only half supports Dart, as it only half supports Urry, who had forced every line (including lines with double rhymes) into ten syllables. The note begins as a careful gloss—

> *Misse-metre*, Tr. L. 5 1795. To destroy the Metre or Numbers in Poetry by incorrect Writing, or wrong Reading. But *Chaucer* having particularly mentioned the fault of Miswriting in the foregoing Verse, it is that to be supposed he means there[21] that of Reading amiss, which generally happens, *for defaute of tonge*, i.e. for want of a perfect understanding of his language.

—but rapidly becomes a general disquisition on Chaucer's meter, apparently conceding Chaucer's unevenness and citing a line (1098 in modern editions) from *The House of Fame*:

> He owns in *Fa. L. 3. 9*, &c. that he chose sometimes to leave a Verse too short by a Syllable, where he had a greater regard to the sense then the Metre.

Thomas then returns on himself, suggesting that an examination of the manuscripts might provide an authentic and fairly regular text without recourse to the expedients adopted by Urry:

> He was not so loose in his Metre, as some may imagine; for by collating any part of his works with MSS. of old Editions, it will appear, that Verses, which in one Copy or Edition are defective, may out of others be made compleat; and that very often without the use of the *i* or *y* prefixt to Verbs, the distinct pronunciation of the final *in* or *é*, or useless Expletives. (46)

Johnson observed in his preface to *The Plays of William Shakespeare* (1778) that "the chief desire of him that comments an author, is to shew how much other commentators have corrupted and obscured him."[22] Thomas used his glossary repeatedly to point out the discrepancy between his preferred MS readings and those given in the text he is supposedly glossing. The predecessor animadverted upon in these comments and scattered annotations is Urry himself.

The pronunciation guides ("the *i* or *y* prefixt to Verbs, the distinct pronunciation of the final *in* or *é*") and, most especially, the use of "useless Expletives" that were Urry's textual trademarks, were also derided in Thomas Morell's edition, *The Canterbury Tales of Chaucer* (1737), which was as concerned to follow Dryden on metrical and critical matters as it was to combat its predecessor.[23] Chaucer's "Numbers," Morell (1703–1784) first suggests in his "Preface," "are, by no Means so rough and inharmonious as some People imagine." Morell was to become Handel's librettist; he presumably uses the term *musical* with care when he goes on to claim that Chaucer's lines "are always musical, whether they want or exceed their Complement" of ten syllables, and in suggesting that, in his example, "two Times" were to be given to a single syllable. He had "observed" that the want of a syllable occurs

> generally at the Beginning of a Verse, when a Pause is to be made, or rather two Times to be given to the first Syllable, as v. 368.
>   *Not* in Purgatory, but in Hell.
> Mr. *Urry*, to make out his ten Syllables, reads it *right* in Hell, which *right*, tho' I am no great Admirer of a Pun, is *wrong*, as it renders the Verse very harsh and dissonant.[24]
> (Morell, xxvi)

CHAUCER, HOMER, AND POPE

Morell's original project (of which only one volume containing the "Prologue" and "Knight's Tale" appeared) was highly innovative, and it is a reverse of that adopted in Dryden's *Fables*. His notion was to follow each section of *The Canterbury Tales* with a version "turn'd into modern language" by an "eminent" recent poet (or failing that by Morell himself). The text of Chaucer was to be an entirely new compilation from "the most authentic manuscripts," presented in old spelling, and including no reading (such as "*right* in hell") that did not have support from the manuscripts. Two sets of annotation were supplied: one set at the bottom of each page of Chaucerian text containing glosses and simple explanations, and another set in an appendix containing "Annotations," which precedes a list of textual variants at the end of the volume.[25] These are described as "chiefly relating to antiquities" (Morell, 349), but, in fact, the matters discussed and information adduced are extraordinarily miscellaneous.

One model for Morell was provided by the "Observations" to Pope's *Iliad*. In some cases, a note by Pope is simply reproduced. So when coming to the list of trees cut down to provide the funeral pyre of Arcite in the "Knight's Tale," Morell in his "Annotations" cited Homer and Virgil ("So *Hom. Il.* 23. *Virg.* 6 180."), but he went on to observe that "*Chaucer* seems more directly to have copied *Statius* in that Description, which Mr. *Pope* esteems one of the best in that Author, and therefore worth the transcribing." Morell quotes twenty-one lines from Statius where Pope had confined himself to nine, and makes clear that the relation between Statius and Chaucer, and Chaucer and ("the excellent") Spenser is one of mutual imitation:

> The particular Description of the Trees our Author has imitated in a Poem called the *Assembly of Fowles*, wherein he is followed by the excellent *Spenser* in his *Fairy Queen*, *l*. I. The sailing Pine, the Cedar proud and tall, *&c*. (Morell, 417–18)

The process seen in the Observations on the *Iliad* is reversed; Pope used Chaucer to illuminate Homer; Morell uses Homer to illuminate Chaucer.

Homer features largely in Morell's edition partly because Morell was convinced, as the following footnote suggests, that Chaucer had read the ancient text in Greek: "I cannot but think *Chaucer* understood that Language, from his Quotations from *Plato* and *Homer*, and particularly from the Use he makes of the *Greek* Fathers in the Parson's Tale" (Morell, xxxiv). For Morell, however, the similarity between Chaucer and Homer is clearest in the two poets' *sentiments*. As Morell seems to have seen it, Chaucer at key moments in the "Knight's Tale" presented an essentially *Homeric* view of life. This is particularly clear when Morell comments on Theseus's account of how the "Movere"

> of his wise Purveyaunce,
> He hath so well besett his Ordenaunce,
> That Species of Thingys, and Progressiounys
> Shullen endurin by *Successiounys*,
> And not eterne. (Morell, 199; italics mine)

This Dryden had represented quite closely in *Palamon and Arcite* (included in Morell's volume):

> This Law th'Omniscient Pow'r was pleas'd to give,
> That ev'ry Kind should by *Succession* live;
> That Individuals die, his Will ordains;
> The propagated Species still remains. (Morell, 344; italics mine)

Morell, in a responding endnote, quotes from Pope's *Iliad*, providing at once an illustration to the sentiment and a genealogy of the poetic history of the terms "succession" and "successive." It appears to be the similarity of wording in Pope's modern version that matters, and that provides the pertinent connection:

> Like Leaves on Trees the Race of Man is found,
> Now green in Youth, now with'ring on the Ground
> Another Race the following Spring supplies,
> They fall *successive*, and *successive* rise.
> So Generations in their Course decay,
> So flourish these, when those are past away. (Morell, 422; italics mine)[26]

The idea connects Homer and Chaucer, the word Chaucer and Pope (via Dryden). Theseus's speech that concludes the tale is heavily illustrated from Pope's Homer—so much so that Morell's "Annotations" end with a tribute to that poem, and even more to the "Observations" on it. This is most strongly marked when Theseus comes to speak of death and honor:

> And serteynly a Man hath most Honoure,
> To deyen in his Excellence and Floure,
> Whan he is sekyr of his godé Name,
> Than he hath done his Frend ne hym no Schame.
> And gladder owith his Frend ben of his Deth,
> Whan with Honoure is yolden up his Breth,
> Than whan his Name apeyrid is for Age,
> For all forgettin is his Vasselage;
> Than is it best, as for a worthi Fame,
> A Man to dey whan he is best of Name. (Morell, 203)

This speech is illustrated by quotations from the praise of honor from "old *Priam*, *Il.* 22, 100," from Hector ("*Il.* 15, 582"), and from Achilles himself:

Such too was *Achilles's* Choice, who was so possessed with the Love of Glory, that he preferred it to Life itself; when he says,
> Here if I stay before the *Trojan* Town,
> Short is my Date, but deathless my Renown:
> If I return, I quit immortal Praise,
> For Years on Years, and long extended Days, *&c.*
Upon this [book 9:535] Mr. Pope has an excellent Comment, to which I refer the Reader, and shall conclude with the noble Speech of *Sarpedon* to *Glaucus*, as translated by the same incomparable Poet, *Il.* 12, 400. (Morell, 423–44)

Pope's "excellent Comment" is an account of Achilles's character and role in the *Iliad* as a whole—and has only oblique bearing on the "Knight's Tale."[27] Turning from Chaucer to Homer as represented by the modern living poet has renewed Morell's sense that there was a profound similarity between the treatment of honor in Chaucer and Homer, and that Alexander Pope is "incomparable" both as a poet and as a critical commentator.

One of Morell's notes linking Chaucer, Homer, and Pope deserves particular attention. Morell seems to have been troubled by the moment in the "Knight's Tale" when Palamon, jealous of his friend's freedom and in despair at his perpetual imprisonment, questions Providence:

> Crewel Goddis, that governe
> This World with Byndyn of your Word, eterne,
> And wretyn in the Table of Athamaunte,
> Throw Parlement, and your eternal Graunte;
> What is Mankynd more unto yow yhold,
> Than is the Schep that rokyth in the Fold? (Morell, 100)

Morell glossed *rokyth* ("to squat or lie down; used in the *North*") at the foot of the page, but in his "Annotations" commented:

> V. 446. Cruel Goddess, *&c.* These Words, transgressing the Bounds of Reason, are to be ascribed to an Excess of Sorrow, like those of *Philætius* in *Homer*, who, in his great Concern for his Master's Sufferings, says,
>
> O *Jove*, for ever deaf to human Cries,
> The Tyrant, not the Father of the Skies;
> Unpiteous of the Race thy Will began,
> The Fool of Fate; thy Manufacture, Man,
> With Penury, Contempt, Repulse, and Care,
> The gauling Load of Life is doom'd to bear.
> *Pop. Odys.* 20, 251. (Morell, 393)

This note seems to represent an invocation of Homer of a slightly different kind from those discussed previously. Morell, on this occasion mindful of his clerical role perhaps, seems to have been disquieted by Palamon's description of a world ungoverned by careless (or malign) gods, and, since neither Chaucer nor Dryden offer any palliation, he appears to have turned to Pope (and Elijah Fenton, who assisted Pope with his *Iliad* notes) for help. Palamon's words, as Morell reads them, come close to blasphemy but should be understood as the expression of his extreme sufferings, "like those of *Philætius* in *Homer*." Philætius, the faithful herdsman, lamented the hard state of life represented by the beggar (Odysseus in disguise) he thinks he sees before him, a state that reminds him of the possible or probable current fate of his master, and the cruelty of the gods. It is not so much the similarity of the sentiments expressed by Palamon and Philætius, however, as the Observation made on them that appears to matter to Morell. Philætius's outburst received explanatory comment in the Observation to this moment in the *Odyssey*:

> These words are to be ascribed to the excess of sorrow which *Philætius* feels for the sufferings of *Ulysses*; for they certainly transgress the bounds of reason. But if we consider the state of Theology in *Homer's* time, the sentence will appear less offensive; "How can *Jupiter* (says *Philætius*) who is our father, throw his children into such an abyss of misery? Thou, oh *Jove*, hast made us, yet hast no compassion when we suffer."

(For the comfort of the reader, these remarks are followed in the Observation by a brief Christian theodicy.)[28] As in the case of Palamon and Morell, a pious objection is removed and turned into appreciation of Homer's human and poetic understanding.[29]

MORELL'S MEANDERINGS: THEOBALD AND WARBURTON

This is not to suggest that Morell's footnote world was confined to Pope's *Iliad*, or that his illustrations are always as interpretatively pertinent as the above—or pertinent at all. Apropos of lines 529–30 on the character of the good "Parsone"

("But *Christys* Lore, and his Apostels twelve, / He taught, but ferst he folwede it hymselve"), Morell's note wanders (almost Dodd-like) into Shakespeare, from Shakespeare back to Chaucer and Dryden's *Character of a Good Parson*, and from there (almost Scriblerus-like) to a contentious remark of Theobald's:

> this reminds me of that excellent Advice, which *Ophelia* gives her Brother in *Haml, p.* 242 and which I shall transcribe, because of two or three old Words often used by our Author.
> —But, good my Brother,
> Do not, as some ungracious *Pastors* do,
> Shew me the steep and thorny Way to Heaven:
> Whilst, like a puft, and careless Libertine,
> Himself the Primrose Path of Dalliance treads,
> And *recks* not his own *Reed.*—
> Upon a Review of this plain and honest Character of a Priest, I think it charming, without having Recourse to the finer Touches, or beautiful Heightening of Mr. *Dryden*. This, indeed, is a *true Priest*, of quite another Stamp from one Mr. *Theobald* calls such in his Not. [*sic*] on *Troil. & Cressid.* Tho', I confess, I had no more Business to bring him in here, than he had to hedge that vile Reflection. (Morell, 378)

The initial connection is made in terms of *excellence*. Chaucer's description of a good parson is excellent, partly because it a wise account of what makes a "true Priest"; its excellence is matched by Ophelia's observations, and its charm does not require Dryden's "beautiful Heightening."

So far so good; the wanderings to Shakespeare and Dryden subserve a valuable critical point, but it is hard to guess what Morell's readers were to make of his further meandering reference to Theobald, which, as Morell confesses, has no "Business" here, and which would take some tracking down. Theobald's note containing the "vile Reflection" that offended Morell concerns the moment in *Troilus and Cressida* when the Trojan priest, Calchas, proposes to the Greeks an exchange of prisoners that would bring the return of his daughter Cressida, and appeals to the assembled Greeks by claiming "*That, through the Sight I bear in Things to come / I have abandon'd* Troy." This is glossed (the square brackets are Theobald's): "Gentlemen, by my Power of Prescience I found my Country must be subdued and ruin'd: and therefore I have left House and Home in Time to [save myself, and] come and serve you." To Theobald this is not convincing:

> the Motives of his Oratory seem to me somewhat perverse and unartful: nor do I know how to reconcile it, unless our Poet purposely intended to make *Calchas* act the Part of a true Priest; and so from Motives of Self-Interest insinuate the Merit of Service.[30]

Theobald's final speculation is a kind of joke, a piece of ironic anticlericalism. But it is not entirely gratuitous. Calchas's plea seems to Theobald to be "perverse and unartful"; his guess is that Shakespeare *intended* it to be so. (In that way, Theobald's interpretation is not unlike that of Morell on the words of Palamon and Philætius.)

Morell's reference, in contrast, is entirely beside the point. Using the phrase "true priest" has led him to recall Theobald's insinuation that *all* priests "from Motives of Self-Interest insinuate the Merit of Service."

Morell, who comes to praise Chaucer, might have had stronger or more clearly *literary* reasons for quarrelling with Theobald, who, although citing Chaucer frequently, does so for mainly philological reasons—and sometimes suggests some denigration of the pre-Shakespearian writer. One of Dodd's few references to Chaucer is again stolen from Theobald, who had observed a similarity between Shakespeare's description of Patience in *Twelfth Night* and one in the Chaucer's *Parliament of Fowls*:

> She pined in thought;
> And, with a green and yellow melancholy,
> She sat like patience on a monument,
> Smiling at grief.
> Mr. *Theobald* observes, on this very fine image in the text, that it is not impossible but our author might originally have borrowed it from *Chaucer*, in his *Assembly of Fowles*.
> And her besidis wonder discretlie,
> Dame *Pacience ysittinge* there I fonde,
> With *facé pale*, upon an *hill* of *sonde*.[31]

As Theobald had presented the comparison, the opportunity was to appreciate the ways that Shakespeare had *improved* on his source.

> If he was indebted, however, for the first rude Draught, how amply has he repaid that Debt in heightning the Picture! How much does the *green* and *yellow Melancholy* transcend the Old Bard's *Face pale*; the *Monument*, his *Hill of Sand*; and what an additional Beauty is, *smiling at Grief*, for which there are no Ground, nor Traces, in the Original![32]

In his 1747 edition of Shakespeare's plays, William Warburton offered an elaborate and spirited defense, quoting Chaucer, paraphrasing Theobald, attempting wit, and pointing to the differences between the descriptions:

> *Shakespear* is speaking of a marble statue of *Patience*; *Chaucer*, of *Patience* herself. And the two representations of her, are in quite different views. Our Poet, speaking of a despairing lover, judiciously compares her to *Patience* exercised on the death of friends and relations; which affords him the beautiful picture of *Patience on a monument*. The old Bard speaking of *Patience* herself, directly, and not by comparison, as judiciously draws her in that circumstance where she is most exercised, and has occasion for all her virtue; that is to say, under the *losses of shipwreck*. And now we see why she is represented as *sitting on an hill of sand*, to design the scene to be the sea-shore. It is finely imagined; and one of the noble simplicities of that admirable Poet. But the Critick thought, in good earnest, that *Chaucer's* invention was so barren, and his imagination so beggarly, that he was not able to be at the charge of a monument for his Goddess, but left her, like a stroller, sunning herself upon a heap of sand.[33]

Warburton's objection was both that Theobald had misunderstood Shakespeare and that he had maligned "the noble simplicities" of Chaucer "that admirable Poet"—although his is a defense in which ingenuity and absurdity go hand in hand. (Who but Warburton, it might be asked, took the sand on which Dame Pacience sits to signal that she was contemplating a shipwreck?) Warburton's discussion moves some distance away from a scholarly determination of Shakespeare's indebtedness to Chaucer. It is from that point of view gratuitous—and highly fanciful.

TYRWHITT, THOMAS WARTON, GEORGE STEEVENS, AND SHAKESPEARE

There is very little that is gratuitous and (almost) nothing that is purely fanciful in Thomas Tyrwhitt's edition of *The Canterbury Tales of Chaucer* (1775–1778), which presents itself as determinedly resisting most of these intellectual procedures and to represent a reaction against the annotatory excesses of his predecessors.[34] To later generations, Tyrwhitt (1730–1786) has seemed to be the true scholar, with a true scholar's critical reticence governed by an exemplary sense of pertinence, of evidence, and of the business immediately in hand. The text and annotations of Tyrwhitt's *Canterbury Tales* were reprinted throughout the eighteenth century and well into the nineteenth.[35]

Tyrwhitt expressed nothing but contempt for Urry's text but made appreciative use of the glossary by Timothy Thomas. He disagreed, too, with the metrical notions he found in Morell's edition. While allowing eleven-syllable lines with a double rhyme, Tyrwhitt was otherwise almost as inflexible as Urry in his demand for equality of numbers, and therefore, as in this footnote to "Essay on the Language and Versification of Chaucer," in absolute opposition to Morell's headless lines (the square brackets are Tyrwhitt's):

> no such liberty can be taken in the Heroic metre without totally destroying its harmony; and therefore when the abovementioned learned Editor says [Pref. p. xxvi.], that the numbers of Chaucer "are always musical, whether they want or exceed their complement," I doubt his partiality for this author has carried him too far. I have no conception myself that an heroic verse, which wants a syllable of its complement, can be musical, or even tolerable. The line which he has quoted from the Knightes Tale [ver. 1228 of this Edition],
>
> *Not* in purgatory but in helle—
>
> however you manage it; (whether you make a pause; or give two times to the first syllable, as he rather advises;)—can never pass for a verse of any form. Nor did Chaucer intend that it should. He wrote (according to the best Mss.)—
>
> Not *only* in purgatory but in helle. (Tyrwhitt, 4:82)[36]

On other matters, Tyrwhitt expresses some admiration for Morell ("the abovementioned learned Editor"), taking the earlier edition as a model for several of his editorial procedures. Half of Morell's project had been carried further in the connected collection of translated tales and links in the three volumes of *The Canterbury Tales of Chaucer, Modernis'd by Several Hands. Publish'd by Mr. Ogle* (1741). Tyrwhitt was, in effect, revising and completing the scholarly part of Morell's intention: providing a text of the whole *Canterbury Tales* based on manuscript sources, and with full explanatory annotation.[37]

In Tyrwhitt's annotations, poetical context is presented almost entirely as a matter of sources or of analogues closely contemporaneous with Chaucer. The working assumption is that only works that were written before (or immediately after) the moment of composition can have much relevance. Where most other editions are declaredly encomiastic, it is only in an aside in a footnote to the "Appendix to the Preface" that a reader of Tyrwhitt might discover that the editor thought that Chaucer was "a great Poet" and that the gifts of writing and appreciating "genuine Poetry" were "only bestowed on the chosen few by the peculiar favour of heaven" (and even then the sentiment is attributed to Milton) (Tyrwhitt, 1:xxviii).

Modern poets are ignored *as poets* and quietly corrected in their factual mistakes.[38] Tyrwhitt is equally polite in his discussions with fellow scholars. Thomas Warton, to take the most pertinent example, is cited respectfully as an authority or a repository of useful information. There are some disagreements, however. One interesting case was inserted in the second edition (published posthumously in 1798) that suggests considerable (if humorous) self-consciousness on Tyrwhitt's part. It concerns some lines in the description of the Clerk of Oxenforde (from the "Prologue," lines 305–8):

> Of studie toke he moste cure and hede.
> Not a word spake he more than was nede;
> And that was said in form and reverence,
> And short and quicke, and ful of high sentence.
>
> Ver. 307. in forme and reverence] *with propriety and modesty.* In the next line *"full of high sentence"* means only, I apprehend, *"full of high,* or *excellent, sense."*—Mr. Warton will excuse me for suggesting these explanations of this passage in lieu of those which he has given in his *Hist. of Eng. Po.* p. 451.[39]

Thomas Warton is carefully corrected because "[t]he credit of good letters is concerned, that Chaucer should not be supposed to have made 'a pedantic formality,' and 'a precise sententious style on all subjects,'" [both are Warton's phrases] the characteristics of a scholar.[40] For all his carefulness, Tyrwhitt seems to have been at equal pains to avoid "pedantic formality" as gratuitous comparison.

There are, however, some exceptions. Tyrwhitt differs from Morell in his absolute certainty that Chaucer knew not a word of Greek. In one note, however, Tyrwhitt, under the influence of some strange impulse, appears to break his own rules. A large part of Tyrwhitt's effort, both scholarly and critical, was to present *The Canterbury Tales* as a cohesive whole. He observes of the setting out of the pilgrims that "the contrivance of appointing the Knight *by lot* to tell the first tale is a happy one, as it affords the Author the opportunity of giving his work a splendid opening." Contemplating the "general satisfaction, which this appointment" of the Knight as first teller is met by the pilgrims, "puts us in mind of a similar gratification to the secret wishes of the Grecian army, when the lot of fighting with Hector falls to Ajax." That similarity is offered "though there is not the least probability that Chaucer had ever read the Iliad, even in a translation" and the moment in the *Iliad* cannot be considered a source, or to contribute anything to scholarly understanding of Chaucer's poem (Tyrwhitt, 4:131–32).

Nor is Tyrwhitt's eschewing of modern poets without exception. For Thomas Warton (and even more for his brother Joseph) an interest in Chaucer was often connected with an appreciation of distinctly modern poetry. Not so Tyrwhitt. In one note, he offers a suggestion he would have made had he not been presented with reasons for not doing so:

> *Yet in our ashen cold is fire yreken*
> There is so great a resemblance between this line and the following of the *Church-yard Elegy*, Dodsley's Coll. vol. 4.
>   Ev'n in our ashes live their wonted fires—
> that I should certainly have considered the latter as an imitation, if Mr. Gray himself had not referred us to the 169 (170) Sonnet of Petrarch, as his original. (Tyrwhitt, 4:247)

The resemblance between the line in the "Reeve's Prologue" and Gray's poem are, nevertheless, presented to the reader for immediate consideration.

And there is one great general exception to Tyrwhitt's abstention from recording the poetical reception of Chaucer's poems beyond Lydgate: Shakespeare. Tyrwhitt's note records his conviction that "Shakespeare's *Host of the Garter*" in *The Merry Wives of Windsor* had a Chaucerian antecedent in the "Pardoner's Prologue":

> Ver. 12246. Said I not wel?] All the best Mss. agree in giving this phrase to the Host in this place. It must remind us of the similar phrase, *said I well?* which occurs so frequently in the mouth of Shakespeare's *Host of the Garter*; and may be sufficient, with the other circumstances of general resemblance, to make us believe, that Shakespeare, when he drew that character, had not forgotten his Chaucer. (Tyrwhitt, 4:306)

The suggestion depends in part on a phrasal similarity; one phrase "must remind us" of another, and that *reminding* is offered as an argument for Shakespeare's not having *forgotten*.

Occasionally, the perception of resemblances appears to come into the mind with almost resistless force, accompanied with obvious pleasure. This is Tyrwhitt's note concerning semi-deities in the "Merchant's Tale" and *A Midsummer Night's Dream*:

> the Machinery of the Faeries, which Chaucer has used so happily, was probably added by himself; and indeed, I cannot help thinking, that his *Pluto* and *Proserpina* were the true progenitors of *Oberon* and *Titania* . . . or rather, that they themselves have, once at least, deigned to revisit our poetical system under the latter names. (Tyrwhitt, 4:161)

Interestingly, Tyrwhitt here abandons the plural of his suggestion about the innkeepers ("which must remind *us*") for the first person singular: "I cannot help thinking." Pedantic formality is abandoned, too, in describing "*Pluto* and *Proserpina*" as "the true progenitors of *Oberon* and *Titania*," and even more in suggesting that these Chaucerian/Classical creations "have, once at least, deigned to revisit our poetical system under the latter names."

Tyrwhitt was himself an annotator on Shakespeare. Several of his comments both on Chaucer and on the playwright were appreciated by George Steevens. Shakespearian annotations affect Chaucer, and Shakespearian annotations affect Chaucer. Steevens, for example, noticed Tyrwhitt's note on Pluto and Proserpina, but he preserves only half Tyrwhitt's play of fancy and turns the *suggestion* into an *observation*:

> The judicious editor of the *Canterbury Tales* of Chaucer, in his *Introductory Discourse*, (See vol. iv. p. 161.) observes, that *Pluto* and *Proserpina* in the *Marchant's Tale*, appear to have been "the true progenitors of Shakespeare's *Oberon* and *Titania*."[41]

Steevens appears to have been led by careful reading of Tyrwhitt's edition to consider poetical indebtedness to Chaucer more widely. Having attributed the establishment of the fact that Drayton in his *Nymphidia* was "the follower of Shakespeare" to the "editor of the *Canterbury Tales of Chaucer*," Steevens drifts into a general refection: "In this century some of our poets have been as little scrupulous in adopting the ideas of their predecessors." Steevens cites an example, a ballad of John Gay's set against a passage in "Chaucer's *Frankeleines Tale*, late edit. v. 11179, &c.," and then drifts into the comment: "and Mr. Pope is more indebted to the same author for beauties inserted in his Eloisa to Abelard, than he has been willing to acknowledge."[42]

Steevens's note here is, strictly speaking, gratuitous. Here we might guess that, having written a series of notes drawing attention to the various resemblances between *A Midsummer Night's Dream* and Chaucer's poems, it had come into his mind that English indebtedness to older poets, and to Chaucer in particular, was more substantial than was generally recognized and this was as good a place as any to make the necessary observation—assuming perhaps that his literary readers might entertain (and enjoy entertaining) similar reflections about Chaucer's influence.

CONNECTIONS IN THE MIND OF THE ANNOTATOR

Steevens does not provide instances of Pope's borrowings from Chaucer. One that *had* been noted was that to some lines from *Eloisa to Abelard*.[43] In his 1757 edition of Pope's *Works*, Warburton had quoted lines attributed to "Chaucer" at the bottom of the page under the section heading "IMITATIONS."[44] Warburton's note was reproduced without comment in the editions of Pope's *Works* of 1806 and 1822,[45] both editions ignoring some objections that had been raised by Philip Neve in his *Cursory Remarks on Some of the Ancient English Poets* (1789):

that couplet of *Pope*, in his Epistle of *Eloisa to Abelard*,

> Love, free as air, at sight of human ties,
> Spreads his light wings, and in a moment flies—

is taken from Chaucer's *Frankeleines Tale*,

> Love wol not be *constreined* by maistrie.
> Whan maistrei cometh, the *God* of Love anon
> *Beteth* his winges, and, *farewel*, he is gon.

Bishop *Warburton*, in his notes on *Pope*, has quoted these lines of *Chaucer*, from that vile edition published by Mr. *Urry*; and they stand,

> Love will not be *confin'd* by Maisterie:
> When Maisterie comes, the *Lord* of Love anon
> *Flutters* his wings, and *forthwith* is he gone.—

by which it is seen, that, in these three lines, are four words, which do not belong to *Chaucer*.[46]

But Warburton's text is *not* Urry's—nor that of any printed edition.[47] Warburton attributes the note to 'P.' [Pope], but Pope's handwriting is easy to read and Warburton's text is unlikely to be a mistranscription.[48] Who is the author of the Chaucerian lines in Warburton's note? Was Pope (or was Warburton) inventing the lines from memory—a memory partially affected by Samuel Butler's use of the word *confined* when borrowing from the same passage in Chaucer?[49] Or was Warburton half remembering (as Pope may have done) Spenser's version?[50]

If such a conflation existed in Warburton's mind it would be representative of the general Chaucerian presence in eighteenth-century annotation, where Chaucer's text (in whatever form) almost joins with that with which it is compared, or with which resemblances are found. The footnote world into which endlessly mutating Chaucerian texts intrude is large on the one hand, and remarkably petty on the other. Theobald is as likely to be cited as Homer and Shakespeare. On the other hand, these annotatory habits allowed a fluidity and wideness of interest that would now be found reprehensible, but which may have reflected the realities of eighteenth-century reading experience.

The all-revealing phrases are, perhaps, those where the connection between poems is described as occurring principally in the mind of the annotator—those that take a form resembling Tyrwhitt's "*I cannot help thinking*" (italics mine). Dodd is perhaps at his most representative when expressing helplessness in the face of his own impulse to provide a redundant opulence of citation: "Tho' perhaps it is *not entirely to the purpose I cannot help quoting* here a fine passage"—in this case from *The Double Falsehood*, the "Shakespearian" play that Theobald claimed to have discovered, and which Dodd esteems highly (italics mine).[51] Of a similar kind would seem to be Morell's admission apropos the good parson that "*this reminds me* of that excellent Advice, which *Ophelia* gives her Brother" (italics mine), or Tyrwhitt's assertion that the "general satisfaction" at the lots falling out in the Knight's favor "*puts us in mind*" (italics mine) of a similar gratification in the *Iliad*. Often, that which is assumed to be shared between annotator and reader is a pleasure in the workings of poetry at its most attractive. Pope cited the "fine Passage" from Statius because it had been copied "by two of the greatest Poets of our own Nation." Johnson drew attention to passages "by two great poets"—assuming that Dryden, though writing very differently, had appreciated Shakespeare to the fullest extent. For many of these annotators the poetical reception of a given work was testimony to and a reflection of its thoughtfulness. The intention is to share highly particularized and localized poetical enthusiasm. In addition, it is frequently hinted that the mental connections that occur in the mind of the critical and scholarly annotator closely resembled those that had occurred, and could not but occur, in the mind of the receiving poet. Tyrwhitt maintained that Shakespeare drawing the character of a Host "had not forgotten his Chaucer." It seems probable that Tyrwhitt, in linking the deities that appear in the "Merchant's Tale" with Oberon and Titania, was responding to Pope's *January and May*—where precisely this conjunction was part of the creative process. Pope, too, perhaps could not help thinking of Oberon and Titania when meeting Chaucer's Pluto and Proserpine, or, like Tyrwhitt, was tempted to see Chaucer's deities as the "true progenitors" of Shakespeare's fairies—or perceiving that these deities had revisited "our poetical system."

By these annotators the apparently arbitrary connections that a mind can make between otherwise unrelated works is treated as of the utmost importance—and as having extraordinary consequences. At a time when many readers regarded Chaucer as unreadably antiquated, the contrary demonstration that the mind could pass happily from his lines to those of Homer, Shakespeare, Dryden, Pope, Gay, or Gray was peculiarly powerful. In this light, the most consequential connection between Chaucer and another poet may have occurred in the mind of Dryden. In the preface to *Fables*, Dryden recalls that, having completed his translations from Ovid, it occurred to him that Chaucer had much in common with the Latin poet, whom he (it now appears) excelled: "Having done with Ovid for this time, it came into my mind, that our old *English* poet *Chaucer* in many things resembled him, and that with no disadvantage on the side of the modern author."[52]

NOTES

1. William Dodd, *The Beauties of Shakespear: Regularly Selected from Each Play. With a General Index, Digesting Them under Proper Heads. Illustrated with Explanatory Notes, and Similar Passages from Ancient and Modern Authors.* 2 vols. (London: Printed for T. Waller, 1752), 1:252.

2. *The Works of Shakespeare, Collated with the Oldest Copies; and Corrected, with Notes, Explanatory and Critical,* ed. Lewis Theobald, 7 vols. (London: Printed for A. Bettesworth et al., 1733), 7:327.

3. Theobald, *Works of Shakespeare,* 7:327.

4. *The Iliad of Homer,* ed. Maynard Mack, vols. 7 and 8 of *The Twickenham Edition of the Poems of Alexander Pope,* ed. John Butt et al., 11 vols. (London: Methuen, 1967), 7:198 (book 3, lines 150, 151); 8:336 (book 18, line 294).

5. Pope's translation is frequently quoted alongside, or as commentary on Homer, in Thomas Newton's editions of *Paradise Lost*, both when Pope is responding to Milton's version (note to book 1, line 764, 1:72) and, as in the case of the fall of Mulciber (note to book 1, line 740, 1:70), when he is studiously avoiding it. Newton sometimes comments on the "beauty of the numbers" in Milton, Homer, and Pope (note to book 2, line 948, 1:149), and (occasionally) on Pope's notes (note to book 2, line 489, 1:113). *Paradise Lost. A Poem, in Twelve Books. The Author John Milton. A New Edition, with Notes of Various Authors*, ed. Thomas Newton, 2 vols. (London: Printed for J. and R. Tonson and S. Draper, 1749).

6. Johnson's note to *Macbeth* act 2, scene 2, quoted from Dodd, *Beauties of Shakespear*, 2:140.

7. Thomas Rymer, trans., "The Preface of the Translator," in *Reflections on Aristotle's Treatise of Poesie*, by Rene Rapin (London: Printed by T. N. for H. Herringman, 1674), a4v–b2r. As indicated in a footnote, Dryden's line had been imitated (at line 386) in the second book of *The Dunciad*: "*And all was hushed, &c.*] Alludes to *Dryden's* verse in the *Indian Emperor*, *All things are hush'd, as Nature's self lay dead.*" *The Dunciad*, ed. James Sutherland, 3rd ed., vol. 5 of *The Twickenham Edition* (1963), 148n. Dryden's lines appear in a footnote to William Wordsworth's "Essay, Supplementary to Preface" of 1815, where they are described as "vague, bombastic, and senseless." *Poems by William Wordsworth: Including Lyrical Ballads, and the Miscellaneous Pieces of the Author. With Additional Poems, a New Preface, and a Supplementary Essay*, 2 vols. (London: Printed for Longman et al., 1815), 1:358–59.

8. Included in Dodd's *Beauties* is a description of a routed army in *Cymbeline* on which Dodd commented: "This description is truly classical, and deserves to be placed in competition with the finest in *Homer* and *Virgil*," but, assuming that such comparisons produce pleasure suggests that readers "may be agreeably amused by turning to the . . . *Iliad*" (1:210).

9. Samuel Johnson, *Lives of the Most Eminent English Poets*, ed. Roger Lonsdale, 4 vols. (Oxford: Clarendon Press, 2006), 4:74. For a full account of Pope's "Observations" on the *Iliad*, see David Hopkins's chapter in this volume.

10. Pope, *The Iliad of Homer*, 23:141n. The passage in the "Assembly of Fowls," as Pope calls Chaucer's poem, occupies lines 176–82 in modern editions.

11. For a discussion of all these editions, see Barrett Kalter, *Modern Antiques: The Material Past in England, 1660–1780* (Lewisburg, PA: Bucknell University Press, 2012), chap. 2.

12. For a full account of Speght's editions, see Derek Pearsall, "Thomas Speght," in *Editing Chaucer: The Great Tradition*, ed. Paul G. Ruggiers (Norman, OK: Pilgrim, 1984), 71–92.

13. A copy of Speght's 1598 edition of Chaucer that was given to Pope at the age of thirteen, which contains marginalia in his earliest hand, is in the Hurd Library at Hartlebury Castle, Worcestershire. See "Pope's Copy of Chaucer" in *Collected in Himself: Essays Critical, Biographical, and Bibliographical on Pope and Some of His Contemporaries*, by Maynard Mack (London: Associated University Presses, 1982), 179–94.

14. Thomas Speght, *The Workes of Our Antient and Learned English Poet, Geffrey Chaucer, Newly Printed* (London: Printed by Adam Islip, at the charges of Thomas Wright, 1598), Bbbb.iii.v.

15. Alice S. Miskimin has pointed out that the praise for Spenser in 1602 (reproduced in 1687) is stronger than that which had appeared in 1598, when Spenser's "much frequenting of Chaucers antient speeches causeth many to allow farre better of him, then otherwise they would." Alice S. Miskimin, *The Renaissance Chaucer* (New Haven, CT: Yale University Press, 1975), 255.

16. John Dryden, preface to *Fables, Ancient and Modern*, in *The Poems of John Dryden*, ed. Paul Hammond and David Hopkins, 5 vols. (New York: Pearson/Longman, 1995–2005), 5:49–50.

17. Dryden, preface to *Fables*, 5:67.

18. Ibid., 5:84.

19. *The Works of Geoffrey Chaucer, Compared with the Former Editions, and Many Valuable MSS*, ed. John Urry (London: Printed for Bernard Lintot, 1721), iv. Subsequent references are cited parenthetically in the text.

20. For the composition of the 1721 edition, see William L. Alderson and Arnold C. Henderson, *Chaucer and Augustan Scholarship* (Berkeley: University of California Press, 1970), chap. 5.

21. Timothy Thomas annotated a copy of Urry's edition that was presented to the British Library by William Thomas (shelfmark 831.l.4-5). On an interleaved page facing this footnote *there* is corrected to *here*.

22. *The Plays of William Shakespeare. In Ten Volumes. With the Corrections and Illustrations of Various Commentators* (London: Printed for C. Bathurst et al., 1778), 1:49.

23. *The Canterbury Tales of Chaucer, in the Original, from the Most Authentic Manuscripts; and as They Are Turn'd into Modern Language by Mr. Dryden, Mr. Pope, and Other Eminent Hands*, ed. Thomas Morell (London: Printed for the Editor, 1737). Subsequent references are cited parenthetically in the text. The volume was reissued (but not in any way altered) as *The Canterbury Tales of Chaucer, in the Original from the Most Authentic Manuscripts; and as They Are Turn'd into Modern Language by Several Eminent Hands. With References to Authors, Ancient and Modern; Various Readings, and Explanatory Notes. The Second Edition* (London: Printed for J. Osborn, 1740).

24. For discussion of headless lines (and other irregularities) in Chaucerian MSS, see Derek Pearsall, "Chaucer's Meter: The Evidence of the Manuscripts," in *Essays on the Art of Chaucer's Verse*, ed. Alan T. Gaylord (London: Routledge, 2001), 131–44.

25. The distinction between footnotes on the page and annotations in the appendix is not always strictly observed. When, in "The Knyghtes Tale," Theseus goes hunting with "Houndys," Morell comments at the foot of the page: "We have a pretty Description of these Hounds in *Shakespear* from *Theseus*'s own Mouth," and goes on to quote extensively from *A Midsummer Night's Dream* (124n).

26. In his own Observation on this passage in book 6, lines 181–86, Pope compared Homer with "Ecclesiasticus Ch.14. V.18.": "*As of the green Leaves on a thick Tree, some fall, and some grow; so is the Generation of Flesh and Blood, one cometh to an end, and another is born.*" Pope, *The Iliad of Homer*, 7:334–35n.

27. For Pope's "Observations" on Achilles, see David Hopkins's chapter in this volume.

28. "It is no easy matter to answer this argument from the heathen Theology, and no wonder therefore if it confounds the reason of *Philætius*; but we who have certain hopes of a future state, can readily solve the difficulty: that state will be a time of retribution; it will amply recompense the good man for all his calamities, or as *Milton* expresses, *Will justify the ways of God to men*." Pope, *The Odyssey of Homer*, ed. Maynard Mack, vols. 9 and 10 of *The Twickenham Edition* (1967), 10:245n (note to book 20, line 251).

29. In this Morell was similar to Joseph Spence, who in "Evening IV" of *An Essay on Mr Pope's Odyssey* has *Antiphaus* observe of this moment in Homer's poem that "upon considering the Afflictions of his Prince, whose Piety and Virtue he was so well assured of," Philætius "falls into a Rant against Providence; in which the Language is as lively and vigorous, as the

Sentiment is ill-grounded and absurd," adding that "we must always take care not to attribute to the Poet, what he speaks under some other Person." Joseph Spence, *An Essay on Mr Pope's Odyssey. In Five Dialogues*, 2nd ed. (London: Printed for S. Wilmot, 1737), 221–22.

30. Theobald, *Works of Shakespeare*, 7:66n.

31. *The Parliament of Fowls*, lines 241–43, Dodd, *Beauties of Shakespear*, 1:124.

32. Theobald, *Works of Shakespeare*, 490.

33. *The Works of Shakespear in Eight Volumes. The Genuine Text (Collated with all the Former Editions, and then Corrected and Emended) Is Here Settled: Being Restored from the Blunders of the First Editors, and the Interpolations of the Two Last: With a Comment and Notes, Critical and Explanatory. By Mr. Pope and Mr. Warburton* (London: Printed for J. and P. Knapton et al., 1747), 3:153–54.

34. *The Canterbury Tales of Chaucer. To Which Are Added, an Essay on His Language and Versification; an Introductory Discourse; and Notes*, ed. Thomas Tyrwhitt, 5 vols. (London: Printed for T. Payne, 1775–1778). Subsequent references are cited parenthetically in the text. The second posthumous edition, *The Canterbury Tales of Chaucer. To Which Are Added an Essay on his Language and Versification, and an Introductory Discourse: Together with Notes and a Glossary*, 2 vols. (Oxford: Clarendon Press, 1798), although sensibly rearranged and beautifully printed, contains few modifications. For a full account of Tyrwhitt's editions, see B. A. Windeatt, "Thomas Tyrwhitt," in Ruggiers, *Editing Chaucer*, 117–43.

35. It should be recorded, however, that in several editions, such as John Bell's *Poets of Great Britain* (1782), and Robert Anderson's *British Poets* (1793), Tyrwhitt's *Canterbury Tales* was combined with Urry's text of the other Chaucerian poems.

36. Urry's line ("Not in Purgatory, but right in Hell") was never reproduced. Tyrwhitt's reading is not found in any of those manuscripts now regarded as the best ("Nought in purgatorie / but in helle" [Hengwrt]; "Nat in my purgatorie / but in helle" [Ellesmere]; "Nought in Purgatori but in helle" [Corpus Christi MS.198]; "Nought in purgatorie / but in helle" [Cambridge Dd.4.24]) or in the early printed editions ("Nought in purgatory / but in hell" [Thynne, 1532]; "Nought in purgatory, but in hell" [Speght, 1598]; "Nought in purgatory, but in hell" [Dryden, 1700]). It was Tyrwhitt's reading, however, that held sway well into the nineteenth century, both in learned and popular editions such as Cowden Clarke's *The Riches of Chaucer* (1735) (which marked the necessary elision "Not only' in purgatory but in hell"), and the edition of *The Canterbury Tales* published in Edinburgh under the care of George Gilfillan in 1760. Thereafter, almost all printings of "The Knight's Tale" have reproduced Morell's headless form of the line.

37. Windeatt lists some admissions by Tyrwhitt in his annotations that he has added some words without manuscript authority; Ruggiers, *Editing Chaucer*, 133.

38. Dryden is called a "great Poet" but one who "was not very conversant with the authors of which Chaucer's library seems to have been composed" (Tyrwhitt, *The Canterbury Tales of Chaucer*, 4:177), and gently mocked for following Rymer in pointing to Provencal influence (ibid., 1:xxv) and for one glaring mistranslation (ibid., 4:229).

39. Tyrwhitt, *The Canterbury Tales of Chaucer* (1798), 2:401.

40. Ibid., 2:401. Warton, in fact, had not glossed but paraphrased the lines on the Clerk: "His unwearied attention to logic had tinctured his conversation with much pedantic formality, and taught him to speak on all subjects in a precise and sententious style." But Warton continues: "Yet his conversation was instructive: and he was no less willing to submit than to communicate his opinion to others." Thomas Warton, *The History of English Poetry, from the*

Close of the Eleventh to the Commencement of the Eighteenth Century, 4 vols. (London: Printed for J. Dodsley, 1774–1781), 1:451.

41. *The Plays of William Shakespeare*, ed. George Steevens (London: Printed for C. Bathurst et al., 1778), 3:31.

42. Steevens, *Plays of William Shakespeare*, 3:29.

43. "How oft', when press'd to marriage, have I said, / Curse on all laws but those which love has made! / Love, free as air, at sight of human ties, / Spreads his light wings, and in a moment flies." Alexander Pope, *Eloisa to Abelard*, in *The Rape of the Lock and Other Poems*, ed. Geoffrey Tillotson, vol. 2 of *The Twickenham Edition* (1962), 2:304–5 (lines 73–76).

44. "*Love will not be confin'd by Maisterie: / When Maisterie comes, the Lord of Love anon / Flutters his wings, and forthwith he is gone.* Chaucer. P*" (where "P" attributes the quotation to Pope himself). Pope, *Eloisa to Abelard, Twickenham Edition*, 2:305n.

45. *The Works of Alexander Pope, Esq.*, ed. William Lisle Bowles, 10 vols. (London: Printed for J. Johnson et al., 1806), 2:39; *The Poetical Works of Alexander Pope, Esq.*, 2 vols. (London: Printed for John Bumpus, 1822), 2:32.

46. Philip Neve, *Cursory Remarks on Some of the Ancient English Poets, Particularly Milton* (London, 1789), 6.

47. Urry reads: "Love wolle not be constreynid by maistry: / Whan maistry cometh, the God of Love anon / Betith his winges, and farewell, is he gone." Urry, *Works of Geoffrey Chaucer*, 108.

48. Pope's *The Temple of Fame* had been accompanied, in the editions of 1736 and 1751, with footnotes containing extensive and (fairly) accurate transcriptions from Chaucer's *The House of Fame* as printed in Speght's edition of 1598.

49. "Love, that's too generous, t'abide / To be against its Nature ty'd; / For where 'tis of it self inclin'd, / It breaks loose, when it is confin'd; / And like the Soul its harbourer, / Debar'd the freedom of the Air; / Disdains, against its will, to stay, / But struggles out, and flies away. / And therefore, never can comply, / T'indure the Matrimonial tye." Samuel Butler, *Hudibras*, ed. John Wilders (Oxford: Clarendon Press, 1967), part 3, canto 1, lines 553–62.29-30.

50. "Ne may loue be compeld by maistery; / For soone as maistery comes, sweet loue anone / Taketh his nimble winges, and soone away is gone." Edmund Spenser, *The Faerie Qveene*, (London: William Ponsonbie, 1590), 398 (book 3, canto 1, stanza 25).

51. Dodd, *Beauties of Shakespear*, 1:83.

52. Dryden, preface to *Fables*, 50.

8

Looking Homeward

Thomas Warton's Annotation of Milton and the Poetic Tradition

Adam Rounce

The reader accustomed to annotation of poetry as self-evident explication will likely be nonplussed by some of the notes in Thomas Warton's edition of Milton's shorter poems (1785). Take the famous sonnet, "Methought I saw my late espoused saint," the informal end of Milton's English poems in Warton's volume. The final line has this note affixed:

> Birch has printed a Sonnet said to be written by Milton, in 1665, when he retired to Chalfont on account of the plague, and to have been lately seen inscribed on the glass of a window in that place. LIFE, p. xxxviii. It has the word SHEENE as a substantive. But Milton was not likely to commit a scriptural mistake. For the Sonnet improperly represents David as punished by a pestilence for his adultery with Bathsheba. Birch, however, had been informed by [George] Vertue, that he had seen a satirical medal, struck upon Charles the second, abroad, without any legend, having a correspondent device.[1]

The relation of this succession of details to "Methought I saw" is not immediately apparent: the scriptural accuracy might be a submerged reference to that sonnet's "purification" of the "old law" in *Leviticus*, accuracy not maintained by the ersatz Miltonic sonnet offered by Thomas Birch in the biography attached to his *Miscellaneous Works of John Milton* (1738), with its mistaken allusion to David and Bathsheba, but not reprinted by Warton (1728–1790). The reference to "sheene" also appears a non sequitur.

It might be inferred that Warton's compendious scholarship and desire for completism make him insert the note here to explain why he is not including the sonnet found by Birch. The attentive reader of Warton's edition might link the mention of "SHEENE" to Milton's use of it near the conclusion of *Comus* (1634), where Warton marks "spangled sheen" by a reference to his earlier *Observations on the Faery Queene* (1762); there, he lists Milton's other poetic deployments of the word, also

151

notes Birch's hypothetical sonnet, and suggests that Milton's "singular . . . usage" of "SHEEN" as a substantive "ought to be admitted as an internal argument in favour of that hypothesis."[2] Twenty-three years later, Warton's return to "SHEENE" in his footnote thus implies (albeit rather gnomically) that this argument has some weight in favor of Milton's authorship, though ultimately the evidence is against it.

Birch had also noted the scriptural error in the sonnet, considering it "only as a very happy Imitation of *Milton's* Style and Manner." It only has ten lines, for one, and does indeed strike the reader as a pastiche of Milton's righteous ire in his own, Petrarchan sonnets:

> Fair Mirrour of foul Times! whose fragile Sheene
> Shall as it blazeth, break; while Providence
> (Aye watching o'er his Saints with Eye unseen,)
> Spreads the red Rod of angry Pestilence,
> To sweep the wicked and their Counsels hence.[3]

The sonnet is, in fact, a spoof by Alexander Pope, sent in a letter to Jonathan Richardson the elder, with the usual disclaimer ("the above was given me by a Gentleman, as I travelld").[4] Its presumed mission (which it accomplished, to some degree) was to fool the many Miltonic collectors and enthusiasts, starting with Richardson, one of the most distinguished.

This footnote is characteristic of Warton's editing in Milton's *Poems upon Several Occasions*. It is suggestively informative, rather than linear or direct, implying a rich, diffuse world of further information. The point is reached by the reader, but the journey is usually not concise or straightforward. There was no "standard" scholarly edition of an English poet in 1785, and Warton's Milton may seem a peculiar model to adopt as one. Yet for all its apparent eccentricities, certain important features of Warton's annotation (such as its allusive range and the purpose behind its critical deliberations) are indicative of the ways in which editing of English poetry would further develop. It will be argued here that Warton's footnotes, like his edition, are both a curio of its learned age and a notable anticipation of a style of editing that would follow, and therefore one of the most significant editions of English poetry in the eighteenth century.

Warton's edition was of no little consequence in the continuing reception of Milton. Collected Miltons (such as Thomas Newton's of 1752, completing his important *Paradise Lost* of 1749) had appeared before, but the shorter poems had been eclipsed by the prominence of *Paradise Lost* and served more as adjuncts to its undoubted centrality in English poetry. Commentators such as Francis Peck (in his miscellaneous 1740 collection of biographical and critical material, apocryphal texts, and notes on Miltonic style as well as influence) had of course remarked on the non-epic poetry. But Warton's voluminous headnotes and annotation would act as a reminder of the significance of such works to contemporary aesthetics, and prove highly influential on its readership, not least in the sort of poetic taste and historical reading it promoted.[5] As Tom Duggett, among others, has noted, Wordsworth shows traces of Warton's phraseology in the "Essay, Supplementary to the Preface" (1815).[6] Leigh Hunt, like Warton a lover of Edmund Spenser, offered the fullest encomium to his labors: "His edition of the minor poems of Milton is a wilderness of sweets. It is the only one in which a true lover of the original can pardon an exuberance of annotation; though I confess I am inclined enough to pardon any notes that resemble it, however numerous. The 'builded rhyme' stands at the top of the page, like a fair edifice with all sorts of flowers and fresh waters at its foot."[7] Why did Hunt not find this wilderness chaotic? It is possible that the very detours of the annotation, adapting the tradition of reading Milton's poetry through the classical, scriptural, and European languages, and augmenting this with many more sources from vernacular English poetry, especially the literature of the earlier Renaissance and medieval periods, was what made the experience of reading the poems so attractive. Warton had spent decades assiduously rediscovering such vernacular literature, in his writings on Spenser, his unfinished *History of English Poetry* (1774–1781), and elsewhere. The notes to the Milton edition are in some ways a low-key culmination of that labor.

Although others would be less complimentary, before considering Warton's extensive annotation in detail, it is worth enumerating the virtues of Warton's approach. The most comprehensive historian of Milton's editors has a very high estimate of the edition and its effects. Ants Oras declared, "it was Warton's destiny to help to establish a more or less adequate valuation of Milton's early works," and to introduce a certain rigor: "critical analyses in Warton's edition are more minute and keener than those in any of the earlier Milton commentaries."[8] Of course, Warton's scholarly background made him "unusually fit for all kinds of historical illustration" (271), and this was his great innovation, particularly with regard to allusion: "Warton is keenly bent on establishing the literary ancestry of Milton's epithets, apparently recognizing that the sources of an expression largely determine its associations" (286). Though some of these sources would not be readily accepted, it is the forensic level of detail applied that is an important step. The incidental consequence is a "rehabilitation of older English literature," which is "the most conspicuous feature of Warton's labours" (296). Oras's general conclusion is that

> Warton's edition realized in a remarkable degree for Milton what Shakespeare scholarship had already accomplished, and in some respects with more instinctive insight and literary skill. The minute inquiries into Elizabethan literature and lore found, for example, in Steevens's contributions to the First Variorum do not convey the same feeling of atmosphere, and deal less with distinctly artistic qualities than Warton's remarks. (18)

Here, the wilderness of notes was a means to an important end: Warton's erudition was not mere allusion spotting but part of his larger critical understanding of Milton's influences, aesthetic, and poetic technique.

"A POETIC IDEAL"

Warton's edition was published in March 1785, to a generally favorable reception.[9] Richard Hurd congratulated him a few weeks later on his "admirable Edition" and hoped Warton will find time to edit *Samson Agonistes* and *Paradise Regained*, the two longer poems not included, "in the same form & manner" in the future. George Steevens, never shy in displaying his own erudition, wrote a longer letter a week later, full of praise and further possible allusions.[10] As will be seen, there was dissent, but mainly related to the quantity of allusion in the footnotes, rather than the wider intention of the volume—to consolidate the significance of Milton's non-epic poetry for contemporary literary culture.

In his prefatory remarks, Warton makes clear the relationship between Milton's shorter poems and the 1780s. The poems are popular now because of their imaginative character: their "fiction and fancy," "picturesque description, and romantic imagery" were previously less appreciated, in the later seventeenth and earlier eighteenth centuries, because "the times were still unpropitious, and the public taste was unprepared for their reception." The reason for this lack of preparation? "Wit and rhyme, sentiment and satire, polished numbers," in other words, a critical position that since the 1740s had led both Thomas and his brother Joseph to posit a more spontaneous reliance on nature and the imagination as an alternative (iii).

Joan Pittock has described how Milton's early poems "seem to Warton the last emanation of those flights of fancy that had figuratively and inventively bodied forth the experiences of life itself, to transmute mundane existence into an artificial but poetical ideal. This faculty has departed with the new insistence on the importance of everyday life and manners."[11] The poems are a more instinctive imaginative form, now unobtainable due to the more self-conscious modern placing of the quotidian as the center of artistic experience. In ironic fashion, this anticipates the notorious "disassociation of sensibility" of T. S. Eliot, who attempted to show the imaginative possibilities lost to English poetry after 1660, supposedly "aggravated by the influence of the two most powerful poets of the century, Milton and Dryden."[12]

For Warton, Milton's shorter, more lyric verse is a crucial imaginative and artistic conduit between the present and the lost past. It is a habit of most editors to distinguish themselves from their predecessors, and point out what they have improved. Warton is less dismissive than most, but he always makes clear the underexplored aspects of both Milton's work and its sources in older English literature. Bentley's infamous suggested improvements to *Paradise Lost* (1732), based on the flawed hypothesis of an incompetent or nefarious amanuensis, would have been better had he paid attention to the rest of Milton's canon: Bentley "never attempts to confirm his conjectures from the smaller poems, written before the poet was blind: and from which, in the prosecution of the same arbitrary mode of emendation, his analogies in many instances might have consequently derived a much stronger degree of authority" (vii). Even if such emendations would still be contentious, they would at least be grounded in Milton's language. A similar omission is noted, politely, in another predecessor: "Doctor Newton, an excellent scholar, was unacquainted with the treasures of the Gothic library. From his more solid and rational studies, he never deviated into this idle track of reading" (xxi). The slightly self-mocking opposition between the rationalistic scholar and the more adventurous antiquarian, rediscovering the obscurities of the past, is overdone, but it is also part of Warton's central thesis. His editing of Milton will introduce a new level of contextual scholarship and explication through its attention to the sort of "gothic" vernacular poetry previously overlooked; Milton "may be reckoned an old English poet; and therefore here requires that illustration, without which no old English poet can be well illustrated" (xxi). In practice, editors such as Newton and his contributors had found elements in Milton of Shakespeare and Spenser (when not drawing on the classics or scripture); Warton's framing of Milton as an English classic took him to their less well-known contemporaries and to the literature of the previous centuries.

Warton placed Milton in a rich, hitherto hardly noticed intertextual world; this required a degree of illustration in his annotation, the extent and validity of which would be debatable. His rationale was that "[t]he best poets imperceptibly adopt phrases and formularies from the writings of their contemporaries or immediate predecessors." The first line edited in the volume, the opening of *Lycidas*, shows this in practice: to "Yet once more," Warton quotes an elegy on Mary Sidney, Countess of Pembroke, "Yet once againe, my Muse" (2). The objection to such a suggestion is the familiar one of intention, or as Coleridge put it, testily, in his marginalia, "Why, in Heaven's name! might not 'once more' have as well occurred to Milton as to Sidney?"[13] The claims for the imperceptible nature of such borrowing are arguably the Achilles's heel of Warton's notes: suggesting that the influence is hardly realized even by the poet adopting the "phrases and formularies," makes it seem all the more tenuous (and therefore unnecessary to trace). A similar example is the start of "Methought I saw my late espoused saint," which recalls

> Raleigh's elegant Sonnet, called a VISION *upon the conceipt of the* Faerie Queene, [which] begins thus,
>   Methought I saw the grave where Laura lay.
> And hence perhaps the idea of a Sonnet in the form of a vision was suggested to Milton. (365)

And hence, perhaps not, of course. The way in which a common phrase, a poetic form, and the idea of the poem all add up to a possibly profound influence is attractive in its assumption of how literary works affect one another; the problem, for some (other than the impossibility of proving such influence) is that such allusion spotting becomes a substitute for critical insight. Of the modern writers on Warton's criticism, Lawrence Lipking has drawn attention to this antiquarian tendency to be interested in sources and derivations in literature for their own sake, but unwilling and unable to synthesize such great learning toward wider significance: "Along with the virtues of comparative source studies, Warton also exhibits their problems. Once the critic has discovered a source, he may tend to overestimate its importance; and

Warton's criticism, like his poetry, often wanders off into the past when it might better clarify the text presently at issue." For Lipking, the result in a poem like *Lycidas* is that "Warton breaks the poem into a collection of literary reminiscences, and his criticism seldom employs any faculty beyond his well-stocked memory of phrases."[14]

Such a critique seems slightly unfair, though it also gives evidence of a tendency to worry over Warton's alleged allusive excesses that has accompanied his editing (and that of his brother Joseph) from his own lifetime. It is a partial truth, in that Warton's lengthy annotations contain all sorts of apparently undirected material, though he also makes repeated practical interventions with regard to potential ambiguities. His editing of *Lycidas* is a touchstone for both positions. Even if, like Coleridge, readers are unconvinced of the utility of "Yet once againe," Warton precedes to contradict the claims of Francis Peck and Newton that "Yet once more" signifies Milton's returning to the elegiac form; "why should it have a restrictive reference," he argues, pointing out that the flowers of the opening are generically pastoral, rather than directly related to elegy (2–3). The pattern is set, whereby prolix and discursive notes are accompanied by those with telling insights and suggestions.

One such instance is the extended note on a famous line: "Look homeward Angel now, and melt with ruth." Warton's long discussion establishes the now accepted reading that the castle island of St Michael's Mount in Marazion, west Cornwall, is the ideal symbolic place for the titular saint to guard the English coast against the threat of Catholic Spain. He also takes on the contention of Robert Thyer, a learned contributor to Newton's 1752 edition, that the "angel" concerned is not Michael but Edward King, an "angel now," looking "homeward." Thyer argues this through allusion:

> So the Pastoral Elegy on Sir Philip Sidney.
> Philisides is dead. O happy Sprite,
> That now in Heav'n with blessed souls dost bide,
> Look down awhile from where thou sitst above &c. *Thyer.*[15]

This elegy (by Spenser's friend Lodowick Bryskett) is a precedent for the superficially attractive reading of the late King looking down from heaven, and an implied reconciliation with his loss. Warton will have none of it: "Thyer seems to suppose, that the meaning of the last line is, 'You, O Lycidas, now an angel, look down from heaven, &c.' But how can this be said to *look homeward?* And why is this shipwrecked person to *melt with ruth?*"[16] It is a good, practical point, ignoring the possible relation of the allusion (which indeed is only relevant if the angel can be identified with King): a pedant might argue that King as angel could look homeward from Cornwall toward Cambridge, or his birthplace of Ireland even, but still it would seem strange for him to "melt with ruth," or pity, at his own loss (and hardly analogous to Sidney sitting happily in heaven). Warton paraphrases the line's apostrophe to the Saint: "look landward, Look *homeward* now, and melt with pity at the melancholy spectacle to which you have been a witness." He also identifies the misidentification with the ambiguities of syntax and the tense. Newton's text of "Look homeward Angel now" allows the present tense to be applied to the supposed beatification of King (i.e., "now you are an angel") rather than the looking. To prevent such misreading in future, Warton will "now for the first time exhibit" the line "properly pointed"—that is, "Look homeward, Angel, now, and melt with ruth" (29). There is no bibliographical justification offered for this "proper" punctuation; the emendation is necessary to solve the problem, and that for Warton is sufficient. Cavalier as this may seem to a modern editor, Thyer's reading has been found wanting and the more plausible meaning established.

Lipking's complaint, that Warton's wandering among his multiple possible sources took him away from any real criticism, is justified in the breach rather than the observance: the general impression is of a proliferation of annotation and allusion, but within this larger pattern Warton repeatedly makes specific significant interventions. Not least of these is with the recently departed Samuel Johnson, whose low opinion of Milton's shorter verse had been recently canonized in the "Life of Milton" (1779), with particular disdain for *Lycidas*:

> It is not to be considered as the effusion of real passion; for passion runs not after remote allusions and obscure opinions. Passion plucks no berries from the myrtle and ivy, nor calls upon Arethuse and Mincius, nor tells of rough *satyrs* and *fauns with cloven heel*. Where there is leisure for fiction there is little grief.[17]

This charge of affected and insincere sorrow would become notorious, and a part of Johnson's prejudiced suspicion of the character of Milton the ambitious Puritan (a suspicion that Warton shared, giving the aesthetic reasons behind his reply more clarity than a riposte based on politics). Warton's response in his notes is to embrace, rather than evade, the challenge: to feel only "leisure for fiction" is to misread poetic effect:

> In this piece there is perhaps more poetry than sorrow. But let us read it for its poetry. It is true, that passion plucks no berries from the myrtle and ivy, nor calls upon Arethuse and Mincius, nor tells of *rough Satyrs with cloven heel*. But poetry does this; and in the hands of Milton, does it with a peculiar and irresistible charm. (34)

It is not the reader's job to judge Milton's sincerity but, rather, to accept the poem as a performance and to appreciate its literary achievement on those terms; in this respect, its effect is more important than its content. Style is not an end in itself, but poetry transfigures experience through its form: such charm might be a trick, but it is a beautiful one, and disarms any potential critique. Warton is equally dismissive of quibbles about the poem's mixture of pagan and religious pastoral: "These irregularities and incongruities must not be tried by modern criticism" (35). To suggest that contradictions should not be attempted to be resolved might seem an odd position for an editor, but Warton as an enthusiast cannot see the point of disabling the imaginative experience for such irritable reaching after fact and reason; those sort of critical urges are for him misplaced.

"MUCH OLD READING"

It is, in many ways, fruitless to judge Warton by the punctilious standards of modern criticism. There is evidence to suggest that many readers were not overwhelmed by Warton's profuse annotation, or at least accepted its excesses rather than openly chastised them. Even Coleridge's rather facetious marginalia show him to be stimulated by Warton's wholehearted presentation of Milton's shorter poetry. Lipking has a point, in that Warton was undeniably diffuse as an editor, but the benefits of such an approach seem to have been thought to outnumber the longueurs.

In such editorial workings, distinctions can and should be made, of course. It is entirely possible to argue that Warton's aims and critical judgments were sound, but that his method sometimes produced results that were out of proportion to the original question. His accumulation of verbal echoes in his annotation is uniformly thorough, but sometimes the means and the end do not match. The opening declaration that Lycidas too knew how to "build the lofty rime" leads to an extended argument with the shade of Zachary Pearce (bishop of Rochester and enemy to Bentley's edition) about the different meaning of "Rhime" (verse generally) and "Rime" (the sound of line endings). Warton accepts that "the lofty verse" and "unattempted yet in prose or rhyme" are synonyms, and quotes from Ariosto's "in *prosa* mai, ne in RIMA," and in Sir John Harrington's translation: "A tale in *prose* ne VERSE yet sung or said" (4). But he dismisses Pearce's citations of Spenser's sonnet to Lord Buckhurst (which distinguishes "rude rime" from "golden verse") and *Faerie Queene* 1.6.13 ("a shepherd's rime") because these are not "at all to the point." Instead, he offers counterexamples of where "Rime" means poetry generally. Pearce should have quoted Spenser's *October*, "Thous kenst not, Percy, how the RIME should rage," and John Fletcher's ode to his wearily prolific collaborator Francis Beaumont, "The wanton Ovid whose enticing RIMES." He queries also why Bentley, knowing the Greek, wanted to substitute "song" for "Rhime." He ends with a near contemporary, Thomas Gray's ceremonial *Ode for Music* (1769), and its Miltonic sense of the word: "And nods his hoary head, and listens to the RHIME" (5).

Enough is accumulated, in Warton's view, to show that Pearce was mistaken to build a theory of Milton's two distinct meanings in the spellings. It is very much of a piece with Warton's method to dig into the footnotes of other editors and suggest to them more pertinent examples (and he was much less rude about it than many), yet the proliferation of illustrations here does not perhaps elucidate as much as confuse. On the other hand, this is perhaps Warton's point: Pearce may have been wrong to demarcate two definite meanings in the variant spellings of the word, and the necessary multiplication of varying examples leads the reader to understand the difficulty of such precise explication. It also shows Warton's abiding sense of the chronology of poetic history by ending with one of the most Miltonic of eighteenth-century poets in Gray.

Warton's annotation often starts with Milton's internal references, and the building of an allusive vocabulary in his own works. Occasionally Warton seems to have an irresistible urge to trace possible further allusions: The line in the *Ode, on the Morning of Christ's Nativity* (1629)—"As all their souls in blissful rapture took"—is compared to the philosophical fallen angels in *Paradise Lost* 2.554–5, who "Took with ravishment / The thronging audience." This possible trace is followed by "I observe, by the way, that RAVISHMENT is a favourite word with Milton" (273). Warton then quotes two examples of the word from *Paradise Lost* (5.46 and 9.541) and one from *Comus* (line 245). When this is compared to Spenser's *Astrophel* ("Secret ravishment"), which is in turn compared back to *Paradise Lost* (9.461, "With rapine sweet bereav'd"), even the patient reader may feel that we have wandered somewhat off-piste.

Leaving aside the differences of tone between holy rapture and less than divine ravishment, what is presented in such footnotes is an exhaustive guide to the connections in Milton's universe; this often shows how Warton possessed a knowledge unsurpassed in the possible density of poetic allusion. Yet, sometimes, it exhausts itself: examples can be tenuous, or indicative of a likelihood for writers to repeatedly use similar words or phrasing. When Warton follows every allusion through, he sometimes seems aware of this potential exhaustion, even though his own curiosity obliges him to reach every possible end, when relevance is waning. In such instances, the charge of excess pedantry is almost ruefully acknowledged. The lengthy response, in *Lycidas*, to "the tender stops of various quills" begins with an apparent ambiguity: "Some readers are here puzzled with the idea of such STOPS as belong to the Organ. By STOPS he here literally means what we now call the HOLES of a flute or any species of pipe." Cited in support is William Browne's *Brittannia's Pastorals* (1613), "What musicke is there in a shepherd's quill, / If but a STOP or *two* therein we spie?" Browne's once-popular work is near enough linguistically to make the point. To confirm it, Warton offers a more famous example of the pipe from the same period, this time as metaphor, with Hamlet confronting Rosencrantz and Guildenstern: "you would *play upon me*: you would seam to know my STOPS, &c." Just in case the point is unclear, he also cites the Prologue to 4 *Henry* 2, where the personification of "Rumour" defines itself: "Rumour is a pipe. . . . And of so easy and so plain a STOP"; this is followed by Michael Drayton, from the *Muses Elizium* (1630): "Teaching every STOP and *kay* / To those that on the pipe do play" (32). Then he moves forward a few decades to *Comus*, "Or found of pastoral reed with oaten STOPS." Moreover, Milton "mentions the stops of an organ, but in another manner, in PARAD. L. B. xi. 561. See also B. vii. 596." Almost as an afterthought, "In Drummond [of Hawthornden], STOP is applied to a Lute, but I think metathetically for *note*." The example, "Each STOPPE a sigh," is then possibly undermined: "unless he means CLOSE, or *interval*" (33).[18] It is charming that Warton cannot rule out either possibility, even if neither helps the footnote's attempt to show why the word means one thing rather than another.

This recreation, in the notes, of such an allusive contextual literary sphere—consisting of Milton's peers, near contemporaries, analogues, followers, possible sources, and clear influences—attempts to present the full richness of the literary, religious, artistic, and historical culture surrounding Milton's writing from before the 1600s up to the present, and is Warton's signal achievement. Where previous editors had suggested some echoes of Miltonic vocabulary, Warton found and traced comprehensive linking patterns of language and images throughout his writings. Where previous writers had noted Shakespearian or Spenserian allusion, he found more pertinent ones, or supplemented them with the likes of Drayton, Fletcher, or Browne. It is, though, the nature of such annotation to be speculative and ultimately uncertain: a clear allusion to one reader is to another a mere coincidence, or an exaggerated attempt to locate the sources behind an act of creation where few, if any, may exist.

Amid the genial good wishes and praise for Warton's edition, the dissenting voices tended to draw attention to his habit of pinning and locating allusions and phrases in somewhat tenuous and often very obscure sources. An anonymous correspondent criticizes in particular the relation of these "similar passages" in the annotation

> where there is only a word or half a phrase to build any likeness upon. I cannot readily persuade myself that Milton and Shakespear borrowed half their thoughts and almost all their expressions from a few insipid Rhymers, who have happened to come down to our times,—who drew from the same sources, and of course wrote in the *same common language*,—because they published their ditties ten or twelve years before them.[19]

The idea is a little mixed, in that the allusions are criticized for being unlikely given their relative brevity, and for the inherent claim that the works of obscure poetasters are an influence on Milton or Shakespeare. It does not take a more egalitarian age to consider this an odd form of snobbery, given that the influence of a work is not dependent on its merit or place in any hierarchy. But the more concrete objection anticipates Coleridge's complaint on the note to the opening of *Lycidas*—there is no reason why such phrases or epithets need to be seen as traces and echoes, when they could be as easily reached independently. The correspondent mocks Warton's tracing a commonplace from the *Tempest* to George Peele's *The Old Wives Tale* (1595); Shakespeare could surely have thought of it "without being *obliged for the Thought to George Peele*." The very notion seems to be as ridiculous as Mozart asking a tone-deaf tradesman to whistle him a melody:

> How ludicrous would the Idea be to You, of a Critic, who, an hundred Years hence, should prove that Pope borrowed from Ambrose Philips, or Gray from Mr Jago, or Wm. Woty!—It is true this observation stands in the Way of much old reading, and quotation; but You have made so much real good use of the writers of those times, in throwing light on old words &c.—that You can more readily give up these trifles.[20]

The distinction is between true poet and dunce—Pope and Philips, Gray and Richard Jago (author of *Edge-Hill*) or William Woty (editor of the *Poetical Calendar*), neither of whom are today dismissed as being so obviously beneath the notice of any serious reader. The mocking prediction of how ludicrous it would be to find criticism still quoting such mediocrities as poetic influences a century hence appears ironic indeed, given the heterogeneity of literary studies since the later twentieth century. But beneath the artificial divide between Warton's "real good use" of language and sources, and these "trifles," is a very serious point: the assumption that Milton could not be influenced by "insipid Rhymers" is a fundamental objection to Warton's method of accumulating as much source material as possible, irrespective of its origins. For who is to distinguish between apparently approved canonical influences and sources, and those that are not fit to accompany Milton's own words on the page?

The correspondent's assumption, that there is an inherent quality of literature that can be related to its ability to influence other works, indeed "stands in the Way of much old reading, and quotation," but such old reading and quotation was the systole and diastole of Warton's annotation, and it was rather tactless to declare its fundamental uselessness. As well as such blanket dismissal of minor authors, there is also the criticism of the particulars of Warton's "old reading" from more than one writer ("old" here meaning pre-1580). Readers who were neither antiquarians nor connoisseurs were happy to patronize medieval literature, for instance, as a tedious farrago. A pamphlet response (1785) to Warton's edition illustrates this. Published anonymously, but attributed to Samuel Darby, this is a long review, rather than an argument, and is often approving, but there is one aspect of Warton's editing that brings forth the manner of Pope's *Dunciad*: "I must beg the Favour of you to be sparing in your Quotations from the English blacke Letter Classics. The present Age has manifested an uncommon Relish for all such Reading as was never read." This may seem an odd complaint to make of a scholar renowned in his poetry and prose for promoting the archaic, the gothic, and the historically obscure in literature, a scholar who had repeatedly exhibited an abiding belief in the cultural significance of those "blacke Letter Classics" often held up to ridicule. Darby's argument is that the supposed reading of such works is an artificial, unnatural taste, and their presence is thus antithetical to the workings of an edition read by the truly educated: "I only object to an unsparing Use of these Materials in *classical Publications*."[21] Whether or not this is intended as a withering sarcasm, it indicates a fault line: "*classical*" works—such as editions of Milton—have no place for the Gothic frippery of the materials that form the narrative of Warton's *History of English Poetry* (1774–1781), and that he has indiscriminately introduced into his editing.

This can be represented by many moments in Warton's Milton, such as the extended gloss to "L'Allegro" (1645), line 11, "But come thou Goddess fair and free":

Compare Drayton, Ecl. iv. vol. iv. p.1401.
   A daughter cleped Dowsabell,
      A maiden FAIR and FREE.
In the metrical romances, these two words thus paired together, are a common epithet for a lady. As in SYR. EGLAMOUR, Bl. Let. Pr. by J. Allde, 4to, Signat. A.iii
   The erles daughter FAIR and FREE.
We have FREE alone, ibid.
   Cristabell your daughter FREE.
Another application may illustrate its meaning, ibid.

He was curteys and FREE.
See also Chaucer, March. T. v. 1655. Urr.
   Rise up my wife, my love, my lady FRE.
So Jonson makes his beautiful countess of Bedford to be "FAIR and FREE, and wise."
EPIGRAM. lxxvi.
I know not how far these instances, to which I could add more, will go to explain a line
in TWELFTH NIGHT. A.ii. S.iv. Edit. Steev. Johns. vol. iv. 204. Of an old Song.
          And the FREE maids that weave their threads with bones,
                    Do use to chaunt it,———. (38)

This moves from Drayton's 1593 *Pastorals* (the fourth eclogue) back to the fourteenth-century romance, *Sir Eglamour of Artois* (Warton cites the 1555 black letter
edition, published by William Copland; its composition is usually dated to c.1350).
He then moves forward, and traces half the "epithet for a lady" in Chaucer's "Merchant's Tale," before jumping forward to Jonson's epigram "On the Countess of
Bedford" (1616), ending on the duke's comment introducing the song "Come away,
death" in *Twelfth Night* (1602).

It is entirely characteristic for Warton to claim that he knows not how these instances may explain the duke's line (the phrase "to which I could add more" is also
not a surprise). The allusions are not meant to lead to any such closure, of course,
and Warton's comment is a polite throat clearing: the instances trace a pattern of an
epithet otherwise obscured, from 1350 to the 1630s. It is not, perhaps, the most
important pattern, and an impatient reader might complain that it is vague and does
not lead to any particular point, but that is to misjudge the intention: the result is a
microcosm of Warton's method, which offers a map that is far more comprehensive
in its awareness of what actually made up British literature, with regard to its sources,
alterations, and transformations. Many of these sources are obscure, or anyway not
especially noteworthy, but the aim is not aesthetic so much as archaeological, representing the full range of vernacular works that influenced Milton to some extent,
and which have left their marks, howsoever indirectly, on modern literary culture.

In many ways, such objections as Darby's draw attention to Warton's real innovation—the introduction of a more comprehensive vernacular canon through his annotation, and the move away from an exclusive sense of recent, post-1600 English
poetry as the source, end, and test of ultimate literary value. Warton's primitive materials also illustrate, and help to initiate a further move away from, the annotation
of English poetry as a sort of extension of classical literature, with regard to materials
and method. That Darby's complaint strikes an odd, old-fashioned, and fusty note
(twenty years after Percy's *Reliques*, and in the aftermath of the Chatterton controversy) shows Warton's greater awareness of the literary zeitgeist.

Darby's objection to a more familiar problem with the edition is a useful summary
of the larger difficulties of over-annotation and the tracing of allusion:

When the Images presented to us are not only beautiful, but new; or when there is
something ingenious and uncommon in the Combination or Application of them to

the Subject, it is often a pleasing Task both to the Critic and to the Reader, to trace the Steps of the Author; to enquire at what Fires his Imagination was kindled; *where* he borrowed his Ideas, and *how* he has improved them. . . . But when the Design of "explaining the Author's Allusions, and pointing out his Imitations," is carried to an unreasonable Length; when Epithets or Images, not unusual among good Writers, are piled on each other, without Count or Measure;—the Book indeed will be swell'd to an enormous Size; the Bookseller, like the Sea, may still call out, "It is not enough;" but, believe me, the Reader will be somewhat more than satiated.[22]

For such readers, the notes become at times not a "wilderness of sweets" but an indulgent surfeit. It is possible to argue that Warton often proves some significant point through his tracings, however random they may appear; it is also the case that there is a serendipity in some of his digressions, in that they lead to an unexpected conclusion or area of insight. Yet in many ways, Darby is right: some of the imitations and allusions are extremely tenuous, and some merely prolix examples of a literary enthusiasm that the reader may not share. The only real defense of this aspect of Warton's work is that partly offered by Leigh Hunt: his profuse annotation has the faults of its virtues, because only with its excesses is Warton able to represent his full idea of the workings of a literary culture, some of which is tedious and tendentious but much extremely pertinent. To forbid him to trace allusions from obscure medieval romances would be as fatal as to remove all references to Spenser or Shakespeare.

"A DURABLE MONUMENT"

Over two hundred years on, in a far more self-conscious age of scholarly editing, the degree to which quantities of annotation are a help or hindrance to a reader remains a critical problem. Warton anticipated such difficulties (though his solution was not that of brevity) and also rather more baldly contravened an orthodoxy of modern critical annotation—that of over-interpretation and the insertion of subjective opinion. Mention in his edition of Milton's politics and his prose works in favor of the Commonwealth is usually enough to produce both effects, as in Warton's comments on the Cromwell sonnet ("Cromwell, thou chief of men"): "The prostitution of Milton's Muse to the celebration of Cromwell, was as inconsistent and unworthy, as that this enemy to kings, to antient magnificence, and to all that is venerable and majestic, should have been buried in the Chapel of Henry the Seventh" (353). His brother Joseph wished in 1792 that "he had softened some of his censures on our divine Poet's politics"; at the time of publication, he was more jocular, but he still warned Thomas that "it will be thought you have mauled the Puritans & their Principles." Darby, too, attacked Warton's lapse of editorial judgment at some length.[23] It remains the one element of the edition that makes it seem dated and outmoded; unlike the sources and allusions, which always have the editor's vast learning somewhere behind them, the caustic criticism of Milton and his supposedly offensive beliefs seems out of place amid the erstwhile urbanity of Warton's prose.

Such acid contempt is, however, related to another element that should seem similarly dated to modern editors but is ultimately the most winning side of Warton's annotation: his admittance of his own subjectivity, and that for the sake of what he is trying to represent, pragmatism must sometimes win over scholarly accuracy. It is encapsulated in an editorial explanation of the placing of quotation marks to demarcate the speakers in the famous sonnet "On his blindness":

> *"Doth God exact day-labour, light deny'd?"* Here is a pun on the doctrine in the gospel, that we are to work only while it is light, and in the night no man can work. There is an ambiguity between the natural light of the day, and the author's blindness. I have introduced the turned commas, both in the question and answer, not from any authority, but because they seem absolutely necessary to the sense. (359)

This is a helpful, concise reading, combined with a justification of his offering an emended text in order to make its meaning more coherent. Warton does not hide behind any imaginary source, but he admits, refreshingly, his utter lack of precedent or authority, and that this text, like any other, is an editorial intervention and interpretation. Even if the result tweaks the text beyond what is acceptable in modern terms, his honesty is bracing, punctures his own pretension, and shows the lack of ego in his scholarship.

Warton's Milton is not a neat or polished work: the end of Milton's poems is greeted by the familiar "finis," an overly optimistic marker. There follows an appendix (on *Comus*), corrections and additions, textual variants, and a bibliography of editions. Warton's volume is a work bursting with matter that is squeezed into notes—headnotes, footnotes, endnotes, and ancillary notes at the end. It impresses information on the reader, tirelessly: the eighty-seven lines of the final poem, the Latin verses to John Rouse (1646), cover twelve pages, with a long final note (pages 586–90) acting as a postscript to the edition, describing Milton's genius, his bigoted prose works, and his central place in poetic posterity. Warton did nothing by halves, and he seems to find it hard to stop.

At first sight, the *Critical Review* was excessive in its praise of the edition and Warton's efforts, calling it "a durable monument, on which his name will appear, though in a different department, with a splendour little inferior to Milton's."[24] This seems too much for the editor of a volume (even an abundantly detailed one), rather than its author. It is also not at all what its subject would have thought appropriate, as Warton seems to have been the least egotistic of editors. Even his disdain for Milton's politics is more in sorrow than a chance to use Milton to place his own personality at the forefront. And for all his occasional superlatives, his annotation is not fey, emptily rhapsodic, or affected; nor is it remotely vain or self-interested. Warton has his diversions and indulgences, but he is too fascinated in the workings of literature to become distracted for too long, or self-involved. And his preoccupation with the details of literary history and poetic reception eventually shines through, even if it is sometimes indirect. In his prefatory pages, he notes that "[w]e are surprised to find [John] Dennis, in his Letters, published 1721, quoting a few verses from Milton's

Latin Poems," thus suggesting an unacknowledged popularity at this early date: "But Dennis had them from Toland's *Life of Milton*," Warton reassures himself (vi). What could seem mere pedantry in Warton is never quite so simple, and here his careful plotting of Milton's posthumous reputation is not troubled by a rogue element: Dennis is assimilated and placed into the scheme of things, albeit through such incidental notes. In such diligent (albeit sometimes superfluously detailed) construction of a narrative explication of Milton's life and works through his annotation, Warton provides a model for the level of scrutiny required by the future scholarly edition, even if his materials proved to be distinctly miscellaneous; the result, in an odd way, is a mighty maze that is entirely justified in often seeming without a plan, and when its future influence on the relationship between established canonical poetry and the vernacular tradition is considered, the annotation to Warton's Milton is one suitable coda to his many labors.

NOTES

1. John Milton, *Poems upon Several Occasions, English, Italian, and Latin, with Translations; with Notes Critical and Explanatory, and Other Illustrations*, ed. Thomas Warton (London: Printed for James Dodsley, 1785), 367. Subsequent references to Warton's edition are cited parenthetically in the text.

2. Warton, 261, citing *Observations on the Faery Queene of Spenser*, 2nd ed., 2 vols. (London: Printed for J. and R. Dodsley, 1762), 2:181–82.

3. *The Complete Collection of the Historical, Political, and Miscellaneous Works of John Milton*, ed. Thomas Birch, 2 vols. (London: Printed for A. Millar, 1738), 2:xxxviii.

4. Alexander Pope to Jonathan Richardson, July 18, 1737, in *The Correspondence of Alexander Pope*, ed. George Sherburn, 5 vols. (Oxford: Oxford University Press), 4:81. The poem appears in *Minor Poems*, ed. Norman Ault, vol. 6 of *The Twickenham Edition of the Poems of Alexander Pope*, ed. John Butt et al. (London: Methuen, 1954), 374.

5. Thomas Newton, ed., *Paradise Regain'd: A Poem, in Four Books. To Which Is Added Samson Agonistes: and Poems upon Several Occasions. The Author John Milton. A New Edition, with Notes of Various Authors* (London: Printed for J. and R. Tonson, 1752); Francis Peck, *New Memoirs of the Life and Poetical Works of Mr. John Milton* (London, 1740).

6. Tom Duggett, *Gothic Romanticism: Architecture, Politics, and Literary Form* (Houndmills, UK: Palgrave Macmillan, 2012), 19.

7. Leigh Hunt, "My Books," in *The Indicator, and the Companion; A Miscellany for the Fields and the Fire-side* (London: Edward Moxon, 1845), 54.

8. Ants Oras, *Milton's Editors and Commentators from Patrick Hume to Henry John Todd (1695–1801): A Study in Critical Views and Methods* (London: Oxford University Press, 1931), 269. Subsequent references to Oras are cited parenthetically in the text.

9. See Thomas Warton to Edmond Malone, February 21, 1785, "My volume of Milton will be published on the Tenth of next month" (and n10, advertised in *London Chronicle*, March 8–10), in *The Correspondence of Thomas Warton*, ed. David Fairer (Athens: University of Georgia Press, 1995), 506.

10. Richard Hurd to Thomas Warton, April 4, 1785; George Steevens to Thomas Warton, April 12, 1785. Fairer, *Correspondence of Thomas Warton*, 517, 519–25.

11. Joan Pittock, *The Ascendancy of Taste: The Achievement of Joseph and Thomas Warton* (London: Routledge & Kegan Paul, 1973), 213.

12. T. S. Eliot, "The Metaphysical Poets," in *Selected Essays* (London: Faber and Faber, 1999), 288.

13. Samuel Taylor Coleridge, *Collected Works*, ed. H. J. Jackson and George Whalley, vol. 12, *Marginalia: Part 6. Valckenaer to Zwick* (Princeton, NJ: Princeton University Press, 2001), 888.

14. Lawrence Lipking, *The Ordering of the Arts in Eighteenth-Century England* (Princeton, NJ: Princeton University Press, 1970), 388. Lipking's wider argument is of a certain philological weakness in the *History of English Poetry*: because Warton regards the English of his day as the norm, he "judges the language and versification of old poets according to their progress towards modern English" (386).

15. Newton, *Paradise Regain'd . . . and Poems upon Several Occasions*, 498n. Lodowick Bryskett, an administrator in Ireland, contributed the poem to the 1595 volume containing Spenser's "Astrophel" and other tributes to Sidney. Robert Thyer (1709–1781), librarian at Chetham's in Manchester and the editor of Samuel Butler's *Remains* (1759), was the most significant contributor to Newton's edition (see Oras, 208–9).

16. Samuel Darby, in his pamphlet response to Warton, agreed that "Thyer's Note is every way wrong certainly. Ruth means Pity—Sorrow for others, not for ourselves." *A Letter to the Rev. Mr. T. Warton, on His Late Edition of Milton's Juvenile Poems* (London: Printed for C. Bathurst, 1785), 2.

17. Samuel Johnson, "Life of Milton," in *The Lives of the Most Eminent English Poets*, ed. Roger Lonsdale, 4 vols. (Oxford: Clarendon Press, 2006), 1:278.

18. Warton cites *Sonnets* [i.e., *Poems*] (1616); the reference is to William Drummond's Sonnet 8, "My lute, bee as thou wast."

19. Anonymous to Thomas Warton, December 1, 1785; Fairer, *Correspondence of Thomas Warton*, 552–53. A bugbear of the correspondent is that many of these more flimsy allusions seem to have been suggested to Warton by his friend John Bowle, known for his annotated edition of *Don Quixote* (1781). Warton (xxii) acknowledged Bowle's help.

20. Ibid., 553; for the allusion in question, see Warton, *Poems on Several Occasions*, 592.

21. Darby, *Letter to the Rev. Mr. T. Warton*, 40.

22. Ibid., 16–17.

23. Joseph Warton to William Hayley, March 12, 1792, quoted in John Wooll, *Biographical Memoirs of the Late Revd. Joseph Warton* (London: T. Cadell and W. Davies, 1806), 403–4. Joseph Warton to Thomas Warton, March 13, 1785, in Fairer, *Correspondence of Thomas Warton*, 508. Darby, *Letter to the Rev. Mr. T. Warton*, 37–39.

24. *Critical Review* 59 (May 1785): 321.

IV

ANNOTATING THE CANON

9

Zachary Grey's Annotations on Samuel Butler's *Hudibras*

Mark A. Pedreira

Although part of the difficulty of editing Samuel Butler's *Hudibras* (1663, first part; 1664 and 1678, second part and third part) is the poem's topicality and "recondite information,"[1] as the editor of the standard edition puts it, the earliest editors found it equally challenging to explain the satirist's numerous allusions to canonical classical and modern sources. As the first prominent editor of *Hudibras*, Zachary Grey (1688–1766) wrote copious annotations on the poem's sources and literary allusions, notes that aim to educate readers about the broad range of literary and satirical contexts behind *Hudibras* and, by situating this poem in these contexts, to establish its canonicity among the great works of classical and modern literature. To this end, I argue that Grey, both in the preface and annotations to his 1744 edition—titled, *Hudibras, in Three Parts, Written in the Time of the Late Wars: Corrected and Amended. With Large Annotations, and a Preface, by Zachary Grey, LL.D.*[2]—presents himself as a "scholar-editor" with distinctive educational aims, most conspicuously, making his readers more knowledgeable about the vast humanistic learning, ancient and modern, underpinning Butler's satirical art. As a scholar-editor, Grey takes the stance of an annotator whose implied reader has some familiarity with the classic texts, ancient and modern, but who nonetheless needs considerable help understanding the subtle literary contexts of Butler's satire. By closely examining some of Grey's more memorable annotations, I attempt to show how the editor makes Butler's subtle literary references and allusions—unfamiliar to some eighteenth-century readers—accessible. Grey's scholarly edition of *Hudibras* achieves the difficult task of satisfying various readers, from the novice to the expert—frequently quoting classical sources in original languages (Homer, Virgil, and Lucan) and citing scholarly editions of modern classics (especially Cervantes and Shakespeare) but also explaining stories from these works possibly unfamiliar to novice readers without offending the sensibility of expert readers. To explain how Grey's 1744 edition makes available for eighteenth-century readers the "once-shared 'linguistic and literary expertise'" of Butler's contemporaries, I rely on the work of Marcus Walsh, Ian Small, and Anthony Grafton,[3] who write about the various perspectives of "scholar-editors" and their authorial, cultural, and aesthetic orientations, to which Zachary Grey makes a contribution.

In his preface to the 1744 edition, Grey praises Butler for his exemplary learning and wit and identifies the poem's implied readers. Noting the appeal of Butler's *Hudibras* to the "generality" of readers on account of his "Sublimity of Wit, and Pungency of Satire," Grey states the following about the relationship of the author to his readers:

> The Poet has surprizingly displayed the noblest Thoughts in a Dress so humorous and comical, that it is no wonder, that it soon became the chief Entertainment of the King and *Court*, after it's [*sic*] publication; was highly esteemed by one of the greatest Wits in that Reign; and still continues to be an Entertainment to all, who have a Taste for the most refined Ridicule and Satire.[4]

To appeal to his own readers' "Taste" for "refined" satire, Grey, as editor, annotates his text with what he refers to (in the title of his 1752 supplement to *Hudibras*) as his "Critical, historical, and explanatory notes."[5] Of these notes, Grey's "historical" notes frequently follow up on the research of Roger L'Estrange (1616–1704), an earlier critic of Butler who identifies (in his "Key to Hudibras" [1715]) the specific individuals that Butler's poem may have satirized.[6] Though he gives some attention to such topical matters, Grey sees one of his most important editorial endeavors as identifying, explaining, and commenting on the satire's numerous allusions to classical and modern authors and texts. This endeavor is sometimes collaborative, drawing on the notes of scholars whom he esteems for their learning. But such collaboration always presents Grey's viewpoints and the shaping influence of his editorial hand. Among his collaborators, Grey gives special credit to the Manchester scholar Christopher Byron, his editorial colleague, for his critical notes, though the best of Byron's notes sometimes become an occasion for Grey's own critical annotations.

In his annotations, Grey generally strives for the kind of editorial precision and judgment that Small and Walsh stipulate as the annotator's craft of writing good footnotes. For Walsh, good footnotes must demonstrate, with scholarly precision, the relevance and significance of what is cited, and such editorial excellence must be motivated by a clear and consistent theoretical orientation for textual editing.[7] As defined and classified in the pioneering work of Peter L. Shillingsburg, there are various types of "orientations" taken by editors—specifically, historical, authorial, cultural, and aesthetic.[8] For Walsh, as for Shillingsburg, these editorial orientations concern how an editor examines texts and relevant textual documents in historical, authorial, cultural, and aesthetic frameworks—regarding the editor's focus, respectively, on historical documents, authorial intentions, cultural perspectives, and aesthetic dimensions of a text. While Grey's annotations on *Hudibras* demonstrate a broad editorial orientation, he obviously lacks the kind of documentary evidence on

Butler's *oeuvre* possessed by later editors, which constrains his editorial approach.[9] Lacking the scholarly materials of Butler's unpublished manuscripts (published, in small part, by Robert Thyer in 1759 under the title *Genuine Remains in Verse and Prose of Mr. Samuel Butler, Author of Hudibras* and comprehensively in the twentieth century by A. R. Waller, René Lamar, and Hugh de Quehen),[10] Grey, in his editing of *Hudibras*, focuses on editorial matters of relevance to his mid-eighteenth-century readers, particularly concerning textual issues of authorial intention and of cultural and aesthetic significance. Most important, Grey as a scholar-editor sees his job as an educator, who instructs his readers about things that they should know if they aspire to be Butler's implied readers as characterized in the preface to his 1744 edition. Grey's annotations emphasize the learning and canonicity of *Hudibras*, as Butler's satire draws, in memorable allusions, on ancient and modern classics (especially Homer, Virgil, and Lucan, among the ancients, and Cervantes, Shakespeare, and John Fletcher, among the moderns). In *Hudibras*, Grey, therefore, turns his editorial acumen on every satirical domain of this poem, including the heroic, historical, and domestic. Whether his notes concern such things as mock-heroic depictions of Hudibras, the protagonist's parodied imitation of Lucan, Trulla's failure at Camilla-like speed, Orsin's inequality to the Homeric Diomedes, or the Widow's scorn of Hudibras's "Poetique Rapture," Grey's notes educate about the diverse literary contexts of Butler's satirical allusions—even drawing on post-Restoration learning when it elucidates Butler's satirical art. To this end, Grey makes every attempt in his annotations to share the learning of Dryden, Addison, and Pope (including their renowned translations) to illuminate Butler's satire.

ANNOTATOR AS "SCHOLAR-EDITOR"

It is easy to forget that Grey is one of the first eighteenth-century editors of *Hudibras* to familiarize readers with Butler's satire, as another scholarly annotated edition did not appear in print until the publication of Treadway Russell Nash's edition in 1793.[11] On the publication of his edition of *Hudibras* in 1744, Grey recognizes his role as one of the earliest editors introducing the characters and themes of Butler's satire to readers, and that despite the popularity of the poem, some of the memorable images that would pose no difficulty for future generations of readers might be less familiar to his own. Take, for instance, one of the most memorable images in part 1, canto 1 of the corpulent Hudibras, whose mock-Virgilian description Butler draws from a heroic scene in the *Aeneid*: Aeneas carrying his father on his back out of besieged Troy. Readers encounter Butler's famous image of Hudibras that Grey annotates with his distinctive editorial style (with his annotations corresponding to lines 289–92):

> His *Back*, or rather Burthen, show'd,
> As if it stoop'd with its own Load.

For as *Æneas* bore his Sire
Upon his Shoulders thro' the Fire,
Our Knight did bear no less a Pack
Of his own Buttocks on his Back. (1.1.287–92)

Readers of classical literature familiar with Virgil's *Aeneid* would recognize in this image Butler's "conceptual integration"—that is, his "conceptual blend," as cognitive linguistics refers to the blending of two "domains" in a third "space" with "emergent structure"[12]—of Virgil's heroic image of the dutiful Aeneas (bearing his father on his back) being conceptually blended with Hudibras's corpulent figure: "Our Knight did bear no less a Pack / Of his own Buttocks on his Back." Rhetorically, this mock-Virgilian conceptual integration—of two spaces, the Virgilian image of Aeneas "[bearing] his Sire" on his back and Hudibras bearing his own corpulent and deformed "Buttocks on his Back"—needs some unpacking. In their encounter with Butler's mock-Virgilian allusion depicting the corpulent Hudibras, Grey's readers, of course, had the visual aid of this caricatured feature of Hudibras displayed in some of Hogarth's illustrations of this character, presented in Grey's edition (as the title states) as a "new set of cuts" (the first cut, depicting Hudibras's arched back, immediately precedes canto 1).[13] But regarding the classical knowledge needed to fully appreciate this allusion, Grey assumes that his readers may vary in educational background. For this reason, in his annotation on Butler's mock-Virgilian allusion, Grey, in two detailed notes, educates his readers on Virgil (with lines from Dryden's *Aeneid*, 1697), compares Butler's image to Homer's deformed Thersites (with lines from Pope's *Iliad*, [1715–1720]), and presents Hudibras satirically as a fashionable subject (with the comical perspective of the *Spectator*).

Concerning his first note on the lines "For as Æneas bore his Sire / Upon his Shoulders thro' the Fire" (1.1.289–90),[14] Grey's annotation, by twenty-first-century editorial standards, gives an overabundance of information on some matters, particularly concerning historical detail on "filial Piety" (with Aeneas's piety toward Anchises being a representative example). But more informatively, Grey begins his note by telling his reader—who is addressed with the familiar pronoun "you"—that "his Story" (the story of Aeneas) "is too long to insert here, and therefore I refer you to *Virgil's Æneids*." Nonetheless, both before and after this comment Grey gives a little of Aeneas's "Story" in a two-sentence summary of Aeneas's genealogy, his fame, and his rescue of "his aged Father *Anchises* upon his Back." Then with no direct relevance to the line being annotated—but with a clear appreciation of Dryden's translation—Grey adds superfluous detail from the epic's larger scene, mentioning the fact (quoted from Dryden) that, while rescuing his father, Aeneas loses his wife, Creusa. In the six lines quoted from book 2 of Dryden's *Æneas*, Grey provides not only the relevant lines about Aeneas's willingness to carry Anchises's "willing Freight" ("Haste, my dear Father ['tis no time to wait,] / And load my Shoulders with a willing Freight") but also the memorable detail about the hero's failure to protect his wife ("My Hand shall lead our little Son, and you / My faithful Consort, shall our Steps pursue").[15] All of this Virgilian detail conveyed in Dryden's translation is vivid and interesting—including Aeneas's failure at protecting his wife—but it is questionable if Grey's inclusion of this material, by today's editorial standards, would be considered relevant or merely dispensable knowledge.[16]

In his second note on Butler's description of Hudibras (specifically, "Our Knight did bear no less a Pack / Of his own Buttocks on his Back" [1.1.291–92]), Grey draws unexpected Homeric parallels, in which a deformed Homeric character, Thersites, is cited from Pope's Homer to show that each author—Homer and Butler—has a character of "the same Make"; and he conjectures, by way of playful annotation (borrowing Richard Steele's comical tone in *Spectator* no. 32), that Hudibras might have been a "fashionable subject" in the *Spectator*'s "Ugly Club."[17] In the six lines that he quotes from Pope's *Iliad* to give the Homeric parallel of Thersites to Butler's misshapen Hudibras, Grey clearly had two lines in mind: "His Mountain Shoulders half his Breast o'erspread, / Thin Hairs bestrew'd his long mis-shapen head."[18] Though the different images compared in these descriptive passages in Homer and Butler might cause skepticism in some readers, Grey nonetheless perceives the image of schematic connection of these two characters—one grotesque, the other comically corpulent—with body parts ("Mountain Shoulders" and large buttocks) being "o'erspread." The Homeric reference presented in Pope's translation is informative and colorful. Immediately following the Popean illustration, Grey gives, more playfully, the following comment about how Hudibras might have been a "fashionable subject" for the "Ugly Club" (blending Steele's satirical words with his own words about Hudibras being a "fashionable subject"): "He would have been a fashionable subject in Richard the Third's days, who set up half the Backs of the Nation and *high Shoulders* as well as *high Noses*, were the top of the Fashion."[19] Whether we take Grey's comment as ironic or serious (either interpretation is possible with the blend of voices), Grey's annotation uses the *Spectator*'s satirical observations to comment on Hudibras's comical appearance, just as he cites the *Spectator* in other contexts (as we will see) to draw on Addison's authority on eighteenth-century culture.

Grey's scholarly attention to Butler's mock-heroic description of Hudibras in part 1, canto 1 is fairly typical of his treatment of Butler's other satirical characters, whose depictions as Hudibras's adversaries in the episodes on bear baiting in part 1, cantos 2 and 3, are similarly measured in comical terms against the epic and historical ideals found in classical literature. Given the priority Grey gives to allusions drawn from classical epic poetry, we will first examine Butler's mock-heroic allusions in part 1, canto 3 and then examine similar editorial concerns in part 1, canto 2 in Butler's parody of historical allusions (specifically, by Lucan). Such generic focus (particularly on classical epic poetry) frequently motivates Grey's annotations—something that Grey himself emphasizes in an opening comment in his preface, in which he claims about *Hudibras*: "it's conformity in some respects to *Epic* Poetry, will be evinc'd, and comparisons here and there drawn from *Homer*, *Virgil*, and *Milton*."[20] Not surprisingly, such comparisons generally focus on the mock-heroic, satirically displaying, with epic references, the disparity between "high" and "low" for its comical effects.

Concerning such generic matters, Grey has a model in the textual and literary criticism of Pope, whose translation of the *Iliad* he frequently quotes and whose criticism he sometimes has in mind. But as will appear, Pope's literary-critical influence on Grey's annotations appears infrequently, with occasional references to Pope's *Essay on Criticism* (1711). Moreover, though Grey's commentary on Homeric and Virgilian images sometimes focuses, like Pope's, on the author or reader's imagination, it rarely does so as extensively as Pope does in his memorable notes in the *Iliad* on Homer's epic similes or on the poet's moving portraits of individuals (such as the memorable parting of Hector and Andromache in book 6).[21]

There are two notes by Grey in part 1, canto 3 concerning the mock-heroic speed and strength of Butler's characters: the one about the nimble yet hardly Camilla-like Trulla, who speedily races to save Bruin, the bear, in a bear-baiting scene; and the other about the mock-heroic strength of Orsin (opponent of Hudibras and Ralph), who, though he cannot hurl huge boulders like Diomedes, almost succeeds in killing Ralph. As a textual critic motivated by literary-critical principles, Grey focuses in these notes, in large part, on the literary-critical axiom that in epic poetry characters should maintain verisimilitude[22] in their actions and speeches: or as Grey calls it, an "Air of Truth and Probability."

Grey's note in part 1, canto 3 on Trulla's lack of Camilla-like speed—befitting the realistic pursuit of a heroine trying to save Orsin's bear, Bruin—exemplifies his editorial method of citing sources to identify and comment on literary allusions. His annotation concerns the lines in which Trulla is running speedily to help Bruin, "the worsted *Bear*," who is being held by fierce "Mastives." The lines under editorial scrutiny about Trulla's speed read: "For *Trulla*, who was light of Foot, / As Shafts which long-field *Parthians* shoot, / (But not so light as to be born / Upon the Ears of standing Corn)" (1.3.101–4). Before presenting his readers with a lengthy annotation on Camilla, Grey, whose annotation on this passage influenced Nash, begins with a note about the simile concerning Trulla's speed. Both Grey and Nash take the allusive expression "long-field *Parthians*" in Butler's extended simile as an epithet (a common epic convention) depicting the forceful *image* of rapid speed over great distance[23]; whereas, a nineteenth-century editor, in a reissue of Nash's edition of *Hudibras* (slightly revised, with bracketed remarks) notes—with a dismissive tone about Grey and Nash's commentary—that "long-field" has no special rhetorical significance but is merely a technical term of archery.[24]

Following his annotation on Butler's "long-field *Parthians*" simile, Grey attends closely, in another note, to Butler's mock-Virgilian allusion on Camilla that rhetorically extends it: "(But not so light as to be born / Upon the Ears of standing Corn)" (1.3.103–4).[25] About this parodic allusion to Virgil, Grey offers his readers a simple comment: "A Satyrical Stroke upon the Character of *Camilla*, one of *Virgil's* Heroines." Then, turning to Virgil's *Aeneid*, he quotes the first line of the relevant passage in Latin—"Hos super advenit Volsca de Gente Camilla, &c."—and thereafter gives the entire corresponding scene (in twenty lines) from Dryden's famous translation.

But the only lines quoted from Dryden's Virgil that are directly relevant to Butler's allusion to Camilla are the following two lines: "Outstripp'd the Winds in speed upon the Plain, / Flew o'er the Fields, nor hurt the bearded Grain."[26] Immediately following his quotation from Dryden, Grey gives bibliographical sources in which the Camilla image appears—including important eighteenth-century texts such as Pope's *Essay on Criticism* and Joseph Trapp's translation of *Virgil* (1731). Among Grey's sources identifying the Virgilian image of Camilla, Pope, perhaps greater than any other, emphasizes (with his iconic representation of energetic verse being Camilla-like; sluggish verse, Ajax-like), the beauty and force of Virgil's poetry: "When *Ajax* strives, some Rocks' vast Weight to throw, / The Line too *labours*, and the Words move *slow*; / Not so, when swift *Camilla* scours the Plain, / Flies o'er th'unbending Corn, and skims along the Main" (lines 370–73).[27] Concerning the beauty of Virgil's (or for that matter Pope's) verses, Grey has no doubt. But he quotes the ambivalent judgment of Christopher Byron about the questionable beauty of Virgil's verses on Camilla, which Byron believes are somewhat compromised by the "impropriety" of Camilla's character. Grey states, "If it was not (says Mr. *Byron*) for the Beauty of the Verses, that shaded the Impropriety of *Camilla*'s Character, I doubt not but *Virgil* would have been as much censured for the one, as applauded for the other."[28] In judging Virgil, Byron's distinction between the aesthetic beauty of Virgil's verse and the rhetorical impropriety of the poet's character Camilla diverges from the perspective on this heroine in Pope's memorable line, which weds sound and sense, aesthetics and rhetoric. Despite citing Pope's *Essay on Criticism* as a poem noteworthy for its depiction of Camilla, Grey agrees with Byron. In fact, given his shared assumptions with Byron about poetic probability and propriety, Grey praises Butler for avoiding "such monstrous Improbabilities" represented by the Virgilian Camilla in the satirist's more believable depiction of Trulla. About the credible nature of Butler's satire, Grey states as a concluding point to his note: "Our Poet has justly avoided such monstrous Improbabilities, nor will he attribute an incredible Swiftness to *Trulla*, though there was an absolute Call for extraordinary Celerity, under the present Circumstances: no less occasion than to save the Bear, who was to be the Object of all the Rabble's Diversion."[29] Grey's editorial judgment on this matter might be questioned by many of his readers, but he is at least clear (and, we will see, consistent) about his literary-critical principles.

In his annotations on the battles of Hudibras and Ralph against the bear-baiters, Grey gives other instances of his literary-critical preoccupation that Butler maintains in his satire an "Air of Truth and Probability." Regarding a memorable scene of Orsin fighting Hudibras's Squire Ralph (also called Ralpho) in part 1, canto 3, Grey, in a note explaining why Butler mock-heroically compares Orsin with Diomedes, comments on the satirist's intentions and the reader's imagination.[30] The lines in this scene examined by Grey display anything but the dignified air of Homeric battle found in the fifth book of the *Iliad* between Diomedes (known as Tydides) and his Trojan opponent, Aeneas. Instead, they display Butler's use of mock-heroic style and his skillful use of parody (here reducing dignified Homeric battle with Hudibrastic verse). The lines read,

> When *Orsin* first let fly a Stone
> At *Ralpho*; not so huge a one
> As that which *Diomed* did maul
> *Æneas* on the Bum withal;
> Yet big enough, if rightly hurl'd,
> T' have sent him to another World. (1.3.491–96)

Grey's comment on this passage reveals his desire, as an editor, to explain Butler's rhetorical motive for his Homeric allusion, which, in his interpretation, concerns the satirist's intention to write both a comical and a credible satire. To this end, Grey claims that in these lines alluding to Diomedes's fierce battle with Aeneas, Butler gives "another Evidence of that Air of Truth and Probability" in *Hudibras* because his Homeric allusion makes it clear (one might say, with intentional irony) that "he would by no means have his Reader's fancy the same Strength and Activity in *Orsin*, which *Homer* ascribes to *Diomed*."[31] In Butler's parodic use of Hudibrastic verse, the "Stone" that Orsin "let fly" at Ralpho hardly compares to its counterpart in Homeric battle as Butler's comical characters sink under the weight of Homeric or Virgilian comparisons. Regarding Butler's mock-heroic allusion, Grey quotes lines in the fifth book of Pope's *Iliad* to show, by way of comparison, the weightiness of Homer's lines in which Diomedes battles Aeneas. Of the fourteen lines quoted from Pope's translation of this scene, four lines, in particular, serve as a clear point of contrast with Butler's mock-heroic allusion: "Then fierce Tydides stoops, and from the Fields / Heav'd with vast force, a rocky Fragment wields; / Not two Strong Men th' enormous Weight cou'd raise, / Such Men as live in these degenerate days" (lines 369–72).[32] By identifying these Homeric lines (forcefully translated by Pope) as the classical source for Butler's satirical allusion on Orsin and Diomedes, Grey's annotation, with its rhetorically sound commentary, persuasively shows how Orsin pales in comparison to Diomedes, just as Ralph heroically diminishes next to his classical counterpart, Aeneas.

Consistent with his educational style of annotation, Grey concludes his note about Butler's mock-heroic comparison of Orsin with Diomedes (and Ralpho with Aeneas) with further contextual detail—one might say peripheral, or dispensable, detail—from Virgil on Aeneas, whose sufferings as the "unfortunate Aeneas" he desires to amplify. About the "unfortunate Aeneas," Grey concludes his note with the following brief comment and paraphrase from book 12 of Virgil's *Aeneid*: "*Turnus* also wields a piece of Rock at him, which *Virgil* says, Twelve Men could hardly raise; tho' the Consequences are not so dismal as in *Homer*."[33] By twenty-first-century editorial standards, Grey, with such peripheral detail, has gone beyond his editorial purpose of explaining Butler's Homeric allusion. But as a scholar-editor, Grey at times cannot resist giving additional information, which he believes might further educate his readers.

ANNOTATOR AS LITERARY HISTORIAN

As an editor, Grey's focus on the classical sources in *Hudibras* is not limited to epic poetry. Given the fact that *Hudibras* satirizes the behavior and speech of the Puritans (of many denominations) during the English civil wars, Grey, not surprisingly, turns his editorial attention to the classical histories that Butler parodied in Hudibras's memorable orations. As a justice of the peace, Hudibras, with his squire Ralph, not only fights the bear-baiters (comically and unheroically); he also addresses them oratorically before he attacks them.[34] In part 1, canto 2, Butler, as Grey notes, alludes to, or parodies, Lucan's *The Civil War* (also *Pharsalia*) in a small part of Hudibras's lengthy speech that criticizes the violence of the civil wars and their aftermath in Britain: the "civil Bloodshed," religious fanaticism, and the bloody sport of bear baiting. It is worth noting, even if to digress for a moment, that Butler's parodic imitation of Lucan in Hudibras's opening oration, gives exigence, later in his speech, for the speaker's pointed rhetorical questions—such as, "For if *Bear-baiting* we allow, / What Good can *Reformation* do?"[35] Some of Hudibras's rhetorical questions conceptually connect with Lucan's criticism of the unnecessary bloodshed of the Roman civil wars. For Hudibras ironically asks the damning rhetorical question: "Shall *Saints* in civil Bloodshed wallow / Of *Saints*, and let the *Cause* lie fallow?"[36]

In his annotations on Hudibras's parodied Lucanian speech, Grey gives limited commentary on the original speech in Lucan, quoting several lines from Lucan's Latin history and providing relevant translations by Sir Arthur Gorges and Nicholas Rowe—the former of which may have loosely shaped in diction and imagery Butler's satirical imitation of Lucan. To annotate Butler's oratorical parody of Lucan, Grey seeks the assistance of another collaborator, Dr. Thomas Brett, who provides occasional historical consultation in Grey's 1744 edition. Collaboratively, Grey and Brett educate their readers about one of the major figures in Hudibras's speech, General William Waller (1597–1668) of the "Rebel Parliament," as well as giving brief detail about Waller's Royalist adversaries who ultimately defeated him in a significant battle during England's first civil war. The lines of Hudibras's speech examined by Grey are as follows:

> What Rage, O Citizens! what Fury
> Doth you to these dire Actions hurry?
> What *OEstrum*, what Phrenetick Mood
> Makes you thus lavish of your Blood,
> While the proud *Vies* your Trophies boast
> And unreveng'd walks _____ Ghost? (1.2.494–99)

Though Grey's curious readers might read further to see Hudibras's larger speech about the broad consequences of the English civil wars, our focus here is on Grey's notes concerning Butler's parodic allusion to Crassus's death in Lucan's *The Civil War* and the relation of this classical allusion to an important English military figure.

In his first note on part 1, canto 2, lines 494–95, Grey begins by quoting in Latin several lines from the second paragraph of *The Civil War*: most famously, "Quis furor, O Cives, Quae tanta licentia ferri" (translated by the Loeb translators, "What madness was this, my countrymen, what fierce orgy of slaughter?").[37] Lucan raises this question because, in the four lines immediately following, he asks how Romans could have waged war against Romans in the face of neighboring enemies triumphing over noble countrymen (particularly Pompey fighting Caesar, after the First Triumvirate dissolves with Crassus's death in Parthia). This concern motivates Lucan to imagine—and Butler to parody in Hudibras's oratorical speech—Crassus's "unavenged" ghost "wandering" ("umbraque erraret Crassus inulta") amid the folly of Roman civil war.[38] Following his quotation of these Latin lines from Lucan's *Civil War*, Grey quotes the same scene in Arthur Gorges's translation of Lucan's work (noting editorially that Gorges's 1614 translation has "the same metre"—or, perhaps more accurately, a similar meter—as *Hudibras*):

> Dear Citizens, what Brainsick Charms,
> What Outrage of disorder'd Arms
> Leads you to feast your envious Foes;
> To see you goard with your own Blows?
> Proud Babylon your Force doth scorne
> Whose Spoyls your Trophies might adorn;
> And Crassus' unrevenged Ghost
> Roams wailing through the Parthian Coast.[39]

And following Gorges's translation, Grey adds, "See likewise Mr Rowe's Translation"—a translation presenting more classical imagery regarding the unavenged "wand'ring Shade" of Crassus (in place of Gorges's "unrevenged Ghost"): "But unatton'd repines the wand'ring Shade!"[40]

Grey's suggestion, in his first note to Hudibras's oration, that Butler's Lucanian scene has some stylistic affinities with Gorges's earlier translation deserves brief attention. This note points up important editorial issues that ultimately become the focus of another note. Though Grey may be inaccurate in his claim that Gorges's earlier translation has a metrical style similar to Butler's *Hudibras*, the editor's point, if extended to include poetic diction, might help us to see how Butler imitates the following vivid lines from Gorges's *Pharsalia*: "And Crassus's unrevenged Ghost / Roams wailing through the Parthian Coast." In fact, Butler's interrogatory line about the causes of England's "mad" civil wars ("What *OEstrum*, what Phrenetick Mood"), foregrounds the war's tragic Lucanian effects (with phrasing remarkably similar to Gorges's "unrevenged Ghost"): "Makes you thus lavish of your Blood, / While the proud *Vies* your Trophies boast / And unreveng'd walks _____ Ghost?" Grey's readers, presented with both Lucan's memorable Latin line, "umbraque erraret Crassus inulta," and Gorges's elegant translation of the "roam[ing]" and "wailing" of "Crassus' unrevenged Ghost," are better prepared for the textual issues presented in Grey's subsequent note. That is, what individual in Hudibras's speech—in lines conceptually integrating the English and Roman civil wars—represents the blank space, "And unreveng'd walks _____ Ghost"?

In the second note on Hudibras's satirical oration (1.2.498), Grey and Brett conjecture about the individual in Butler's Lucanian parody who conceptually integrates (or fills) the blank space occupied by Crassus's unavenged shade (or ghost) in Lucan's history. To provide their readers with an answer, Grey and Brett examine the historical evidence motivating Butler's Hudibrastic couplet. Here, the blank space is part of Butler's conceptually integrated space, drawn from Lucan and the English civil war, of prominent individuals, Crassus and "_____," who suffer the fate, metaphorically speaking, of a "ghost" (either death or the death of reputation). As the collaborative annotation by Grey and Brett makes clear, no one but General Waller—who suffered a devastating loss and career blow in the Battle of Roundway Down near Devizes (also called Vies, as it is in Butler's poem) in July 13, 1643—could fill the blank space of this line. Grey and Brett give both historical and literary evidence, educating their readers about this pivotal battle that motivates Butler's parody of Lucan concerning the follies of civil war. Like any good historian, Brett begins with the most evident facts concerning Butler's couplet about the boasted trophy of "proud *Vies*" (first controlled by the Parliamentarians, but later regained by the Royalists) and about the unnamed and "unreveng'd" ghost who is historically identified with this place. About the first part of Butler's couplet, "While the proud *Vies* your Trophies boast," Brett states, "This refers to the great Defeat given to Sir *William Waller*, at the *Devises*, of which the Reader may meet with an account, in Lord *Clarendon's History of the Rebellion*" as well as in "[Laurence] *Echard's History of England*."[41] Immediately following, Brett identifies Waller—who is conceptually blended with Lucan's suffering ghost of Crassus, who died ignominiously at the hands of the Parthians—as "*Waller's Ghost*," the unspecified presence (filling the blank) in Butler's line. Concerning this crucial historical identification in Butler's Lucanian parody, Brett, as Grey's collaborator, gives reasons that contemporary readers would find informative and incontrovertible: "the Blank is here to be fill'd up with the Word *Waller's*, and we must read *Waller's Ghost*: for though Sir *William Waller*, made a considerable figure among the Generals of the Rebel Parliament, before this Defeat, yet afterwards he made no Figure, and appear'd but as the *Ghost* or Shadow of what he had been before."[42] As a skillful collaborator, Brett concisely explains that before Waller's "defeat" at Devizes, he "made a considerable figure" (Clarendon, in his *History*, depicts Waller's previous successes at the Battle of Lansdown and in the early stages of the battle of Devizes, when he was strongly fortified on Roundway Down, overlooking Devizes).[43] But Brett notes that "afterwards" Waller became, metaphorically speaking, "the *Ghost* or Shadow of what he had been before," losing this decisive battle against such adversaries (in Grey's words) as the "famous Sir Ralph Hopton."[44]

In the same coauthored note, Grey quotes a song allegedly written by Sir John Denham (though without proof of attribution)—in *A Collection of Loyal Songs Written against the Rump Parliament*—a song depicting the courage of Sir Ralph Hopton (1596–1652), the Cavalier general who not only survives a large gunpowder explosion but later, as depicted in Clarendon's *History*, helps win the Battle of Devises against William Waller.[45] As elsewhere in his notes and preface to *Hudibras*, Grey, in his presentation of the Royalist poetical song, "A Second Western Wonder," does not hide his own Royalist politics, extolling the courage of "the famous Sir *Ralph Hopton* [who] was in danger of being kill'd."[46] Grey cites the following vivid lines (occupying two distinct quatrains in the 1731 edition of *A Collection of Loyal Songs*) about "honest Sir Ralph." Grey's quotation varies from the 1731 edition of the *Loyal Songs* that he cites as his source, changing "Miracles" to "miraculous" and "Beard" to "Head":

> You heard of that Wonder, of the Lightning and Thunder,
> Which made the Lye so much the louder,
> Now list to another, that miraculous [*sic*] Brother,
> Which was done by a Firkin of Powder.
> Oh what a damp, it struck thro' the Camp
> But as for honest Sir Ralph,
> It blew him to the Vies, without Head [*sic*] or Eyes.[47]

As his eighteenth-century readers might appreciate, Grey's quotation of this song presents vivid historical detail that contextually connects with the focus of his note—the battle of Devies (or Vies)—as well as subtly insinuating Grey's affinity to Butler's Royalist politics in the satirical world of *Hudibras*.

ANNOTATOR AS LITERARY CRITIC

In addition to educating his readers about literary allusions in the domains of the heroic and historical in *Hudibras*, Grey also proves an adept editor when annotating the satire's comical scenes concerning the Lady Widow's parody of Hudibras's professions of love. In one of Butler's most memorable scenes in part 2, canto 1, Grey identifies and explains the literary significance of the modern allusions motivating the Widow's parody of Hudibras's professions of love, which she mocks for their hyperbole and insincerity. Most significantly, Grey examines Butler's satiric allusions to Cervantes, Shakespeare, and Fletcher (among other sources) in the Widow's parody of Hudibras's fustian style of courtship (or in her words, his "*Poetique Rapture*" and "high *Heroick* Fustion" [2.1.586; 590]). In her memorable lines in part 2, canto 1, the Widow parodies the kind of bold figurative rhetoric in love (Hudibras's "*Poetique Rapture*") that enables the male poet (or rhetor) to dominate, and even objectify, the female subject, making her, as the Widow ironically puts it in subsequent lines, "a *Desk* to write upon" ("She that with *Poetry* is won, / Is but a *Desk* to write upon" [2.1.591–92]).[48] Grey gives detailed annotations on Butler's allusions in the following lines by the Widow (lines that, from her perspective, typify male love poetry):

> Her Mouth compar'd t' an *Oyster's*, with
> A Row of *Pearl* in't, stead of *Teeth*;

> Others make *Posies* of her *Cheeks*,
> Where *Red* and *Whitest* Colours mix;
> In which the *Lilly*, and the *Rose*,
> For *Indian* Lake, and Ceruse goes.
> The *Sun*, and *Moon*, by her bright Eyes
> Eclips'd, and darken'd in the *Skies*,
> Are but *black Patches*, that she wears,
> Cut into *Suns*, and *Moons*, and *Stars*: (2.1.603–12)

In several notes on this passage, Grey unpacks the allusions in the Widow's parody of the hyperbolical comparisons used by male writers—particularly poets and dramatists—to idealize female beauty.

Regarding the Widow's parodied speech in part 2, canto 1, lines 603–4 (concerning the female mouth and teeth), Grey gives various possible sources for Butler's oyster-mouth imagery in the two initial lines, but he gives precedence to Cervantes, as well as considerable attention to John Taylor (1578–1653), a popular early seventeenth-century poet in the comic tradition. As Grey frequently does when discussing satirical sources, he frames his discussion of Butler's allusion to Don Quixote as the satirist's "sneer" (one of Grey's favorite expressions) on Cervantes's protagonist, a term defined in Nathan Bailey's 1730 *Dictionarium Britannicum* (cited frequently by Grey) as "to laugh foolishly or scornfully" at something.[49] Concerning the Widow's parodied description of the female mouth (with "A Row of *Pearl* in't, stead of *Teeth*"), Grey gives both comments and extensive quotation. He states, "This description, is probably a sneer upon *Don Quixote*, for his high-flown Compliments upon his Mistress."[50] In this comment, Grey refers contextually to Don Quixote's memorable description of Dulcinea found in a famous episode that begins with local shepherds praising Marcella, their country beauty, a description that ultimately motivates Don Quixote's encomium on Dulcinea—an episode that Grey cites (among others) from chapter 5, volume 1, of Peter Motteux's translation of *Don Quixote* (5th ed., 1725).[51] Don Quixote's "high-flown Compliments," as Grey must have recognized, imitate the rhetoric of male lovers who, in the Widow's words, are given to "*Poetique Rapture*" and "*Heroick* Fustion"—for Dulcinea's mouth, like the Widow's parodied female figure, has *pearls for teeth* (and other idealized features of beauty). Regarding Dulcinea's beauty, Don Quixote states (in Grey's quotation):

> The curling Locks of her bright flowing Hair of [*sic*] purest Gold; her smooth Forehead, The *Elysian Plain*: Her Brows are Two Celestial Bows; her Eyes, Two glorious Suns; her Cheeks, Two Beds of Roses: her Lips are Coral; her Teeth are Pearl, her Neck is Alabaster, her Breasts, Marble, her Hands, Ivory; and Snow would lose it's [*sic*] whiteness near her Bosom.[52]

About such idealized beauty (especially the image of *teeth as pearls*), Grey, in the same note, cites other examples from early seventeenth-century poets and prose writers, whose writings Butler would undoubtedly know. In fact, in the remainder of his note, interspersed with brief citation of scholarly sources useful in their reference to the female body (such as Robert Burton's cornucopian text *The Anatomy of Melancholy* [1621]) Grey focuses largely on Taylor, known famously as the "Water Poet" (a Thames waterman).[53] Regarding Taylor's comical poem titled *A Whore* (1630), Grey speaks of Taylor's "great humour" about the poetical flattery of female beauty. For the reader's enjoyment, Grey quotes extensively from Taylor's *A Whore*, a poem that, consistent with the editorial focus of his note, satirizes flattery ("Flattery makes a Whore to seem a Saint") and describes female beauty, much like Cervantes, in hyperbolized terms ("Her Teeth, to Oriental Pearls a Row").[54]

Of Grey's remaining four notes on the Widow's parody of Hudibras's "*Poetique Rapture*," three are worth examining concerning the editor's identification of allusions and useful scholarly references (the other note simply cites Bailey's *Dictionarium Britannicum*, to define, in part 2, canto 1, lines 605–8, the "Indian Lake" and "Ceruse" that become, in the parodied female, *mixed* colors in the "*Posies* of her *Cheeks*"). In three separate notes giving literary and cultural contexts of the Widow's parodied speech, Grey comments extensively on the following lines: "The *Sun*, and *Moon*, by her bright Eyes / Eclips'd, and darken'd in the *Skies*, / Are but *black Patches*, that she wears, / Cut into *Suns*, and *Moons*, and *Stars*" (2.1.609–12). Concerning his note on the Widow's lines parodying the idealized female's "bright Eyes" ("The *Sun*, and *Moon*, by her bright Eyes / Eclips'd, and darken'd in the *Skies*," lines 609–10), Grey claims that Shakespeare in *Romeo and Juliet* "has something like this" (that is, Shakespeare has something similar to Butler's lines). To examine Butler's possible allusion to Shakespeare, Grey quotes (with the bracketed text signifying misquotation or elided text) relevant lines spoken by Romeo in the opening of act 2, scene 2 in *Romeo and Juliet*:

> But soft! What Light thro' yonder Window breaks?
> It is the East, and *Juliet* is the Sun.
> Arise, fair Sun, and kill the envious Moon,
> Who is already sick, and pale with grief,
> That thou her Maid, art far more fair than she,
> Be not her Maid, since She is envious.
> Her vestal Livery is but sick [and green],
> And nought [*sic*] but Fools do wear it,—cast it off.[55]

While these lines spoken by Romeo in Shakespeare do not have an actual "eclipse" like Butler's line ("Eclips'd, and darken'd in the *Skies*"), Shakespeare nonetheless provides Butler with a classic topos about incomparable beauty to parody (for Romeo, Juliet's beauty, like any incomparable beauty, eclipses all else). In this specific note, Grey does not, however, attend to the comedy involved in the metaphorical extension of Butler's line, a line that, as we recall, involves not just a typical eclipse (or even a Shakespearian eclipse about female beauty) but a parodied eclipse consisting of "black Patches" in astrological dimensions: "The *Sun*, and *Moon*, by her bright Eyes / Eclips'd, and darken'd in the *Skies*, / Are but *black Patches*, that she wears, / Cut into *Suns*, and *Moons*, and *Stars*." Grey's annotation on lines 609–10 about the power of the female beauty's "bright Eyes" to eclipse the sun and the moon focuses exclusively on Butler's possible allusion to Shakespeare, saving any editorial comments about the further metaphorical extension of these lines for subsequent annotations.

In his subsequent notes, Grey cites sources from other writers (Addison, Fletcher, and Sir Kenelm Digby) that help interpret the Widow's parodied lines, identifying additional allusions and explaining relevant contextual detail. Here Grey's commentary focuses on cultural and literary details, explaining, with Addison and Digby's authority, the cultural phenomenon of "black Patches" and their specific comical appearance in Fletcher's play *The Elder Brother: A Comedie* (1651). In his note to line 611, "Are but *black Patches*, that she wears," Grey gives quotations from the writings of Digby and Addison that show the zeal for "black patches" among women in the seventeenth- and early eighteenth-centuries. He begins with a spurious story about "black patches" from medical science told by Digby, a story found in *The First Treatise Declaring the Nature and Operation of Bodies* (originally published in *Two Treatises* [1645]).[56] In his skillful paraphrase of Digby's story, Grey, to educate his readers on "black patches," notes Digby's story about how the "fantasie" of parents (here on black patches) "doth oftentimes worke strange effects in their issue." Grey states,

> Sir *Kenelm Digby* makes mention of a Lady in his acquaintance, who wore many Patches: upon which he used to banter her, and tell her that the next Child she should go with, whilst the solicitude and care of those Patches was so strong in her Fancy, would come into the World with a great *Black Spot* in the midst of it's [*sic*] Forehead; which happened accordingly.[57]

In Grey's paraphrase, Digby presents his warning to "a Lady a kinswoman of mine" about her excessive fondness for patches (with the comical consequence that her child may therefore be born with one); and Digby even notes at the end of his story (though Grey omits this detail), that there are "witnesses," adding, with a hint of irony, that the "young Lady her selfe" gives testimony to this story.[58] In the same note, Grey gives another comical example from Addison's *Spectator*. Drawing on Addison's writings on the female custom of wearing black patches, Grey cites the essayist's first publication on this custom, which presents the writings of four Iroquois kings who had observed this custom in their diplomatic visit to Queen Anne in London in 1710.[59] Though perhaps not intended as comical (as allegedly recorded in Addison's Iroquois source), Grey, like Addison, notes the "Humorous" nature of "the opinion of the *Indian Kings*, concerning the Patches worn by our *English Ladies* (*Spectator, No. 50*)."[60] Grey cites the penultimate paragraph of this number by Addison on the testimony of the Indian kings (quoting his source, though varying the punctuation by adding dashes—in the first instance to mark a break, or elision, in the text—as well as revising Addison's grammar, pronouns, and prepositions, and omitting Addison's words, as noted in the second bracketed text):

> As for the Women of the Country—they [*sic*] look like Angels, and would be more beautiful than the Sun, were it not for the little black Spots, that [are apt to] break out

in their Faces: and sometimes rise in very odd Figures—I have observed, that those little Blemishes wear off very soon; but when they disappear in one part of the Face, they are very apt to break out in another, insomuch, that I have seen a spot in [*sic*] the Forehead in the Afternoon, which was upon the Chin in the Morning.[61]

Grey's quotation from Addison's Iroquois kings is culturally interesting and editorially relevant to the Butler passage under scrutiny; for these black patches, worn by fashionable Londoners, not only appear in every part of the female face but also "rise in very odd Figures"—much, we shall see, like the odd figures ("Cut into *Suns*, and *Moons*, and *Stars*") explained in Grey's final note on the Widow's parody of Hudibras's poetic rhapsody in his love suits.

In his final note to the Widow's parody of Hudibras's poetic raptures in love, Grey explains the concluding line of the Widow's extended metaphor about the idealized female's "bright Eyes" eclipsing and darkening the sun and the moon—in which such eclipse, or darkening, becomes (through poetical hyperbole) "*black Patches*, that she wears, / Cut into *Suns*, and *Moons*, and *Stars*" (2.1.611–12). Regarding Butler's line, "Cut into *Suns*, and *Moons*, and *Stars*," Grey, in his vast familiarity with the English literary canon, identifies the precise (and only possible) allusion to Fletcher's *The Elder Brother* ("revised and completed by Philip Massinger").[62] Grey quotes selectively from this comedy, eliding five lines (i.e., five lines following the first quoted line) not deemed directly relevant to his concern about Butler's allusion to Fletcher. In his note, Grey states, "Thus *Angelina* to *Eustace*, (*Beaumont and Fletcher's* Comedy, intitled *The Elder Brother*, act 3, scene 11) ''Tis not a Face I only am in Love with—No nor Visits each day in New Suits: nor your Black Patches you wear variously: some cut like Stars, some in Half Moons, some "Lozenges.""[63] In these lines and those that immediately follow, Angelina explains why she prefers Charles, the "elder brother," to Eustace; for though Eustace (with his "New Suits" and fashionable "Black Patches") is more refined than his scholarly older brother, he lacks Charles's maturity, honest love, and large inheritance. In Fletcher's comedy, Eustace's "Black Patches"—like those eclipsed astrological bodies ("*Suns*, and *Moons*, and *Stars*") worn as patches by Butler's parodied Beauty—are worn decorously (one might say foppishly), "some cut like Stars, some in Half Moons, some Lozenges." An editor less knowledgeable than Grey might have failed to make the precise allusion to Fletcher's comedy, a play that comically depicts, among other things, the external world of cultural fashion (the black patches of the beau monde). Here and elsewhere, Grey's annotations precisely identify Butler's satirical allusions and when necessary comment on their textual and contextual meanings.

Readers of Butler's *Hudibras* have always enjoyed the learning and allusive playfulness of his seventeenth-century satire. Though much of the best editorial work on Butler occurred in the second half of the twentieth century (benefiting from the textual criticism of Wilders and de Quehen), Zachary Grey had no small influence, as one of the pioneering editors of *Hudibras*, on our understanding of Butler's satire as part of the seventeenth-century satirical tradition and of the modern literary canon. Many of the most memorable scenes in *Hudibras* have been expertly annotated by

Grey, educating his contemporary and future readers about the subtle literary and historical allusions, ancient and modern, that identify Butler's satire with an enduring literary tradition. If his annotations on *Hudibras* are sometimes superfluous or dispensable by twentieth- and twenty-first century editorial standards, Grey's editorial practices are guided by a sense that his implied readers—broadly educated though challenged by this highly allusive poem—need as much help as he could offer them. As an editor, Grey rarely fails to oblige his readers' educational needs or curiosity, and his scholarly annotations on *Hudibras* will always have a lasting place in the reception of this satirical masterpiece.

NOTES

1. Samuel Butler, *Hudibras*, ed. John Wilders (Oxford: Clarendon Press, 1967), xli.

2. *Hudibras, in Three Parts, Written in the Time of the Late Wars: Corrected and Amended. With Large Annotations, and a Preface . . . Adorn'd with a New Set of Cuts*, ed. Zachary Grey, 2 vols. (Cambridge: Printed by J. Bentham for W. Innys et al., 1744). Hereafter, references to lines in Grey's edition will be given in parenthetical citations (citing part, canto, and line number). References to Grey's annotations, however, will generally be cited in endnotes.

3. See Marcus Walsh, *Shakespeare, Milton, and Eighteenth-Century Literary Editing: The Beginnings of Interpretative Scholarship* (Cambridge: Cambridge University Press, 1997). Ian Small and Marcus Walsh state, "The aim of the editor is to enable the modern reader to become as 'competent' as the original intended readership, by making available again a once-shared 'linguistic and literary expertise.'" Ian Small and Marcus Walsh, eds., *The Theory and Practice of Text-Editing: Essays in Honour of James T. Boulton* (Cambridge: Cambridge University Press, 1991), 8. Anthony Grafton, *The Footnote: A Curious History* (Cambridge, MA: Harvard University Press, 1997), 1–33.

4. Grey, preface to *Hudibras*, xxi.

5. Zachary Grey, *Critical, Historical, and Explanatory Notes upon Hudibras, by Way of Supplement to the Two Editions Published in the Years 1744, and 1745 . . . to Which Is Prefixed, a Dissertation upon Burlesque Poetry* (London: Printed for C. Norris, J. Beecroft, and W. Thurlbourn, 1752).

6. Samuel Butler, *Posthumous Works in Prose and Verse, Written in the Time of the Civil Wars and Reign of K. Charles II. . . . With a Key to Hudibras, by Sir Roger L' Estrange. In Two Volumes. The Third Edition* (London: Printed for Sam. Briscoe, 1715). L'Estrange's "Key to Hudibras" appears in 2:259–92.

7. See Walsh, *Shakespeare, Milton, and Eighteenth-Century Literary Editing*, 4–29.

8. See Peter L. Shillingsburg, *Scholarly Editing in the Computer Age: Theory and Practice*, 3rd ed. (Ann Arbor: University of Michigan Press, 1996), 15–27.

9. For an extensive bibliography of primary sources on Butler (with select secondary sources), see Mark A. Pedreira, "Samuel Butler," in *The Encyclopedia of British Literature 1660–1789*, ed. Gary Day and Jack Lynch, 3 vols. (Oxford: Wiley-Blackwell, 2015), 1:198–205.

10. *Genuine Remains in Verse and Prose of Mr. Samuel Butler, Author of Hudibras. Published from the Original Manuscripts, Formerly in the Possession of W. Longueville, Esq; with Notes*, ed. Robert Thyer, 2 vols. (London: Printed for J. and R. Tonson, 1759); Samuel Butler, *Characters and Passages from Note-Books*, ed. A. R. Waller (Cambridge: Cambridge University Press,

1908); Samuel Butler, *Satires and Miscellaneous Poetry and Prose*, ed. René Lamar (Cambridge: Cambridge University Press, 1928); and Butler, *Prose Observations*, ed. Hugh de Quehen (Oxford: Clarendon Press, 1979).

11. Samuel Butler, *Hudibras, a Poem: In Three Cantos*, ed. Treadway Russell Nash (London: Printed by T. Rickaby for J. Edwards, 1793).

12. For seminal work on conceptual integration (also known as conceptual blending), see Mark Turner, *The Literary Mind* (New York: Oxford University Press, 1996); Gilles Fauconnier and Mark Turner, *The Way We Think: Conceptual Blending and the Mind's Hidden Complexities* (New York: Basic Books, 2002); Mark Turner, "Conceptual Integration," in *The Oxford Handbook of Cognitive Linguistics*, ed. Dirk Geeraerts and Hubert Cuyckens (New York: Oxford University Press, 2007), 377–93; and Zoltán Kövecses, "Metaphor and Blends," in *Metaphor: A Practical Introduction*, 2nd ed. (New York: Oxford University Press, 2010), 267–83.

13. In Grey's edition of *Hudibras*, the plate signed by Hogarth, depicting Hudibras and Ralph riding horses, is marked "P II." Hogarth's caricatured features of Hudibras's back is probably motivated by Butler's lines, "His *Back*, or rather Burthen, show'd, / As if it stoop'd with its own Load" (1.1.287–88).

14. Grey, *Hudibras*, 1:36.

15. Ibid. Cf. book 2, lines 962–67 in *Virgil's Aeneid*, trans. John Dryden, ed. Frederick M. Keener (London: Penguin Books, 1997), 57.

16. For the problem of using "punctilious standards of modern criticism" to judge the editorial style of another eighteenth-century editor, Thomas Warton, see Adam Rounce's chapter in this volume.

17. Grey, *Hudibras*, 1:37.

18. Ibid; cf. Alexander Pope, trans., *The Iliad of Homer*, ed. Steven Shankman (London: Penguin Books, 1996), 84.

19. Donald F. Bond, ed., *The Spectator*, 5 vols. (Oxford: Clarendon Press, 1965), 1:135.

20. Grey, preface to *Hudibras*, i.

21. See Pope, *The Iliad of Homer*, 332–33.

22. Regarding "verisimilitude" in seventeenth-century criticism, see Barbara Warnick, *The Sixth Canon: Belletristic Rhetorical Theory and Its French Antecedents* (Columbia: University of South Carolina Press, 1993), 49.

23. Grey asks in 1744, "Might he [Butler] not call them Long Field *Parthians* from the Great Distance they shot, and did Execution with their Arrows?" (200). Nash concurs with Grey's viewpoint (though without giving him credit), and he even states, contra other editors, his "unwilling[ness] to alter" "this epithet." *Hudibras, by Samuel Butler; With Notes . . . a New Edition, in Two Volumes*, ed. Treadway Russell Nash (London: John Murray, 1835), 1:156. Wilders and de Quehen, in apparent agreement with Grey and Nash concerning the rapidity and dexterity of the Parthian horsemen, give the following annotation on the "Parthians": "an ancient kingdom whose soldiers shot their arrows backwards as they rode away from the enemy." John Wilders and Hugh de Quehen, eds., *Samuel Butler, Hudibras Parts I and II and Selected Other Writings* (Oxford: Clarendon Press, 1973), 67.

24. In the 1835 edition of Nash's edition of *Hudibras* (1793), the editor of the revised edition states (in bracketed text): "*Long-field* is a term of archery, and a *long fielder* is still a hero at a cricket match." *Hudibras, by Samuel Butler; With Notes by the Rev. Treadway Russell Nash*, 1:156.

25. See Grey, *Hudibras*, 1:201–2.

26. Grey, *Hudibras*, 1:201; cf. book 7, lines 1100–1101 in Dryden, *Virgil's Aeneid*, 210.

27. *Pastoral Poetry and* An Essay on Criticism, ed. E. Audra and Aubrey Williams, vol. 1 of *The Twickenham Edition of the Poems of Alexander Pope*, ed. John Butt et al. (London: Methuen, 1963), 282.

28. Grey, *Hudibras*, 1:202.

29. Ibid.

30. See Grey, *Hudibras*, 1:223–24.

31. Ibid., 1:223.

32. Grey, *Hudibras*, 1:224; cf. Pope, *The Iliad of Homer*, 237.

33. Grey, *Hudibras*, 1:224.

34. See Grey, *Hudibras*, 1:142–43.

35. Ibid., 1:146.

36. Ibid., 1:144.

37. Grey, *Hudibras*, 1:142. Lucan, *The Civil War*, trans. J. D. Duff, Loeb Classical Library (Cambridge, MA: Harvard University Press, 1928), 3.

38. Grey, *Hudibras*, 1:142.

39. Grey, *Hudibras*, 1:142; cf. Arthur Gorges, trans., *Lvcans Pharsalia: Containing the Ciuill Warres betweene Caesar and Pompey. Written in Latine Heroicall Verse by M. Annaevs Lvcanus. Translated into English Verse by Sir Arthur Gorges* (London: Printed for Edward Blount, 1614), 2.

40. Grey, *Hudibras*, 1:143. Nicholas Rowe, trans., *Lucan's Pharsalia. Translated into English Verse by Nicholas Rowe* (London: Printed for Jacob Tonson, 1718), 4.

41. Grey, *Hudibras*, 1:143.

42. Ibid.

43. Edward Hyde, Earl of Clarendon, *The History of the Great Rebellion*, ed. Roger Lockyer (London: Oxford University Press and the Folio Society, 1967), 135–36.

44. Grey, *Hudibras*, 1:143.

45. Hyde, *The History of the Great Rebellion*, 143–44.

46. Grey, *Hudibras*, 1:143.

47. Ibid. 1:143; cf. *A Collection of Loyal Songs Written against the Rump Parliament, between the Years 1639 and 1661*, ed. Alexander Brome, 2 vols. (London: Printed for J. Stone, 1731), 1:107.

48. Jaclyn Geller, "A Lock without a Key: Satiric Metaphor in Samuel Butler's *Hudibras*," *1650–1850: Ideas, Aesthetics, and Inquiries in the Early Modern Era* 18 (2011): 275.

49. Nathan Bailey, *Dictionarium Britannicum; or, A More Compleat Universal Etymological English Dictionary Than Any Extant* (London: Printed for T. Cox, 1730), s.v. "sneer."

50. Grey, *Hudibras*, 1:332.

51. *The History of the Renowned Don Quixote De la Mancha. Written in Spanish by Miguel de Cervantes Saavedra. Translated by Several Hands*, ed. Peter Motteux, rev. J. Ozell, 5th ed., 4 vols. (London: Printed for J. Knapton et al., 1725).

52. Grey, *Hudibras*, 332–33. In his citation of Motteux's edition of *Don Quixote*, Grey has a minor misquotation in the first clause, which in Motteux reads as follows: "The curling Locks of her bright flowing Hair *are* purest Gold" (italics mine). Motteux, *The History of the Renowned Don Quixote*, 1:109.

53. See John Taylor, *All the Workes of John Taylor, the Water Poet* (1630; repr., Menston, UK: Scolar Press, 1976).

54. Grey, *Hudibras*, 1:333.

55. Grey misquotes two lines in his citation of *Romeo and Juliet*. In the edition by Theobald used by Grey, the misquoted lines (with errors and elided text noted in bracketed text) actually read, "Her vestal livery is but sick and green, / And none but fools do wear it; cast if off—". *The Works of Shakespeare: In Seven Volumes*, ed. Lewis Theobald (London: Printed for A. Bettesworth et al., 1733), 7:153.

56. Kenelm Digby, *Two Treatises: In the One of Which, the Nature of Bodies; In the Other, the Nature of Mans Soule Is Looked Into: In Way of Discovery of the Immortality of Reasonable Soules* (London: Printed for John Williams, 1645).

57. Grey, *Hudibras*, 1:334.

58. Digby, *Two Treatises*, 405–6.

59. See Bond, *The Spectator*, 1:211n4.

60. Grey, *Hudibras*, 1:334.

61. Grey, *Hudibras*, 1:334; cf. Bond, *The Spectator*, 1:214.

62. *The Elder Brother: A Comedie. . . . Printed According to the True Copie. Written by Francis Beaumont and John Fletcher. The Second Edition, Corrected and Amended* (London: Printed for Humphrey Moseley, 1651).

63. Grey, *Hudibras*, 1:335; cf. Fletcher, *The Elder Brother*, 35.

10

William Hymers and the Editing of William Collins's Poems, 1765–1797

Sandro Jung

Two editions of William Collins's poems, by John Langhorne and Anna Barbauld,[1] with memoirs of the author and explanatory notes on the poetry, were published before 1800. Laying significant foundations for subsequent editions of Collins's works, they defined editorial standards and procedures that characterize an ambitious edition-in-the-making that was under way in the 1780s. In the summer of 1783, its editor, William Hymers of Queen's College, Oxford,[2] "was circulating *proposals* for an Edition of Collins with Notes (pr. by Cooke & Prince, Oxon) but . . . died Curate of (& at) Ampthill" in 1785.[3] On his death, Hymers (b. 1758) left unfinished his edition, for which he had compiled an interleaved octavo volume of notes and commentaries that explained and elucidated Collins's compositions. Scholars of Collins have only rarely mentioned this album, which is held by the Beinecke Rare Book and Manuscript Library at Yale University,[4] and no attempt has been made to study the volume and contextualize Hymers's work in the light of the scholarly practice of the two editions that were published in 1765 and 1797.[5] Yet Hymers's edition-in-progress exemplifies and reflects his own participation in the process of canonizing Collins's oeuvre: he connects the poet with the "Gothic" and unrefined, vernacular literary past (embodied by Shakespeare and Spenser) that late eighteenth-century readers identified especially in his "Ode on the Popular Superstitions of the Highlands of Scotland," but also emphasizes the "polite" Miltonic and Popean poetic currency of his verse.[6] Engaging as a keen reader with the task of making sense of the reception of Collins's works from their first publication to the early 1780s, Hymers had to negotiate his own awareness of their peculiar qualities and the opportunity of embedding them into a narrative of the most recent literary history and aesthetic trends.

The aims of this chapter are twofold: after an exposition of the publishing contexts and editorializing of Collins from the 1760s to the late eighteenth century, I will introduce Hymers's edition-in-the-making and examine in what ways he contextualizes Collins as an original poet of descriptive and allegorical verse. I will briefly sketch some of the principal statements that Langhorne and Barbauld make regarding Collins and his poetry, and then discuss Hymers's interpretative and contextualizing accounts of the poems to illustrate his appreciative account of the poet's productions that contrasted strikingly with the generally lyrico-sceptic stance of Johnson. Compared with Johnson's description of Collins as preoccupied with allegorical fictions and superstitions, the "flights of imagination which pass the bounds of nature,"[7] Hymers approaches Collins as a modern classic who, like Gilbert West's Pindar, requires the best available editorial treatment.

Langhorne's and Barbauld's editions defined criteria according to which the Romantics would assess Collins's works, and Hymers's edition-in-the-making offers an insight into a young clergyman's perception (and understanding) of the not necessarily coherent new trends in literary production and historiography, as well as the ways in which he could situate Collins within the two competing narratives of literary progress and decline that Jonathan Brody Kramnick has examined.[8] Those advocating progress strove to formulate ideals of politeness, regularity, and harmony that clearly improved upon the Pindaric and Gothic lack of control in earlier English writing; others—especially from the 1740s onward—tried to counteract the commodification of polite literature by encouraging scholarship on oral culture and the sacred impulses in literature that had fallen victim to the secularization that social politeness had introduced into the consumption of literary texts. Langhorne, Hymers, and Barbauld, while cognizant of the conservative narrative of progress, favor an account that emphasizes and contextualizes Collins's successful mediation of the two models of literary historiography.

JOHN LANGHORNE AND THE FIRST ANNOTATED EDITION OF COLLINS

The edition of Collins's poetical works by John Langhorne (1735–1779) was the first complete edition providing annotation and commentary. His aims were more ambitious than those of Francis Fawkes and William Woty, who had published Collins's poems in the twelve-volume *Poetical Calendar* (1763).[9] *The Poetical Calendar* advertised itself as "Intended as a Supplement to Mr. Dodsley's Collection" and reprinted a large variety of miscellaneous poems from the seventeenth century to the 1760s. With the exception of Collins's poems, the editors did not include any poet's complete works. Not only did they print the majority of poems by Collins in volume 11 but volume 12, apart from including two more poems (the James Thomson ode and "To Miss Aurelia"), carried the only biographical notice printed in the *Poetical Calendar* as a whole. It is not clear whether Fawkes and Woty owned the copyright for Collins's poetry (which is unlikely); Langhorne's edition, issued by Thomas Becket in the following year, improved upon the canon of Collins's poetry assembled by Fawkes and Woty, offering, for the first time, extensive observations and a defense of Collins as a man and writer. The single-author edition format that Langhorne chose for Becket and Peter Abraham De Hondt offered an affordable text—sold in a range of variant editions from 2s. 6d. to 3s.—to middle-class readers who were actively participating in the revaluation of Collins that had been initiated by the editors of the *Poetical Calendar*. Langhorne had published verse in the late 1750s with H. Payne and W. Cropley, but Ralph Griffiths, editor of the *Monthly Review*, then recommended Langhorne to Becket, who published *Theodosius and Constantia* "as a trial-piece."[10] From 1761 to 1768, he was one of Griffiths's principal reviewers. Apart from being an aspiring poet and editor, he translated Milton's Italian poems and worked with his brother, William, on the six-volume edition of Plutarch's *Lives* (Becket and De Hondt, 1770).

Andrew Millar had purchased the *Odes on Several Allegoric Subjects* "at a *very hand-some price*"[11] and, according to the Statute of Anne, held the copyright for fourteen years, up until 1760, when Collins had been dead less than a year.[12] Becket, Millar's former apprentice, set up his shop at Tully's Head in January 1760 and was joined in a business partnership by De Hondt by the end of the year.[13] While Langhorne stated in his "Memoir" of Collins that the poet, in response to the poor sales of his odes, and "conceiving a just indignation against a blind and tasteless age, burnt the remaining copies with his own hands" (xi–xii), Ralph Griffiths in his review of Langhorne's edition clarifies that, as soon as Collins inherited funds from his uncle, he reimbursed Millar for the printing costs. It is doubtful, however, whether he bought back the copyright that Millar had acquired when purchasing his odes, especially as Becket and De Hondt appear to have drawn on this copyright to produce their successive editions of Langhorne's poetical works of Collins.

Langhorne's edition was paradigmatic for successive generations of editors in that he established a pattern for his edition that would be adopted by most late eighteenth- and nineteenth-century editors of modern poetry. He scaled down the extensive commentary that characterized biblical scholarship and earlier eighteenth-century editions of Shakespeare, Spenser, and Milton, and offered a minor but classic near-contemporary poet the features of short biography and commentary that would, in nineteenth-century editions of Collins, be elaborated, and supplemented with notes. Importantly, Langhorne's edition is probably the first edition of its kind, and similar editions of the poetical works of, among others, Matthew Prior and Samuel Butler were produced in the 1770s.

In his edition, Langhorne acknowledges an emerging literary historiography of vernacular rather than classical authors. Drawing implicitly on such a groundbreaking work as Joseph Warton's *Essay on the Genius and Writings of Mr. Pope* (volume 1, 1756), he did not need to contextualize Collins primarily in terms of the classics. Rather, he read Collins's poems as manifestations of an oral poetics focusing on harmony and skillfully deployed classical forms and conventions. The hybrid mixture of past and present literary tenets made it possible for Collins to be appreciated as an original vernacular poet. While reviews were appreciative of the edition and of Langhorne's editorial skill, commending specifically his "new" and "ingenious" "thoughts on the origins of allegorical poetry,"[14] it was recognized that, in addition to "many judicious criticisms," "the ingenious author has endeavoured to obviate the invidious reflections of the world."[15] These "reflections" would certainly have concerned statements regarding Collins's idleness and extravagance, characteristics that admiring critics from Langhorne to Alexander Dyce and beyond sought to mediate by rewriting the life of Collins in terms of the poet's inability to master the social pressures on misunderstood genius.

SUBLIMITY AND THE MYTH OF THE POET: LANGHORNE'S AND BARBAULD'S RECASTING OF COLLINS

In fact, Langhorne was successful in partly refashioning the image of Collins that Johnson had drawn in his "character" for the *Poetical Calendar*; while, in 1757, James Grainger in his review of the *Oriental Eclogues* (1757) had done the "neglected author of Odes on several Subjects, descriptive and allegorical" a service by judging "the images wild, the language correct, and the versification harmonious,"[16] Langhorne, drawing on James Hampton and Johnson's "Account of the Life and Writings of Mr. William Collins,"[17] prioritized some aspects over others and eliminated the largely moralizing conservative critique of the poet; Langhorne was keen that readers' attitudes toward the sentimentalized figure of "poor Collins" should change. He embedded Collins in a myth of unjustly neglected worth and madness that, in its sensational import, would especially appeal to readers fascinated with the mythicized lives of Christopher Smart and Thomas Chatterton. Langhorne's sympathetic account of Collins paved the way for the recognition that Collins's works would receive in the 1780s and 1790s, especially when William Hayley, who has also been associated with Hymers's edition-in-the-making, negotiated the erection of a monument designed by John Flaxman in Collins's native Chichester.[18] Langhorne's edition was issued in three different formats in 1765 and reprinted in 1771, 1776, and 1781. In 1784, Joseph Wenman reproduced Langhorne's "Observations" without acknowledging their author. The number of editions of Langhorne's poetical works of Collins offers evidence of readers' continued engagement with the poet's productions; as a result, early Romantics such as Wordsworth and Charlotte Smith carefully imitated Collins, appropriating him as a poet of mood to their own desire to place themselves within a tradition of pure poetry.[19]

The first biographical sketch of Collins in the *Poetical Calendar* set the elegiac tone of lament that would preoccupy Johnson for his revised and expanded account of Collins in 1781. Even then, however, the poet's mental disorder is related to his excessive imagination, for the "powers of this gentleman's imagination were unfortunately so great, that he lost his reason, at a time of life when common minds possess it in its greatest perfection."[20] The myth of Collins's madness—"that depression of mind which enchains the faculties without destroying them"[21]—spun in the memoir of the *Poetical Calendar* (and encompassed by Johnson's denominating his late friend "poor Collins") was carefully rewritten by Langhorne.

When Barbauld produced her prefatory essay on Collins's poems, she reread the productions as infused with "tenderness, tinged with melancholy," terming the poet "delicate and sentimental"[22] and assigning his malady to his condition as a struggling and anxious writer, rather than to the "dissipation" that Johnson mentioned in his "Life of Collins." Barbauld's edition for Cadell and Davies included four full-page copper-engraved plates by Thomas Stothard, illustrating, among others, "Ode to Mercy" and "The Passions," thereby clearly distinguishing itself from Langhorne's and Johnson's editions, which did not carry illustrative engravings. Even before working on the preface, Barbauld had attentively read Collins's odes; in 1773, she published her debut collection of *Poems* that contained imitations of Collins, including "Ode to Spring," "To Wisdom," and "Hymn to Content."[23] By the time she produced her essay on Collins's poems, she had adopted a more conservative, Johnsonian stance, especially regarding the need for rhyme in poetry (to which notion she had not subscribed in her highly successful *Poems*, published more than twenty years earlier). However, in her account she is "pleading for understanding," offering a sympathetic approach to Collins's assumed "idleness."[24] In her defense of Collins, Barbauld outlines the ideal condition for "the undisturbed exercise of the [poet's] faculties" and notes that he "requires long intervals of ease and leisure; his imagination should be fed with novelty, and his ear soothed by praise."[25] Formally, both Langhorne and Barbauld emphasize the harmony of Collins's verse and thereby contrast strikingly with Johnson's verdict that the poet's "diction was harsh, unskilfully laboured, and injudiciously selected," as well as occasionally characterized by "obscurity."[26] In fact, Barbauld redefines Burkean obscurity as a quality that best encompassed Collins's genius, for his poetry "deals in splendid imagery, bold fiction, and allegorical personages. It is necessarily obscure to a certain degree; because, having to do chiefly with ideas generated within the mind, it cannot be at all comprehended by any whose intellect has not been exercised in similar contemplations."[27] Implicitly, she reveals herself to be a qualified judge of this kind of obscure poetry, as—at least in her 1773 *Poems*—she strove to produce sublime verse herself.[28]

WILLIAM HYMERS'S EDITION: PROBING THE CONTEXTS OF COLLINS'S WORKS

Hymers's volume reveals a textual approach that relies heavily on the identification of both classical and modern sources, and a large number of intertextual references are listed in the pages of the manuscript. It represents a record of Hymers's own reading as well as the ways in which other readers had responded to Collins. The interleaved album comprises a copy of the duodecimo edition of Collins's works that reproduced

Langhorne's commentary.[29] He copiously annotated the pages of Langhorne's edition with comments that clearly engage with Langhorne's textual criticism. At times, he crosses out sections from Langhorne's "Observations"; at others, he supplements them with comments of his own. Hymers also adds queries about which he intended to consult John Ragsdale, one of Collins's London acquaintances.[30] In July 1783, Ragsdale had provided Hymers with information on Collins, such as the poet's producing some of his poems at his house, of which both Langhorne and Johnson, writing his "life" of Collins for the *Lives of the English Poets*, had not been aware.[31] Besides drawing on Ragsdale's recollections of Collins, Hymers also corresponded with Thomas Warton, the brother of Joseph Warton, Collins's Winchester College schoolfellow, who in 1782–1783 furnished him with further biographical information. Toward the end of 1782, Thomas Warton communicated to Hymers that his brother had then in his possession "a few fragments of some other Odes, but too loose and imperfect for publication, yet containing traces of high imagery."[32] In the same letter, Warton also mentioned "an *Ode to Mr. John Hume*" (the "Popular Superstitions" ode), detailing some of the striking images such as "a beautiful description of the Spectre of a Man drowned in the Night"; and he referred to the now lost poem "The Bell of Aragon."[33] Furthermore, he recalled manuscript variants of Collins's poems—such as the manuscript of the "Ode on the Death of Colonel Ross," "with many interlineations and alterations."[34]

After Hymers's death, the Reverend Alexander Dyce, a Collins enthusiast, who owned the copy of Collins's *Persian Eclogues* (1742) that the author had inscribed to Joseph Warton,[35] and edited Collins's poetical works, mentioned Hymers's undertaking in the preface to his edition, and it is possible that he drew on Hymers's edition-in-progress for his own editorial work.[36] Hymers's notes offer an insight into the ways in which a near-contemporary of Collins with scholarly ambitions responded to the poet's language, ideas, use of earlier literary models, and tropes. He does not discuss the "fragments" that Joseph Warton had in his possession but shows an awareness of variants of Collins poems that had been published in Dodsley's *Collection of Poems by Several Hands* and the *Museum*, the periodical that Mark Akenside edited for Dodsley.[37] Nor does he extensively discuss the *Oriental Eclogues* or the *Epistle to Hanmer*, although he annotated the former poem in the copy of Langhorne's edition that he had bound into the album.

Hymers's interleaved manuscript volume deserves to be examined in the light of new concerns with what constituted the proper language of poetry, the formation of a canon of vernacular eighteenth-century poetry, and the fields of philological and biographical scholarship that were emerging in the last two decades of the century. The many new editions of Thomson's *The Seasons* that were published in the last three decades of the century frequently included, from 1777 to 1793, explanatory notes, biographical prefaces, or extended discussions of the poem and its language by such authors as George Wright, John Aikin, Robert Heron, and Percival Stockdale, and responded to the central concern with the definition of the nature of modern poetry and how it should be understood. The number of these essays testifies to the process of defining midcentury poetics, and they were in part inspired by Johnson's recent *Lives of the English Poets*, in which he had offered conservative accounts of the poetry of his contemporaries that did not often advance the narrative of progress found in the scholarship of the Warton brothers.

Hymers's edition may be best understood in the context of Thomas Warton's edition of Milton's minor poems, under way from early 1783 and published in 1785. As Hymers was in touch with Warton regarding Collins, it is likely that he would have been aware of the Milton edition-in-progress and would have reflected a similar late eighteenth-century approach—although not as fully developed as Warton's—to discussing aesthetic trends and models of poetic production. Warton set out to read Milton as a poet using both classical literary models and "the Gothic library," and his general procedure is remarkably similar to the one that Hymers adopted in his manuscript album; the function of Warton's annotation is explained in detail in the preface:

> The chief purpose of the Notes is to explain our author's allusions, to illustrate or to vindicate his beauties, to point out his imitations both of others and of himself, to elucidate his obsolete diction, and by the adduction and juxtaposition of parallels universally gleaned both from his poetry and prose, to ascertain his favourite words, and to shew the peculiarities of his phraseology.[38]

L. C. Martin has termed Warton's edition "a model of discriminating taste aided by extensive learning," observing that it should be "valued because it illustrates the condition of English scholarship and taste, and the relations between the two, at an important stage in English poetic history."[39] Martin comments that Warton

> admired the early poems of Milton with an enthusiasm depending in part upon their incompatibilities with the ruling taste of his time; he was attracted by their romantic glamour and subtly emotive evocations, the qualities which a little later, by analogy with some other romantic performances, were to encourage the notion that in Milton whatever is, is right. But Warton was very far indeed from pleading that Milton is above reproach [. . .]. He maintained [. . .] a double alliance.[40]

This "double alliance" is characteristic of Hymers as well and distinguishes him from critics such as Johnson and John Langhorne, the latter of whom had not attempted the ambitious editorial treatment that Hymers projected.

HYMERS'S ANNOTATION OF COLLINS'S POEMS

Hymers's edition is here introduced by means of a discussion of selected notes on and interpretation of Collins's poems, as well as the ways in which the editor responded to textual and ideational obscurities by working within the traditions established by Johnson and Langhorne. Ultimately, the objective is to offer an introduction to

Hymers's volume and to recognize its literary-historical significance both for textual editing of poetry in the late eighteenth century and for the reception of Collins's poems specifically. In his edition-in-progress, Hymers does not attempt to negotiate Collins's illness, but he offers the sympathetic approach to the poems that Langhorne had used in his "Observations." Hymers's commentary, notes, and queries are primarily textual, and his analytical apparatus is more ambitious than Langhorne's, thereby denominating his work as a scholarly edition but also reflecting the growing institutionalization of literary scholarship, changes in editorial practice, and the redefinition and politics of the edition.[41]

He sets out his editorial objectives by stating that "Each Ode I ~~design~~ intend to preface with an argument ([or brief analysis],) similar to those of Mr. West."[42] Gilbert West had published his translations of the *Odes of Pindar* with Robert Dodsley in 1749; the edition included a detailed dissertation on the Olympic Games, prefatory arguments giving thematic summaries and contextualizing information, the individual translations of each ode following the argument, and a large number of explanatory notes. One of West's declared aims in the preface was to contribute to the understanding of the ode as a genre; later critics praising Collins's odes repeatedly return to West's discussion to understand the poems' "proud irregularity of greatness."[43] In fact, Robert Potter, a late eighteenth-century critic of Johnson quoted by Hymers, argues that "Collins was the first of our poets that reached its [the ode's] excellence," while Langhorne insists that he was "capable of every degree of excellence in lyric poetry."[44] Most late eighteenth-century responses to Collins situate him within an alternative tradition of the lyric that differs significantly from Johnson's narrative in the *Lives*. Readers from John Aikin to Anna Barbauld discussed Collins's contribution to the lyric in terms of his characteristic use of personification, and his poems served as models for imitations to a whole generation of Romantic poets who commended Collins in their productions, excerpted lines for their fiction, and labored to define him, as William Hazlitt did, as a poet who "had that true *vivida vis*, that genuine inspiration, which alone can give birth to the highest efforts of poetry."[45]

Hymers's initial acknowledgment that the "genius of Collins was cramped by imitation" (fol. 24r) prefaces the extended lists of intertexts that he identifies throughout the volume. Apart from a range of Greek authors, Hymers excerpts extensive passages from the *Spectator* and Chambers's *Cyclopædia*, which he probably intended for illustrative purposes to exemplify and explain the uses of figures of speech and ideas. He establishes the kind of map of textual sources and echoes that would inform Roger Lonsdale's editorial practice of annotation in the excellent 1969 Longman edition of the poems of Collins, Gray, and Goldsmith. In his attempt to fashion Collins as a learned and polite poet, Hymers linked his subject's immersion in classic modern (that is, early eighteenth-century) popular texts with those consumed by Collins's middle-class readers. Specifically, as Kramnick has pointed out, the *Spectator* served as a model of politeness, and Hymers's repeated references to the periodical indicate that he used Addison to anchor his reading of Collins as a polite poet; for his reading of the poet as reworking an alternative tradition, however, he refers to authors such as the Warton brothers and Thomas Percy, thus apparently making a seamless connection between the two competing literary-historiographical models of progress and decline.

Hymers's most finished section, containing a preface, extended commentary, and ample annotation on the pages of Langhorne's edition, is the one that he dedicates to the "Ode on the Poetical Character." He relates Collins's personification Fancy to Venus, who "by investing a favourite with her girdle could communicate a portion of her own charms" (fol. 56v). His comments offer information on the mythological frameworks that Collins constructs and reveal Hymers as a sensitive reader capable of insightful practical criticism. In addition, he references the depiction of the creation of the cestus of Venus in Homer's *Iliad*, book 14, and does not comment, as most succeeding readers would, on Collins's misreading of Spenser.[46] Instead, he defines the magical qualities of the cestus and its power to inspire love and control the "effects of the passion." He glosses line 21 ("the cest of amplest power is given")— "From the magic virtue of this Cestus the poet derives that divine enthusiasm which constitutes the essence of the poetical character"—implicitly connecting love, inspiration, and creativity. From his ideational discussion of the poem's myth, he moves on to comment on the structure and often difficult syntax that Collins uses, and observes that the sentence introducing Fancy's "cest of amplest power" is "too long and complicated, a fault that Collins is too frequently guilty of. The same fault occurs towards the conclusion of the Ode" (fol. 35v). In other instances, he highlights obscurities that he glosses elaborately. Hymers interprets the speaker's vision of Eden at the end of the ode as "a day dream" (fols. 36r–37r), linking the dream with Collins's desire for inspiration yet, at the same time, acknowledging its impossibility. The editor's (fairly finished) "Preface" to the ode, given here, represents a contextualizing headnote in the manner of West and characterizes the poem in terms of its occasion and subject matter:

> As the three preceding Odes were written in consequence of a Design the Poet had of writing Tragedy; so this seems to have been composed at a time when (his imagination heated by Milton) he had entertained the like resolution of attempting sacred Poetry—we have indeed an intimation of this towards the conclusion of the ode [. . .]. The complexion of it is sacred, both in its sentiment & imagery. He does not represent Fancy such as she is thought to be by the generality of Poets; but makes her that (divine) heavenly Being whom the Almighty himself is delighted to converse with, and who bore a principal part in the formation of the universe. He calls her divinest name, and attributes to her the Cest of amplest power which was prepared and bathed in Heaven. This description of the manner in which this cest was form'd, is truly sacred and sublime. The divine perfections are only admitted to be present on the occasion, and likewise those blissful spirits who reside in heaven [. . .]. A charm of [. . .] hallowed virtue could only be given to a poet who wrote on sacred thoughts and therefore to enjoy the privilege of wearing it, it is necessary that he sh^d attempt—as Milton—to wear her magic girdle, & desires to follow his steps to the place where he rested (?) for that inspiration, but recollecting himself, he is conscious of the difficulty of the task, and of his being entirely capable to undertake it. (fols. 41v–42r)

Hymers's reading of Fancy as a "heavenly Being" recognizes the sacred, mystic, and mythological nature of the deity and reflects his attempt—in his interpretation—at encompassing both a pseudo-classic mythology and the introduction of the Creator. He does not regard these two mythologies as mutually exclusive, as Barbauld would, but—rather uncritically—seems to read Fancy as an emanation of God's own creativity. While Fancy is constructed as having (or having had) primordial and unmediated access to God and his creation, she has to serve the poet as a means to overcome the boundaries of rational thinking and human limitations to access the shades of inspiration. Again, Hymers links love and creativity when he glosses line 69 ("From Waller's myrtle shade retiring") by stating that the "the Poet had free access to the 'myrtle Shades' of Waller, but he was not permitted to enter the hallowed Bower of Milton" (fol. 40r). Waller's amoric poetry is thereby contrasted with the sublime poetry of Milton; access to the sublime realm of Milton will be possible only through an epiphanic encounter between deity and Collins's speaker, which is a recurrent topos in the poet's odes.

The preface is the only fairly completed attempt to produce a coherent account of a poem that goes beyond the large number of jotted-down comments and references that dominate the volume. It also goes beyond the shorter discussions that Langhorne offered in his edition and anticipates the detailed readings that Richard Edgeworth provided in *Poetry Explained for the Use of Young People* (1802), where he introduced Collins's "Ode to Fear."[47] Unlike Barbauld's readings, Hymers's notes—despite his position as a clergyman—do not overtly aim to inculcate Christian morality through his interpretations. He does not share her rejection of the poem's religion or creation myth.[48] Rather, he evaluates the poem on its own mythopoeic terms.

Hymers discusses the odes in the order in which they occurred in Langhorne's edition but devotes little commentary to the odes to Fear and Pity. Citing Addison's *Spectator* no. 397, he states that "Pity is nothing else but Love softened by a degree of Sorrow" (fol. 28r). He also references John Hughes's depiction of the grotto of Pity from *Spectator* no. 501, and defines "enthusiast" and "enthusiastic," terms that Collins relates to the inspired poet. He holds that the poet's "enfeebling lute" is the "instrument of *Indolence*" and that the lute is "a woman's instrument, weak, feeble, soft." The editor relates his general contextualizations of Collins's divinities to classical traditions, repeatedly introducing the mythic figure of Venus as a connecting figure between some of the odes. He briefly states in a note: "Venus' lutes good—mellowness (which is the most excellent satisfaction from a lute): the Athenians encompassed the funeral monument with garlands of parsley and myrtle." By linking the odes through his discussions of motifs, ideas, or mythic emanations of Natura, he implicitly identifies an order and structuring principle underlying Collins's odes.[49]

He comprehends Pity in terms of the double role of priest and "prayist" (not in the *OED*), arguing that "Both the one and the other receive and transmit the communications of their respective divinities" (fol. 67r). Collins's poet-speaker as praying creator figure desiring inspiration is likely to combine the two aspects of priest and prayist. In his formal readings of the odes, especially the "Ode to Fear," Hymers implicitly refers to the essay on the ode that West prefixed to his edition of Pindar:

> This division of the Ode ought to be intitled Strophe. The excellent translator of Pindar in retaining the names of Strophe & Antistrophe did it, he informs us, on purpose to imprint more strongly on the mind of the English reader, the exact regularity observed by Pindar in the structures of his odes. (fol. 71r)

He provides a number of detailed glosses for individual lines from the ode and offers information that contextualizes Collins's poetry as spiritual and abstract, what Barbauld terms the embodiment of "the fleeting forms of the mind."[50] Hymers is interested in the representational technique that the poet employs to give shape to the inanimate and queries whether Collins succeeds in fashioning "an exact language of the inanimate" and whether "his sentiments [are] acknowledged by every breast" (fol. 73v). His micro-textual examination of the odes devotes special attention to figures of speech and ideas that later editors of Collins's poetical works did not explicate. Explaining the poet's phrase "pebbled bed," for instance, he states that "G. Agricola reports of a certain kind of spirits, that converse in minerals," thereby offering contextual evidence for his reading of the spiritual character of Collins's mythic world in which nature, in all its emanations, is suffused with life and spiritual essence.

HYMERS'S EXPLICATION: COLLINS'S STYLE AND MYTHOPOEIA

Possibly responding to Johnson's charge regarding Collins's obscurity, Hymers undertakes a detailed explication of ambiguous syntax and allusions, puns, or figures of speech.[51] In his view, the "Ode to Liberty" deserves extensive commentary, not primarily because of its ideational makeup, but because of its syntactic obscurity.[52] It is characterized as representing three distinct classical styles, the Doric, Phrygian, and Lydian.[53] Referring to Johannes Winkelmann as his authority, he reads Liberty as one of the conditions for the thriving and "prosperity of art," a progress also traced in the "Ode to Simplicity," where Collins centrally outlines his notion of *haplotes*. In his attempt to render the complex meaning of Liberty, Hymers identifies a range of references that are linked with free, republican countries. He complains, however, that Collins does not describe the goddess of Liberty in more serious terms, for "Collins would have Liberty a general Mistress—There is something frivolous, affected & incoherent in this conception. Let us hear, how the ancients arrayed and characterized such a personage" (fol. 51v). He objects to the erotic impulse in some of Collins's hymnal prayers—means of approximation between speaker and deity—and does not appreciate the complex mythopoeic structure that Collins constructs out of a fusion of traditional myths and secular impulses for privacy and intimacy.

While his mythopoeic readings of the odes published in *Odes on Several Descriptive and Allegoric Subjects* highlight the spiritual and pseudo-classical qualities of the deities, Hymers is alert to the possibility of contextualizing the "Ode on the Death of Mr. Thomson" in terms of both the antiquity of national, bardic identity and the elegance of early eighteenth-century poetry. Discussing the ode, he points out that "[t]he Druidical is a genuine ancient British Character," thereby implicitly denominating Thomson as a patriotic British poet. Hymers also relates the mythical figure of the druid to the close rapport that he is assumed, by the Romantics, to have entertained with nature. He thereby fashions an image of Collins's friend Thomson as the poet-priest of Nature.[54] The editor also notes that "Collins hath employed several of Thomson's words, combinations and phrases in the present ode" (fol. 82r). Not only has Collins succeeded in placing himself in the genealogy of the most important vernacular English poets but he has gone beyond Thomson in that he has fused both the literary present and the past and is therefore, in the 1780s, an appropriate poet to figure in the new historiography of midcentury literature.

Among the questions of style and language, as well as literary actuality, that Hymers raises, he interrogates the particular kind of descriptiveness used in the odes: "Have his descriptions always some peculiarities gathered by contemplating things as they really exist?" (fol. 112v). He partially responds to the question by drawing on John Gilbert Cooper's statements regarding personified characters.[55] In *Letters Concerning Taste*, Cooper had attended to the neglect that Collins's odes had experienced; he commended the "Ode to Evening" for being "animated by proper Allegorical Personages, and coloured highly with incidental Expression," noting that it "warms the Breast with a sympathetic Glow of retired Thoughtfulness."[56] Hymers repeatedly traces Collins's descriptions back to Greek models. In his critique of the "Ode to Evening," for instance, he likens Collins's power of description to Homer's, insisting that "[t]he dewy-fingered Eve of Collins will not be disgraced by a contrast with the rosy-fingered Morn of Homer." His discussion of style further considers questions of form that he had already addressed in his notes to the "Ode to Fear." In that regard, Hymers characterizes the "Ode to Simplicity" in terms of its use of the tail-rhyme stanza, thereby going beyond Langhorne's note that Collins deploys the "measure of the ancient ballad," which results in "an air of simplicity not altogether unaffecting."[57] According to Hymers, the "measure of Milton omits the disproportioned couplet at the close of each phrase. I believe not a ballad occurs in all Percy's collection; conceived in this measure.—I examined 2 vol. for this purpose and found none" (fol. 92v).

Hymers was clearly familiar with the publishing history of Collins's odes and the (published) variants of the poems, and it is possible that he had gleaned further information from the Wartons regarding Collins's unpublished drafts and fragments. He briefly discusses the poet's "Dirge" and observes: "This Poem is called in Dodsley's Collection a Song from Shakespear's Cymbeline &c which, if not absurd, is certainly unhappy, and justly superseded by the present title" (fol. 80r). In his brief discussion of the poem, he also references "Percy's Ballads Vol. 3. P. 176" (fol. 81r). Other critics he consults include James Beattie and Hugh Blair, as well as Collins's friend John

Gilbert Cooper. Beattie and Blair serve as authorities to support his argument that Collins's use of personification is proper and that rhyme is generally needed for lyric poetry. The second half of the album includes a large number of quotations from mid-to-late eighteenth-century criticism on poetry that he most probably wanted to integrate into the final version of the edition. In his notes, he compares Gray with Collins, commenting on their use of Milton, and has transcribed quotations from "Criticisms of Gr. El." (fol. 56v)—John Young's *A Criticism on the "Elegy Written in a Country Church Yard"* (1783).[58] He also examines the hypotextual transposition process informing Collins's reading of Milton: "The beetle of Collins and Gray is the 'grey-fly' of Milton that in the pensive man's ear 'winds his sultry horn.' Collins has changed the epithet into <u>sullen</u> by a happy <u>misremembrance</u>" (fol. 56r). Largely following Johnson, he considers Gray "a copyist" "of Thomson, of Pope, of Collins," identifying him as "deficient in general view—[and] determined by particular objects." In discussing the originality of Collins's poems, Hymers uses the by then conventional juxtaposition of Collins and Gray. While Gray was repeatedly criticized for his imitativeness in the 1780s, a trend emerged in literary historiography that not only privileged Collins over Gray but, by the mid-nineteenth century, culminated in such strictures as Algernon Swinburne's, who observed that "as a lyric poet Gray was not worthy to unloose the latchets of his [Collins's] shoes."[59]

Hymers's edition-in-the-making does not include any discussion of the poet's juvenile *Persian Eclogues*—although he lightly annotates the text in Langhorne's edition; he briefly deals with the "Epistle to Hanmer," Collins's patronage poem that he produced while at Oxford University, and jots down notes for further information that he aims to obtain.[60] His work is primarily focused on the odes, and the commentaries demonstrate that he has extensively examined Langhorne's criticism, familiarizing himself at the same time with very recent literary criticism, such as Potter's. Hymers goes further than Langhorne and Barbauld in his stylistic analyses of Collins's poems and demonstrates a new philological concern that the Warton brothers applied and promoted in their criticism. His ambition was to produce a scholarly edition on the scale and model of West's; unlike his model, however, Hymers contextualized Collins in terms of two narratives of literary historiography. His notes—and especially his "Preface" to the "Ode on the Poetical Character"—reveal him as a reader of Collins's mythopoetics; he interprets the poet's productions as products of a past vernacular tradition of obscurity *and* a recent tradition of politeness. Deliberately transforming, through criticism, some of Collins's obscurities into manifestations of poetic achievement, Hymers—like Langhorne before and Barbauld after him—comprehends Collins as a poet of genius. It is likely that he agreed with Langhorne's lament that an enthusiastic poet is destined to suffer, thereby inscribing Collins's mental disease with a quality of genius that the Romantics favored. Unlike Barbauld, however, Hymers does not indicate an attempt at embedding the poet in a moralizing narrative. Hymers's Collins is a learned poet—familiar with the classics, Spenser, Shakespeare, Milton, and Pope—who had the gift of amalgamating poetic traditions and creating original, mythic poetry.

This chapter is a reprint of the following article: Sandro Jung, "William Hymers and the Editing of William Collins's Poems, 1765–1797," *Modern Language Review* 106, no. 2 (2011): 333–54. Reprinted with the permission of the Modern Humanities Research Association (MHRA).

NOTES

1. *The Poetical Works of Mr. William Collins; with Memoirs of the Author; and Observations on His Genius and Writings*, ed. John Langhorne (London: Printed for T. Becket and P. A. De Hondt, 1765), and *The Poetical Works of Mr. William Collins; with a Prefatory Essay by Mrs. Barbauld* (London: Printed for T. Cadell and W. Davies, 1797).

2. The son of John Hymer (Humber) of Ormesby, Hymers (b. May 11, 1758) entered Queen's College as a battler (paying for his room and tuition, but not for his food) on June 17, 1775, aged seventeen, and took his BA in 1779. The Batells Book shows that he paid to remain a member of the college after his graduation and that, in 1783, he resided at Queen's. He is then referred to as "Dominus" Hymers, indicating that he had not taken the MA. I am grateful to Michael Riordan, the archivist of Queen's College, for supplying this information. Hymers was reputed to be "a very good Greek and Latin scholar, particularly clever at versification in both languages, and of amiable manners." See *Letters of Richard Radcliffe and John James of Queen's College, Oxford, 1755–83; with Additions, Notes, and Appendices*, ed. Margaret Evans (Oxford: For the Oxford Historical Society at the Clarendon Press, 1888), 254n1.

3. *The Correspondence of Thomas Warton*, ed. David Fairer (Athens: University of Georgia Press, 1995), 476n2. I have been unable to trace these proposals. In a letter of July 1783, Joseph Golding writes to John James Jr.: Hymers "only stays to publish his proposals for his edition of Collins, after which he goes to reside at Ampthill in Bedfordshire, where he intends to settle for life." See Evans, *Letters of Richard Radcliffe and John James*, 258.

4. Osborn c380. Material from this manuscript is cited by permission of the Beinecke Rare Book and Manuscript Library, Yale University.

5. *The Works of William Collins*, ed. Richard Wendorf and Charles Ryskamp (Oxford: Clarendon Press, 1979), contains a brief mention of the volume (126).

6. The "Ode" was written c. 1749 but published in 1788, long after the trend for "primitive" literature and the fragmentary, as well as the interest in Gaelic or Ossianic productions, had been consolidated in the 1760s. See Sandro Jung, *The Fragmentary Poetic: Eighteenth-Century Uses of an Experimental Mode* (Bethlehem, PA: Lehigh University Press, 2009), 26–59.

7. Samuel Johnson, *The Lives of the Most Eminent English Poets; with Critical Observations on Their Works*, ed. Roger Lonsdale, 4 vols. (Oxford: Clarendon Press, 2006), 4:121.

8. In Jonathan Brody Kramnick, *Making the English Canon: Print-Capitalism and the Cultural Past, 1700–1770* (Cambridge: Cambridge University Press, 1999).

9. See Sandro Jung, "'In Quest of Mistaken Beauties': Samuel Johnson's 'Life of Collins' Reconsidered," *Études anglaises* 57, no. 3 (2004): 284–96; Richard Wendorf, "The Making of Johnson's 'Life of Collins,'" *Papers of the Bibliographical Society of America* 74, no. 2 (1980): 95–115; and Mary Margaret Stewart, "William Collins, Samuel Johnson, and the Use of Biographical Details," *SEL: Studies in English Literature* 28, no. 3 (1988): 471–82.

10. *European Magazine* 17 (1790): 164.

11. Ralph Griffiths's review of Langhorne's edition, *Monthly Review* 32 (April 1765): 294.

12. Millar entered Collins's *Odes* at Stationers' Inn on December 19, 1746. See page 7 of the volume of "A Register of the Copies of Books Beginning the 29th Day of September 1746." I am grateful to Mary Margaret Stewart for communicating this information to me.

13. See H. R. Plomer, G. H. Bushnell, and E. R. McC. Dix, *A Dictionary of the Printers and Booksellers Who Were at Work in England, Scotland and Ireland from 1726 to 1775* (London: Bibliographical Society, 1968), 20–21.

14. *Monthly Review* 32 (April 1765): 293–98 (297).

15. *Critical Review* 19 (March 1765): 214–15 (215, 214). The edition was also reviewed in the *Candid Review* 1 (1765): 302–7.

16. *Monthly Review* 16 (June 1757): 486–89 (489, 487).

17. Initially published in volume 12 of the *Poetical Calendar*, the account was republished in the *Gentleman's Magazine* 33 (January 1764): 33–34, and the *Monthly Review* 30 (February 1764): 121–23. It was also republished, in March 1765, in the *British Magazine*.

18. Following his activities in the late 1780s to promote interest in Collins and to erect his monument in Chichester Cathedral, in 1796 Hayley corresponded with William Roscoe and revealed his ongoing interest in the poet. He stated: "one of my early companions informed me that an elder brother of his (intimate with Collins) had heard him read a preliminary discourse of great merit, which he intended to prefix to the work in question [history of Leo X]." See Henry Roscoe, *The Life of William Roscoe* (Boston: Russell, Odiorne, and Company, 1833), 225n. I have been unable to identify Hayley's "early companion." The card catalogue at the Beinecke Library has a note stating that Hymers's album also features manuscript annotation in a second hand, possibly Hayley's.

19. See Sandro Jung, "Wordsworth and Collins," *ANQ: American Notes and Queries* 22, no. 1 (2009): 19–24. For Collins's reception during the Romantic period, see Edward Gay Ainsworth, *Poor Collins: His Life, His Art and His Influence* (Ithaca, NY: Cornell University Press, 1937).

20. *Scots Magazine* 26 (August 1764): 439.

21. Johnson, *Lives of the Most Eminent English Poets*, 4:122.

22. Barbauld, *Poetical Works of Mr. William Collins*, xli. Robert Potter, *An Inquiry into Some Passages in Dr. Johnson's Lives of the Poets: Particularly His Observations on Lyric Poetry, and the Odes of Gray* (London: Printed for J. Dodsley, 1783), 15, also characterizes Collins's poems with the phrase "tender melancholy."

23. See William McCarthy, *Anna Letitia Barbauld: Voice of the Enlightenment* (Baltimore, MD: Johns Hopkins University Press, 2008), 109, 367.

24. See McCarthy, *Anna Letitia Barbauld*, 368.

25. Barbauld, *Poetical Works of Mr. William Collins*, xlix, viii.

26. Johnson, *Lives of the Most Eminent English Poets*, 4:122. See also Sandro Jung, "A Poet with a 'Bad Ear'? Reflections on the Harmony of William Collins's *Ode to Evening*," *English Studies* 88, no. 3 (2007): 288–97.

27. Barbauld, *Poetical Works of Mr. William Collins*, iv.

28. See Steven Shankman, "Anna Barbauld, William Collins, and the Rhetoric of the Sublime," *Hellas* 7 (1997): 159–67.

29. London: Printed for T. Evans, 1781.

30. "Mr. Ragsdale will inform me—Many of the Odes were written at his house" (fol. 17r).

31. John Ragsdale, "Particulars of Mr. William Collins," *Monthly Magazine* 21, no. 144 (July 1806): 498. The text of this account was a letter, dated July 1783, which Ragsdale had sent to Hymers.

32. Fairer, *Correspondence of Thomas Warton*, 470. See also J. S. Cunningham, "Thomas Warton and William Collins: A Footnote," *Durham University Journal* 46 (1953): 22–24; and *William Collins: Drafts and Fragments of Verse*, ed. J. S. Cunningham (Oxford: Clarendon Press, 1956).

33. Fairer, *Correspondence of Thomas Warton*, 469. See also Claire Lamont, "William Collins's 'Ode on the Popular Superstitions of the Highlands of Scotland': A Newly Recovered Manuscript," *Review of English Studies* 19, no. 74 (1968): 137–47.

34. Fairer, *Correspondence of Thomas Warton*, 470.

35. This copy (Dyce M8vo) is now in the Dyce collection at the Victoria and Albert Museum.

36. *The Poetical Works of William Collins*, ed. Alexander Dyce (London: William Pickering, 1827), 24. Today, the Forster Collection at the Victoria and Albert Museum holds a copy of the 1765 edition of Collins's poetical works with the manuscript annotations of two editors of Collins's poems, John Mitford and Thomas Park (shelfmark: Forster 1865).

37. See James E. Tierney, "*The Museum*, the 'Super-Excellent Magazine,'" *SEL: Studies in English Literature* 13, no. 3 (1973): 503–15. Tierney states that Dodsley's "literary periodical" "reflects the tastes of the times" (506) and "*The Museum*'s poetry was always original" (505). In fact, Dodsley largely included only those poems for which he held the copyright—as he would do in his *Collection*. On the different variant states, see *The Poems of Gray, Collins, and Goldsmith*, ed. Roger Lonsdale (Harlow: Longman, 1969), 455. Poems by Collins had been published in Thomas Warton's anthology *The Union* (1753) and the second edition of Dodsley's *Collection* (1:327–32). Dodsley included variants of three odes that had been published in Collins's *Odes on Several Descriptive and Allegoric Subjects*: "Ode to a Lady" (327–29; previously published in the *Museum*, 1:215–17), "Ode. Written in the Same Year" (330), and "Ode to Evening" (331–32). See also Michael F. Suarez SJ, "Trafficking in the Muse: Dodsley's *Collection of Poems* and the Question of Canon," in *Tradition in Transition: Women Writers, Marginal Texts, and the Eighteenth-Century Canon*, ed. Alvaro Ribeiro SJ and James G. Basker (Oxford: Clarendon Press, 1996), 297–313.

38. John Milton, *Poems upon Several Occasions, English, Italian, and Latin, with Translations; With Notes Critical and Explanatory, and Other Illustrations*, ed. Thomas Warton (London: Printed for James Dodsley, 1785), xx, xix.

39. L. C. Martin, "Thomas Warton and the Early Poems of Milton" (Warton Lecture on English Poetry), *Proceedings of the British Academy* (1934; repr. Nendeln: Kraus Reprint, 1977), 26, 28. I am grateful to David Fairer for information on Warton's edition.

40. Martin, "Thomas Warton," 27.

41. See Marcus Walsh, "Literary Scholarship and the Life of Editing," in *Books and Their Readers in Eighteenth-Century England: New Essays*, ed. Isabel Rivers (London: Continuum, 2001), 191–216.

42. Osborn c380, fol. 25r. I will reproduce superscripts, alternative readings (in brackets), and eliminations as they appear in the manuscript album. Subsequent references to Hymers's album are cited in the text.

43. Potter, *Inquiry*, 14.

44. Potter, *Inquiry*, 15; Langhorne, *Poetical Works of Mr. William Collins*, 137. See Herbert J. Wright, "Robert Potter as a Critic of Dr. Johnson," *Review of English Studies* 12, no. 47 (1936): 305–321.

45. William Hazlitt, *Lectures on English Poets: The Spirit of the Age* (London: Dent, 1910), 115.

46. Collins's "Ode on the Poetical Character" has been the subject of a large number of articles and has been discussed extensively. See, for example, Sandro Jung, "William Collins, Grace and the 'Cest of Amplest Power,'" *Neophilologus* 91, no. 3 (2007): 539–54; John Sitter, "William Collins, 'Ode on the Poetical Character,'" in *A Companion to Eighteenth-Century Poetry*, ed. Christine Gerrard (Oxford: Wiley-Blackwell, 2006), 265–76; Earl R. Wasserman, "Collins' 'Ode on the Poetical Character,'" *ELH: English Literary History* 34, no. 1 (1967): 92–115; Heidi van de Veire, "The Ordering of Vision in Collins's 'Ode on the Poetical Character,'" *Essays in Literature* 15 (1988): 165–75. In his rendering of the *Iliad*, Pope discusses the different uses of the cestus that Homer and Spenser make. See his "Observations on the Fourteenth Book," in Alexander Pope, trans., *The 'Iliad' of Homer*, 6 vols. (London: Printed for T. J., 1719), 4:54–56.

47. See also Sandro Jung, "William Collins's *Ode to Evening* and R. L. Edgeworth," *Notes & Queries* n.s. 49, no. 3 (2002): 386–88.

48. Barbauld's religious strictures also extend to Collins's "Ode to Mr. Thomson." She explains: "To the sanguinary and superstitious Druid, whose rites were wrapped up in mystery, it was peculiarly improper to compare a Poet whose religion was simple as truth, sublime as nature, and liberal as the spirit of philosophy" (Barbauld, *Poetical Works of Mr. William Collins*, xliii).

49. See Ricardo Quintana, "The Scheme of Collins's *Odes on Several Descriptive and Allegoric Subjects*," in *Restoration and Eighteenth-Century Literature: Essays in Honor of Alan Dugald McKillop*, ed. Carroll Camden (Chicago: University of Chicago Press, 1963), 371–80.

50. Barbauld, *Poetical Works of Mr. William Collins*, vii. Hymers glosses "While Vengeance in the hurried air" in the following terms: "Collins, as usual, improves upon his author [Horace]—The exposed & bare arm is more forcible, than the gloomy dismal more right-hand turn and when we discern it impending in the hurried air, looks more terrible" (fol. 72r).

51. Apart from his macro-textual reading of the ode, Hymers also adds a useful note on the meaning of the stork, remarking that it "was in the number of Egyptian deities and had divine honour also at Thebes."

52. He glosses "Where Orcas howls, his wolfish mountains rounding": "The participle rounding in the sentence depends upon wild waves, and not upon Orcas. The meaning of the sentence is, that the waves (or waters) of the ocean did not then flow towards the Baltic through the English channel, as they do now, but **round** the promontory of Preas, there being no other passage for them till Britain was parted from the Continent. Wolfish mountains may signify either wild & savage, or barking like wolves with the continuing dashing of the waves;—but the former I take to be the better sense, if the epithet do not, as I conjecture, include both" (fol. 49r). He further comments: "Orcas, independent of its wolves, is surrounded with objects of terror and desolation—the frequency of hurricanes, the distraction and concourse of tide-gates, the violence and height of the surges—the thunder and the lightning so prevalent in winter—the eddies, the whirlpools, amazing and terrifying to inexperienced seamen" (fol. 49v).

53. His definitions follow: "1. The Dorick *mode* was a mixture of impossible gravity and mirth, invented by Thamycias of Thrace; 2. The Phrygian *mode* was adapted to the kindling of rage; invented by Marsyas the Phrygian; 3. The Lydian mode or tone was proper for funeral songs; invented, according to Pliny, by Amphin."

54. "The name of druid imports Priest of the groves; and their verdant cathedrals are never omitted" (fol. 51r).

55. See fol. 113v.

56. John Gilbert Cooper, *Letters Concerning Taste, and Essays on Similar and Other Subjects* (London: Printed for R. and J. Dodsley, 1757), 47.

57. Langhorne, *Poetical Works of Mr. William Collins*, 155.

58. John Young, *A Criticism on the "Elegy Written in a Country Church Yard." Being a Continuation of Dr. J---n's Criticism on the Poems of Gray* (London: Printed for G. Wilkie, 1783), 16.

59. Beinecke Rare Books and Manuscript Library, Yale University, Algernon Swinburne Collection, GEN MSS 303, Series III, vol. 6, folder 118, fol. 2r. Cited by permission of the library.

60. On fol. 79v, for instance, he queries: "Sir Thomas Hanmer died May 7 1746—A mural monument at Hanmer, the principal seat of the family—Pennt. North Wales P. 219. Did Pope die before the publication of this poem? [Pope died May 3d. 1744. The epistle is dated Oxf. Dec. 3. 1743]" (the bracketed text was added in different ink).

11

Paratexting Beauty into Duty

Aesthetics and Morality in Late Eighteenth-Century Literary Collections

Barbara M. Benedict

Professional annotations, generally intended as helpful tools to steer readers' responses in the right direction, have appeared in editions of written literature for over seven centuries. Manuscript annotation existed from at least the medieval period, but annotations for current or recent works became popular later, particularly for classical translations that refer to unfamiliar historical or mythical material, and for poetry, which typically possesses a seriousness, concision, and imagistic rhetoric that readers can find difficult.[1] In the eighteenth century, however, annotations flourish in a new form: as a printed part of the text itself, supplied by the author or, more usually, the editor. While midcentury editors confined themselves to brief prefaces and occasional footnotes to clarify specific words or passages, more ambitious paratexts appeared in the Restoration and the Regency designed to mold readers' understanding of an entire text and promote a "reverence" for literature akin to that evoked by biblical exegeses.[2] Indeed, printed annotations were coming to replace the reader's personal notes.[3] This use of annotation to prompt an enveloping interpretation of a work became the practice of many late eighteenth-century editors as the roles of both the editor and the reader changed in a more professional print marketplace catering to more diverse readership.[4]

The practice of annotation has troubled several twentieth-century critics. In their famous New Critical attack on reading poetry biographically or psychoanalytically, "The Intentional Fallacy" (1946), W. K. Wimsatt and Monroe C. Beardsley argue that although critics may use the paratexts an author has published with a poem as guides to interpretation, when editors add their own glosses, the function of interpretation slides away from the reader's control.[5] This, indeed, was the intention of many early editors, and it resulted from the cultural need—or desire, at least—to police textual meaning in an England rocking under an explosion of print and readers in what one historian terms "the age of the reader" itself.[6] Glosses become a means for writers and booksellers to position their texts in a competitive marketplace, yet their disciplinary nature also holds the potential to alienate rather than educate readers.

Annotations need not be in language. In her late eighteenth-century parody of Oliver Goldsmith's *History of England* (1764), titled *The History of England . . . by a Partial, Prejudiced, & Ignorant Historian* in the second volume of her *Juvenilia* (c.1787–1793), Jane Austen includes a small, colored sketch of a bad-tempered Queen Elizabeth I, and William Blake adorned his own poems with colored illustrations. This practice also dates back at least to medieval times, when scribes and monks enhanced their literary transcriptions and biblical commentary with decorations from calligraphy to miniature landscapes. As records of the interaction between individual author or reader and replicated text, these show the personalization of public material. Later, as the book trade professionalized, however, other physical aspects of books were used interpretatively: book design, including format, font variety, ornamentation, and illustration, became important features of a volume, signaling genre and reading process. At the same time, readers still employed the commonplace technique of noting down their sources, including page numbers, and composing indexes. Indeed, the range of paratexts expands with the possibility of printing them in the book, and recent critics have urged an approach to literature that realigns "literary criticism, textual criticism and the history of the book."[7]

Paratextual apparatus became an important part of booksellers' marketing strategy during the last decades of the eighteenth and beginning of the nineteenth centuries because the torrent of previously copyrighted material freshly available for printing gave rise to various new ways of marketing literature. Following the landmark copyright bill of *Donaldson v. Becket* in 1774, which released much earlier eighteenth-century literature from copyright restriction, booksellers issued a burst of poetic anthologies. As Ina Ferris and Paul Keen point out, in the last third of the eighteenth century, "print . . . became entrenched in the culture," while "the physical book (its format, paper, type, etc.) became the subject of commentary in both private and public discourse."[8] Although collections of miscellaneous verse had regularly appeared in print since the Restoration, now booksellers were widely targeting a new audience: children, school-age youth, and self-educated or inexperienced readers with little leisure or means. Many of these collections use inexpensive engravings and explanatory prefaces to attract specific audiences; many also guide readers' interpretations by running heads, forewords, footnotes, and marginalia. These late eighteenth-century to early nineteenth-century compendia straddle two conflicting objectives. On the one hand, poetry appears as ethical education, a moral path to civic and religious virtue; on the other, it appears as a training in aesthetics designed to lift readers' social standing. These different objectives reflect the shifting status of verse as the notion of a distinctively English literary tradition began to surface, thanks to the comprehensive publications of John Bell (1745–1831) and George Kearsley (1739–1790). Collections include—and sometimes combine aspects of—school anthologies, self-help books, handbooks suitable for commonplacing, and cribs to literary culture. They typically, albeit not always, contain works by many authors, and so benefit from editorial assistance to help readers move between different subgenres and topics. Moreover, during the later eighteenth into the early nineteenth century as the number of circulating libraries, bibliophiles, book collectors, and commentators spiked, the notion of a national literary and book history took hold, and this also helped normalize editorial annotation.[9] What once sold as beauty now sold as moral and cultural improvement.

This chapter explores the shifting functions of annotation in some eighteenth-century poetic collections by examining a range of techniques—prefaces, illustrations, epigraphs, footnotes, indexes, and advertisements—used by three late-century figures: the Reverend George Glyn Scraggs, the headmaster and rector Dr. Vicesimus Knox, and the bookseller John Roach. Whereas the former two, both idealistic and committed Christian pedagogues, aim to make literature into lessons in civic virtue, Roach, neither pious nor high minded, presents canonical poems as examples of nationalistic morality, felt sensitively and aesthetically by author and reader. Knox presents literature as aesthetic experience that inculcates virtue; Scraggs sells it as cultural and moral education; Roach sees poetry as social opportunity. These differences appear particularly in the editors' approach to genre. Since he is focused on Christian and social morality, Scraggs interweaves poetry and prose indifferently: he cares less for the form than the message. Knox, more concerned with education, differentiates the two, while preferring poetry as more efficacious precisely because it is more beautiful. As a professional in the book trade, however, Roach preserves a still narrower generic category of canonical British verse in order to profit from a niche market. All three, however, negotiate the problem of matching moral to tale that annotations present and that is epitomized by the form of the fable.

FINDING THE MORAL:
THE PROBLEM OF JOHN GAY'S *FABLES*

Eighteenth-century fables, often published and sold with penny-ballads and chapbooks, borrow from a tradition of children's Christian poetry aimed primarily at readers not deeply familiar with classical literature, like youths and women, and almost always appear in numbers as a form of poetic collection.[10] Although an ancient genre, stemming from Aesop, specifically aimed at presenting lessons by means of a simple narrative, fables actually possess an ambiguity that confutes simple explication. Thus, they epitomize the problem that faced eighteenth-century annotators: the balance between readerly freedom of interpretation and editorial intervention. Angela Yannicopoulou points out that "fables are capable of accepting more than one interpretation of their moral truth and it is the task and joy of the reader to try to reveal it," yet many translators preface or append didactic "promythia" or epimythia to restrain this freeplay.[11] Such attached moral sayings work as annotations to dispel fables' obscurity and marshal them into conformity with traditional proverbs. They typically adorn translations of Aesop's fables, which had become popular for their classical roots, simplicity, and morality: early on, Joseph Addison remarks that fables "have been still highly valued, not only in times of the greatest Simplicity, but among the most polite Ages of Mankind."[12] Yet he also identifies readers' resistance to the sanctimonious, dictatorial, or smug advice embodied in snippets of ham-handed moral direction: "among all the different Ways of giving Counsel, I think the finest, and that which pleases the most universally, is *Fable*, in whatsoever Shape it appears. If we consider this way of instructing or giving Advice, it excells [*sic*] all others, because it is the least shocking, and the least subject to those Exceptions which I have before mentioned" of being reproached, condescended to or "treat[ed] . . . like Children or Ideots [*sic*]."[13] At the same time, Aesop's fables are marked, as Jayne Elizabeth Lewis observes, by an "unvarying division between story and moral," which corresponds to the division between poem and annotation.[14]

Fables' veil of allegory, traditional anonymity, fluidity, and didacticism produces an irony that made them hospitable to political satire early in the century.[15] John Dryden's political fables and Bernard Mandeville's *Fable of the Bees* (1714) exemplify this use of the genre. However, these very features also contribute to a moral ambiguity that, though delightful to Augustan readers, invited suspicion from later editors.[16] Especially after John Locke's endorsement of fables as a pedagogical genre made them common in schools, moral clarification became essential, and this was often achieved by illustration and simple annotative conclusions. For example, one of dozens of late eighteenth-century fables for children, the tiny sixteen-fable *Fables for CHILDREN with Suitable MORALS; By Mr. Wise. Adorned with Cuts* (1795), uses engaging and simple woodcut illustrations and concludes each fable with a separate "*MORAL*." Fable 1, which describes the gruesome death of a monkey, blown up while investigating a gun, concludes with, "Moral: Beware of being over curious; nor meddle with any thing, with which you are unacquainted: for in Curiosity there is always danger, and not unfrequently death."[17] Despite the clear warning, however, ambiguity remains since the gun goes off when the monkey, "in a great rage," flings it to the ground, and thus the story seems rather to illustrate the hazards of impatience. Again, the final fable of the sixteen, "The Wicked Judge, the Sky-Lark, and the Kite," relates the discouraging tale of a corrupt Judge, bribed by the evil Kite to decide against the innocent Lark, after which the Judge promptly slits the Lark's throat. It concludes with the unconvincing "*MORAL*: Riches and power, will frequently get the better of justice and honesty, but persevere in the truth, and that reward which is given to virtuous minds, will certainly be your portion."[18] Similarly, the frontispiece bears an illustration of two men desperately attempting to part a pair of dogs savagely fighting over a sheep in a courtyard: beneath appears the advice, "Those who in quarrels interpose / Must often wipe a bloody nose." This is puzzling, since, although fable 6, "The Old Horse and the Young Horse," and fable 8, "The Good Knight and the Bad Knight," both address the futility of goodness in a world of selfish creatures, there is no other fable to which the frontispiece remotely applies, and the illustration itself does not depict the dire consequences the epimyth intones.

This ambiguous and fluid relationship between the fable and its moral inspires the popular *Fables* of John Gay (1685–1732). These appeared eventually in two volumes. While the later, 1738 volume constitutes political allegory, the 1727 volume revels in social satire. Although dedicated to the Young Duke of Cumberland, it presents fifty lessons for youth concerning "reputation, gossip, and vanity" with an "underlying cynicism" alien to children.[19] Even the seventy beautiful copper-plate engravings by John Wootton (1682–1764) possess an elegance probably lost on the young. Gay further harnesses the ambiguity of this audience to the ambiguity of the genre by an initial fable, "The Shepherd and the Philosopher," that serves as an "Introduction to the *Fables*." This debate on wisdom takes the eighteenth-century conventional question of whether nature or art teaches morality best, and predictably the Shepherd wins by arguing that

> ev'ry object of creation
> Can furnish hints to contemplation;
> And from the most minute and mean
> A virtuous mind can morals glean.
>   Thy fame is just, the sage replies,
> Thy virtue proves thee truly wise;
> Pride often guides the author's pen;
> Books as affected are as men;
> But he, who studies nature's laws,
> From certain truths his maxims draws;
> And those, without our schools, suffice,
> To make men moral, good, and wise.[20]

As a dramatic representation of an abstract argument denigrating book learning, this passage not only conflates text and paratext but also destabilizes the moral authority of the *Fables*. Similarly, fable 10, "The Elephant and the Bookseller," by discussing the vices of booksellers and authors in a profit-mad marketplace, invites readers to reevaluate the wisdom of their own book purchase. The eerie title-page illustration of *Fables*, which appears in all subsequent eighteenth-century editions, reinforces this open-endedness (see figure 11.1). It resembles an oracular warning: elaborately decorated capital letters, surrounded by ink-whirls, surmount a large, unnerving blank mask with curling Medusa locks, and a grimacing mouth and eyes, both ominously enlarged, are open and hollow, through which shines blistering sunburst.[21] Gay mocks the didacticism of the fable form.

Because of this multivalent ambiguity, Gay's *Fables* invite vigorous editing. One response was *Gay's Fables Epitomiz'd: With Short Poems Applicable to Each Occasion, Extracted from the Most Celebrated Moralists Antient and Modern, for the Use of Schools* (1733) by Daniel Bellamy the younger (1717–1788), a writer with a strong interest in preaching. Prefaced with an introduction consisting of Addison's passage from the *Spectator* on the merits of the fable genre to teach us "by Surprise" to "become wiser

Figure 11.1.
Title page, *Fables by Mr. Gay*, 7th ed. (London: Printed
for J. Tonson and J. Watts, 1727).

and better unawares," the edition includes rough copies of Wootton's original illustrations, and thirty fables, each reduced to a ten-line verse ending with a moralistic
couplet.[22] Opposite each of these, an unattributed verse paragraph of between six
and eighteen lines, and headed with a simple, clarifying sentence—"ART IMPROVES
NATURE; OR, THE FORCE OF EDUCATION. A SIMILE," "THE TORMENTS OF AVARICE;
OR, THE ANXIOUS MASTER," etc.—explicates the moral.[23] The efficacy of this moral
crib may be judged from the script annotations in the British Library edition written
by a Miss Barlow in 1755, who numbered the pages, and compiled on the title-page
overleaf a commonplace index of the thirty fables, each listing the short moral headings and the corresponding page number.

Bellamy himself needs as much room to explain Gay's moral points as Gay does.
Gay's original seventy-six line fable 10, "The Elephant and the Bookseller," concludes:

> They [men] unprovok'd will court the fray;
> Envy's a sharper spur than pay:
> No author ever spar'd a brother,
> Wits are game-cocks to one another. (50)

Shrunk to ten lines, it appears as fable 2 in Bellamy's version:

> An *Elephant* in Days of Yore
> (So *Pliny* says) on Books would pore,
> Visit the Shops, learn'd Volumes spread,
> And make Remarks on what he read.
> A *Bookseller*, who heard him speak,
> And with just Accent mouth the *Greek*,
> Addrest him thus:—Exert your Skill
> Against *Mankind*, I'll pay you well.—
> No, Sir, let *Man* commence to Fray;
> "*Envy*'s a sharper Spur than *Pay*." (3)

Bellamy's version represents the annotating Elephant as a moral agent indicting envy, yet fails clearly to explain the relationship between the learned beast and the bookseller's offer. In a further effort to distill Gay's moral, Bellamy appends a bitter, highly allusive declaration ultimately to give up or suffer:

> The *Slander-Selling Bookseller*; or, MERIT creates ENVY.
>
> Censure will blame, her Breath was ever spent,
> To blast the Laurels of the Eminent.
> Had Pope with grov'ling Numbers fill'd his Page,
> Dennis had never kindled into Rage.
> 'Tis the Sublime that hurts the *Critick*'s Ease;
> Write Nonsense, and he read and sleeps in Peace.
> Were Prior, Congreve, Swift and Pope unknown,
> Poor *Slander-selling* Curll would be undone.
> "He who would free from Malice pass his Days,
> "Must live obscure, and never merit Praise. (4)

Whereas Gay's fable ironically illuminates the ignorance of booksellers and the rapacity of literary culture, Bellamy's paratext stresses the parasitical abuse of great poets whose names and quarrels seem hardly likely to engage young readers. Similarly, Bellamy's fable 9 reprises Gay's "The Shepherd and the Philosopher," here titled "Nature's the Best Guide; or, The Happy Scholar":

> How truly blest are they, and only they,
> Who *Nature*'s wise Instructions can obey!
> Who within Bounds their Appetites confine,
> Nor drink too deep of Pleasure's heady Wine!
> Whom free from Business too, the Leizure find,
> To dress the little Garden of their Mind.
> That grateful Tillage best rewards our Pains,
> Sweet is the Labour, certain are the Gains.
> The rising Harvest never mocks our Toil,
> Secure of Fruit, if we manure the Soil. (18)

Bellamy's verse reinterprets Gay's ironic praise of nature as a lesson in Horatian moderation and Voltairean self-cultivation that ignores the purpose of reading for knowledge altogether. The moral intention of the *Fables* remains unclear.

Editors were aware of the problem of incongruous epimythia, and several responded by prefatory discussions of their editorial principles. All agree that the primary goal remained to impress the appropriate moral lesson on readers, but the difficulty was how to do this without alienating them. Among the best received of such prefaces was *An Essay on Fable* (1762) by the poet, sometime footman, and distinguished publisher Robert Dodsley (1704–1764). Dodsley's own verse collection, *The Muse in Livery; or, The Footman's Miscellany* (1732), and his periodicals the *Museum*, published with Mark Akenside, and the *World*, produced under Edward Moore, all contain fables defined as "beast fable, oriental tale, myth, parable, and allegory"; in addition, Dodsley published six volumes of fables and moral tales, including Edward Moore's *Poems, Fables, and Plays* (1756) and the critically acclaimed edition of *Aesop's Fables* in 1753, reprinted several times before a final, lavish Baskerville edition in 1764.[24] Like many others, Dodsley extols the fable as a pedagogical tool: "Whoever undertakes to compose a fable, whether of the sublimer and more complex kind, as the epick and dramatick; or of the lower and more simple, as what has been called the Esopean; should make it his principal intention to illustrate some one moral or prudential maxim. . . . 'Tis the very essence of a Fable to convey some *Moral* or *useful* Truth, beneath the shadow of an *allegory*" (lvii–lviii). Shortly before, Samuel Richardson had sketched out a similar idea: in his preface to *Aesop's Fables* (1740), which includes "*Instructive Morals and Reflections*," some of which head the fable, he quotes Sir Roger L'Estrange's objection to a rote learning that omits a moral even while also warning editors that erroneous morals may misrepresent or bowdlerize the author's meaning.[25] Richardson's solution is to append a paragraph of "Reflection" explicating the fable as a parable.

Dodsley's conventional view of the fable as moral vehicle clearly informs the *Fables for the Female Sex* (1744) by Edward Moore (1712–1757). This imitation of Gay's *Fables*, to which Henry Brooke contributed three fables, was published anonymously in 1744 and ran though sixteen editions in the eighteenth century. Moore opens his volume with some verses announcing the moral intention:

> THE moral lay, to beauty due,
> I write, Fair Excellence, to you;
>
> Truth under fiction I impart,
> To weed out folly from the heart,
> And shew the paths that lead astray
> The wandring nymph from wisdom's way.[26]

The statement of allegorical method is illustrated by an engraved frontispiece vignette depicting a goat-legged Pan figure at a masquerade, standing before a mirror holding a mask, sternly looking behind him at attentive, finely dressed ladies, and gesticulating at the reflected image of one. As Gay had done, Moore dedicated the book to a young noble—the Princess of Wales—and the fine illustrations opposite each fable along with the final page of advertisements for Francklin's books, including Moore's play *The Foundling* (1748) and the popular "*Spectacle de la nature* [designed to] form the Minds of youth," indicate the youthful audience sought by the publisher. Nonetheless, Moore's subject resembles Alexander Pope's in *An Epistle to a Lady* (1735) rather than Aesop's more adult and general topics: Moore declares, "The proud, the envious, and the vain, / The jilt, the prude, demand my strain."[27] This incongruous match of subject matter and audience again reflects the ambiguity of the fable form.

Despite his moral view, Dodsley considered the fable a sophisticated genre, composed with skill to be read with care, exhibiting and demanding intellectual prowess: "A perfect fable, even of this inferior kind, seems a much stronger proof of genius than the mere narrative of an event. The latter indeed requires *judgment*; the former, together with judgment, requires an effort of the *imagination*" (lviii). Like Addison and the critic Charles LaMotte,[28] Dodsley rejects overt moralizing:

> The *Truth* to be preferred on this occasion should neither be too obvious, nor trite, nor trivial. Such would ill deserve the pains employed in Fable to convey it. As little also should it be one that is very dubious, dark, or controverted. It should be of such a nature, as to challenge the assent of every ingenious and sober judgment; never a point of mere speculation; but tending to *inform* or *remind* the reader, of the proper means that lead to happiness, or at least, to the several duties, decorums, and proprieties of conduct, which each particular Fable endeavours to enforce. . . . 'Tis the peculiar excellence of Fable to *wave* this air of superiority; it leavs [*sic*] the *reader* to collect the moral (lix).

At the same time, Dodsley realizes that readers, especially inexperienced ones, need guidance: "Strictly speaking then, one should render needless any *detached* or *explicit* moral. . . . However . . . [i]t must be confessed, that every story is not capable of telling its own Moral," especially one intelligible to youth: "In a case of this nature, and this only, it should be *expressly* introduced" (lix–lxii). Dodsley recommends editors rather to "*prefix* [Morals] as an *introduction*, than *add* them as an *appendage*" in order to control the reader's interpretation from the start (lxii). He thus reveals the ambivalence of many fable editors who wish at once readerly freedom and editorial control.

At the end of the century, the political writer and novelist William Godwin (1756–1836) still more strongly urged didacticism in relating fables to children. Reprinted several times, his popular *Fables Ancient and Modern* (1805) constitutes traditional stories elaborated and addressed directly to the young audience. Although the first edition of two volumes bore seventy-three copper-plate engravings, presumably to focus children's attention, the preface addresses parents with a justification for his explanatory details and happy endings.[29] These are closely tied to the problem of finding the fables' moral: Godwin remarks in his preface, "I have long thought that fables were the happiest vehicle which could be devised for the instruction of children [due to their simplicity, brevity, and use of animals]. Yet these advantages are too often defeated by the manner in which fables are written, and in which they are read." He explains that they are too short, "end in an abrupt and unsatisfactory manner," and contain insufficient background information and descriptive detail to convey "clear and distinct ideas" to the young reader.[30] The *Fables'* paradoxical ambiguity, while "empowering" the reader thus prompts annotation.[31]

IMPLYING THE MORAL: KNOX'S PARATEXTUAL PANOPLY

The rector and schoolmaster Vicesimus Knox (1752–1821), one of the most successful anthologists of the period, largely resists direct annotations in his verse anthologies. Rather, he guides his young readers by means of frontispiece illustrations, broadly descriptive subcategories, and occasional topical headings, all of which represent his books as packages of "useful" and improving literature, "entertaining" yet useful for moral and social discipline. His famous school text, the voluminous *ELEGANT EXTRACTS; or, Useful and Entertaining PIECES of POETRY, Selected for the Improvement of Youth, in Speaking, Reading, Thinking; Composing; and in the Conduct of Life* (1784), corrected, altered, and reprinted several times, with a new edition in 1790, contains hundreds of works arranged under four generic subtitles that also serve as running heads: "Sacred and Oral" ("Oral" is corrected to "Moral" in subsequent editions); "Didactic, Descriptive, Narrative and Pathetic"; "Dramatic, Chiefly from Shakespeare"; and, finally, "Epic and Miscellaneous." Each edition reworks the organization and shifts the order of entries, but most appear in some form in every edition. Since each entry is organized by author, whose name appears at the end of the line identifying the work's title, the book partly works as a literary crib. Knox seems to believe that, since the book contains "the best pieces [that] are usually the most popular," no further annotations are required: "To confess a humiliating truth," he admits, "in making a book like this, the hand of the artisan is more employed than the head of the writer."[32] In contrast, his prose *Epistles, Elegant, Familiar & Instructive* (1791) includes copious headnotes and footnotes providing historical, geographical, and biographical background for both writers and recipients.

Annotation does, however, creep in. Knox also heads every entry with an annotation identifying the main subject, like "Description of the Poor Man's Funeral. Crabbe" (2.272). In the final section, the running head "Divine Songs" shifts to "Moral Songs," headed by topical titles, like "The Danger of Delay" (4.712); "Against Idleness and Mischief" (4.713); "Against Pride in Clothes" (4.714); and "Obedience to Parents" (4.714). Although some concern virtues, like "Love between Brothers and Sisters," most constitute warnings and strictures (4.713). In addition, the poetic *Elegant Extracts* bears an instructive title-page paratext (see figure 11.2). This large oval illustration by Edward Francisco Burney (1760–1848), engraved by James Heath (1757–1834), shows a youth reading a large book (*Elegant Extracts*), seated on a river bank, and leaning against a tree; another youth sits beside him, leaning his head on one hand and holding a quill in the other, with a sheet of paper beside him on the mossy bank, staring dreamily up into the sky for inspiration. A

Figure 11.2.
Title page, Vicesimus Knox, *Elegant Extracts; or, Useful and Entertaining PIECES of POETRY* (London: Printed for C. Dilly and Poultry, 1789).

third boy, the youngest, with another copy of *Elegant Extracts* open beside him, propped up by two other volumes, looks meditatively down, touching the tips of his two index fingers. The engraved epigraph reads: "While some on earnest Business bent / Their murmuring Labours ply—Gray." This serves literally to illustrate the ways in which the book should be used for promoting "Reading, Thinking," and "Composing" while implying the imaginative delights it will supply. These paratexts hence package literature as morality and education, as well as culture.

For adults and instructors, moreover, Knox supplies an elaborate preface that justifies poetry. It declares that "poetry has ever claimed the power of conveying information in the most effectual manner, by the vehicle of pleasure," and that youth are led on by enjoying poetry into serious pursuits of philosophy and science (i–ii). Significantly, Knox identifies his main audience as gentry unconcerned with "what they call the MAIN CHANCE," making money, declaring that one who sees an opposition between poetry and profit has not "the mind of the gentleman, or the man of a liberal profession"; although he admits that some of "the mercantile classes, at least of the higher order," should be allowed to enjoy it. Centrally, he declares, "it will be readily acknowledged, that ideas and precepts of all kinds, whether of morality or science, make a deeper impression when inculcated by . . . poetical language. And what is thus deeply impressed will also long remain," especially since "[a] great part of the Scriptures is poetry and verse" (iii–iv). Most important, Knox argues that, "as to morals," poetry instills goodness, quoting Sir Philip Sidney's *A Defense of Poetry* (1582–1583), which recommends its narrative and descriptive detail as a "gentle yet certain method of allurement [that] leads both to learning and to virtue" (ii). He thus largely trusts verse alone to do the work of moral inculcation while explaining this to schoolmasters and parents.

Nonetheless, Knox saw the opportunity to mold readerly experience even as he acknowledged readers' resistance. In the three-volume collection of his own prose works titled *Winter Evenings; or, Lucubrations on Life and Letters* (1788), he includes an essay that is titled in later editions as "On the Use and Abuse of Marginal Notes and Quotations" and subtitled "Apologies for them—If not always useful, yet commonly ornamental—If troublesome or unintelligible, may be neglected."[33] The essay focuses on readers' individual *process* of reading both as an intellectual and as an aesthetic enterprise. Knox disparages the seventeenth-century passion for paratexts for violating the aesthetics of print presentation, as well as diluting the content of the text: marginalia such as "notes, quotations, and mottoes" may distract a reader, dampen "that ardour which he might have contracted in continual reading," or even shame him, especially if they appear in a language other than English (91, 89). By deriding the "fashion" of the "laborious writers of the last century" for crowding the pages of their "bulky folios" with "a small letter, a large page, a narrow margin, and a great abundance of notes and citations," he suggests that the contemporary practice of providing "many volumes" with margins large enough to accommodate more text than the book itself, yet "without . . . a single quotation" to "violate" "the uniformity of the beautiful page," presents the book as high art (88). His own meticulous organization reflects this value for "uniformity," a clarion call at the time as an English literary tradition was being formed. In addition, Knox observes that booksellers "craftily" "swell" a volume and increase its price by stuffing the text with peripheral material extracted from "Indexes, Dictionaries, *Florilegia* [gathered flower], *Spicilegia* [gleaned ears of corn], *Ecloga* [short poems], and Synopses" (90–91). Yet his prose *Elegant Epistles* bristles with such gleanings. Knox's contradictions reflect the problematic relationship between texts, paratexts, and parasitical genres as new readers attempted to understand a complex literary heritage. By noting the physical layout of the page, Knox also reveals the contemporary sensitivity to printed books as objects of art that echoes the conception of poetry as beauty. Later in the essay, Knox compares quotations to paintings as "ornamental and amusing to the fancy, instructive to the understanding, and, in some measure, prove the [bibliophile] traveller's authenticity" (94). Books thus appear as items of luxurious consumption, and his own ornate title pages, in turn, represent reading as a visual experience.

The focal point of this consumption remains the reader, who is free to read as he or she wishes. A reader, he points out, can ignore notes but can also contemplate quotations "without the trouble of recurring to his library; a pleasant circumstance, which saves both time and trouble, and, I should think, could not fail of being agreeable to the indolent student of modern times, who only reads on his sofa over his chocolate, or as he lolls in his chariot, or under the hair-dresser" (92). If books are luxury items equivalent to chocolate, readers here appear privileged and leisured consumers of fashionable experience. Moreover, annotation provides social, as well as literary, context. While condemning self-important and autodidactic (often French and atheistic) authors who include quotations as "pedantic ostentation," he approves editorial apparatus as a means for socializing the lonely habit of reading (96). Indeed, he mourns the loss of a friendly editorial presence: "Formerly," he sighs, "as you journeyed through a book, elucidations in the margin attended your progress like lamps by the road side; but now, it may be presumed, books shine like phosphorus, or the glow-worm, with an internal lustre, and require not the assistance of extrinsic illumination" (88). Thus, Knox defends editing practices as social accompaniments in order to negotiate the central problem facing all contemporary editors: the tension between licensing individual interpretation and presenting literature as part of an authoritative national culture.

FORCING THE MORAL: SCRAGGS'S SOLUTIONS

Whereas Knox aims to broaden readers' imaginative engagement in literary culture at large, many annotators have a narrower pedagogical or religious agenda. John Kerrigan notes that the Renaissance editor of the *Works of Seneca* (1620), Thomas Lodge, suggests that "[t]he editing reader should be prudent, lest he multiply error. But the text is his to use, to modify and select from. 'What a Stoicke hath written,' Lodge advises, 'Reade thou like a Christian.'"[34] Especially in the frightened, reactionary wake of the French Revolution, cultural critics leapt to revise or bowdlerize the often raunchy material of the early eighteenth century into fare for the mixed audience of the Regency pious. Among the most interventionist and energetic of such editors was the Reverend G. G. Scraggs. His two-volume *Instructive Selections; or, The Beauties of Sentiment*, published in 1801, was reprinted the next year and followed by a second edition in 1812. On October 28, 1809, Robert Southey, reproaching Samuel Taylor Coleridge for his essayistic prolixity, quoted an advertisement for Scraggs's book: observing that, in the current climate, "every thing must be short," he cited the prospectus for what he called "the Beauties of Sentiment," which promised that "the extracts are always complete sense, not very long, and yet not too short."[35] This (probably ironic) exchange between the two Romantic poets suggests that Regency writers were very conscious of the changing habits and preferences of readers. As the reading matter itself dwindled to bite-sized excerpts, the need for editorial guidance increased.

Scraggs's anthology promises a digest of literary and moral culture. While volume 1 is designed to recommend religion, the second supplies "information and entertainment," serving as "a *book of reference*, and as an *help to conversation* . . . well adapted to be made a *school book*."[36] Although Scraggs had written a book of fables intended to instill "The Love of Virtue" in children, this book offers more sophisticated fare.[37] In his preface, Scraggs earnestly assures readers that he has avoided all religious or political bigotry, and urges them as evidence to compare entries on "Party, Spirit, Brotherly Love" and so forth as evidence: he thus seeks a general audience without "much money . . . or time to consult larger works."[38] The volume supplies excerpts from both poetic and prose writers ranging from "Philosophers, ancient"—in other words, Seneca—to such contemporaries as Johann Caspar Lavater and Knox himself, and Scraggs structures this array by means of a systematic apparatus of paratexts. The title page provides a detailed advertisement of the contents with a descriptive title produced in a medley of fonts, from gothic to italic: "INSTRUCTIVE SELECTIONS; *OR,* 𝕿𝖍𝖊 𝕭𝖊𝖆𝖚𝖙𝖎𝖊𝖘 𝖔𝖋 𝕾𝖊𝖓𝖙𝖎𝖒𝖊𝖓𝖙. BEING STRIKING EXTRACTS FROM THE BEST AUTHORS, ANCIENT AND MODERN, *IN PROSE AND VERSE*, ON A GREAT VARIETY OF SUBJECTS, *Divine, Moral, Literary, and Entertaining*, ON A NEW METHODICAL PLAN. ALSO, A LIST OF THE BEST BOOKS ON THE PRINCIPAL SUBJECTS, and *THE NAMES OF THE AUTHORS AFFIXED TO THE EXTRACTS*." While neither the touting nor the variety of fonts are themselves particularly original, the declaration that attributions are "affixed to the Extracts" is: albeit a common practice, this statement underscores the editor's intention to provide readers with authoritative literary information, as well as apt quotes for showing off in conversation.

Scraggs clearly believes that European literary culture is consistent with a broad and comprehensive morality. In his preface, he argues:

> It was the opinion of Lord Bacon, that if a judicious collection could be made of the theological sentiments of the most eminent British divines, it would form the best system of divinity in the world. If we consider also what a number of excellent writers in divinity have appeared since [that] time . . . the remark will appear still more striking. The same observation will extend with equal propriety to *morality and literary* matters, and therefore the Editor has compiled this work . . . Although [it] contains many short wise sayings and sentences, yet it is by no means to be considered only as a *book of maxims*, [since] the greatest part of these volumes contains extracts that are large, and . . . placed in such order, that by putting together the quotations here inserted, a judicious person many, in a short time, and with very little trouble, have a comprehensive view of any important subjects which he wishes to understand. (1:iii–iv)

Through a process of selection, editing, and annotation that emphasizes the moral uniformity of literature through the ages, Scraggs thus intends to provide moral and cultural knowledge.

Accordingly, Scraggs's annotation takes two forms: attribution and commentary. He declares that the "wise sayings and sentences" in the book constitute a concise compendium of cultural knowledge, some apparently common knowledge and therefore impossible (and unnecessary) to attribute to one author:

> In a work of this kind it cannot be expected that there should be found many long *poetical* extracts, however some of the most striking verses from the very best British poets are inserted almost on every subject. . . . For the satisfaction of the reader, the names of the authors are placed at the end of most of the extracts, but in such a *great* variety of quotations, it is very likely the Compiler has put a wrong name to some of them, especially as the *same* sentence is frequently ascribed to different authors. (Preface, 1:v–vi)

Despite this assertion of editorial probity and scholarly accuracy, however, Scraggs overrates the accuracy of either his sources or his memory, including unattributed excerpts from Pope's *Essay on Criticism* (1711), among other texts, and sometimes revises or cuts the quotations to suit what he imagines to be a Regency sensibility and feminine audience.[39] To him, precise information is less important than general concept.

Throughout the book, Scraggs also provides direct commentary for scholarly and moral guidance, but many of these annotations are misleading or clearly tailored to convey what he considers the correct attitude toward a topic. Scraggs begins the lesson, as it were, by heading most of the entries with a brief, often tendentious, definition of the term discussed. For example, he explains "ABILITIES, *OR ACCOMPLISHMENTS*" as "Signify[ing] such mental gifts, endowments, or talents, as render some persons superior to others, and more fit for usefulness" (2:1). This note fuses natural talents with learned skills, and defines both by their social value, as rendering their possessors "useful": behind the rhetoric lurks a didactic direction to readers to work hard for society's benefit. Again, Scraggs explains that "AMUSEMENTS," subtitled *"DIVERSIONS OR PASTIMES,"* "[s]ignify any kind of temporary games, sights, or pleasures," and further indicates the appropriate way to regard them by his first illustration: he writes, "Demartus, the Lacedemonian, being asked his opinion of a famous singer, only said 'that he seemed to trifle very well'; this is all we can say of players, and all kinds of diversions are but trifles" (2:20). After a disparaging remark on Venus, he proceeds to quote William Wilberforce by announcing: "Religion prohibits no amusement or gratification that is *really* innocent. The question however of its innocence must not be tried by the loose maxims of worldly morality, but by the Bible, the genius of christianity [*sic*], and the temper and disposition of mind enjoined on its professors" (2:21). A selection of short poetic warnings against amusements as impoverishing by Dryden, Benjamin Franklin, and Edward Young follow, with a final, italicized recommendation: *"See more under Pleasure."* Thus, Scraggs weaves the quotations in the book into a series of associations that promote a socialized Christian morality.

Scraggs often meanders away from quotation altogether to advise readers on various topics. For example, after the comments on "Authors and Books," Scraggs writes, "Our books may be said to be our *dead counsellors*, and are better than many living advisers, for they without flattery or fear give good advice" (2:20). His snippets of wisdom serve to direct readers in how to navigate the chaotic world of print to continue independently their own education. One of the longest on "*Good Judges of Poetry very rare*" declares, somewhat illiterately:

> The term poetry is very comprehensive, as it not only includes a great variety of subjects, and so many different metres, but as it is governed by very different rules to what prose is, and as it has likewise such an amazing number of peculiar similies [*sic*], epithets, phrases, and allusions. To be a judge of these various species of poetry, a person should be conversant with the nature of each, and the rules by which that kind is governed, as well as he should possess almost universal knowledge in learning, men, and manners. How few such critics are to be found? But if these requisites be allowed them, there are more still wanting to complete their sufficiency. Genius and taste are necessary ingredients in a poetic critic, which are the gifts of nature, and to be sought in vain by study and toil. A critic in poetry must likewise have a fine and delicate ear, a quality which many learned men have not, and which indeed every man of genius and taste does not possess in perfection. (2:219–20)

This mishmash of banal critical opinion derives from Pope's *Essay on Criticism*, Samuel Johnson's *Rasselas* (1759), and the clichés of many lesser critics. It serves here to provide readers with a shorthand account of the topic, without the need for direct quotation. Indeed, the entries on "Learning" and "Poetry" consist almost entirely of Scraggs's own *pensées*, as he considered himself an expert on composition.[40]

All of Scraggs's paratexts function intertextually to weave his book into a seamless fabric of literary culture. His index reverts to the commonplace formula for organizing the material by theme: the eighty-five entries in volume 2, for example, range from "Abilities" to "Youth," and include the usual topics of moral commentary, both abstract and specific: "Covetousness," "Masters and Servants," "Pride," "Wit," "Women," and so forth. On the reverse, Scraggs lists the fifty-nine extracted authors, noting at the top of the page that "[m]any Extracts are taken from those marked thus +," which includes fifteen: Addison, Blair, Cowper, Dryden, Fielding, Goldsmith, Johnson, Knox, Lavater, Locke, Seneca, "Spectator" (i.e., the *Spectator*), Lyscombe Maltbee Stretch (editor of a well-received edition of historical beauties showing pictures of vice and virtue for youth), Thomson, and Nathaniel Wanley (a vicar and author of an anthology of moral qualities also designed for youth). In addition to the definitive headers and inserted commentary, Scraggs ends many selections with "Select Books," recommended reading for further study, including the *London Catalogue*, Lackington's *Catalogue*, and the "Monthly and other Reviews." Since his concern to educate and enfranchise an underprivileged audience prohibits Scraggs from regarding his book as an art object, he boasts of its "small and very close" print, which makes it "cheap and comprehensive," and available to "all classes of readers" (Preface, 1:v). Despite his stringent critique of poetry and good poetic judgment, his practices present literature as a transhistorical expression of moral truths and civic virtue.

FEELING THE MORAL: ROACH'S BEAUTIFUL BEAUTIES

John Roach (1753/4?–1832?) was an entrepreneurial bookseller whose list of publications included *Roach's Authentic Memoirs of the Green Room, Containing the Lives of All the Performers of the Theatres Royal* (1796) and, with Henry Ranger, the scandalous catalog of prostitutes, *Harris's List of Covent-Garden Ladies* (1793). At much the same time as the latter, he published a part publication of six-penny pamphlets, twenty-four in all, each eighteen pages and issued monthly, titled *Roach's Beauties of the Poets of Great Britain; Carefully Selected & Arranged from the Works of the Most Admired Authors* (1791–1792). Like other books for readers without their own libraries, these featured illustrations and decorative devices: Roach's are highly ornamented, with elaborate title pages for each volume, part, and each of the four sections in each part, often cartouches portraying a bust of the author, and internal vignettes of scenes from the poems that work to isolate moments of emotion from the narrative, suspending causality and, thus, morality. Although readers could collect each part and assemble their own library of English classic verse, Roach issued the entire series, with slightly different titles, in six-volume sets in 1791–1792, 1793–1794, and 1794–1795. All editions present verse as visual beauty while their annotations provide supplementary prompts to feeling and morality.

Roach was an enthusiastic annotator, and his glosses cover the range of possibilities, from interpretative meditation to historical information and linguistic definition, but all present poems as emotional prompts to civic virtue. He supplies epigraphs, footnotes, and introductory essays, sometimes poetic quotations or references to biblical passages; some footnotes provide definitions or allusions, but many of these annotations do not merely identify figures, places, and events but prompt readers' sentimental responses. Most he has written himself, but some are cribbed from other sources. For example, on the first page of the first part, he prefaces the first selection, a proto-Romantic and pious meditation on the vanity of human wishes titled "Evening Reflections Written in Westminster Abbey," with this introduction by the anonymous G. W., a source for another of Roach's annotations: "The following Reflections, suggested by a contemplative walk among the Monuments in WESTMINSTER ABBEY, as they hold out lessons of moment and importance to men in general, are worthy the remembrance and regard of all." In addition, Roach adds, signaled by an asterisk, the footnote, "*The long drawn aisles and pensive vaults of this venerable pile of Gothic magnificence, diffuse over the mind a pleasing melancholy; while the eye is on every side attracted by the storied urn and animated bust, which commemorate the virtues of the monarch, the abilities of the statesman, or the achievements of the hero." Sandwiched between these copious annotations stands a single four-line stanza of the fifteen that constitute the poem:

> HAIL, sacred Fane! amidst whose stately shrines,
> Her constant vigils Melancholy keeps;*
> (Whilst on her arm her grief-worn cheek reclines)
> And o'er the spoils of human grandeur weep. [*sic*][41]

Roach's footnote not only attempts to explain the metaphorical meaning behind the personified Melancholy but serves as an introduction to the imagery in the rest of the poem. These annotations indicate Roach's estimation of his audience: readers whose grasp of poetic language might not extend to neoclassical devices, and who probably lack firsthand knowledge of Westminster Abbey. Given such limitations, why did Roach choose to open with this apparently inaccessible poem at all? The answer partly lies in its earlier publication as a pamphlet by J. Wooding in 1789, titled *Evening Reflections Written in Westminster Abbey to Which Are Added Night Thoughts in a Country Church Yard and The Grave by R. Blair with Occasional Notes and Illustrations*, which perhaps prompted the enterprise. At any rate, it works well to begin the almost hyperbolically sentimental content, marked by exclamatory and tragic rhetoric and images of death and decay, which supersede the specificity of the poem's references. Melancholy was the popular mode of the day.

Moreover, Roach consistently urges the universal application and wide appeal of his selections. He follows this poem with a paragraph-long, prose extract from Addison on the universality of death and consolation of the resurrection, called "Tombstone Lectures. Addressed to All," which he does not cite by name in the series' index of "Contents." Bearing the epigraph, "A lecture silent, but of sov'reign use," attributed to Young, this passage serves itself as an annotation to the poem it follows (1, no. 1, 17–18), and precedes, "Night Thoughts among the Tombs. By the Late Mr. Moore, of Cornwall"—perhaps so scrupulously identified to differentiate him from the famous poet and playwright—that reworks the same theme (1, no. 1, 19–23). Following this is Young's eleven-line verse, "The Rich Man's Dream;* or, Death Levels All," which concludes with the maxim, "Pride was not made for Men" (1, no. 1, 24). Roach hastens to clarify this with Young's own footnote: "*Night visions may befriend. YOUNG." Again, the next poem, Robert Blair's "The Grave" (1743) includes an instructive preface by G. W.:

> In the following well known Poem (written by a clergyman of Edinburgh, and first published in the year 1743) many important admonitions are held out, and solemn truths inculcated and enforced.
>
> Most of the characters which mankind sustain in the present state; many of the pursuits of men in general here below, together with the vanity and emptiness of every earthly pleasure and enjoyment, are herein pourtrayed in the most lively and striking colours; well deserving the attention and regard of you, of me, of all. G.W. (1, no. 1, 25)

Like many of Roach's prefatory annotations, whether quotations by poets themselves or prose notes, this serves both to advertise the following selection and to define its salient themes in sentimental language.

As well as spurs to spiritual feeling, Roach's annotations serve to inform his youthful or undereducated audience. Some footnotes also serve this purpose. For example, following Blair's description of a superstitious schoolboy fleeing a ghastly apparition, Roach footnotes: "This natural and striking picture well deserves general admiration"—possibly a hint to read the passage aloud (1, no. 1, 28). Later, he footnotes

Blair's portrait of the life-disgust of the aged with, "Well may it be said, a serious look at things temporal looks them into nothing" (1, no. 1, 51). Others digest the poem's meaning. The final selection, Thomas Gray's *Elegy Written in a Country Churchyard*, bears an epigraph by Samuel Johnson, "The church-yard abounds with images, which find a mirror in every mind, and with sentiments, to which every bosom returns an echo" (1, no. 1, 54).

Some footnotes function simply to define words fallen from common use: for example, he footnotes Blair's term "solder" (line 89) with "Strengthener, or uniter," a somewhat less graceful and scarcely clearer term (1, no. 1, 28). Again, Blair's "invigorating tube" is glossed as "The Telescope" (1, no. 1, 36). The first line of Gray's poem, "The *curfew tolls the knell of parting day," prompts the historical footnote: "An evening bell appointed by William the Conqueror, to remind people to rake out their fires and put out their lights" (1, no. 1, 54). Further footnotes include a note on "for ever" referring to the book of Revelations (1, no. 1, 55), and a gloss on "But knowledge to their eyes her ample page, / Rich with the spoils of time did ne'er unrol*" reading, "Whatever abilities persons may be possessed of, if there are no opportunities of displaying them, will be of little or no service either to the possessors of them, or the community" (1, no. 1, 57). These annotations supply information as interpretation.

There may be reason to believe that such vigorous annotation either limited or alienated the audience, or became too labor intensive to continue, for although some historical, contextual, and definitional footnotes persist, they lessen substantially in the following five volumes. However, perhaps Roach's audience grew to include readers in no need of such notes. This thesis may gain some support by the terse footnote to canto 3 of Alexander Pope's *The Rape of the Lock* (1714–1717), which describes the fatal snip. Here, Roach merely points readers to understand "The Peer now spreads the glitt'ring forfex wide" (3, no. 9, 20) by the footnote, "*See the Plate*," which reproduces Isaac Cruikshank's vignette of the lustful baron with indecently spread legs.[42] This may also serve as an internal advertisement, since Roach had been indicted for selling obscene prints in July 1787 (his sentence in 1795 to a year in jail was commuted) and was known to keep a sheaf of pornographic prints in his shop, which his wife would allow housemaids and boys to see for a penny-purchase a peek. Further evidence may lie in the fact that an earlier three-volume 1792–1793 edition of *Beauties of the Modern Poets*, Roach had included even more and more didactic notes. Much more coarsely printed, it bears a stunning frontispiece vignette—subsequently reused—with Muses and cherubs (see figure 11.3), headed with epigraph in tiny script: "Taste shewing Britannia the Beauties of Modern Poets," and an epitaph from Goldsmith, somewhat ironic considering Roach's enterprises and history:

> And thou sweet Poetry! Thou loveliest maid,
> Still fist to fly where sensual joys invade:
> Unfit, in these degen'rate times of shame,
> To catch the heart, or strive for honest fame. Goldsmith.[43]

The title-page engraving shows a tomb with the inscription on the front panel, "Verily man at his best estate is altogether vanity. Dust thou art & unto Dust thou must return" and Memento Mori engraved beneath. Underneath the picture is "Earth's highest station ends in Here he lies." Moreover, after G. W. is a passage from Young as second epigraph:

> We read their monuments; we sigh; and while
> We sigh we sink, and are what we deplor'd;
> Lamenting or lamented, all our lot.—Dr. Young.

Figure 11.3.
Frontispiece, designed by Isaac Cruikshank, engraved by
Inigo Barlow, *Roach's Beauties of the Poet's [sic] of Great
Britain; Carefully Selected & Arranged from the Works of
the Most Admired Authors*, comp. John Roach (London:
By and for J. Roach, 1794).

In addition, Roach glosses "Evening Reflections" extensively, explaining, for example, "Here terminate ambition's airy schemes" (stanza 4, line 1) with: "+ Hitherto Job xxxviii. 1.1 mayst thou go, but no farther, and here shall thy proud waves be stay'd" (1, no. 1, 2). Other glosses from Pope, Young, Horace, John, Revelations, and Genesis, among others—thirteen footnotes in all for a sixty-line poem, most identifying the poet's sources—provide a comprehensive if rather bludgeoning apparatus for interpretation, which may have been overkill for new readers.

The nationalistic moralism of Roach's annotations appears throughout. In the prefatory note to Oliver Goldsmith's mournful depiction of the ruin of the traditional English countryside, *The Deserted Village* (1770), which appears in both the 1793 and 1794 editions, for example, Roach adds, "In this much admired POEM, the author paints in the strongest colours, the baleful effects of luxury, and overgrown wealth on states, kingdoms, and individuals; Heaven prevent Great Britain being ruined by them" (1, no. 3, 1). Here, Roach represents Goldsmith's attack on enclosure and industrialization as a general portrait of the ill-effects of opulence rather than a specific lament for lost England. Later, he observes, "The poet here happily characterises the vanity and emptiness of all honorary titles and distinctions among men; what is fame but *breath?*" (referring to stanza 5, line 4). Again, he glosses Goldsmith's sentimental praise of the poor with a patriotic hint, "An honest industrious tradesman or mechanic is more valuable to the community or nation to which he belongs, than half a dozen idle *Lords* or *Gentlemen*" (1, no. 3, 3). His footnote for Goldsmith's lines admiring the wise who retire from the world, "*No surly porter stands in guilty state, / To spurn imploring famine from the gate*" is "*The insolence of servants in great families is as notorious in the present day, as to become almost proverbial; set a beggar on horseback, and he will ride to the Devil—so much for Jacks in office*"—an odd comment combining the banal complaints of the last century with weak political satire (1, no. 3, 6). Finally, the remarks on the description of a lass who followed her sire into the city for work "*left a lover's for her father's arms*" intones, "*A remarkable instance of filial affection this, very rarely to be met with I believe in the* present *day*" (1, no. 3, 17). British poetry appears as a pious and nationalistic narrative of sentimental virtue.

The annotations and paratexts of these three collections reveal the shifts in the conception of the social, aesthetic, and moral value of poetry, and in the reading habits and processes of audiences, from the mid-eighteenth century to the Regency. Whereas Knox aims to educate readers in developing their own abilities and sensitivity in order to practice virtue, Scraggs seeks to bring spiritual and cultural enfranchisement to inexperienced and disadvantaged readers. Roach, however, seeks to represent famous British works as examples of an aesthetically responsive and deeply moral, contemporary sensibility: beauty *as* duty. All three, speaking to new and previously neglected readers—children, the self-educated, and the mercantile classes—negotiate through multiple paratexts the claims of aesthetics, practical use, and religious and civic virtue to present poetry as national morality.

NOTES

1. J. Paul Hunter, *Before Novels: The Cultural Contexts of Eighteenth-Century English Fiction* (New York: Norton, 1990), 87.

2. Esther Yu, "From Judgement to Interpretation: Eighteenth Century Critics of Milton's *Paradise Lost*," *Milton Studies* 52 (2012): 202.

3. William H. Sherman, "What Did Renaissance Readers Write in Their Books?," in *Books and Readers in Early Modern England*, ed. Jennifer Andersen and Elizabeth Sauer (Philadelphia: University of Pennsylvania Press, 2001), 119–22. Andrew Piper points out that miscellanies produce "more writing," providing a model for the recipient "to create her own miscellany." See *Dreaming in Books: The Making of the Bibliographic Imagination in the Romantic Age* (Chicago: University of Chicago Press, 2009), 134.

4. See Jon Klancher, *The Making of English Reading Audiences, 1790–1832* (Madison: University of Wisconsin Press, 1987); William St. Clair, *The Reading Nation in the Romantic Period* (Cambridge: Cambridge University Press, 2004), 237–47, passim; Christopher Flint, *The Appearance of Print in Eighteenth-Century Fiction* (Cambridge: Cambridge University Press, 2011), 42–43, passim.

5. W. K. Wimsatt and Monroe C. Beardsley, "The Intentional Fallacy," in *The Verbal Icon: Studies in the Meaning of Poetry*, by W. K. Wimsatt (Lexington: University Press of Kentucky, 1954), 3–18.

6. Gabrielle Watling, "The Enlightenment," in *The Cultural History of Reading*, ed. Gabrielle Watling, 2 vols. (Westport, CT: Greenwood Press, 2009), 1:194.

7. Maureen Bell, "Introduction: The Material Text," in *Re-constructing the Book: Literary Texts in Transmission*, ed. Maureen Bell et al. (Aldershot, UK: Ashgate, 2001), 1. See Janine Barchas, *Graphic Design, Print Culture, and the Eighteenth-Century Novel* (Cambridge: Cambridge University Press, 2003); and Sandro Jung, "Packaging, Design and Colour: From Fine-Printed to Small-Format Editions of Thomson's *The Seasons*, 1793–1802," in *British Literature and Print Culture*, ed. Sandro Jung, Essays and Studies (Cambridge: D. S. Brewer for the English Association, 2013), 97–124.

8. Ina Ferris and Paul Keen, introduction to *Bookish Histories: Books, Literature, and Commercial Modernity, 1700–1900*, ed. Ina Ferris and Paul Keen (Houndmills, UK: Palgrave Macmillan, 2009), 5.

9. Jon Klancher, "Wild Bibliography: The Rise and Fall of Book History in Nineteenth-Century Britain," in Ferris and Keen, *Bookish Histories*, 19–40, esp. 21–30. See also Viccy Coltman, *Classical Sculpture and the Culture of Collecting in Britain since 1760* (Oxford: Oxford University Press, 2009).

10. Jayne Elizabeth Lewis, *The English Fable: Aesop and Literary Culture, 1651–1740* (Cambridge: Cambridge University Press, 1996), 162.

11. Angela Yannicopoulou, *Fables and Children: Form and Function* (Liverpool: Manutius Press, 1993), 66.

12. Donald F. Bond, ed., *The Spectator*, 5 vols. (Oxford: Clarendon Press, 1965), 2:219.

13. Bond, *The Spectator*, 4:317.

14. Lewis, *The English Fable*, 1, 3.

15. M. H. Pritchard, "Fables Moral and Political: The Adaptation of the Aesopian Fable Collection to English Social and Political Life, 1651–1722" (PhD thesis, University of Western Ontario, 1976), 176; passim; mentioned in Lewis, 21, and Yannicopoulou, 71. See Annabel Patterson, *Fables of Power: Aesopian Writing and Political History* (Durham, NC: Duke University Press, 1991).

16. Lewis, *The English Fable*, 3, 13.

17. *Fables for CHILDREN with Suitable MORALS; By Mr. Wise. Adorned with Cuts* (London: Printed and Sold by G. Thompson, 1795), 4. The British Library edition bears the contemporary script "Anna Jackson Chappell, Feb. 22 1826" on the title page, suggesting it became a family volume, passed down through the generations (shelfmark RB.23.a.7749).

18. *Fables for CHILDREN*, 70.

19. Thomas Noel, *Theories of the Fable in the Eighteenth Century* (New York: Columbia University Press, 1975), 36–37; see also Lewis, *The English Fable*, 3, 13.

20. John Gay, *Fables by John Gay, with a Life of the Author and Embellished with Seventy Plates*, 2 vols. (London: Printed for John Stockdale, 1793), lines [69–80].

21. Lewis contrasts this title page "mask of ambiguous race and gender" with the two-volume frontispiece, which "dominated by an image of Gay's own imposing monument . . . is a canonizing ploy" (Lewis, *The English Fable*, 13, 174).

22. Bond, *The Spectator*, 4:318.

23. [Daniel Bellamy], *Gay's Fables Epitomiz'd: With Short Poems Applicable to Each Occasion, Extracted from the Most Celebrated Moralists Antient and Modern, for the Use of Schools* (London: Printed for B. Creak, [1733]; British Library shelfmark 1164.h.35), n.p. [2, 6]. Subsequent references are cited parenthetically in the text.

24. Jeanne K. Welcher and Richard Dircks, introduction to *An Essay on Fable*, by Robert Dodsley, Augustan Reprint 112 (1764; repr., Los Angeles: William Andrews Clark Memorial Library, 1965), i–ii.

25. Samuel Richardson, preface to *Aesop's Fables. With Instructive Morals and Reflections, Abstracted from All Party Considerations, Adapted to All Capacities. And Design'd to Promote Religion, Morality, and Universal Benevolence. Containing Two Hundred and Forty Fables with a Cut Engrav'd on Copper to Each Fable. And the Life of Aesop Prefix'd by Mr. Richardson* (London: Printed for J. Rivington et al., [1740]), i–xiv.

26. Henry Moore, *Fables for the Female Sex*, 3rd ed. (London: Printed for R. Francklin, 1749), 1.

27. Moore, *Fables for the Female Sex*, 2.

28. See Charles LaMotte, *An Essay upon Poetry and Painting* (London: Printed for F. Fayram, 1730).

29. David L. Greene, preface to William Godwin, *Fables Ancient and Modern*, 2 vols. (1805; repr., New York: Garland, 1976), vii.

30. Edward Baldwin [William Godwin], preface to *Fables Ancient and Modern, Adapted for the Use of Children from Three to Eight Years of Age. Adorned with Thirty-Six Copper-Plates*, 2 vols. (London: Printed for Thomas Hodgkins, [1805]), iii–v.

31. Lewis, *The English Fable*, 162–64.

32. Vicesimus Knox, preface to *Elegant Extracts; or, Useful and Entertaining PIECES of POETRY* (London: Printed for C. Dilly and Poultry, 1789), iii. Subsequent references are cited parenthetically in the text.

33. Vicesimus Knox, ["On the Use and Abuse of Marginal Notes and Quotations"], in vol. 1 of *Winter Evenings; or, Lucubrations on Life and Letters. In Three Volumes* (London: Printed for Charles Dilly, 1788), 88–96. Subsequent references are cited parenthetically in the text.

34. John Kerrigan, "The Editor as Reader: Constructing Renaissance Texts," in *The Practice and Representation of Reading in England*, ed. James Raven, Helen Small, and Naomi Tadmor (Cambridge: Cambridge University Press, 1996), 117.

35. Robert Southey to Samuel Taylor Coleridge, October 28, 1809, *The Collected Letters of Robert Southey, Part Three: 1804–1809*, ed. Carol Bolton and Tim Fulford, n3; http:\\www. rc.umd.edu/editions/southey_letters/Part_Three/HTML/letterEEd.26.1704.html.

36. Reverend G. G. Scraggs, *Instructive Selections; or, The Beauties of Sentiment. Being Striking Subjects from the Best Authors, Ancient and Modern, in Prose and Verse, on a Great Variety of Subject, Divine, Moral, Literary, and Entertaining, on a New Methodical Plan. Also a List of the Best Books on the Principal Subjects, and the Names of the Authors Annexed to the Extracts*, 2nd ed., 2 vols. (London: Printed by C. Whittingham, 1802), 1:vi–vii. Subsequent references are cited parenthetically in the text.

37. See Rev. G. G. Scraggs, comp., *A Father's Instructions to His Children: Consisting of Tales, Fables, and Reflections; Designed to Promote the Love of Virtue, a Taste for Knowledge, and an Early Acquaintance with the Works of Nature*, 2nd ed. (London: Printed for J. Johnson, 1776).

38. Reverend G. G. Scraggs, comp., *Instructive Selections; or, The Beauties of Sentiment. Being Striking Subjects from the Best Authors, Ancient and Modern, in Prose and Verse, on a Great Variety of Subject, Divine, Moral, Literary, and Entertaining, on a New Methodical Plan. Also a List of the Best Books on the Principal Subjects, and the Names of the Authors Annexed to the Extracts*, [1st ed.], 2 vols. (London: Printed by C. Whittingham, 1801), 1:vii, ix.

39. Barbara M. Benedict, "'Admiring Pope No More Than Is Proper': Romanticizing Alexander Pope in Late-Eighteenth-Century Booksellers' Beauties," in *Women, Gender, and Print Culture in Eighteenth-Century Britain: Essays in Memory of Betty Rizzo*, ed. Temma Berg and Sonia Kane (Bethlehem, PA: Lehigh University Press, 2013), 217.

40. See Rev. G. G. Scraggs, *English Composition, in a Method Entirely New, with Various CONTRASTED EXAMPLES, FROM CELEBRATED WRITERS, THE WHOLE ADAPTED TO Common Capacities, and Designed as an Easy Help to Form a Good Style, and to Acquire a Taste for the Works of the Best Authors. To Which Are Added, an Essay on the Advantages of Understanding Composition, and a List of Select Books for English Readers with Remarks* (London: For H. D. Symonds, 1802), which is also directed to a crossover audience.

41. James Roach, comp., *Roach's Beauties of the Poet's* [sic] *of Great Britain; Carefully Selected & Arranged from the Works of the Most Admired Authors* (London: By and for J. Roach, 1794), vol. 1, no. 1, page 13. Subsequent references are cited parenthetically in the text by volume, number, and page.

42. The Cruikshank frontispiece appears in the 1794 edition printed at the Britannia Record Office, New Drury Theatre Royal.

43. James Roach, comp., *Roach's Beauties of the Modern Poets of Great Britain, Carefully Selected and Arranged in Three Volumes* (London: Printed by and for J. Roach, 1793), title page. Subsequent references are cited parenthetically in the text by volume, number, and page.

Index

References to tables and figures are in italics.

Addison, Joseph, xxviii, 196, 224; "Essay on the Georgics," 7–9, 11, 25; *The Spectator*, 173, 183–84, 198, 210, 211–12

Aikin, John, 8, 194, 196

Akenside, Mark, 4, 5, 9–10, 194, 214

Allatius, Leo, 110

annotation (printed): defined, xiv; and canon formation, xiv, xxxvii–xviii, 11, 13–15, 33, 47–64, 67–68, 75–76, 78, 80–83, 132, 153–65, 169–85, 189–202, 209; and decorum, 4, 25–27, 34, 119–23; and historicism, xviii, 15, 131–32, 152–60; and illustration (visual), xv, xvii, 24, 75, 81–82, 172, 209, 210, 212, 215, 216, 223; and specialization, xviii–xix, 7–9, 14–16, 23–40; and translation, 105–124

annotation, consequences for: linear reading, xx, 10; literary property, xvii–xviii; marginalia (handwritten), xx; reading aloud, xx; cultural memory, 72–75

annotation, functions of: authentication, xiv, 55, 73–74, 80–83, 90, 145, 158, 181–82; explanation of allusion, xvi,

xviii, 14, 16, 33, 67, 82, 129–46, 151–65, 169–85, 195; explanation of cultures, 67–83, 97–98, 108, 110–12, 117–18; explanation of languages, 25–27, 35–39, 49–51, 54–69, 112–13, 158–63; explanation of technical jargon and procedures, 15–16, 23–40; explanation of versification, 51–52, 55–56, 61–63, 133–35, 141, 178; instruction, xxiii, 7–8, 15–16, 23, 40, 51–56, 169–85, 207–27

annotation, opinions on: compulsory, xxi, xxiii; disenchanting, xv–xvi, 13, 142; distracting, xiii, xx, xxi, xxii, xxiii, 78; excessive, xxii, 3, 70–72, 129–30, 139–41, 156–63; irrelevant, 142–44, 155–56, 160–61, 163; limiting, 29–31, 34; optional, xx, xxiii, 110, 219; pedantic, xiii, xxi, 109–10, 219; pleasurable, xxi, xxii, xxiii, 3–4, 78, 107, 131, 153; subjective, 145–46, 163–64

annotation, placement of: advertised, xvi, xvii, 25, 76–77; decided by booksellers or printers, xvii, xix, 87n75; endnotes made footnotes, xv, xvii, 105; endnotes preferred to footnotes, xiii, xix, xxii, 5,

18n12, 153; footnotes made endnotes, xiii, 5, 78; headnotes, 60, 61, 69, 100, 113–14, 152, 164, 197, 216; multiple systems of annotation, xiv, 5, 25n9, 20n38, 135, 148n25, 164; notes expanded in later editions, 11, 19n26, 31; notes reduced in later editions, xvii, 35, 191

annotation, social aspects: aesthetic considerations, xix–xx, xxiii, 218; collaboration, xvi, 110, 133, 138, 154, 170, 177–80; commercial considerations, xv, xvii, xviii, xx, 5, 107; national identity, xxv, 67–83, 47–64, 94–96, 100, 200; novice readers, xviii, xxvii, xxviii, 28, 169, 207–27; poetic identity, 90–91, 92, 99–101, 200; professional identity, 8, 25–26, 35–36; rivalry (with main text), xiii, xvi, 3, 9–10, 130, 134; rivalry (between annotators), xiii, xvi, 130, 154, 158, 194; women, xxix

annotation, types of: aesthetic, xx, 110, 195; antiquarian, xiv, 52–53, 63, 73, 78, 80–83 (*see also* editing: ballads); authorial vs. non-authorial, xv, 5–16; dialogic vs. referential, 9, 11; mock, xiii, xv, 50; scientific, xxiv, 7–8, 15–16; topographical, 67–83

antiquarianism. *See under* annotation, types of

Ariosto, Ludovico, 89, 158

Armstrong, John, 4

Arnold, Cornelius, 5

Arnold, Matthew, 125n6

Austen, Jane, 208

Bacon, Francis, 220

Bailey, Nathan, 181, 182

ballads. *See* annotation, types of: antiquarian; editing: ballads

Bancks, John, xvii

Barbauld, Anna, 189–202, 205n48

Barbour, John: xxii, xxv–xxvi, 68, 77–83

Barlow, Inigo, *226*

Barnes, Joshua, 110, 112

Bayle, Pierre, xiv

Beattie, James, xix, 200–201

Beaumont, Francis, 132, 184

Becket, Thomas, 191

Beckford, William, 89, 101n2

Bell, John, 208

Bellamy, Daniel, the younger, 211–14

Bentley, Richard, 106, 112, 154, 158

Beowulf, 47, 55, 63–64

Birch, Thomas, 151–52

black letter classics, 56, 57, 161–62

Blair, Hugh, 7, 15, 200–201,

Blair, Robert, 224–25

Blake, William, 24, 208

Blanckley, Thomas, 37

Blind Hary's *Wallace,* 79–80

Boethius, 60

Boileau-Despréaux, Nicolas, 12, 123

Boivin, Jean, 105

Bossu, René Le, 114

Boswell, James, 25

Brett, Thomas, 177, 179

Brooke, Henry, 214

Broome, William, 110

Browne, William, xxvii, 159, 160

The Bruce (Barbour), 68, 77–83. *See also* Pinkerton, John

Bryskett, Lodowick, 156, 166n15

Buchan, Earl of. *See* Erskine, David Steuart

Burney, Edward Francisco, 216

Burney, William, 37, 41n6

Burns, Robert, 24

Burton, Robert, 182

Butler, Samuel, 145, 191; *Hudibras,* xxvii, 169–85

Byron, Christopher, 170, 175

Byron, George Gordon, 100

Castillo, Bernal Diaz del, 97

Cervantes, Miguel de, 171, 180, 181–82

Chambers, Ephraim, 26, 196

Chapman, George, 111, 124

Chardin, Jean, 89

Chatterton, Thomas (Thomas Rowley), 70

Chaucer, Geoffrey, xxvi–xxvii, 55, 63, 129–46; *See also* Morell, Thomas; Speght, Thomas; Tyrwhitt, Thomas; Urry, John

The Chronicle of Robert of Gloucester, xxv, 47–64; *See also* Hearne, Thomas
Clarke, James Stanier, 24
Coleridge, Samuel Taylor, xxv, 48, 61, 62–63, 66n40, 91, 98, 155, 160
Collins, William, xxviii, 189–202, 203n18
Colman, George, the elder, xxii
commentary, as distinguished from annotation, xiv
Concanen, Matthew, xxi, xxiv
Congreve, William, 213
Cooper, John Gilbert, 200, 201
Cowper, William, 124
Creech, Thomas, xxi
Creech, William, 77
Crowe, William, 9, 10
Cruikshank, Isaac, 225, *226*
Cuperus, Gisbertus, 110
Curll, Edmund, xvi, 213
Cyder (Philips), 4, *11*, 14–16

Dacier, André, 122
Dacier, Anne, 110, 117–18, 122, 126n22
Dante, Alighieri, 79
Darby, Samuel, 161–63, 166n16
Dart, John, 133–34
Darwin, Erasmus, xix, 14
De Hondt, Peter Abraham, 191
Denham, John, 8, 13, 179
Dennis, John, 164–65, 213
Desaguliers, John Theophilus, xix
Digby, Kenelm, 183
Dodd, William, 129–31, 140, 145, 147n8
Dodsley, Robert, 5, 190, 194, 196, 200, 204n37, 214–15
Donaldson v. Becket, 208
Donaldson, Alexander, xvii
Drayton, Michael, xviii, 144, 159, 161–62
Drummond, William (of Hawthornden), 159
Dryden, John, xvii, xxi, 111, 115, 130–35, 136, 139, 146, 149n38, 154, 210, 221
  Aeneid translation, 171–72, 174–75
  Fables, Ancient and Modern, 133–34;
  Georgics translation, 3–4, 5

The Dunciad (Pope), xiii, xiv, xv, xvi, xviii, xxix, 12, 50–51, 161
Dunster, Charles, xxiv, 4, 14–16
Dyce, Alexander, 192, 194
Dyer, John, 5, 25

Edgeworth, Richard, 198
editing: ballad, xix, 48–49, 68, 73, 75–76; classical, xiv, xviii, xix, xxix, 105–24; emendation, 154, 156–57, 164; excerpting, xix, 14, 196, 219–22; misquotation, 182, 187n52, 188n55; textual variants, 11–13, 57, 135, 164, 194; theory of, 67, 170–71. *See also* annotation; annotation, types of: antiquarian
Edwards, Thomas, xxi
Eliot, T. S., 154
Elphinston, James, 5
endnotes. *See under* annotation, placement of
Enfield, William, xvii
Ennius, 55, 115
Erskine, David Steuart, 11th Earl of Buchan, xxii, 75, 77–78, 80, 83, 86n53
Eustathius, 110, 117, 118

Fables (Gay), 209–15, *212*
Falconer, William, 26, 35, 42n30;
  The Shipwreck, xv, xxiv–xxv, 8, 23–40, *29, 30*; *An Universal Dictionary of the Marine*, xxv, 23, 34, 35–40
Fawkes, Francis, 190, 191
Felton, Henry, xxi
Fenton, Elijah, 138
Ferriar, John, 92
Fielding, Jonathan, 222
Flaxman, John, 192
Fletcher, John, 160, 171, 180, 183–84
footnotes. *See under* annotation, placement of
Foster, Birket, 24
Foulis, Robert, xix
Franklin, Benjamin, 221

Garth, Samuel, 14
Gay, John, xiv, 4, 144, 209;

Fables, 209–16, *212*
Gellius, Aulus, 110
Genette, Gérard, xv–xvi, 53, 65n25. *See also*
    paratexts
georgic poetry, xxiv–xxv, 3–16, *6*, *11*,
    23–40; annotation and genre in, 4–5,
    11–16; generalist vs. specialist in, 25–26,
    38–39; preference for footnotes in, 5
Gibbon, Edward, xvi, 95; *The History of the
    Decline and Fall of the Roman Empire*,
    xiii, xv, 100
gloss. *See* annotation
Gloucester, Robert of. *See* The Chronicle of
    Robert of Gloucester
Godwin, William, 215
Goldsmith, Oliver, xxii, xxviii, 24, 208,
    225, 227
Gómara, Francisco López de, 97
Gorges, Arthur, 177, 178
Grainger, James, xxii, 3–4, 192;
    The Sugar-Cane, 3–4, 5, 8, 10, 25
Gray, Thomas, xvi, xix, xxii, xxvii, 13, 32,
    143, 158, 160, 201, 225
Grey, Zachary, xxvii–xxviii, 169–85,
    186n23, 188n55
Griffiths, Ralph, 191
Grose, Francis, 74

Hamilton, James, 7
Hampton, James, 192
Hawkesworth, John, xvii
Hayley, William, 192, 203n18
Hazlitt, William, 196
headnotes. *See under* annotation, placement
    of
Heaney, Seamus, 63
Hearne, Thomas, xxv, 47–64, *57*, *58*
Heath, James, 216
Henley, Samuel, 100
Henryson, Robert, 63–64
The Hermit of Warkworth (Percy), xxv,
    67–75, 81–83
Heron, Robert, 194
Hesiod, 7
*The History of the Decline and Fall of the
    Roman Empire* (Gibbon), xiii, xv, 100
Hobbes, Thomas, 110, 124

Hodgson, Francis, xxiii, xxiv
Hogarth, William, 172
Holinshed, Raphael, 95
Homer, xxvi, xxvii, 13, 105–24, 130–33,
    135–38, 171, 172, 173–76, *Iliad*, 79,
    105–8, 109, 111, 114, 118, 119, 120,
    123–24, 130, 131, 136, 143, 145,
    175–76, 197; *Odyssey*, 106, 118, 138.
    See also under Pope, Alexander
Hopton, Ralph, 179–80
Hudibras (Butler), xxiii, xxvii, 169–85. *See
    also* Grey, Zachary
humanist scholarship, xiv–xv, 119, 169
Hume, David, xiii, xvi, 78
Hume, Patrick, xiv–xv
Hunt, Leigh, xxiii, 153, 163
Hurd, Richard, 154
Hymers, William, xxviii, 189–202, 202n2,
    202n3, 205n50, 205n51

Jago, Richard, 10, 160
Jamieson, John, 60
Johnson, Samuel, xx, 8, 24, 25, 69, 74,
    108, 112, 146, 194, 195–96, 199, 201,
    222; annotation, remarks on, xiii, xvii,
    xxi, 106–7, 134; criticism by, 130–31,
    157, 190, 192–93, 195–96, 199, 225;
    Dictionary, 37–38, 60
Jonson, Ben, 162
Juvenal, xxiii

Kearsley, George, 208
King, Edward, 156–57
Kitchin, Thomas, 24
Knapton, John, xix
Knight, Richard Payne, 5
Knox, Vicesimus, xxiii, xxviii, 209, 216–19,
    217, 227

L'Estrange, Roger, 170, 214
Lamb, Charles, xxiii
LaMotte, Charles, 215
Langhorne John, 3–4, 189–201
Lavater, Johann Caspar, 220, 222
Lintot, Bernard, xvii
Llwyd, Richard, xv
Locke, John, 210

Lodge, Thomas, 219
Longinus, 123
Lucan, 169, 171, 177–79
Lucretius, xxi, 10, 14, 115

Macpherson, James (Ossian), 70, 73
Macrobius, 110
Madden, Frederic, 63
Madoc (Southey), xv, xxvi, 89–101
Mandeville, Bernard, 210
Manwayring, Henry, 37
marginalia, as distinguished from
    annotation, xiv
Martyn, John, 3, 5, 7
Mason, William, 5, 11
Massinger, Philip, 184
meter. *See* annotation, function of:
    explanation
Millar v. Donaldson, xvii
Millar, Andrew, xvii, 24, 31, 191
Milton, John, 113, 117, 119, 121, 142,
    173, 197–98, 200–201; *See also* Dunster,
    Charles; Hume, Patrick; Newton,
    Thomas; Peck, Francis; Thyer, Robert;
    Warton, Joseph
Monmouth, Geoffrey of, 51, 54
Moore, Edward, 214–15
Morell, Thomas, xxvii, 135–42, 145
Morganwg, Iolo. *See* Williams, Edward
Morison, Robert and James, 78, 80
Motte, Antoine Houdar de la, 106, 122
Motteux, Peter, 181

Nash, Russell Treadway, 171, 174, 186n23,
    186n24
Neve, Philip, 144–45
Newton, Thomas, xvii, 155, 156
Nichol, George, 78
Nichols, John, 77
notes. *See* annotation

Ogilby, John, 110, 112, 124
Ossian. *See* Macpherson, James
Ovid, 12, 113, 146, 158
paratexts, 56–59, 65n25, 105, 207–27; as
    distinguished from annotation, xv. *See
    also* Genette, Gérard

Parnell, Thomas, xiv, 105
Paton, George, 67, 76, 77
Pearce, Zachary, 158
Peck, Francis, 152, 156
Peele, George, 160
Pennant, Thomas, 74, 81–82
Percy, Thomas, xxviii, 48, 76, 200; *Reliques
    of Ancient English Poetry*, 60–62, 69, 70,
    71–72; *The Hermit of Warkworth*, xxv,
    67–75, 81, 82–83
Philips, Ambrose, 160
Philips, John, xxiv; *Cyder*, 14–16
Pindar, 190, 196, 199
Pinkerton, John, xxii, xxiv, xxv–xxvi, 75–83
Plato, 119
Plutarch, 118
Pocock, Nicholas, 24
Pope, Alexander, xviii, xix–xx, xxi, xxviii,
    9, 25, 132, 152, 160, 171, 175, 201,
    213, 226; annotations, xiv, xvi, xvi,
    xvii, xxi, xxvi, xxix, 8, 11, 105–24, 130,
    131, 135–37; annotation, remarks on,
    xviii, xxi, 50, 109–110; *The Dunciad*,
    xiii, xiv, xv, xvi, xviii, xxix, 12, 50–51,
    161; *Eloisa and Abelard*, 144–46; *Essay
    on Criticism*, xvi, 107, 108, 174, 175,
    221, 222; *Epistle to a Lady*, 215; *The
    Iliad*, Pope's translation, xvii, xxvi, xxvii,
    105–24, 130–31, 135–38, 172, 173–74,
    176; *The Rape of the Lock*, 225; *Windsor-
    Forest*, xiv, 3, 4, 8, 9, 11–14, 15, 16.
    See also Wakefield, Gilbert; Warburton,
    William; Warton, Joseph

Postlethwayt, Malachy, 26
Potter, Robert, 14, 196, 201
Prior, Matthew, 191, 213
prosody. *See* annotation, functions of:
    explanation
Pye, Henry James, 14

Quincey, Thomas de, xxiii

Ragsdale, John, 194
Ranger, Henry, 223
Reliques of Ancient English Poetry (Percy),
    60–62, 69, 70, 71–72, 162

Richardson, Jonathan, the elder, 152
Richardson, Samuel, 214
Roach, John, 223–27, *226*
Rowe, Nicholas, xxiii, 177, 178
Rowley, Thomas. *See* Chatterton, Thomas
Rymer, Thomas, 131

Sánchez, Tomás Antonio, 79
Scaliger, J. C., 110
Scotland, 49, 53, 68–83
Scott, James, 36
Scott, Walter, 100
Scraggs, George Glyn, xxviii, 209, 219–22, 227
self-annotation. *See* annotation, types of: authorial vs. non-authorial
Seneca, 220
Settle, Elkanah, xiv, 50
Seward, Anna, xxii
Shakespeare, William, xxvii, 33, 95, 108, 124, 139, 141, 143–44, 145–46, 153, 163, 169, 189, 191, 201, 216; allusions to, annotated 33, 130–31, 143, 155, 171, 180, 182–83; annotated, xvi, xxi, xxiii, 130, 134, 140, 144, 160; *Cymbeline*, 200; *Hamlet*, 129, 130, 159; *Henry IV, Part 2*, 159; *Macbeth*, 130; *The Merry Wives of Windsor*, 143; *A Midsummer Night's Dream*, 143, 144; *The Tempest*, 160; *Twelfth Night*, 140, 162; *Romeo and Juliet*, 182–83
Shenstone, William, xxii
The Shipwreck (Falconer): popularity of, 23–24
Sidney, Mary, 155
Sidney, Philip, 156, 218
Simon, Richard, xiv
Sir Eglamour of Artois, xxvii, 161–62
Sir Gawain and the Green Knight, 47, 63
Skelton, John, 71
Smart, Christopher, 25, 192
Smith, Charlotte, 3, 5, 18n12, 192
Smollett, Tobias, xxii
Somervile, William, 13, 19n32
Southey, Robert, xv, xxvi, 89–101; *Madoc*, xxvi, 89–101

The Spectator, 173, 183, 196, 198, 211, 222
Speght, Thomas, 59, 131–34; 147n13
Spence, Joseph, xxi, 106
Spenser, Edmund, xiv, xxvii, 9, 13, 131–33, 136, 145, 153, 155, 158–63, 189, 191, 197, 201
Sponde, Jean de (Spondanus), 110
Staël, Germaine de, xxiii
Statius, 131, 135–36, 146
Steele, Richard, 173
Steevens, George, 144, 153, 154
Stephen, Leslie, 106
Stockdale, Percival, xxii, 194
Stothard, Thomas, 193
Strahan, William, xvi
Stretch, Lyscombe Maltbee, 222
The Sugar-Cane (Grainger), xxiv, 3–4, 5, 8, 10, 15, 16, 25, 192
Swift, Jonathan, xvi, 49, 62, 213
Swinburne, Algernon, 201
Switzer, Stephen, 26

Taylor, John, 181, 182
Taylor, William, 89
Tennyson, Alfred, 63
Theobald, Lewis, 50, 129–30, 131, 138–40, 145
Thomas, Timothy, 133, 141
Thomas, William, 133
Thomson, James, 4, 14, 31, 190, 194, 200, 201
Thorkelin, Grímur Jónsson, 63
Thyer, Robert, 156–57, 171
Tibullus, xxii
Tonson v. Walker, xvii
Tonson, Jacob, the elder, xvii, xxiii
Tonson, Jacob, the younger, xvii
Trapp, Joseph, 5, 17n7, 175
typography, 48, 50–51, 56–59, 66n29, 220. *See also* black letter classics
Tyrwhitt, Thomas, xxvii, 78, 141–46

An Universal Dictionary of the Marine (Falconer), xxv, 23, 35–40
Upton, John, xiv, 9
Urry, John, 9, 133–35, 141, 145

Valterie, abbé de la, 110
Vida, Marco, 119
Virgil, 4, 7, 10, 14, 108, 109, 115, 119,
120, 123, 133, 135, 169, 173; *Aeneid*,
xvii, xxvii, 171–72, 174–75, 176;
allusions to, annotated, xxiv, 10, 12–13,
15–16, 171–72, 174–75; *Georgics*,
annotations to, 3, 5, 7. *See also under*
Dryden, John

Wakefield, Gilbert, 12–13
Wales, 49, 91, 94–96, 101
Waller, Edmund, 198
Waller, William, 177, 179, 180
Walpole, Horace, xxii
Wanley, Nathaniel, 222
Warburton, William, xix–xx, xxi, 12–13,
16, 50, 58, 140–41, 144–45
Warrington, William, 95
Warton, Joseph, xxviii, 4, 5, 12–14, 15,
143, 191, 194, 197, 200, 201
Warton, Thomas, xxviii, 76, 82, 142–43,
149n40, 194, 197, 200, 201; annotation
of Milton, xxii, xxiii, xxvii, 151–65,

195; objections to his shorter Milton,
160–61, 163
Weekes, Nathaniel, 5, 9, 19n31
Wenman, Joseph, 192
West, Gilbert, xxviii, 196, 197, 199, 201
Westall, Richard, 24
Wilberforce, William, 221
Williams, Edward (Iolo Morganwg), 96
Windsor-Forest (Pope), xiv, 3, 4, 8, 9, 11–14,
15, 16
Wootton, John, 211, 212
Wordsworth, William, 153, 192
Woty, William, 160, 190–91
Wright, George, 194
Wright, William Aldis, 52
Wynn, John, 94

Xenophanes, 119

Young, Edward, 221, 224, 226
Young, John, 201

Zoilus, 119

About the Contributors

Barbara M. Benedict holds the Charles A. Dana Chair in English at Trinity College, Connecticut. She has published *Framing Feeling: Sentiment and Style in English Prose Fiction, 1745–1800* (1994); *Making the Modern Reader: Cultural Mediation in Early Modern Literary Anthologies* (1996); and *Curiosity: A Cultural History of Early Modern Inquiry* (2001). She coedited Jane Austen's *Northanger Abbey*, with Deirdre Le Faye (2006). She is currently writing on collecting, advertising, early modern sciences, and sentimental fiction.

Michael Edson is assistant professor of English at the University of Wyoming, and associate editor of *Eighteenth-Century Life*. He has published articles on eighteenth-century poetry in the *Journal for Eighteenth-Century Studies*, *Eighteenth Century*, *European Romantic Review*, and *Studies in the Literary Imagination*. His Festschrift, *Publishing, Editing, and Reception: Essays in Honor of Donald H. Reiman*, appeared in 2015.

David Hopkins is emeritus professor of English Literature and Senior Research Fellow at the University of Bristol. His publications include books on Dryden, Milton, and English poets' relations with the Greek and Roman classics, as well as editions of Dryden and Abraham Cowley. He is the coeditor (with Paul Hammond) of *John Dryden: Tercentenary Essays* (2000), coeditor (with Stuart Gillespie) of volume 3 of *The Oxford History of Literary Translation in English* (2005), and co–general editor (with Charles Martindale) of *The Oxford History of Classical Reception in English Literature* (2012–).

William Jones is emeritus professor at the University of Newcastle and professor at the University of Leicester. He has worked in university continuing education all his career. His teaching subject is English literature, and his research is on poetry of the eighteenth century, with a special interest in maritime literature. His definitive edition of the poetical works of William Falconer was published in 2002.

Sandro Jung is Stirling Maxwell Fellow at the University of Glasgow, Senior Fellow of the Alexander von Humboldt Foundation at the Herzog August Bibliothek Wolfenbüttel, and Hiob Ludolf Fellow at the Forschungszentrum Gotha. His publications include: *David Mallet, Anglo-Scot: Poetry, Politics, and Patronage in the Age of Union* (2008), *The Fragmentary Poetic: Eighteenth-Century Uses of an Experimental Mode* (2009), *James Thomson's The Seasons, Print Culture, and Visual Interpretation, 1730–1842* (2015), and *The Publishing and Marketing of Illustrated Literature in Scotland, 1760–1825* (2017).

Tom Mason retired in 2015 after some thirty-five years teaching in the English Department of the University of Bristol. He supervised research on Chaucer, Shakespeare, Dryden, and Johnson, as well as research on English responses to Catullus, Virgil, and Ovid. He has published on Anacreon, Cowley, Dryden, and Johnson.

Mark A. Pedreira is professor of English at the University of Puerto Rico. He has published essays on Johnson, Cowley, and Samuel Butler. He has also edited a special feature, "Metaphor in the Poetry and Criticism of the Restoration and Early Eighteenth Century," for volume 18 of *1650–1850: Ideas, Aesthetics, and Inquiries in the Early Modern Era* (2011). He is currently writing a monograph on Johnson's theory and practice of metaphor, which places Johnson in a broad philosophical and rhetorical tradition extending from antiquity to the eighteenth century.

Adam Rounce is associate professor in English Literature at the University of Nottingham. He has written extensively on various seventeenth- and eighteenth-century writers, including Dryden, Pope, Johnson, and Charles Churchill. He is coediting two volumes for the ongoing Cambridge edition of the writings of Swift, as well as writing a separately published *Chronology*. He is the author of *Fame and Failure, 1720–1800: The Unfulfilled Literary Life* (2013).

Jeff Strabone is associate professor of English at Connecticut College where he teaches the eighteenth century, British Romanticism, and African fiction. His articles and reviews have appeared in *English Literary History*, *Eighteenth-Century Life*, and *Eighteenth-Century Scotland*. His book *Poetry and British Nationalism in the Bardic Eighteenth Century: Imagined Antiqueties*, a study of the Romantic construction of the British nations from Allan Ramsay to Samuel Taylor Coleridge, will be published in 2017.

Thomas Van der Goten is a PhD candidate and a member of the Centre for the Study of Text and Print Culture at Ghent University. His dissertation offers a revisionist, genre-theoretical study of the history of the British ode in the eighteenth century. He has recently published on the Lilliputian Ode, the research of which forms part of a quantitative, print-cultural analysis of ode publications produced in the first half of the century.

Alex Watson is associate professor at the Graduate School of Humanities at the University of Nagoya. His monograph, *Romantic Marginality: Nation and Empire on the Borders of the Page* (2012), is the first book-length study of Romantic-era annotation. He is currently editing a volume that considers the reception of British Romanticism in Asia and writing a monograph that explores how the image of ruins provided an unstable cultural and epistemological foundation for the British Empire.

Karina Williamson is Honorary Fellow at the Institute for Advanced Studies in the Humanities, University of Edinburgh. She has edited *The Poetical Works of Christopher Smart* (1980–1996), *Marly; or, A Planter's Life in Jamaica* (2005), and *Contrary Voices: Representations of West Indian Slavery, 1657-1834* (2008), and has published articles on English, Scottish, and Caribbean literature.